Gifts, Romance, and Consumer Culture

How do people communicate their romantic feelings? Gift-giving is one way. Giving and receiving of gifts is a characteristic of intimate relationships. Gifts are a message, a form of communication with a tangible material object, about love, affection, or concern for the recipient. The "romantic gift" evokes a multitude of intertwined meanings: passion, intimacy, affection, persuasion, care, celebration, altruism, and nostalgia. They can also connote the negative images of obligation and reciprocity. Romantic gift-giving may be practiced at rituals, during rites of passage, or for casual occasions, to affirm the continued importance of the romantic relationship. We may even romanticize the giving of gifts to the self, to nonhuman companions, and to others we do not know personally. If loving and giving are a practice, then romantic gift-giving is a practice of loving with intimate—or would-be intimate—others.

This book addresses gift-giving among consumers attempting to express and construct romantic love. It lies at the intersection of consumption, markets, and culture. In societies shaped by the globalizing neoliberal economic order, increasing wealth disparity, and a partially digitized social environment that they help to co-construct, it may be time to rethink romantic love. Gift-giving is a key arena to do so, as gifts make love tangible and act as carriers of meaning as well as cultural symbols.

In gift-giving, the meanings of romance are renewed, renegotiated, and reconstructed. *Gifts, Romance, and Consumer Culture* demonstrates a wide variety of scholarly work bearing on romantic gift-giving using an interpretive consumer research perspective. The book introduces critical studies by scholars in this unfolding and new interdisciplinary field.

Yuko Minowa is Professor of Marketing at Long Island University, USA.

Russell W. Belk is Professor of Marketing at the Schulich School of Business, York University, Canada.

Routledge Interpretive Marketing Research

Recent years have witnessed an "interpretative turn" in marketing and consumer research. Methodologists from the humanities are taking their place alongside those drawn from the traditional social sciences.

Qualitative and literary modes of marketing discourse are growing in popularity. Art and esthetics are increasingly firing the marketing imagination.

This series brings together the most innovative work in the burgeoning interpretative marketing research tradition. It ranges across the methodological spectrum from grounded theory to personal introspection, covers all aspects of the postmodern marketing "mix," from advertising to product development, and embraces marketing's principal sub-disciplines.

Consumption, Psychology, and Practice Theories
A Hermeneutic Perspective
Tony Wilson

Gifts, Romance, and Consumer Culture
Edited by Yuko Minowa and Russell W. Belk

Also available in Routledge Interpretive Marketing Research series

Representing Consumers
Voices, Views, and Visions
Edited by Barbara B. Stern

Romancing the Market
Edited by Stephen Brown, Anne Marie Doherty and Bill Clarke

Consumer Value: A Framework for Analysis and Research
Edited by Morris B. Holbrook

Marketing and Feminism
Current Issues and Research
Edited by Miriam Catterall, Pauline Maclaran, and Lorna Stevens

For more information about this series, please visit: www.routledge.com/
Routledge-Interpretive-Marketing-Research/book-series/RIMR

Gifts, Romance, and Consumer Culture

Edited by Yuko Minowa and Russell W. Belk

Routledge
Taylor & Francis Group

LONDON AND NEW YORK

First published 2019 by Routledge

2 Park Square, Milton Park, Abingdon, Oxon, OX14 4RN
605 Third Avenue, New York, NY 10017

Routledge is an imprint of the Taylor & Francis Group, an informa business

First issued in paperback 2020

Library of Congress Cataloging-in-Publication Data
Names: Minowa, Yuko, editor. | Belk, Russell W., editor.
Title: Gifts, romance, and consumer culture / edited by Yuko
    Minowa and Russell W. Belk.
Description: New York, NY : Routledge, 2019. | Series: Routledge
    interpretive marketing research | Includes index.
Identifiers: LCCN 2018034612 | ISBN 9781138500709 (hardback) |
    ISBN 9781315144658 (ebook)
Subjects: LCSH: Gifts. | Courtship. | Consumer behavior. |
    Consumer research.
Classification: LCC GT3040 .G55 2019 | DDC 394—dc23
LC record available at https://lccn.loc.gov/2018034612

ISBN: 978-1-138-50070-9 (hbk)
ISBN: 978-0-367-73334-6 (pbk)

Typeset in Sabon
by Apex CoVantage, LLC

It's all I have to bring to-day,
    This, and my heart beside,
This, and my heart, and all the fields,
    And all the meadows wide.
Be sure you count, should I forget,—
    Some one the sum could tell,—
This, and my heart, and all the bees
    Which in the clover dwell.

Emily Dickinson (ca. 1858)

Contents

List of Illustrations   x
List of Contributors   xi
Acknowledgments   xix

SECTION I
Overview   1

1 Introduction   3
   YUKO MINOWA AND RUSSELL W. BELK

SECTION II
Romantic Gift-Giving: The Nature of Love   17

2 Are We a Perfect Match? Roles for Market Mediators in
   Defining Perfect Gifts   19
   TONYA WILLIAMS BRADFORD

3 Romantic Gift-Giving of Mature Consumers: A Storgic
   Love Paradigm   37
   YUKO MINOWA AND RUSSELL W. BELK

4 If You Love Me, Surprise Me   65
   ADITYA GUPTA AND JAMES W. GENTRY

5 Characteristics and Meanings of Good and Bad Romantic
   Gifts Across Cultures: A Recipient's Perspective   80
   SYDNEY CHINCHANACHOKCHAI AND THEERANUCH PUSAKSRIKIT

SECTION III
Romantic Gift-Giving Contexts   99

  6 Practicing Masculinity and Reciprocation in
    Gendered Gift-Giving Rituals: White Day in Japan,
    1980–2009   101
    YUKO MINOWA, RUSSELL W. BELK, AND TAKESHI MATSUI

  7 Romantic Gifts as an Expression of Masculinity Amongst
    Young Men With Disabilities in Zimbabwe   126
    TAFADZWA RUGOHO

  8 Gift-Giving Within Adult Daughter-Mother Dyads   141
    CHIHLING LIU, XIN ZHAO, AND MARGARET K. HOGG

  9 Crunch My Heart! It Falls for You: Carnal-Singularity
    and Chocolate Gift-Giving Across Language Contexts   153
    MARJAANA MÄKELÄ, SHONA BETTANY, AND LORNA STEVENS

SECTION IV
Romantic Gift-Giving: Unselfishness and
Self-Interest   171

 10 The Romantic Potential of Money: When Credit
    Becomes a Gift   173
    DOMEN BAJDE AND PILAR ROJAS GAVIRIA

 11 From Strangers to Family: How Material and
    Nonmaterial Gift-Giving Strategies Create Agapic
    Relationships Over Time   184
    LYDIA OTTLEWSKI

 12 Romantic Self-Gifts to the "Hidden True Self": Self-Gifting
    and Multiple Selves   204
    SAORI KANNO AND SATOKO SUZUKI

 13 For You and for Me: Creative Experiences as Gifts   218
    EIRINI KORONAKI, ANTIGONE G. KYROUSI, AND ATHINA Y. ZOTOU

CONCLUSION 235

14 **Reflections on Romantic Gift Exchange: An Intersectional Conversation** 237

CELE C. OTNES AND ROBERT ALFONSO ARIAS

EPILOGUE 253

15 **Four Gift Poems** 255

JOHN F. SHERRY, JR.

Index 258

Illustrations

Figures

2.1	Gift-Giving With the Market as a Resource	32
2.2	Gift-Giving With the Market as a Participant	33
4.1	A Conceptual Framework for Surprise Romantic Gifts	74
6.1	An Ad With the "White Day as an Event for Gender Performance" Theme (*Shukan Sankei* March 2, 1984)	110
6.2	An Ad With the "White Day as a Rite of Institution" Theme (*Asahi Shinbun* March 4, 1993)	114
11.1	Gift-Giving Spiral Based on Sahlins (1972) and Belk and Coon (1993)	198
13.1	Gifts of Creative Experiences	224

Tables

3.1	Aging Influences on Romantic Gift-Giving	42
3.2	A Comparison of Three Gift-Giving Paradigms	45
5.1	Top Three Perfect Gifts, Good Gifts, and Bad Gifts	88
5.2	Summary of the Cross-Cultural Comparison of Three Types of Gifts	94
12.1	Summary Profile of Informants	208
14.1	Questions for Future Research on Gift-Giving	250

Contributors

Robert Alfonso Arias is a fifth-year marketing doctoral candidate in the Gies College of Business at the University of Illinois at Urbana-Champaign. Prior to entering the doctoral program, he earned his bachelor's degree at DePaul University in Chicago. In his research, he studies how consumers navigate experiences of belonging and exclusion within social contexts. Specifically, he is interested in how consumers leverage resources in the marketplace to facilitate belonging pursuits. Moreover, he explores how consumers navigate tensions within a dysfunctional brand community. Robert primarily uses qualitative methods in his research, but also uses experimental methods as well. As face-to-face human interactions decrease and technology increases our capability for digital human connection, Robert sees a changing and intriguing future for research topics pertaining to belonging and exclusion within the consumer behavior discipline.

Domen Bajde is Associate Professor at the University of Southern Denmark, where he heads the Consumption, Culture, and Commerce research unit. He has published extensively on morality and consumption, charitable gift-giving, and actor-network theory. His current research focuses on the development of moralized markets and high technology markets.

Russell W. Belk is York University Distinguished Research Professor and Kraft Foods Canada Chair in Marketing, Schulich School of Business, York University. A fellow, past president, and Film Festival co-founder in the Association for Consumer Research, he has a number of awards, including the Paul D. Converse Award, two Fulbright Fellowships, Fellow in the Royal Society of Canada, and the Sheth Foundation/ *Journal of Consumer Research* Award for Long Term Contribution to Consumer Research, and he has over 600 publications. His research involves the extended self, meanings of possessions, collecting, gift-giving, sharing, digital consumption, and materialism.

Shona Bettany is Professor of Marketing and Associate Dean for Research, Liverpool Business School, UK. Her research focuses on ethnographic studies of consumption cultures, particularly related to the family, technology, and sexualities. Her work also encompasses critical studies employing feminist and post-humanist approaches. She has published in the *European Journal of Marketing*, the *Journal of Business Research*, *Marketing Theory*, the *Journal of Marketing Management*, *Advances in Consumer Research*, and *Consumption, Markets, & Culture*.

Tonya Williams Bradford researches rituals, communities, and identity across phenomena, including gifting (e.g., registry, organ, charitable), relationships with money, communities (e.g., tailgating and support), acculturation, and brand loyalty. She earned a BA in Anthropology from Northwestern University, an MBA from the Kellogg School of Management, Northwestern University, and a doctoral degree in Marketing from Northwestern University. Her research is published in the *Journal of Consumer Research*, the *Journal of Marketing*, the *Journal of Retailing*, the *Journal of Business Research*, the *Journal of Interactive Marketing*, and *Research in Consumer Behavior*. She serves as a reviewer for several journals, in addition to serving on the editorial review board for the *Journal of the Academy of Marketing Science*. Professor Bradford presented her research at various marketing conferences, including the Consumer Culture Theory, the Association for Consumer Research, and the American Marketing Association Winter Educator's Conference. Prior to joining the academy, she worked nearly 20 years in the financial services sector, domestically and abroad.

Sydney Chinchanachokchai is Assistant Professor of Marketing in the College of Business Administration at the University of Akron. Her primary research interests are in the areas of cross-cultural consumer behavior, multitasking, mind wandering, and attention. She has published articles in the *Journal of Business Research* and *Computers in Human Behavior*.

Pilar Rojas Gaviria is an assistant professor of marketing at Pontificia Universidad Católica de Chile. Her work focuses on understanding the role of consumption in the construction of multicultural collective identities and solidarities. She draws on philosophical theories, poetry, and research on consumer behavior. She has published her work in *Consumption, Markets & Culture*, the *Journal of Business Research*, *International Marketing Research* and the *Journal of Consumer Behavior*.

James W. Gentry is Professor of Marketing and the Maurice J. and Alice Hollman Professor of Marketing in the College of Business at the

University of Nebraska-Lincoln. He has a bachelor's degree in Civil
Engineering from Kansas State University and an MBA and DBA
from Indiana University. He has taught at Kansas State University, Okla-
homa State University, the University of Wisconsin-Madison, and the
University of Western Australia and has been with UNL since 1987.
While at Oklahoma State University, he was named the Outstanding
Graduate Instructor on campus, and he was awarded the Excellence
in Graduate Education Award in 2007 from UNL's Graduate Studies.

Jim's research early in his career focused on behavioral decision
theory, using survey research and experimental methods, but in the
last two decades he has concentrated on family, gender, aging, and
cross-cultural consumer issues. He has published in a wide variety
of journals.

Aditya Gupta is a PhD candidate in the Marketing Department of the
College of Business at the University of Nebraska-Lincoln. He has a
bachelor's degree in Economics from Delhi University in India and
a master's degree in Marketing from the S.P. Jain Institute of Management and Research, also in India.

His research interests lie in the domain of consumer behavior and
include hedonic and eudaimonic approaches to consumption, the
role of surprise and uncertainty in gift-giving, and the differences
between experiential and material purchases. He has presented his
research at venues such as the Winter AMA Conferences, the Association for Consumer Research Conference, the Annual Macromarketing Conference, and the Haring Symposium. He has also represented
his department at academic events such as the AMA-Sheth Doctoral
Consortium and the Paul D. Converse Symposium and has served
as a reviewer for the AMA, ACR, and SCP conferences.

Margaret K. Hogg holds the Chair of Consumer Behavior and Marketing
in Lancaster University Management School. She studied Politics and
Modern History (Edinburgh University) and completed her PhD at
Alliance Manchester Business School, UK. Her principal research
interests lie in the relationship between identity, self, and consumption. She has been Associate Editor (Buyer Behavior) for the *Journal
of Business Research* since 2013. Her work has appeared in the
Journal of Advertising, the *Journal of Business Research*, *Consumption, Markets, & Culture*, the *Journal of Services Marketing*, the
European Journal of Marketing, the *International Journal of Advertising*, and *The Sociological Review*. She edited six volumes on Consumer Behavior in the SAGE *Major Works* series (2005 and 2006)
and is a co-author of the 7th European Edition of *Consumer Behavior:
A European Perspective* (Pearson, in press). In 2017 she won the
Student-led Teaching Award for Postgraduate Teaching/Supervision
at Lancaster University.

Saori Kanno is Professor of Marketing at the Faculty of Business Administration at Komazawa University, Japan. Her research focuses on brand relationships, self-concept and consumptions, and cultural influence on consumer behavior.

Eirini Koronaki is an academic and researcher in the field of marketing and holds a PhD in Business Administration (Subject: Luxury Branding) from the Athens University of Economics and Business. She currently works as a Part-Time Faculty in the Marketing Department of Deree—the American College of Greece, has received an Academic Scholarship for teaching and research from Athens University of Economics and Business, and works as a Visiting Professor for ECS Rennes School of Business. Her research interests lie in the fields of luxury branding, marketing communications, and cross-cultural research. She has co-authored chapters in books and has presented papers in several conferences. She has professional experience as a Business Development Manager for Eurodiet Med.

Antigone G. Kyrousi is an academic and researcher in the field of marketing. She currently works as Adjunct Faculty in the Marketing Department of Deree—The American College of Greece. She holds a PhD in Business Administration (Subject Area: Advertising) from the Athens University of Economics and Business (AUEB), where she has also conducted postdoctoral research under grant funding. Her research interests lie in the field of consumer behavior, as well as marketing communications. Her doctoral research has been funded by the EU, and she has received distinctions for research papers presented at academic conferences. Her work has been published in journals such as the *International Journal of Advertising* and *Corporate Communications: An International Journal*, and she has presented several papers at conferences such as the *American Marketing Association Conference*, the *International Conference on Research in Advertising*, and the *International Conference on Corporate and Marketing Communications*. She has also co-authored chapters in books and research volumes.

Chihling Liu is an assistant professor of consumer behavior and marketing in the Department of Marketing at Lancaster University Management School, UK. She obtained her PhD at Alliance Manchester Business School, UK. Her primary research interests lie in exploring the relationship between identity, self, and consumption, with a specific focus on improving consumer welfare and making a positive social impact. Her research areas include self-presentation, gifting, and stigma management in the contexts of family and gendered consumption. Her current teaching involves courses on Advanced Topics on Consumer Behavior, Marketing Research, and Marketing Research and Consultancy Projects at both the undergraduate and postgraduate levels. She has been an editorial board member of the *Journal of Business Research* since 2016. She is also a member of Association of Consumer Research (ACR) and Consumer Culture Theory (CCT). Her research has been published in the *Journal of Business Research*, *Advances in Consumer Research*, and *Research in Consumer Behavior*.

Marjaana Mäkelä works as Principal Lecturer at the Haaga-Helia University of Applied Sciences (Helsinki, Finland), lecturing in culinary French and coordinating pedagogical development. She is also consulting in projects on the Finnish export of education.

Marjaana's scholarly interests are discourse studies, the French language, food consumption trends, and consumer culture. She is preparing an interdisciplinary PhD on totemic foods at the University of Westminster. This research has a Consumer Culture Theory-oriented approach of linguistics, sociology, and marketing, with chocolate and chili as key foods. Marjaana holds a Licentiate of Philosophy degree in French linguistics, an MA in Romance philology and gender studies, and an MSc in sociology and business administration. Her publications are mainly French on contemporary issues of working life (L'Harmattan Paris 2006, 2008, 2008, 2011), with recent contributions in English and Finnish on work-based learning in higher education (2017, 2018) and foodie consumption (2017).

Takeshi Matsui is Professor of Marketing at the Graduate School of Business Administration, Hitotsubashi University, Japan. Matsui received his BA in Commerce and his PhD in Commerce and Management from Hitotsubashi University. His research tends to be sociological and cultural and involves market creation through language, global marketing of creative products, and theory and methods in the sociology of culture and Consumer Culture Theory. Matsui published *Language and Marketing: A Social History of the "Healing Boom" in Japan* (Sekigaku-sha) in 2013. His *Selling Japanese Comics in the United States: A Global Marketing of Creative Products* is forthcoming from Yuhikaku Publishing Co., Ltd. He has received the Japanese Society of Marketing and Distribution Encouragement Book Award, the Global Marketing Conference Best Paper Award, the Yoshida Hideo Memorial Foundation Encouragement Award, and other awards.

Yuko Minowa is Professor of Marketing in the School of Business at the Brooklyn Campus of Long Island University in New York. She earned her PhD from Rutgers, the State University of New Jersey. She was a Visiting Scholar at the Jerome A. Chazen Institute of International Business/ Graduate Business School of Columbia University. Her research involves theoretical study of consumption phenomena and consumer behavior with a focus on consumption rituals, interpretive research methods, semiotic analysis of cultural media, and historical research in marketing and consumer behavior. Her research is published in the *Marketing Theory*, the *Journal of Business Research*, the *Journal of Macromarketing, Consumption, Markets & Culture, Visual Communications Quarterly*, and the *Journal of Historical Research in Marketing*, and in the edited volumes *Brand Mascots* and *Global and Multinational Advertising*.

Cele C. Otnes is Professor of Marketing and the Anthony J. Petullo Chair of Business Administration in the Gies College of Business at the University of Illinois at Urbana-Champaign and Adjunct Professor at the Norwegian School of Economics. Her research focuses on how micro, macro, and marketplace factors shape consumption rituals such as gift-giving, holidays, and culturally embedded occasions. She is the co-author of *Royal Fever: The British Monarchy in Consumer Culture* (with Elizabeth H. Pleck) and *Cinderella Dreams: The Allure of the Lavish Wedding* (with Pauline Maclaran). Her research appears in the *Journal of Consumer Research*, the *Journal of Consumer Psychology*, the *Journal of the Academy of Marketing Science*, the *Journal of Advertising*, the *Journal of Retailing,* and other journals and edited volumes. Her current research explores consumers' quests for tranquility-inducing products, services, and experiences, with funding from the Marketing Science Institute and the Transformative Consumer Research initiative.

Lydia Ottlewski is a doctoral candidate in Marketing and a research associate at the Institute for Customer Insight at the University of St. Gallen, Switzerland. Her research interests are gift-giving, elderly consumers, social innovation, and alternative family constructions. Her master's thesis was supervised by Professor Domen Bajde at the University of Southern Denmark in Odense. Her PhD research was supervised by Professor John Schouten.

Theeranuch Pusaksrikit is Assistant Professor of Marketing at the School of Business, University of the Thai Chamber of Commerce, Thailand. She completed her PhD at the University of Manchester, UK. Her research interests lie in the area of cross-cultural gift-giving behavior, religious consumption, consumer acculturation, and consumer rights. Her prior articles appeared in the *Journal of Consumer Psychology* and the *Journal of Business Research*.

Tafadzwa Rugoho is a part-time lecturer at Great Zimbabwe University and a doctoral candidate with University of KwaZulu-Natal, where he is specializing in the participation of persons with disabilities in empowerment initiatives in Zimbabwe. He holds an MSc in Development Studies and an MSc in Strategic Management. He has vast experience in disability issues, having worked in the field for more than ten years. He has authored a number of scientific journal papers and several book chapters. Tafadzwa is also a disability activist. Tafadzwa is a family therapist and offers his services for free to fellow people with disabilities. He is more interested in the sexual relationships of people with disabilities.

John F. Sherry, Jr. is Herrick Professor of Marketing at the University of Notre Dame. He studies brand strategy, experiential consumption, and retail atmospherics. He is a Fellow of the American Anthropological Association and the Society for Applied Anthropology, a past President both of the Association for Consumer Research and the Consumer Culture Theory Consortium, and a former Associate Editor of the *Journal of Consumer Research*. Sherry has edited and written ten books and authored more than 100 widely reprinted articles and chapters. He has won awards for his scholarly work and poetry.

Lorna Stevens is Associate Professor of Marketing at the University of Bath. Her research, which adopts a qualitative, interpretive approach, focuses on feminist perspectives and gender issues in marketing and consumer behavior. She is particularly interested in experiential and media consumption, as well as in the cultural aspects of contemporary consumption, often exploring the underpinning ideological aspects of texts such as advertisements. Her work has been published in a range of publications, including the *Journal of Retailing*, the *Journal of Advertising*, the *Journal of Strategic Marketing*, and the *Journal of Macromarketing*. She has also contributed to a number of edited books, including *Gender, Culture, and Consumer Behavior* (Taylor & Francis, 2012), *Marketing Management: A Cultural Perspective* (Routledge, 2012), *Motherhoods, Markets, and Consumption* (Routledge, 2014), and *Brand Mascots* (Routledge, 2014). She is Associate Editor of the *Journal of Marketing Management* and is on the Review Board of *Marketing Theory*.

Satoko Suzuki received her MBA and DBA from the Graduate School of International Corporate Strategy, Hitotsubashi University, and is Associate Professor at Hitotsubashi University Business School, where she teaches Marketing and Design Thinking. She conducts interdisciplinary research on topics related to culture, consumer behavior, and marketing management. Her current research focuses on how various cultural dimensions, both at individual and societal levels, affect consumer behavior and marketing. She has a strong interest in Japanese women's consumer identity project, and her works appear in *Advances in Consumer Research*. Her other works appear in scholarly journals and other media, including the *International Journal of Psychology*,

Cognition, and Emotion, Frontiers in Psychology, the *International Journal of Innovation Management*, and *Food Quality and Preference*.

Xin Zhao is Senior Lecturer of Marketing at Lancaster University Management School, UK. His research focuses on communal consumption, semiotics, consumption rituals, gift exchange, and social media in China. His previous work has been published in the *Journal of Consumer Research*, the *Journal of Retailing*, the *Journal of Advertising*, and the *Journal of Advertising Research*.

Athina Y. Zotou received her PhD in Marketing from Athens University of Economics and Business. She holds a bachelor's degree in Social Sciences from the Aristotle University of Thessaloniki, Greece, and a master's degree in Mass Communications from London Metropolitan University, UK. Her research interests focus on marketing and communications, advertising, and consumer behavior and related areas. She is currently teaching in Cyprus University of Technology, Limassol, Cyprus. Several pieces of her work have been published in international conferences' proceedings and in refereed academic journals.

Acknowledgments

The chapters that appear in this volume mostly originated in conversations with the contributors at the Association for Consumer Research Gender Conference in Paris, the Consumer Culture Theory Conference in Lille, France, the Association for Consumer Research Conference in Berlin in 2016, and the Consumer Culture Theory Conference in Anaheim, California, in 2017. This book was made possible by the enthusiastic contributors, who prepared manuscripts with zest and love.

Each chapter was reviewed by two scholars in the field of consumer research. We would like to particularly thank the following external reviewers who generously contributed their time: Aaron Ahuvia, Michelle Barnhart, Michael Beverland, Gokcen Coskuner-Balli, Eileen Fischer, Ahir Gopaldas, Annamma Joy, Junko Kimura, Tina Lowrey, Pauline Maclaran, Jean-Sebastien Marcoux, Rebecca Mardon, David Mick, Nacima Ourahmoune, Victoria Rodner, Daiane Scaraboto, Jonathan Schroeder, and David Wooten.

In preparing the book proposal and chapters, the help provided by the staff at Taylor & Francis was valuable. We especially thank David Varley for believing in this project and Megan Smith and Mary Del Plato for offering continuous support in preparing this edited volume. We also thank Sanford Kryle for conducting copyright searches.

Last, but not least, we would like to send thousands of thanks and love to our family and friends, who made the sun shine even on gray days.

Yuko Minowa
Russell W. Belk
May 2018

Section I

Overview

1 Introduction

Yuko Minowa and Russell W. Belk

"How do I love thee? Let me count the ways." Elizabeth Barrett Browning's (1986 [1850]) sonnets—her very personal expressions of love—were not meant for publication, but as a gift to her husband Robert as a token of her devotion. There are different ways to communicate romantic feelings. Gift-giving is one. Giving and receiving of gifts is characteristics of intimate relationships. It is a message, a form of communication, through a tangible material object, about love, affection, and concern about the recipient. The "romantic gift" is a provocative subject. It evokes a multitude of intertwined meanings: passion, intimacy, affection, persuasion, care, celebration, altruism, and nostalgia. It can also connote negative images of obligation and reciprocity. Romantic gift-giving may be practiced within rituals, such as Valentine's Day, during rites of passage, such as weddings, or for casual occasions to affirm the continued importance of the romantic relationship. It can be used for an instrumental purpose to initiate and maintain an intimate relationship. We may even romanticize the giving of gifts to the self, to nonhuman companions, and to others we do not know personally. If loving and giving are practices, then romantic gift-giving is a practice of loving with intimate—or would-be intimate—others.

The Objectives of the Volume

This book addresses gift-giving among consumers attempting to express and construct romantic love. It lies at the intersection of consumption, markets, and culture. In societies shaped by the globalizing neoliberal economic order and increasing wealth disparity, and mediated by a partially digitized social environment that they help to co-construct, it may be time to rethink romantic love. Gift-giving is a key arena in which to do so, as gifts make love tangible and act as carriers of meaning as well as cultural symbols (Belk and Coon 1993). In gift-giving, the meanings of romance are renewed, renegotiated, and reconstructed. Love is problematized and conceptualized through cultural and social media and often involves giving gifts (Illouz 1997, 2007). Practices of intimacy and reciprocity produce emotional, exotic, and cultural capital. On the other hand, in the sexualized culture of affluent modern societies, erotic capital is exploited by some for upward social mobility (Hakim 2010). There is a seemingly inescapable relationship of intimacy and reciprocity with economic capital as well and a necessary translation of economic resources into symbolic resources (Zelizer 2005). Consumers are in search of intimacy in this precarious world, both in everyday reality and in virtual spheres. Under such social conditions, do consumers still "fall in love"? With whom? Can "love" still be agapic and storgic, or merely erotic and pragmatic? Does the ideology of "the perfect gift" (Belk 1996) still apply?

Gifts exist with their "social ontology"—an intermixing of human thought and materiality, springing from social and material relations (Gosden 1994). Traditional romantic gift-giving rituals (e.g., Capellanus 1960; Davis 2000) die while new ones emerge in a fragmented consumer culture. The marketplace is now the crucible of rhetoric that legitimizes new gift-giving rituals as a rite of social practice interacting with marketplace institutions. The inalienable romantic gift objects that once encapsulated memory, created identity, and stirred romantic imagination may be replaced by intangible gifts in this age of digitization, overconsumption, and anti-consumption. Gift-giving itself may be marginalized or replaced by sharing and downsizing. Alternative gift economies and market systems may emerge as a result. The objective of this edited volume is to demonstrate a wide variety of scholarly work bearing on romantic gift-giving using an interpretive consumer research perspective. The book introduces critical studies by a mixture of well-established and emerging scholars in this interdisciplinary field.

Gifts, Romance, and Consumer Culture consists of four sections, ranging over several social scientific disciplines, reflecting the many faces of romance in relation to the gift. After this introduction in Section I for overview, Section II focuses on the nature of love, focusing on social psychological theories, and empirical and conceptual research on romantic gift-giving in both Western and Eastern societies. The focus of Section III is on studies of the contexts of romantic gift-giving based on sociological and anthropological perspectives: the premise is that romantic gifts are a means to achieve a cultural and social cohesion. The main themes of Section IV are altruism versus self-interests that underlie the core of romantic gift-giving. These sections are followed by the conclusion and the epilogue.

Romantic Gift-Giving: The Nature of Love

"What is love?" Is it Eros or Agape? Plato in the *Symposium* argues, through the story of Socrates, that love is our means to try to attain goodness. The concept of love is not singular. Altruistic agapic love, for instance, is considered not as universal but rather as one type of love (Belk 1996, 2005; Belk and Coon 1993). Love is multidimensional. It may be defined in terms of the expression of feelings and attitudes and may manifest in emotional and physical affinities (Hetsroni 2012). Although the English word "love" is used with great frequency, no consensus on its meaning is found in the arts and sciences (Hunt 1959), and a detailed consideration has been neglected in consumer and marketing research as well (Batra, Ahuvia, and Bagozzi 2012). Various theories of love indeed exist (Fisher 2004; Hendrick and Hendrick 1986; Illouz 1997; Lewis 1960; Zelizer 2005). Stendhal posits four kinds of love—mannered love, physical love, vanity-love, and passionate love (Stendhal 1975 [1822]), while, theologically inspired, Lewis (1960) classifies love into affection, friendship, eros, and charity. Love may be classified based on the chemical systems in the brain into lust, romance, and attachment (Fisher 2004). According to "attachment theory," biological systems divide love into sexuality, attachment, and caregiving (Ackerman 1994). Sternberg's (1986) "triangular theory of love" emphasizes three components: intimacy, passion, and decision/commitment, considered to be the "prototype of love" (Aron and Westbay 1996).

Based on earlier sociological studies, Lee (1973) postulated a model of six love styles, on a "colour wheel of love." His typology consists of three primary hues—Eros (passionate love), Ludus (game-playing love), Storge (friendship-like love)—and three secondary hues as blends of the primary ones—Pragma (practical love), Mania (possessive love), and Agape (altruistic love). All these six love styles have been found to exist, each shaped by the nature of the relationship with another person (Hendrick and Hendrick 1986) or companion animal (Belk 1996; Hirschman 1994). There is a relationship between these love styles and personality and attachment styles (Heaven et al. 2004), desire for closeness (Goodboy and Booth-Butterfield 2009), jealousy-evoking behaviors (Goodboy, Horan, Booth-Butterfield 2012), and TV viewing habits (Hetsroni 2012). They exist with intercultural and intracultural variations. Asians, for instance, are inclined to be pragmatic (Neto et al. 2000). In Asian arranged marriages, love is seen to develop after marriage. Gender differences in love styles have been claimed: women tend to be more storgic, manic, and pragmatic, while men tend to be more ludic (Hendrick, Hendrick, and Slapion-Foote 1984). While behavioral manifestations of love and emotional expressions may be socially cultivated and culturally construed, the fundamental components of romantic love—attraction and attachment—are primarily panhuman emotions and not a Western invention or phenomenon. The ideal of romantic love has been suggested to be a cultural universal (Jankowiak 1997).

Romantic gift-giving has been studied in diverse contexts and disciplinary perspectives from psychology (Areni, Kiecker, and Palan 1998; Saad and Gill 2003), sociology (Zelizer 2005), and gender studies (Gould and Weil 1991; Newman and Nelson 1996), to consumer research (Belk

1996; Belk and Coon 1993; Minowa and Gould 1999; Minowa, Kho-menko, and Belk 2011; Minowa, Matsui, and Belk 2012, 2013; Otnes, Ruth, and Milbourne 1994; Otnes, Zolner, and Lowrey 1994; Rugimbana et al. 2003). Belk and Coon (1993) divide gift-giving among couples into three models of giving: (1) economic exchange, (2) social exchange, and (3) as an expression of agapic love. Their study broadened the realm of gift-giving research by adding selfless romantic giving to the exchange paradigm. Based on the analysis of altruistic gift-giving by young adults in literary works, Belk (1996) further examined symbolic properties of "the perfect gift" as an expression of the selfless, altruistic love of the giver. It is characterized by: luxury, surprise, appropriateness, an extraordinary sacrifice by the giver, a wish to please the recipient, and as fulfilling the desire of a recipient who is delighted by the gift. Such a gift defines gift-giving and receiving ideals among couples.

In Chapter 2, Tonya Williams Bradford examines the roles of market mediators in defining the perfect gift in the context of living organ donation. People use their bodies as gifts in various forms of sexual encounters, conception, surrogate motherhood, and household labor. Bodily generated gifts do not always require market participation. For the gift of an organ, however, the market is a necessary participant in gift-giving, as it coordinates givers and recipients. Bradford's discussion of gifted kidneys among two married couples provides an opportunity to better understand how market mediated gift-giving influences romantic love and vice-versa.

In Chapter 3, based on in-depth interviews, Yuko Minowa and Russell W. Belk investigate the different meanings of romantic gift-giving for mature consumers in an aging cohort comprised of Baby Boomers in Japan. The emergent storgic love model, characterized by caring, appreciative, and empathetic companionate love, illustrates that gifts may be used: to enhance affectionate relationships by enriching everyday experiences; to facilitate a new consumption style—downsizing; and to convey empathy for recipients' frailty, to defy aging, and to impart knowledge and skills for the Fourth Age.

In Chapter 4, Aditya Gupta and James Gentry discuss surprise gifts and love. Surprise has been posited as an integral element of "the perfect gift" (Belk 1996). What makes surprise interesting is its association with delight, another prerequisite for a gift to be perfect. While surprise has been researched as an element of emotion, the transient nature of surprise makes it an elusive emotion to study. In this chapter, the authors take a closer look at surprise—both good and bad surprise—and its relationship with delight. They also explore the role that surprise can play in the "magic" of romantic gift-giving.

Is surprise always an element of "the perfect gift" across cultures? In Chapter 5, Sydney Chinchanachokchai and Theeranuch Pusaksrikit empirically examine characteristics and meanings of perfect, good, and bad romantic gifts from a recipient's perspective. Comparing the data collected from Thai and American gift recipients, they found similarities and differences between the East and the West. The common characteristics/themes for perfect gifts for recipients from both countries are the gifts that represent relationship and sacrifice. While surprise is appreciated in the West, Asian respondents valued it less due to cultural emphasis on uncertainty avoidance. Their findings also reveal that American recipients emphasized material gifts while Thai respondents valued the giver rather than gifts themselves.

Romantic Gift-Giving Contexts

CHREMYLUS: For to money all things pay obedience. . . . They say too of the Corinthian courtesan, that, if a poor lover attacks them, they will not even lend him an ear: but when a rich lover presents himself before them, they will themselves present anything to him.
CARIO: They say that boys will present too: not for the sake of their lovers, but of money.
CHREMYLUS: You speak of prostitutes, not the worthier sort: for those never ask for money.
CARIO: Why, what do these ask for?
CHREMYLUS: One will accept a fine horse, another a pack of hounds.
CARIO: O then it is probable they are ashamed to ask for the money: they are pleased to cover their inquiry with the name of a present.
—Aristophanes, 1812 [388 BCE], 144–45

Love in the exchange of material gifts, rather than money, is not a unique phenomenon of contemporary capitalist society. As Aristophanes' comedy *Plutus* (Wealth) demonstrates, such exchange is ancient. And it is perhaps global, beyond Athens, wherever wealth exists. Human ambition and avarice are omnipresent across times and places. From a sociological perspective, love is socially situated, and thus, a socially distributed emotion (Cheal 1987). Love and intimacy in capitalist society is a subject of interrogation by sociologists and economists: the motive of love relates to the construction and sustenance of marriage, family, and home economy (Lee 1973). There is a renewed realization that money, gifts, and emotions are profoundly interrelated (Cheal 1987). Illouz (1997, 2) argues that "practices of romance are intertwined with [the] duality of capitalism": the schism between every individual's opportunity to participate in consumption activities and the inequitable concentration of wealth as well as the legitimation of social divisions. Love is also problematized and conceptualized through cultural and social media, some of which involve giving gifts as well (Illouz 1997, 2007).

Different pictures of romantic gift-giving from social psychological perspectives can be drawn from sociological and anthropological approaches. Classical anthropological theories of gift exchange regard gifts as fulfilling crucial functions for the continuation of society and culture. Anthropologists have concluded that feelings of indebtedness lead to patterns of reciprocity in gift exchange. Mauss (1967 [1925]), the key theorist, argued that obligations to give, receive, and repay underlie every gift exchange in both non-Western and Western cultures. Similarly, Malinowski's (1970 [1922]) functionalist approach and Levi-Strauss' (1989 [1949]) structuralist approach emphasize the principles of "give and take" and reciprocity as fundamental parts of developing and maintaining shared meaning in culture. Thus, what Malinowski (1984 [1922], 177) called "pure gifts"—regular gifts from a husband to a wife—were, from Mauss' perspective, a fallacy; they were a payment for the sexual services she rendered to him (Scott and Seglow 2007). Sociologists have contributed to our understanding of the social functions of gift-giving, by emphasizing the concept of faithfulness, gratitude, and reciprocity (Komter 1996; Simmel 1964 [1908]; Visser 2008). In Goffman's (1971, 65–6, 1977; cited in Cheal's 1987, 152) terms, gift-giving is an opportunity through which we display "identificatory sympathy" and engage in interpersonal courtesies. In studying gift-giving among couples, Belk and Coon (1993) discuss economic and social exchange models of the dating gift, as well as giving as an expression of agapic love. Both social and economic exchange models regard gift-giving as an instrumental act for accomplishing a certain goal. While economic exchange is concerned with the financial value of the gift object, social exchange involves the symbolic value. Thus, in the case of social exchange, the giver and the recipient would value a preserved red rose that reminds them of their first date more than an expensive luxury brand leather wallet. Economists, in contrast, are apt to see the whole process of gift-giving as a foolish waste of money, since it fails to fulfill the desires of the recipient as much as a self-gift would (Waldfogel 2009).

In Chapter 6, Yuko Minowa, Russell W. Belk, and Takeshi Matsui investigate the practice of masculinities and reciprocation in a gendered gift-giving ritual, White Day in Japan. Through employing Foucauldian discourse analysis, they educe the hidden presumptions of discourses encompassed in editorials and advertisements involving gifts in Japanese print media. They find that White Day is an opportunity for male consumers to negotiate power relations with women through material objects. The consumer holiday also functions a rite of institutionalization that consecrates the boundary between men and women and shapes collective masculinity through gendered practice. The intertextual interplays show that the "reality" of masculinity is socially constructed through gendered consumer rituals with socially effective language in discursive media.

Romantic gifts are an expression of masculinity across cultures and subcultures with different connotations. In Chapter 7, Tafadzwa

Rugoho discusses romantic gifts among young men with disabilities in Zimbabwe. In most African communities, men with disabilities are generally regarded as feminine and weak. To demonstrate their masculinity, they play the breadwinner role to their romantic partner and give expensive romantic gifts to show their dominance. Some with disabilities have multiple relationships, but it does not prove their masculine worthiness. Buying romantic gifts is considered an ultimate test for young men with disabilities in Zimbabwe.

In Chapter 8, the empirical study by Chihling Liu, Xin Zhao, and Margaret Hogg examines adult daughter-mother dyads in which gift-giving may evoke conflicts and ambivalence rather than appreciation. Underpinned by the study by Otnes, Lowrey, and Kim (1993), the authors explore: 1) what are the different social roles gift-givers express specifically within the mother-daughter dyad, and 2) how might gift-givers influence the dynamics of mother-daughter relationships through gift-giving while expressing their different social roles. They found three social roles—the guardian, the mender, and the keeper—that were not formerly reported by Otnes et al. (1993). They highlight the role of gift-giving in intergenerational influence unique to such intimate relationships as the mother-daughter dyad.

The focus of Chapter 9 is the social ontology of a romantic gift—chocolate—interrogated by Marjaana Mäkelä, Shona Bettany, and Lorna Stevens. By using a material-semiotic approach, the authors extend "singularity" concept of the gift and its recipient (Kopytoff 1986) and develop carnal-singularity. They show how the gift, chocolate, not only becomes de-commodified due to the profusion of meaning and symbolism in social and material relations, but effectively also becomes imbued with the body of the recipient (and giver), and hence with their sexual agency. Their study is cross-cultural. Through a multi-sited netnography, they analyze the gendered nature of chocolate and gift in English, French, and Finish chocolate discourses.

Romantic Gift-Giving: Unselfishness and Self-Interest

The essence of human nature has been a question long debated by philosophers and political economists. One aspect of human nature is its possibility of altruism without displaying another aspect of human nature involving reward seeking. Jencks (1979) defines selfish people as those whose subjective definition of their own welfare does not take the welfare of others into consideration; or whose actual behavior shows that they are not concerned with the welfare of others; or whose concern with the welfare of others is merely instrumental in order to aid their own longer-term selfish goals. Love for the self has been considered sinful, while love for others is virtuous, as those two types of love are considered mutually exclusive and not able to coexist

(Fromm 1956). Thus, self-love has been equated with selfishness. In Freud's term, self-love is narcissism, the manifestation of the libido directed towards the self. On the other hand, Fromm (1956) argues if it is a virtue to love others, it must be a virtue to love the self as well, because the self is also a human being. The self is as much an object of love as another person. And, the individual who can affirm his own life, happiness, growth, and freedom has capacity to love both the self and others. Thus, selfishness is seen by Fromm to be caused by a lack of self-love.

On the other hand, Jencks (1979) defines the unselfish (altruistic) person as someone who considers and acts as if the long-term welfare of others is important, apart from its effects on their own welfare. There are different altruisms, reflecting different motives. Three possible sources of unselfishness are: empathy, community, morality. Empathetic unselfishness tends to occur when individuals "identify" with people outside of themselves. When the interests of others are incorporated into the subjective welfare functions of the self, their interests become part of those of the self. Selfish interests dismantle. The individual "loves" the other whose welfare becomes part of the concern of his or her own. Communitarian unselfishness also involves the identification of the self with, not specific individuals, but a collectivity, such as family, social institutions, and the nation-state. Finally, moralistic unselfishness entails the inclusion of moral ideals into the sense of "self." Such moral ideals are defined by the collective culture of the individual. Once the ideals are internalized, we may be willing to sacrifice our self in order to avoid attitudinal or moral conflict. Jencks (1979) postulates people are likely to act altruistically because they empathize with the person they will eventually become and feel guilty if they act imprudently. In other words, unselfishness is motivated by selfish concerns about the welfare of the self over time. Thus, a person's self-regard may rationally produce reasons for altruism (Schmidtz 1993).

Can humans be generous and be able to help others without seeking return? According to social exchange theorists, the observable generosity in gift-giving is an obvious display of altruism. Altruistic giving, in reality, may be motivated by the expectation of some direct reward, such as power, or an indirect reward, such as recognition (Cheal 1988). Such givers may be considered reciprocal altruists (Niall and Seglow 2007). On the contrary, the giving by pure altruists is voluntary, unrewarded, uncoerced, and creative. Altruistic giving, in which a giver chooses to not sell but give, and the givers and recipients are strangers, as exemplified by blood donation (Titmus 1971), binds the strangers together as a civilized human community, and strengthens communitarian virtues of solidarity and fellowship. Gift-giving can also be practiced as part of the institutionalization of social cohesion within a moral economy. A moral economy involves "a system of transactions which are defined as socially desirable (i.e. moral), because through them social ties are recognized, and balanced social relationships are maintained" (Cheal 1988, 9). Within such a moral economy, the transfer of gifts is a desirable practice in order to construct and maintain these social relationships. Social supports through gifts—transfers of resources—occurs in order to create a better relative distribution of well-being in society. Such transfers are a natural behavior among the members of a "part-society," which consists of a small world of personal relationships that is the emotional core of the individual's social experiences. Beneficence thus increases the stability of relationships in the small social world, although we should not imply that this is necessarily voluntary; it can be socially mandated, as with the gift-giving cases examined by Mauss.

In Chapter 10, Domen Bajde and Pilar Rojas Gaviria argue that money and microloans act as romanticized gifts. Based on an extensive investigation of online microlending platforms, they discuss how microloans involving small monetary loans to disadvantaged borrowers, obtain a uniquely romantic character and come to be framed as perfect gifts to the poor. Furthermore, the authors link the romantics of money to the romantics of capital and credit. By stimulating the futuristic and romantic features of credit-capital, they posit, microfinance institutions sublimate microlending for lenders. In the end, the authors reflect on the role that money and credit "romance" plays in the financialization of development aid and humanitarianism.

In Chapter 11, Lydia Ottlewski examines how material and nonmaterial gift-giving strategies transform and foster agapic relationships between strangers over time. She interrogates this in the context of a non-commercial elderly-student home share program called "Housing for Help." Underpinned by Sahlins' (1972) kinship distance and reciprocity model and Belk and Coon's (1993) agapic love model, she proposes a spiral of reciprocity model that explains how strangers transform their transactional market exchanges into close family-like relationships and friendship bonds. This model contributes to understanding romantic gift-giving by incorporating both the longitudinal emergence and reformulation of relations between alternating givers and recipients.

The focus of Chapter 12 shifts from romantic gifts for selfless love to the gifts given out of self-love: self-gifts (Mick 1996). Saori Kanno and Satoko Suzuki explore romantic self-gifts—a wish solely to please oneself through special indulgences—that reconcile the discomfort and inconsistency of multiple selves. Based on phenomenological interviews with female informants about their most memorable self-gift, the authors examine the reasons and process with which Japanese women engage in self-gift behavior. They argue that a romantic self-gift is a present to the "hidden true self" for Japanese women.

In Chapter 13, Eirini Koronaki, Antigone Kyrousi, and Athina Zotou argue that creative experiences can be gifted. They postulate that such creative experiences are the positive affective outcomes or hedonic benefits produced from activities involving esthetic products. The authors suggest that creative experiences can be gifted to a valued other, as an agapic love gift, celebrating the relationship and expressing the uniqueness of the gift recipient. They posit that creative experiences can also be gifted to the self in order to fulfill the individual's desire for self-actualization and serve to fulfill self-indulgence.

Cele Otnes and Robert Alfonso Arias in Chapter 14 conclude this volume with their reflections on select topics that emerge in the book. Through their dialog, they explore their divergent perspectives and attribute them to the intersectionality: the distinct differences in their demographics, professional status, and life course. They also generate ideas for future gift-giving research. To elucidate their points, they offer an abridged transcript of their discussions around six themes: surprise gifts, masculinity and White Day, creativity and gift-giving, self-gifting, gifts of chocolate, mother/daughter (parent/child) giving, and gifts of time.

The epilogue of this volume is the icing on the cake: four gift poems by John Sherry. With mesmerizing embroidery of powerful word plays and rhymes, Sherry's poems transport us to the evoked world of romantic gift-giving. Love and gifts are heartache, poets would say. May the minstrels of the bard heal our heart and elevate our spirit.

Conclusion

"Belovèd, thou hast brought me many flowers," begins the last in the sequence of Browning's sonnets. Loving is a practice, so is romantic gift-giving. While romantic gift-giving has many faces, our knowledge of this subject tends to be limited and fragmentary. By assessing this multivalent and polysemic subject from divergent theoretical perspectives, we attempt to integrate pieces of a jigsaw puzzle and better understand the landscape of romantic gift-giving. Our hope is that this book on the romantic gift-giving and its various meanings can enrich future enquiries and prompt interdisciplinary conversations on this provocative subject.

References

Ackerman, Diane (1994), *A Natural History of Love*, New York: Random House.
Areni, Charles S., Pamela Kiecker, and Kay M. Palan (1998), "Is It Better to Give Than to Receive? Exploring Gender Differences in the Meaning of Memorable Gifts," *Psychology and Marketing*, 15 (January), 81–109.
Aristophanes (1812 [388 BCE]), "Plutus, *the God of Riches*," in *Comedies of Aristophanes*, ed. Henry Fielding, London: Lackington, Allen, and Co., 113–267.
Aron, Arthur and Lori Westbay (1996), "Dimensions of the Prototype of Love," *Journal of Personality and Social Psychology*, 70 (3), 535–51.

Batra, Rajeev, Aaron Ahuvia, and Richard P. Bagozzi (2012), "Brand Love," *Journal of Marketing*, 76 (March), 1–16.

Belk, Russell W. (1996), "The Perfect Gift," in *Gift Giving: A Research Anthology*, ed. C. Otnes and R. F. Beltramini, Bowling Green, OH: Bowling Green State University Popular Press, 59–84.

——— (2005), "Exchange Taboos from an Interpretive Perspective," *Journal of Consumer Psychology*, 15 (1), 16–21.

Belk, Russell W. and Gregory Coon (1993), "Gift Giving as Agapic Love: An Alternative to the Exchange Paradigm Based on Dating Experiences," *Journal of Consumer Research*, 20 (December), 393–417.

Browning, Elizabeth Barrett (1986 [1850]), *Sonnets from the Portuguese: A Celebration of Love*, New York: St. Martin's Press.

Capellanus, Andreas (1960), *The Art of Courtly Love*, New York: Columbia University Press.

Cheal, David (1987), "'Show Them You Love Them': Gift Giving and the Dialectic of Intimacy," *Sociological Review*, 35 (1), 150–69.

——— (1988), *The Gift Economy*, New York: Routledge.

Davis, Natalie (2000), *The Gift in Sixteenth-Century France*, Madison, WI: Wisconsin University Press.

Fisher, Helen (2004), *Why We Love: The Nature and Chemistry of Romantic Love*, New York: Henry Holt and Company.

Fromm, Erich (1956), *The Art of Loving*, New York: HarperCollins.

Goffman, Ervin (1971), *Relations in Public: Microstudies of the Public Order*, London: Allen Lane.

——— (1977), "The Arrangement between the Sexes," *Theory and Society*, 4 (3), 301–31.

Goodboy, Alan K. and Melanie Booth-Butterfield (2009), "Love Styles and Desire for Closeness in Romantic Relationships," *Psychological Reports*, 105 (1), 191–7.

Goodboy, Alan K., Sean M. Horan, and Melanie Booth-Butterfield (2012), "Intentional Jealousy-Evoking Behavior in Romantic Relationships as a Function of Perceived Partner Affection and Love Styles," *Communication Quarterly*, 60 (3), 370–85.

Gosden, Christopher (1994), *Social Being and Time*, Oxford: Blackwell.

Gould, Stephen J. and Claudia E. Weil (1991), "Gift-Giving Roles and Gender Self-Concepts," *Sex Roles*, 24 (9/10), 617–37.

Hakim, Catherine (2010), "Erotic Capital," *European Sociological Review*, 26 (5), 499–518.

Heaven, Patrick C. L., Tatiana Da Silva, Christine Carey, and Janet Holen (2004), "Loving Styles: Relationships with Personality and Attachment Styles," *European Journal of Personality*, 18 (2), 103–13.

Hendrick, Clyde and Susan Hendrick (1986), "A Theory and Method of Love," *Journal of Personality and Social Psychology*, 50 (2), 392–402.

Hendrick, Clyde, Susan Hendrick, Franklin H. Foote, and Michelle J. Slapion-Foote (1984), "Do Men and Women Love Differently?," *Journal of Social and Personal Relations*, 1 (2), 177–95.

Hetsroni, Amir (2012), "Associations between Television Viewing and Love Styles: An Interpretation Using Cultivation Theory," *Psychological Reports*, 110 (1), 35–50.

Hirschman, Elizabeth (1994), "Consumers and Their Companion Animals," *Journal of Consumer Research*, 20 (4), 616–32.

Hunt, Morton M. (1959), *The Natural History of Love*, New York: Minerva Press.

Illouz, Eva (1997), *Consuming the Romantic Utopia: Love and Cultural Contradictions of Capitalism*, Berkeley, CA: University of California Press.

——— (2007), *Cold Intimacies: The Making of Emotional Capitalism*, Cambridge, UK: Polity Press.

Jankowiak, William (ed.) (1997), *Romantic Passion: A Universal Experience?*, New York: Columbia University Press.

Jencks, Christopher (1979), "The Social Bias of Unselfishness," in *On the Making of Americans: Essays in the Honor of David Riesman*, ed. H. J. Gans, N. Glazer, J. R. Gusfield, and C. Jencks, Philadelphia: University of Pennsylvania Press, 63–86.

Komter, Aafke E. (1996), *The Gift: An Interdisciplinary Perspective*, Amsterdam: Amsterdam University Press.

Kopytoff, Igor (1986), "The Cultural Biography of Things: Commoditization as Process," in *The Social Live of Things: Commodities in Cultural Perspective*, ed. Arjun Appadurai, Cambridge: Cambridge University Press, 64–91.

Lee, John Alan (1973), *Colours of Love: An Exploration of the Ways of Loving*, Toronto: New Press.

Levi-Strauss, Claude (1989 [1949]), "The Principle of Reciprocity," in *Sociological Theory: A Book of Reading*, 5th edition, ed. L. W. Coser and B. Rosenberg, Prospect Heights, IL: Waveland Press, Inc., 94–4.

Lewis, Clive Staples (1960), *The Four Loves*, New York: Harcourt, Brace & World, Inc.

Malinowski, Bronislaw (1970 [1922]), "The Principle of Give and Take," in *Crime and Custom in Savage Society*, London: Routledge and Kegan Paul, 39–45.

——— (1984 [1922]), *Argonauts of the Western Pacific: An Account of Native Enterprise and Adventure in the Archipelagoes of Melanesian New Guinea*, Prospect Heights, IL: Waveland Press, Inc.

Mauss, Marcel (1967 [1925]), *The Gift: Forms and Functions of Exchange in Archaic Societies*, ed. Ian Cunnison, New York: W. W. Norton & Company.

Mick, David G. (1996), "Self-Gifts," in *Gift Giving: A Research Anthology*, ed. C. Otnes and R. F. Beltramini, Bowling Green, OH: Bowling Green State University Popular Press, 99–120.

Minowa, Yuko and Stephen J. Gould (1999), "Love My Gift, Love Me or Is It Love Me, Love My Gift: A Study of The Cultural Construction of Love and Gift-Giving among Japanese Couples," in *Advances in Consumer Research*, Vol. 26, ed. Eric J. Arnould and Linda M. Scott, Provo, UT: Association for Consumer Research, 119–24.

Minowa, Yuko, Olga Khomenko, and Russell W. Belk (2011), "Social Change and Gendered Gift-Giving Rituals: A Historical Analysis of Valentine's Day in Japan," *Journal of Macromarketing*, 31 (1), 41–56.

Minowa, Yuko, Takeshi Matsui, and Russell W. Belk (2012), "'I Would Want a Magic Gift': Desire for Romantic Gift Giving and the Cultural Fantasies of Baby Boomers in Japan," in *NA: Advances in Consumer Research*, Vol. 40, ed. Zeynep Gürhan-Canli, Cele Otnes, and Rui (Juliet) Zhu, Duluth, MN: Association for Consumer Research, 901–2.

—— (2013), "'Make Someone Happy': Romantic Gift Giving of Teenagers in Japan," in *European Advances for Consumer Research*, Vol. 10, ed. Gert Cornelissen, Elena Reutskaja, and Ana Valenzuela, Duluth, MN: Association for Consumer Research, 219–20.

Neto, Felix, Etienne Mullet, Jean-Claude Deschamps, José Barros, Rosario Benvindo, Leôncio Camino, Anne Falconi, Victor Kagibanga, and Maria Machado (2000), "Cross-Cultural Variations in Attitudes Toward Love," *Journal of Cross-Cultural Psychology*, 31 (5), 626–35.

Newman, Peter J. and Michelle R. Nelson (1996), "Mainstream Legitimization of Homosexual Men through Valentine's Day Gift-Giving and Consumption Rituals," *Journal of Homosexuality*, 31 (1/2), 57–69.

Niall, Scott and Jonathan Seglow (2007), *Altruism*, New York: Open University Press.

Otnes, Cele, Tina M. Lowrey, and Young Chan Kim (1993), "Gift Selection for Easy and Difficult Recipients: A Social Roles Interpretation," *Journal of Consumer Research*, 20 (2), 229–44.

Otnes, Cele, Julie A. Ruth, and Constance C. Milbourne (1994), "The Pleasure and Pain of Being Close: Men's Mixed Feelings about Participation in Valentine's Day Gift Exchange," in *Advances in Consumer Research*, Vol. 21, ed. Chris T. Allen and Deborah R. John, Provo, UT: Association for Consumer Research, 159–64.

Otnes, Cele, Kyle Zolner, and Tina M. Lowrey (1994), "In-Laws and Outlaws: The Impact of Divorce and Remarriage upon Christmas Gift Exchange," in *Advances in Consumer Research*, Vol. 21, ed. Chris T. Allen and Deborah Roedder John, Provo, UT: Association for Consumer Research, 25–9.

Rugimbana, Robert, Brett Donahay, Christopher Neal, and Michael Polonsky (2003), "The Role of Social Power Relations in Gift Giving on Valentine's Day, " *Journal of Consumer Behaviour*, 3 (1), 63–73.

Saad, Gad and Tripat Gill (2003), "An Evolutionary Psychology Perspective to Romantic Gift Giving of Young Adults," *Psychology and Marketing*, 20 (9), 765–84.

Sahlins, Marshall (1972), *Stone Age Economics*, New York: Aldine de Gruyter.

Schmidtz, David (1993), "Reasons for Altruism," in *Altruism*, ed. E. F. Paul, F. D. Miller, and J. Paul, Cambridge: Cambridge University Press, 52–68.

Scott, Niall and Jonathan Seglow (2007), *Altruism*, Maidenhead, UK: McGraw-Hill Education.

Simmel, Georg (1964 [1908]), "Faithfulness and Gratitude," in *The Sociology of Georg Simmel*, ed. K. H. Wolff, New York: The Free Press.

Stendhal (Marie Henri Beyle) (1975 [1822]), *Love*, Trans. Gilbert Sale and Suzanne Sale, New York: Penguin Books.

Sternberg, Robert J. (1986), "A Triangular Theory of Love," *Psychological Review*, 93 (2), 119–35.

Titmuss, Richard M. (1971), *The Gift Relationship: From Human Blood to Social Policy*, New York: Pantheon Books.

Visser, Margaret (2008), *The Gift of Thanks: The Roots, Persistence, and Paradoxical Meanings of a Social Ritual*, New York: HarperCollins.

Waldfogel, Joel (2009), *Scroogenomics: Why You Shouldn't Buy Presents for the Holidays*, Princeton, NJ: Princeton University Press.

Zelizer, Viviana A. (2005), *Purchase of Intimacy*, Princeton, NJ: Princeton University Press.

Section II
Romantic Gift-Giving
The Nature of Love

2 Are We a Perfect Match?

Roles for Market Mediators in Defining Perfect Gifts

Tonya Williams Bradford

Market mediation permeates much of everyday life, as firms employ algorithms to identify which offerings to complement a recent purchase or to recommend new offerings based on positive reviews by similar others. The prevalence of market mediation makes the engagement and acceptance of market partners to manage the most intimate aspects of life commonplace, such as identifying who to date, having children through artificial reproductive technologies, or identifying one's "true" ancestry through DNA testing. Market mediation is optional for some transactions, however, there are others where such mediation is necessary, and even mandated, as with living organ donation. How does mandated market mediation influence experiences of gift-giving rituals within intimate relationships?

Western notions of romantic love inspire (and social norms require) individuals to demonstrate affection to one another in varying forms, including gift-giving. A quintessential exemplar of a gift inspired by romantic love is depicted in *The Gifts of the Magi* (Henry 1906). In this classic tale, an impoverished couple desires to provide one another with perfect gifts for Christmas. Each has a prized possession: the wife treasures her long hair, and the husband cherishes a gold watch that was passed down to him from his father and grandfather before him. The wife cuts her hair to obtain enough money to purchase a chain for her husband's watch. The husband sells his watch to attain the amount of money necessary to buy the combs his wife has long admired to adorn her hair. Upon exchanging the gifts at Christmas, each realizes the other no longer has means to fully utilize their gifts, yet they each appreciate the romantic love represented by their respective gifts. The role of the market provides both the inspiration to represent and communicate love through specific offerings, as well as the outlets to fulfill those desires for these lovers. And, as gifts are more often purchased than made (Cheal 1988), opportunities for market involvement in gift-giving has become more prevalent.

While gifts generally convey emotion relative to a relationship between the gift-giver and their recipient, gifts between romantic partners also have an expectation that the gift parallels the unique and intimate relationship between the partners (Belk and Coon 1993; Sherry 1983). Gifts between loved ones may be given for a range of reasons including the commemoration of momentous occasions (e.g., planned gifts for anniversaries, birthdays, Sweetest Day, Valentine's Day), as well reminders of their shared affection (e.g., spontaneous gifts of cards, flowers, candy). Be it spur of the moment or special occasions, archetypal gifts reflect thoughtful creation by a gift-giver to suit a particular gift-recipient, and to convey specific messages to that recipient within the context of the relationship. Consumer researchers adopt a view of gift-giving as a key social exchange, and explain gift-giving as a process, define roles for participants within the process, identify varying conditions which add to the complexity found in this form of exchange, and codify consequences for gift-giving (Belk and Coon 1993; Bradford and Sherry 2013; Joy 2001; Otnes, Lowrey, and Kim 1993). Across relationship types, the notion of giving the perfect gift is present (Belk 1996). While a perfect gift may nurture affection within romantic relationships, how does the (necessary) involvement of market mediators in determining the perfect gift influence the roles of gift-giver and gift-recipient?

Organ donation is, by definition, the perfect gift. It is a gift of luxury as it uniquely addresses a specific need, requires extraordinary sacrifice on behalf of the gift-giver, and may be met with delight by the recipient (Belk 1996). Transplantation of an organ may be perceived by most as a medical procedure, however, the laws governing living organ donation in the United States require that individuals freely gift an organ to another without payment or expectation of reciprocity. Further, institutions encouraging organ donation employ the language of "gift of life" when promoting living organ donation. Gifts of organs are like other gifts in that they require thought, convey affection, and are relevant for a specific recipient.

Organs, as gifts, differ from other types of gifts in that the market is not a resource for a gift, but rather a central participant. More specifically, market mediators employ clinical criteria to determine within whom a perfect gift resides, and to whom that gift may be given. Market mediators define the conditions under which the gift may be given, and dictate the relative timing of its presentation. And, gift-receipt is partitioned by market mediators as they segregate incorporation from reciprocation, and mediate opportunities to express appreciation. The incorporation of the gifted organ into the recipient's lived experience is jealously guarded and managed by market mediators who continuously track the gifted organ's performance. And, a gifted organ may be physiologically rejected, even as the gift is embraced emotionally. Finally, any notion of reciprocation is annihilated beginning with the donor qualification process that includes an assessment of one's motives for participating to ensure that the organ is provided freely. Each component of the gift-giving process exists within organ donation, yet, the necessary participation of market mediators obfuscates the gift-giving process. Thus, organ donation provides an opportunity to explore how market mediation influences gift-giving.

A formal category of romantic relationship is marriage, where partners often state vows committing to stand by one another through varying conditions including "in sickness and in health." Many partners are content to abide by the health aspect of the commitment, however, the sickness component is often unimaginable when the vow is made. Organ failure is one such manifestation of sickness that is most often not predictable (nor predicted). It is a relatively slow process that culminates in the need of a functioning organ. And for some spouses, the vow to remain with their partner through sickness engenders the desire to give an organ to their partner as the gift-giver anticipates such a gift will provide an opportunity for health to return. Thus, the desire to gift an organ is a function of a recipient's medical condition (vs. gift occasion), and a potential gift-giver's market defined match (vs. gift-giver knowledge of the recipient). This chapter considers how the necessitated presence of market mediators influences gift-giving processes, roles, and enactments in romantic love relationships as that love is under the physical, emotional, social, and psychological scrutiny of the market.

Organs as Gifts

Objects are perceived as neutral until transformed into gifts symbolic of fences or bridges within the realm of relationships (Douglas and Isherwood 1979). By virtue of transmitting the hopes, wishes, and desires of the gift-giver into an offering, it is transformed into a gift that is imbued with symbolism (Gregory 1982; Hyde 1979; Mauss 1967), and its meaning is valued more than the benefits accrued from use of the material object (Belk 1996; Wolfinbarger 1990). As symbols, gifts represent relational ties and communicate expectations from the giver to the recipient (Bradford 2009; Caplow 1984). Gifts establish and maintain roles in social relationships (Otnes et al. 1993), fortify social bonds (Mauss 1967), alter relationships (Cheal 1988), and serve higher-order needs of love, self-esteem, or self-actualization (Belk 1996; Offer 1997).

Studies of gift-giving first entered into the consumer behavior literature over three decades ago and emphasized the gift-giver (Belk 1976). Scholars characterize gift-giving as a social exchange and communication process (Giesler 2006; Mauss 1967; Sherry 1983; Wooten 2000) and theorize it primarily with dyads of givers and recipients (Belk and Coon 1993; Lowrey, Otnes, and Ruth 2004; Sherry 1983; Wooten 2000). As described by Sherry (1983), the process of gift-giving is composed of three parts: gestation, prestation, and reformulation. Gestation is defined as the transformation of a commodity into a gift. Gestation is orchestrated by the gift-giver and most often necessitates interaction between individuals and the market primarily retailers that are selected by gift-givers on a range of criteria (e.g., gift occasion, assortment, convenience, price). Prestation tends to be a more private moment when the gift-giver presents the gift to the gift-recipient, and, ideally, they accept it. Reformulation is governed primarily by the recipient, as gifts may be embraced as hoped by the gift-giver or disposed of through re-gifting, resale, or destruction (Sherry 1983; Sherry, McGrath, and Levy 1992). That gift-giving model parallels the consumption process of the gift-giver's acquisition (gestation), use (prestation), and disposal (reformulation) of market offerings selected and given as gifts.

The sharing of emotions through gifts communicates messages about the relationship between the giver and the recipient. Expressive gifts—those communicating meaning and affect—are more likely to be given in the context of intimate relationships, such as those with family and close friends. Instrumental gifts—those addressing social norms and obligations—are most likely given in the context of more distant relationships (Joy 2001; Sherry 1983). Gifts are used to socialize recipients into appropriate values and behaviors (Bradford 2009); to engage in relationships that are important, and thus, ought not be taken for granted (Caplow 1982); to acknowledge close others in furtherance of strengthening relationships (Joy 2001); and, to guide and control the behaviors of others (Bradford 2009; Camerer 1988; Schwartz 1967).

There are different perspectives of the body when considering organ donation, and explicit in each perspective is that such a donation is a sacred gift (Belk 1990). Social norms for gift-giving in romantic relationships dictate that individuals give expressive gifts that are stripped of market essence to convey love. Though, it is unlikely that a gift-giver will repackage a gift acquired from Tiffany and packaged in its signature box and bow because such an affiliation contributes to the gift's symbolism and essence. Organs do not have market brands, however, as they are sourced from individuals, each organ does have an indelible marker of belonging represented by one's DNA, a personal brand. When individuals experience organ failure, the "brand" of gifted organ best suited to help them is one that is a clinical match, most likely found in a blood relative.

A perfect gift is one that encompasses extraordinary sacrifice by gift-givers, represents luxury for gift recipients, and inspires surprise and delight for recipients (Belk 1996). Such gifts occur due to foreknowledge of the recipient by the gift-giver, which likely involves study (Caplow 1984; Cheal 1988; Davis 1972; Otnes et al. 1993; Sherry et al. 1992; Sherry et al. 1993). Forethought is evident in planning, searching, shopping, selecting, preparing, and investing objects with love and care (Sherry et al. 1992). Planning and searching include contemplation of the desired response from the recipient that is sought by a gift-giver. The formulation of a desired response is informed by the gift-giver's evaluation of the recipient with respect to the categories of value, esteem, and appreciation (Wooten 2000). Shopping and selecting reflect investments of time and money (Belk 1996; Sherry 1983). Each stage serves to imbue meaning and affect into objects thereby transforming them into gifts, where meaning is transferred to recipients with the presentation of gifts. Though several types of gift-giving and gifts are identified by consumer researchers, gift-givers are particularly challenged when creating gifts for the infirm where the perfect gift is that of health (Otnes et al. 1993).

Organ donation is possible with a perfect match. This match is determined first by a clinical match that is defined by the market, tested by market mediators, and managed by the same. Such a match is a rare occurrence—even between siblings—making the possibility for gift-giving between loved ones even more awe-inspiring. And, when one member of a romantic relationship is in need of a kidney, it is most often the other member who immediately volunteers to gift the organ. What roles do market mediators play in gift-giving when individuals who are romantically involved are inspired to volunteer for such gift-giving? How does the necessity of market mediators influence gifts and gift-giving?

Two Cases of Living Organ Donation

Living organ donation is a multifaceted medical process where healthy organs are removed from an individual to replace the function that is lacking in another. Such replacement results from an extensive clinical matching and clearance protocol, followed by organ harvest and transplantation. Opportunities for living organ donation are becoming common practice as medical innovations, together with health care policies and procedures, provide opportunities for sharing organs between genetically unrelated individuals (Bradford 2013; Rothman, Rozario, and Rothman 2007). Clinical matches are rare between biologically unrelated individuals (such as with spouses) though they do occur. To better understand the relationship between market mediators and gift-giving, living organ donation is explored within married couples where one member of the couple successfully donated to the other. Social norms for gift-giving within romantic relationships suggest that gift-givers avoid offerings which may be considered instrumental. Yet, when an individual experiences organ failure the gift that is most desired is an organ to restore the body and purse life more fully, an instrumental gift.

This research is informed by accounts collected from married couples where one person was the organ donor and the other the recipient. A total of nine (9) couples whose accounts are included in a broader study on organ donation provide the basis for the exploration into understanding market mediators, as central participants in gift-giving. These couples and their marriages were established prior to one member in the couple needing a transplant. Within each couple, one partner needed a kidney, and the other volunteered to give, was found to be a match, and gave their kidney to the other. Where many studies focus on outcomes of the transplant itself, the intention of this research is to understand the impact on gift-giving when there is a market mediator at the center of the ritual. While these individuals and their circumstances do not represent the general population of organ donors, for the objective of the current inquiry, this is a relevant data set.

The objective of this research is to explore the impact of market mediators on gift-giving. To ensure a broad set of experiences in the analysis, positive and negative relationship outcomes, as well as a female and male gift-giver were included. This chapter will focus on the experiences of two married, heterosexual couples, whose pseudonyms are the Andersons and the Baxters. For the Andersons, both husband and wife describe the impact of this market mediated gift as one that enhanced their relationship. The husband as donor and his wife as recipient were initially interviewed together, with follow-up interviews with the donor alone. Those interviews were audio recorded, and transcribed. Where there were many instances of positive relationship outcomes, including a marriage resulting from a donation, it was more challenging to find those individuals for whom the gift resulted in a negative relationship outcome. The Baxters, a couple whose story was reported in the news after successful transplantation, represent a case of a negative relationship outcome. The recipient regained health and filed for divorce from his wife, the donor. She then sought to sue for the return of the donated kidney. While the wife donated her kidney with an intention of restoring her husband to act as a full partner in their marriage, the husband had a different view. Their story was captured through television interviews and news articles. The recorded interviews were transcribed and supplemented with text from news articles. The text of each couples' experiences comprise the primary data for this analysis.

Anna and Alex Anderson were married for several years prior to Anna being diagnosed with renal failure. They do not have children, and, therefore, Anna's options for a blood relative donor were limited to her siblings, parents, and extended family. Her doctor advised that she join the national transplant wait list, and to inquire among family if there was anyone willing to be tested to gift her a kidney. Alex, her husband, asked that he be tested first. Upon completing the medical, psychological, and social testing, he was deemed a match for Anna. Though Anna felt accepting a kidney from Alex was too much to ask, even as his wife, she graciously accepted the offer. He successfully donated to Anna, and they continue to live a full marital life. They are active in living organ donor communities, a part of which is telling their story to others to inspire living organ donation. Alex describes his gift as an additional nuance in their union, such that where they were once perpetually united spiritually, he believes they now also are united in a perpetually physical manner.

Like the Andersons, Bette, and Bob Baxter were married when Bob was diagnosed with renal failure. Bob has children from a prior union, and Bette described her desire to do all she could to enable Bob to live a life where he would see his children grow up, and also be an active participant in the lives of his future grandchildren. Like Alex, Bette completed a battery of tests and was found to be a suitable match to gift a kidney to Bob. Bette was excited to gift her kidney to Bob, though Bob was far less enthusiastic to have her give, even as he spent many miserable hours each week on dialysis. After the transplant, Bob felt better immediately, whereas Bette felt horrible. Bette, like most kidney donors, was healthy prior to the surgery which removed one of her two kidneys while also leaving her body to recuperate from the surgical invasion, and the reduced kidney filtering function. Beyond the expected recovery, Bette noticed her relationship with Bob seemed to change. She recalls her first post-gift encounter with Bob and in particular how he looked at her. She says when she looked in his eyes, she saw that he was no longer in love with her. It was a look she did not see when he was fighting to stay alive. Bob shared that he was unable to reconcile the level of indebtedness he felt toward Bette. The Baxters are now divorced, and Bette unsuccessfully sued Bob for the return of the kidney she gifted to him.

When viewed as social exchange, an act of gift-giving communicates emotions at every stage of the process, beginning with the giver's motives for creating the gift (Belk 1976; Sherry 1983). Motives for gift-giving range from agonistic, where gift-givers seek to maximize their own pleasure, to altruistic, where givers seeks to maximize the pleasure of the recipient (Sherry 1983). Lowrey et al. (2004) developed a typology of ten social influences that motivate gift-giving and addressed the impact those influences have on the giver's relationship with the recipient. That typology of influences identifies five core relational processes gift-givers engage in furtherance of their motives: maintaining equality through social comparison; adjusting to disrupted relational traditions; accessing social support; following relational rules; and initiating and severing relationships. Couple these communications with motives, and the possible relationship outcomes may range from enhancement to termination.

Both Alex and Bette point to their gift of a kidney as the impetus for changing their relationship. Regardless of the outcome, it is the personalization by market mediators that makes such a gift possible. How is it that the market mediation that supports such personalization in gift-giving? How does that personalization influence gift-giving?

Market-Mediated Gifts

The three stages of the gift-giving process—gestation, prestation, reformulation—are evident in living organ donation. The findings from this comparative case analysis primarily provide insight into gestation, and its influence on roles within the ritual. In particular, the findings are categorized as: hopes to embody a perfect gift; instrumental gifts contribute to romantic love; and market mediators as partners in gift-giving.

Hopes to Embody a Perfect Gift

The gift-giving process begins with gestation, the origination of the gift. Each individual arrives at the decision to gift an organ along a distinct path. Common across these organ gift-givers' experiences are a conscious anticipation and imaginative elaboration of life without their recipient. As romantic partners, Bette and Alex express the impetus to give an organ stems from their desire to do whatever was necessary to re-establish the health of their spouses so they could return to being vibrant participants in life.

The preparation to become this particular type of gift-giver is impacted by accentuating and attenuating factors. A factor that heightens the desire to give is learning that their partner's organ function is declining. This is often accompanied by observing how that decline alters the individual's (and the couple's) quality of life. This knowledge may be accompanied with the recognition that their partner will begin dialysis, which can significantly impact their daily routines, including personal fulfillment through professional endeavors, as well as social engagements. Another amplifying factor for gift-giving is the emotional attachment between spouses, particularly as the healthy spouse contemplates life without their loved one. While those factors generate desires to gift an organ, others attenuate that drive. There are likely to be concerns related to the gift-giver's overall health, and the possibility of future complications given the gift-giver will be left with one kidney. An element of the gift-giving process that garners significant attention relates to possible consequences resulting from the surgery to harvest the kidney. As with any surgery, longer term consequences are possible, ranging from minor negative health outcomes to death. In sum, the gift of an organ provides benefits for the recipient that come at some loss of functionality for their gift-givers, such that this particular gift embodies observable sacrifice, unlike that employed in the creation of other gifts.

The decision to gift an organ manifests once a market mediator deems a transplant is a viable option. Unlike other gifts where an occasion may be determined between a gift-giver and a recipient, for organ donation, the occasion is identified by the market mediator along with the recipient. Once the gift is identified as necessary, it only then is possible for a gift-giver to contemplate the idea, and share their decision to participate in gift-giving with a transplant coordinator. Engagement with the transplant coordinator is the first of a complex web of market mediators who actively orchestrate this gift-giving process. The transplant coordinator initiates the protocol to assess the potential gift-giver as a clinical match for their recipient, as well as to evaluate the nature of the motives that drive an individual to voluntarily risk their life to improve the health of another. The clinical match is necessary to determine that the gift-giver and recipient share enough biological matter to make the transplant viable, and reduce the likelihood of rejection. The clinical match process is intrusive, and may prove inconvenient as it requires visits to various labs and specialists and, often, modifications to routines to complete tests along the schedule defined by market mediators.

Understanding the psychological and social motives is more complex than clinical testing where results are binary—clinical results are acceptable, or they are not. With the psychosocial evaluation, potential gift-givers are questioned by various market mediators as to what the givers perceive the benefits may be should they give a kidney to their desired recipient. Each market mediator works to assure the potential gift-giver that there are no right or wrong answers throughout the psychosocial evaluation. Yet, each potential gift-giver sees the market as a form of obstacle course to get through so they might be deemed an acceptable gift. Alex and Bette each describe how they convinced social workers and psychologists of their deep love for their spouses, the altruistic nature of their gift, and the overall benefit to others if they were able to gift their kidneys to their loved ones. They shared memories of their marital past and plans for their collective future in the hopes that the market mediator would assess their love as genuine, their intentions pure, and their marriage worthy. After much testing, contemplation, and designation as a "perfect" match, a potential organ gift-giver may then decide to continue with the process.

The Andersons and Baxters represent a small portion of couples where one partner desires to give a kidney to the other, and is cleared to do so. Like others who strive to donate to their spouse, both Alex and Bette share that they wanted to give their kidney to their spouse as a means of improving their spouse's quality of life and to bolster the possibility that they would have a richer life together. As the gift-givers contemplated their anticipated gift and how it would impact their individual and collective lives, Alex and Bette became even more committed to giving their gift. Each undertook additional preparations to become gift-givers. Bette joined a gym and began a weight loss program to demonstrate her commitment to her overall health. Alex was already healthy, however, he began a workout regimen as he was determined to become "the best specimen" to donate. In sum, they exert effort to ensure their evaluations result in the market mediators determining them to be the perfect match to give their gift!

Instrumental Gifts Contribute to Romantic Love

The market is a source of many types of gifts that range from being principally expressive to primarily instrumental. Social norms for romantic gifts provide guidance on which type of gifts are ideal—the expressive ones. Expressive gifts tend to be the gold standard in romantic gift-giving in that those gifts intuitively confirm intimate knowledge of the beloved recipient, provide a form of luxury for the recipient to enjoy and convey deep affection to the recipient through sacrifice by the gift-giver (Belk and Coon 1993). Instrumental gifts are a bit of an oxymoron in that they tend to reflect what is required versus desired by the recipient. The instrumentality of the gift is most evident when viewing how a gifted organ restores overall physiological, emotional, and social functioning, which together allow an individual to resume their lifestyle. The expressiveness of the gift manifests through the gift-giver's sacrifice when an individual is deemed uniquely suitable to give. The gift of an organ lies at the intersection of expressiveness and instrumentality as it allows the gift-giver and recipient to both imagine and pursue their new life.

The experiences of Bette and Alex illuminate how the notions of instrumentality and expressiveness are united within living donation. Alex describes his journey to gift his kidney in pragmatic terms—acknowledging the desire for his wife, Anna, to live her life free of dialyzing machines and to be her best self. Further reflection of his goals for the gift morphed into more intangible desires for changes in Anna's life. Alex spoke of the joy emanating from her laughter and the intricacies of her personality. He described feeling a void when she was at dialysis and the degree to which she expressed disdain when missing out on those things that made her life enjoyable. For Bette, she thought of how important it was to her that Bob see his children learn life lessons from him as they enter adulthood. When contemplating life together, she could not imagine their possible future, as Bob was physically incapacitated due to dialysis. His declining health contributed to his bitterness, transforming him into a person Bette did not recognize. Bette expressed how she anticipated feeling joy when she could once again see light in his eyes, as an indication that his passion for living returned. Though these individuals risked their own well-being to enhance that of another, they also sought to sow a life-generating love into their recipient to benefit themselves, as well as their family and friends.

Secrecy is a norm in gift creation, and is thought to bolster the expressive value of gifts. Yet, it is transparency that is necessitated for determining who can gift an organ, and ultimately give the gift. The notion of surprise, as a component of the perfect gift, is unimaginable for those giving an organ to a romantic partner. The types of tests required, as well as accepted metrics to determine a match differ by transplant centers, and therefore, is best coordinated with the recipient's transplant team. Once a potential gift-giver is designated as a match for their recipient by the market mediator, the recipient must formally accept the gift prior to it being created or given. The gift-giver and recipient work with the market mediators to identify when the gift will be given. Once the transplant is complete, the recipient's physical body is carefully managed and monitored by the market mediators. More specifically, to ensure that the intended gift is operating as expected, the gift-recipient must comply with extensive testing by the market mediators upon release from the hospital. In accordance with privacy laws governing health care, the gift-giver is devoid of communication regarding the efficacy of their gift beyond that which may be observed, or communicated to them by their recipient. Except for the monitoring of the organ once gifted, the process is more transparent than most gift-giving occasions. This transparency does little to dampen the essence of the gift, but rather elevates its perceived magnificence, perfection, and sacrifice, transforming instrumentality which results in functionality, into expressiveness most often yielding awe and affection.

Market mediators instill transparency in the process, and an unintended consequence is the striking awareness of the sacrifice resident in the gift. For most gifts, a recipient can at best infer the extent of sacrifice involved in its creation. The requisite transparency in organ donation makes the degree of sacrifice, and the inability to reciprocate it conspicuous. And, it is likely this transparency which effectuates an enduring bond between Alex and Anna, and creates a wedge loosening Bob from Bette. Thus, the transparency infused in the process by market mediators serves to amplify the status of the relationship. Anna was overwhelmed by Alex's magnanimity in gifting a kidney, and accepted the gift as an opportunity to grow in their union. This perspective allowed Anna and Alex opportunities to enjoy and share in the expressiveness of the gift. Bob also was struck by Bette's altruism, yet, he felt burdened by the inability to satisfy what he viewed as an insurmountable debt. Bob's view of the debt intensified the instrumental nature of the gift. He viewed Bette less as his partner and more as a means to his path to achieving health and a new life without her. With instrumentality in the foreground, Bette demanded a (proverbial) return of the gift in their divorce. If such an extraction were legal (and ethical), the result would be to strip Bob of a dialysis-free life and, in her estimation, fully separate versus allowing Bob to retain possession of the gift that she refers to as "my kidney!"

Market Mediators as Partners in Gift-Giving

Gifts may be given to the self, between exchange partners, or within broader gift communities (Belk and Coon 1993; Bradford and Sherry 2013; Mick and DeMoss 1990; Weinberger and Wallendorf 2012). No matter the type of gift relationship, these gifts are often facilitated by market participants as offerings are sourced and transformed from commodities into gifts. Typically, shopping is a key to obtaining the perfect gift, and the market is a resource in the process. Organ gift-giving is less driven by shopping to find the perfect gift, but rather about meeting criteria to be identified as the perfect gift. That criteria are established by market mediators who serve as intimate parties in identifying, creating, and presenting a gift with the gift-giver to their recipient. The mediators serve in roles as gatekeepers, facilitators, and monitors to determine if and when a gift may be given, as well as by and to whom.

For organ gift-givers, mediation by market participants infuses the process with anxiety beyond what may be typically experienced in selecting a gift (Wooten and Wood 2004). More specifically, where traditional gift-giving may result in the rejection of a gift by a recipient, with organ donation, market mediators may reject a possible gift due to physical or psychological criteria which are not always well known or understood by the potential gift-giver. For romantic partners where one is in renal failure, the healthy partner sees how decreasing functionality impacts their loved one, and their life together. In addition, the healthy partner is impacted through their involvement in caregiving, particularly if their partner is on dialysis. Observing the need for a gift, desiring to be the gift-giver and relying on market mediators to determine their ability to give a gift lead to anxiety for gift-givers, as giving their desired gift requires relinquishing control over the process itself.

Traditional gift-giving generates anxiety due to selecting and giving a gift. With gifts of organs, anxiety may develop as individuals acknowledge there are few opportunities for the potential gift-giver to influence the outcome of the selection, presentation, or incorporation gift-giving stages. Recognizing a kidney transplant may be possible is determined by market mediators who assess the likelihood that a transplant would be of benefit. Awaiting this proclamation is met with mixed emotions. Negative emotions result as individuals learn that the organ failure has advanced significantly, thus necessitating a transplant. Positive emotions emerge as individuals contemplate a return to health. These mixed emotions are experienced differently within the couple, and tend to initiate reactions. For most, the inclination of the healthy partner is to volunteer to donate. And, for the ailing partner, they experience dread contemplating possibilities for their gift-giver as a result of giving their gift. Where these partners likely have an extensive and complex gift exchange history, their experience of desiring to give, and doing so, is significantly altered as they enjoin with market mediators to consider, assess, and pursue gift-giving.

The market primarily serves as a resource in traditional gift-giving, where an occasion recognized between a gift-giver and recipient most likely inspires a gift-giver to employ money, time, and effort to secure an offering in the market that may be transformed into a gift (see Figure 2.1). Yet, in living organ donation market mediators become crucial participants who circumscribe much of the process. As participants in the intimate social process of gift-giving, market mediators strive to infuse the process and their roles with the essence of the giftness. Market mediators reframe organ failure into a gift occasion for which they declare criteria for a perfect gift, identify a gift-giver, and celebrate their generosity (and compliance).

Market mediators transform a surgical process to transplant an organ into that of the gift of life. This transformation is most often facilitated through language (Otnes, Ilhan, and Kulkarni 2012) and in particular the employment of words and phrases that serve to minimize the clinical nature of the experience, while emphasizing the life-giving benefits of the gifted organ for the recipient. Market mediators employ language to assure gift-givers of their primacy in driving the gift process, even as mediators dictate the process. Analogies are employed to reframe the loss of kidney function, as an opportunity for the body's miraculous capability for regeneration to accommodate their gift. Though the word "sacrifice" is rarely used, the notion of sacrifice is amplified through expressions of appreciation from market mediators throughout the process. And, to reframe their role of gatekeeper, market mediators adopt an advocacy role to support individuals should they successfully qualify to donate through the screening process. Thus, market mediators are embedded in the process and embraced by relationship participants as figurative and literal miracle workers.

Through the screening process, potential gift-givers are educated about the complexity of match criterion, as well as the difficulty in achieving such a match. This education also serves to develop an aura of sacredness associated with organ gift-giving that is transferred from market mediators and taken up by gift-givers. This infusion continues in the ways market mediators communicate with individuals who are accepted to become organ gift-givers. This communication is framed as a milestone worthy of celebration, as they are now deemed as the perfect gift for their recipients. The period between solidifying the match and giving the gift (the surgical harvest and transplant) is precarious as the market mediators strive to balance clinical efficacy and efficiency with the excitement—their own, the gift-giver's, and the recipient's—that precedes the actual gift presentation. Celebrations that occur in advance of the actual gift-giving are necessary as the presentation of the gift occurs at the hands of the market, which also ultimately determines the efficacy

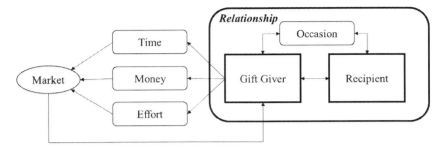

Figure 2.1 Gift-Giving With the Market as a Resource

of the gift they identified as perfect based on (less than romantic) criteria such as urine output and creatinine levels. When market mediators, through the screening process, indicate a match between the spouses, it contributes to the notion that their marital union is, in fact, perfect.

Gift-givers also employ language as a means of elevating their role in the process. Gift-givers, particularly those in romantic relationships, seek to contribute to personalization of their gift as they customize how they share the news they are willing and able to donate to their recipient. Many employ the notion of being a "perfect match," a determination made by market mediators that is adopted by relationship partners to infuse the essence of the gift into the process.

Market players recognize the concerns experienced by donors and recipients related to the various components of gift-giving. By serving as a guide to securing the perfect gift, these market mediators carefully navigate the qualification process advising potential gift-givers that should they not be a match, it is for their own well-being. Thus, they also transform the negative associations derived from not participating in giving, into a positive one of self-care. Throughout the process, market mediators stage this gift process as orchestrated by the donor even as it is significantly controlled by the market.

General Discussion

The present research explores the market as a central participant in gift-giving, namely as mediator. Prior research finds offerings are imbued with meaning through sacrifice by gift-givers, where they employ time, effort, and money to create what they perceive to be approaching perfect gifts (see Figure 2.1). These gifts are provided for occasions observed by the gift-giver and their recipient. The present research explores roles for the market under conditions when the market is a necessary participant in gift-giving. In such circumstances, it is the market that defines what may be perceived as near perfect gifts, and how they will be created. Thus, the market defines the gift, and the occasion which results in the prescription and extraction of sacrifice in the forms of time, effort, and money from the gift-giver to imbue the market defined gift with meaning (see Figure 2.2). This research contributes an explanation of how gift-giving roles and processes are influenced when the market serves as a mediator in gift-giving rituals.

An individual desiring to gift an organ is at the mercy of market mediators. Prior research finds that when gifts are necessarily part of the market and gift economies, the gift-giver strives to imbue the offering with an aura of giftness to enable that gift to circulate within the gift economy along with the affection and symbolism it represents (Bradford 2009). In the present study, the marketplace and players are active managers of the gift-giving process versus resources within the process. When market mediators necessarily define an occasion and determine its terms, as with organ donation, they displace the gift-giver as the orchestrator in the gift-giving process. As such, market mediators may embrace an ad hoc role of relationship partner as they identify the relevant gift, and orchestrate how the gift is generated from the gift-giver for the recipient. In addition, market mediators may employ language (Otnes et al. 2012) to transform the appropriated experience into one that retains an essence of gift-giving. Unlike prior research that explores different types of gift-giving (e.g., monadic, dyadic, systemic), this research explores market mediated gift-giving and identifies how such mediation influences roles in the process. It is important to note that though the market may serve as mediator in some gift-giving rituals, it is likely that market mediation is the exception within gift-giving such that those mediators are only temporarily participating as relationship partners.

Gift-giving rituals support relationships, where couples are more likely to exchange gifts to nurture romantic love. They give gifts sourced from the market, and employ their bodies as gifts of communication, sexuality, and labor. Where most bodily generated gifts do not require market participation, the gift of an organ does. The body is sacred in nature (Belk

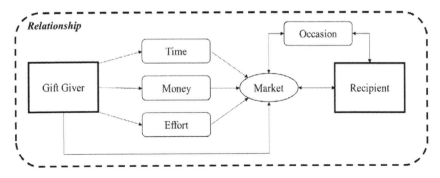

Figure 2.2 Gift-Giving With the Market as a Participant

1990), and market mediators in transplantation acknowledge this as they employ language to sacralize the individual giving the gift, as well as the organ itself. The organ gift-giving process makes transparent the notion of the gift-giver's sacrifice, a central component of gift creation. That sacrifice imbues an aura of giftness throughout the process. Prior research finds market participants may behave differently when providing routine offerings versus gifts (Davis 1972). For example, a general surgeon will likely be assigned to remove a kidney from a gift-giver. Market mediators may introduce the surgeon as a "transplant surgeon" to convey uniqueness to the gift-giver, whereas with a more routine surgery (i.e., appendectomy), a special moniker is deemed unnecessary, and is therefore unlikely employed. Thus, market mediators strive to eradicate any taint of the marketplace essence that may be evident in the gift-giving process, even as the entirety of the process occurs within the market.

Prior studies find gift-givers engage the market as a resource for offerings that individuals may transform into gifts. The present study explores roles for market mediation within gift-giving. The experiences of the Andersons and Baxters provide insight into the extent to which market mediators may impact gift-giving processes and roles. The management of the gift-giving process for organ by market mediators is necessarily inescapable given the specialized skills required to identify a match to gift, present the gift through the surgical transplant, and to sustain the gifted organ through follow-up care. Those characteristics allow market mediators to seize control of the process from the gift-giver and eradicate secrecy from the process as the perfect gift is pursued. In addition to gift-giving, there are other social processes that are prone to such market mediation such as choosing romantic partners (e.g., casual dating, marriage), increasing one's family membership (e.g., adoption, artificial reproductive technologies), caretaking of family members (e.g., children, parents, and pets), or crafting customized vacation experiences (e.g., babymoons, family reunions). The extent to which an instrumental gift may also be expressive, and have long-standing consequences after the departure of market mediators, is likely similar in the aforementioned arenas as well. Thus, there are several opportunities worthy of further study with respect to the influence of market mediators in social processes.

The engagement of market mediators in social processes has the potential to change how individuals, beyond those in romantic relationships, interact through social exchanges, and influence the trajectory of relationships over time. People seek their unique version of happily ever, at times through market mediated offerings, in support of interactions with family, friends and "framily." As the market becomes more embedded within these intimate spaces, there will be additional opportunities for market mediators to wrestle (and individuals to relinquish) control within relationships, and the processes that nurture them.

Endnote

Special thanks of Vinisha Kothari, Research Assistant, University of California, Irvine, for her support in data collection.

References

Belk, Russell W. (1976), "It's the Thought That Counts: A Signed Digraph Analysis of Gift-Giving," *Journal of Consumer Research*, 3 (3), 155–62.

——— (1990), "Me and Thee Versus Mine and Thine: How Perceptions of the Body Influence Organ Donation and Transplantation," in *Organ Donation and Transplantation: Psychological and Behavioral Factors*, ed. James Shanteau and Richard Jackson Harris, Washington, DC: American Psychological Association, 139–49.

——— (1996), "The Perfect Gift," in *Gift Giving: A Research Anthology*, ed. Cele Otnes and Richard Francis Beltramini, Bowling Green, OH: Bowling Green State University Popular Press, 59–84.

Belk, Russell W. and Gregory S. Coon (1993), "Gift Giving as Agapic Love: An Alternative to the Exchange," *Journal of Consumer Research*, 20 (3), 393–417.

Bradford, Tonya Williams (2009), "Intergenerationally Gifted Asset Dispositions," *Journal of Consumer Research*, 36 (1), 93–111.

Bradford, Tonya Williams and John F. Sherry, Jr. (2013), "Orchestrating Rituals through Retailers: An Examination of Gift Registry," *Journal of Retailing*, 89 (2), 158–75.

Camerer, Colin (1988), "Gifts as Economic Signals and Social Symbols," *The American Journal of Sociology*, 94 (Supplement), S180–S214.

Caplow, Theodore (1982), "Christmas Gifts and Kin Networks," *American Sociological Review*, 47, 383–92.

——— (1984), "Rule Enforcement without Visible Means: Christmas Gift Giving in Middletown," *American Journal of Sociology*, 89 (6), 1306–23.

Cheal, David (1988), *The Gift Economy*, Cambridge, MA: Harvard University Press.

Davis, J. (1972), "Gifts and the U.K. Economy," *Man*, 7 (3), 408–29.

Douglas, Mary and Baron Isherwood (1979), *The World of Goods*, New York: Basic Books.

Giesler, Markus (2006), "Consumer Gift Systems," *Journal of Consumer Research*, 33 (2), 283–90.

Gregory, Chris. A. (1982), *Gifts and Commodities*, Cambridge: Academic Press.

Henry, O. (1906), "The Gifts of the Magi," in *The Four Million*, ed. O. Henry, New York: Doubleday, Page & Company, 16–25.

Hyde, Lewis (1979), *The Gift: Imagination and the Erotic Life of Property*, New York: Vintage Books.

Joy, Annamma (2001), "Gift Giving in Hong Kong and the Continuum of Social Ties," *Journal of Consumer Research*, 28 (2), 239–56.

Lowrey, Tina M., Cele C. Otnes, and Julie A. Ruth (2004), "Social Influences on Dyadic Giving over Time: A Taxonomy from the Giver's Perspective," *Journal of Consumer Research*, 30 (4), 547–58.

Mauss, Marcel (1967), *The Gift*, New York: W. W. Norton & Company.

Mick, David Glen and Michelle DeMoss (1990), "Self-Gifts: Phenomenological Insights from Four Contexts," *Journal of Consumer Research*, 17 (3), 322–32.

Offer, Avner (1997), "Between the Gift and the Market: The Economy of Regard," *The Economic History Review*, 50 (3), 450–76.

Otnes, Cele C., Behice Ece Ilhan, and Atul Kulkarni (2012), "The Language of Marketplace Rituals: Implications for Customer Experience Management," *Journal of Retailing*, 88 (3), 367–83.

Otnes, Cele C., Tina M. Lowrey, and Young Chan Kim (1993), "Gift Selection for Easy and Difficult Recipients: A Social Roles Interpretation," *Journal of Consumer Research*, 20 (2), 229–44.

Rothman, Sheila M., Natassia Rozario, and David J. Rothman (2007), "What Body Parts Do We Owe Each Other?," *Society*, 44 (5), 24–9.

Schwartz, Barry (1967), "The Social Psychology of the Gift," *American Journal of Sociology*, 73 (1), 1–11.

Sherry, John F., Jr. (1983), "Gift Giving in Anthropological Perspective," *Journal of Consumer Research*, 10 (2), 157–68.

Sherry, John F., Jr., Mary Ann McGrath, and Sidney J. Levy (1992), "The Disposition of the Gift and Many Unhappy Returns," *Journal of Retailing*, 68 (1), 40–65.

Sherry, John F., Jr., Mary Ann McGrath, and Sidney J. Levy (1993), "The Dark Side of the Gift," *Journal of Business Research*, 28 (1 November), 225–44.

Weinberger, Michelle F. and Melanie Wallendorf (2012), "Intracommunity Gifting at the Intersection of Contemporary Moral and Market Economies," *Journal of Consumer Research*, 39 (1), 74–92.

Wolfinbarger, Mary Finley (1990), "Motivations and Symbolism in Gift-Giving Behavior," in *Advances in Consumer Research*, Vol. 17, ed. Marvin Goldberg, Gerald Gorn, and Richard W. Pollay, Provo, UT: Association for Consumer Research, 699–706.

Wooten, David B. (2000), "Qualitative Steps toward an Expanded Model of Anxiety in Gift-Giving," *Journal of Consumer Research*, 27 (1), 84–95.

Wooten, David B. and Stacy L. Wood (2004), "In the Spotlight: The Drama of Gift Receipt," in *Contemporary Consumption Rituals: A Research Anthology*, ed. Cele C. Otnes and Tina M. Lowrey, London: Lawrence Erlbaum Associates, Inc., 213–36.

3 Romantic Gift-Giving of Mature Consumers

A Storgic Love Paradigm

Yuko Minowa and Russell W. Belk

> He bought me a ring for our 30th anniversary. . . . I thought he was still thinking of me. After 35 years, yes, love is there, but I think it is the kind of love where we are taking care of each other.
>
> (Izumi, female informant in her early 60s)

> I decided to go back to the Honolulu marathon again at the age of sixty five. . . . And this is the necklace I received from my wife when I made the decision. . . . And she was like "Let's wear this and go to the marathon together."
>
> (Hideo, male informant in his early 60s)

How might aging influence the romantic gift-giving of now mature consumers? The subject of love is of primary importance and philosophers, authors, poets, and scientists have focused on romantic love over millennia. Discovering the meaning of love, exploring sexuality, and overcoming struggles in romantic relationships are often considered to largely be accomplished before entering old age. Moreover, erotic love and raging libidos in later life can be a subject of ridicule and indignity, as exemplified in literary characters such as Shakespeare's Falstaff (1997 [1602]) and Tanizaki's Mad Old Man (2004 [1965]). The above vignettes of two consumers in their early sixties, however, suggest that there are different kinds of love and that love may transform from one type to the other over their life course. Accordingly, while romantic gifts may be appreciated irrespective of age, aging seems to influence gift meanings for a couple.

The purpose of this study is to investigate the influence of aging on romantic gift-giving by mature consumers. The theoretical contributions is to diversify the gift-giving paradigm and expand romantic gift-giving as an expression of "storgic" love in addition to "agapic" love (Belk and Coon 1993). We use data from in-depth interviews conducted in Japan and illustrate how the romantic gift-giving of mature consumers is related to their life course, beyond the dyadic exchange process that consists of three distinct stages: gestation, presentation, and reformulation (e.g., Belk 1979; Belk and Coon 1993; Sherry 1983).

The organization of the paper is as follows: First, we offer a literature review on romantic gift-giving in consumer research and identify the shortcomings of the existing literature in order to outline the theoretical groundwork for our interrogation. Second, we describe both the methods of the study and the context of baby boomers in Japan as our empirical inquiry. Then, we illustrate the emergent storgic love model that embodies the mature "perfect gift" experience, distance of intimacy, and concern for well-being. We conclude with implications of the present study for extant theories of romantic gift-giving in consumer research and a discussion of possible future studies.

Literature Review

In classical anthropological and sociological studies, gift exchange is considered a "total social phenomenon" (Mauss 1990 [1925]; Hyde 1983). The ritual goes beyond the dyadic exchange and embodies diverse social, economic, and cultural meanings. Consumer researchers have investigated the subject underpinned by anthropological and socio-logical theories (e.g., Belk 1979; Sherry 1983). Gift-giving can vary from formal rituals as rites of passage and progression (Rook 1985) to post-modern symbolic consumer behavior (Otnes and Beltramini 1996). Motivations for these rituals vary depending on situations, contexts, and perceived relationships. In the cycle of giving and receiving, consum-ers formulate, reformulate, and strengthen or weaken their relationships (Ruth, Otnes, and Brunel 1999). Gender plays a crucial role in gift-giving rituals. It is largely women who carry out the rituals, and these are often construed as women's work (Fischer and Arnold 1990). Cultural differ-ences in gift-giving norms and traditions exist. In China for instance, varying levels of intimacy alter gift relationships, following the cultural rules regarding reciprocity, face, and sentiment (Joy 2001). Hashimoto (1996) also emphasizes similar rule of gift-giving in Japan, with greater degrees of interdependence than among Americans who struggle to be independent, even in old age.

Research on romantic gift-giving has been conducted in psychology (Saad and Gill 2003), sociology (Zelizer 2005), gender studies (Gould and Weil 1991), and consumer research (Belk 1996; Belk and Coon 1993; Minowa and Gould 1999; Minowa, Matsui, and Belk 2012, 2013; Otnes, Ruth, and Milbourne 1994; Otnes, Zolner, and Lowrey 1994; Rugimbana et al. 2003). Belk and Coon (1993) broadened the realm of gift-giving research by adding selfless romantic giving to the eco-nomic and social exchange paradigm. Belk (1996) further examined "the perfect gift" as an expression of the selfless, altruistic love of the giver. Such a gift defines gift-giving and receiving ideals among couples. In exploring differences in giving and receiving experiences between Japa-nese women and men, Minowa and Gould (1999) found the similarity of the characteristics of Japanese couples' most memorable gift to the "perfect gift" (Belk 1996) as well as culturally distinct aspects.

Love in Later Life

"Each time of life has its own kind of love" (Tolstoy 1965 [1859], 210). Love in later life is characterized dominantly as storgic love, defined as friendship-based rather than hot, passionate love (Barusch 2008; Gibson 1997). Etymologically, storge in Greek means affection or fondness (Stavropoulos 1995, 822). Storge is "evolutionary" rather than "revolutionary" (Hendrick and Hendrick 1986, 400). The ancient Greeks used this word to mean the affection that develops between siblings and childhood friends (Gibson 1997). It is enduring love, the hardy love of Penelope for Odysseus, truer as it grows out of sympathy rather than desire, in which one finds peace rather than agony (Heaven et al. 2004; Lee 1973; Tolstoy 1965 [1859]). Storge is associated with kindness and sociability without emotional or sexual arousal (Kanemasa et al. 2004). It is un-self-conscious affection, "the humblest and most widely diffused of loves" (Lewis 1960, 53). Lee (1973, 77) describes it as "love without fever or folly, a feeling of natural affection." It is characterized as not ecstatic, dramatic, or anguishing as Eros, Mania, and Ludus are. Storgic love may grow as time passes, instead of being a state that lovers "fall in" at a particular moment of comfortable familiarity (Lee 1973). It grows into partnership, or soulmateship, based on a mutuality of values and attitudes, which is more important than physical attraction and sexual satisfaction as a couple wants to establish long-term commitment (Hetsroni 2012). Storge overlooks the imperfections of the beloved. Successful marriages are thought to be fundamentally storgic. Yancey and Berglass (1991) found that Agape and Storge relate to greater overall life satisfaction, and, in particular, Agape is for women and Storge for men. For both life satisfaction and mature love, commitment is critical (Fromm 1956; Sternberg 1986). Despite all these typologies and aspects of love, and Storge in particular, there is no comprehensive study on romantic gift-giving in later life.

Aging and Consumer Behavior

On the other hand, the consumer behavior of aging population has gained attention because of global population aging and the increasing interest in studying this rapidly growing segment (Drolet et al. 2010; Elder, Johnson, and Crosnoe 2003; Moschis 1991, 2012) that contains active "healthy indulgers" who are still evolving after retirement rather than becoming "fragile, vulnerable, and slouching toward insignificance" (Schau, Gilly, and Wolfinbarger 2009, 256). Previous studies have focused on age as a variable (Holbrook and Schindler 1989, 1996), aging at a particular stage of the lifecycle, or socio-historically contextualized individual negotiation of age-related behavior (Bode and Østergaard 2011). Other studies have found chronological age problematic as a predictor of attitudes and behavior of mature consumers and suggest self-perceived cognitive age as an alternative (Barak and Gould 1985; Barak and Schiffman 1981). Barak et al. (2001) found the existence of cognitive and desired age in the Far East on four functional dimensions of the self—psychological (feelings), biological (looks), social (actions), and cognitive (interests). Their study finds evidence that no significant gender and cross-cultural differences from "ageless" American society exists. Thus, while cultural differences exist, "cognitive age is a universal characteristic, irrespective of the cultural background" (Kohlbacher and Chéron 2012, 184).

Moschis (2007, 295) contends that "studies that demonstrate age-related differences do not show changes in consumer behavior or how previous experiences affect present patterns of consumer behavior, because individual consumers or segments are not examined relative to earlier experiences or stages of life within historical and cultural contexts." Sociologists conceptualize life course theory based on the nexus of five paradigmatic principles: The principle of life span development, the principle of agency, the principle of time and place, the principle of timing, and the principle of linked lives (Elder et al. 2003; George 1993). A key aspect of the life course is that the micro-level aspects of individual negotiation, interpretation, and selection of one's own path through life is constrained by, or intertwined with, social changes on a macro-level, thereby providing social and personal meaning to the passage of biological time (Bode and Østergaard 2011). Other principles of life course theory are life transitions—changes in roles, status or identity—and their trajectories, and interdependently experienced shared relationships (Elder et al. 2003). Some stressful transition experiences are reported with lifelong consequences. In consumer research, such factors as family structure, socialization, and stressful life events have been found to have lifelong influences on materialism, compulsive buying, and consumer preferences (Mathur, Moschis, and Lee 2008; Moschis 2007; Baker et al. 2011; Nguyen, Moschis, and Shannon 2009). However, there seems no extant research that dissects the romantic gift-giving of mature consumers by incorporating a life course perspective.

This literature review leads to two research questions: What is the nature of the love paradigm in romantic gift-giving among older Japanese? And, in what ways does this paradigm manifest in gift-giving meanings and practices?

The Context of the Study

We investigate the romantic gift-giving by mature consumers in the context of the baby boomers in Japan—the nation with the oldest median age in the world and a projected population with nearly 40% who will be age 65 years or older in 2050 (Chéron 2011). Japan has long valued gift-giving rituals (Francks 2009; Ito 2011; Rupp 2003; Yamaguchi 2012). Yet, there is limited research on romantic gift-giving (Creighton 1993; Minowa and Gould 1999; Minowa, Khomenko, and Belk 2011; Minowa et al. 2012, 2013).

Modern studies of Japanese gift-giving evolved in ethnology and anthropology. Japanese ethnologists claim that dyadic gift-giving exchange originated in the pre-modern religious practice of commensalism—the rite of sharing votive foods for ensuring and strengthening the sense of cooperation and solidarity among communal members. No other culture predominantly uses foods as items of gift exchanges throughout its history as much as Japan (Ito 2011). The traditional, obligatory ritual gift exchange in general is termed *zōtoh*, written with two kanji characters "send" and "respond." On the other hand, gift-giving as an expression of affective feeling is called *purezento*, the Japanese way of pronouncing the English word present. In this regard, Minowa and Gould (1999) explored differences in giving and receiving experiences between Japanese women and men. While their informants ranged in age from 25 to 69, the median was 35, and no attention was paid to age differences.

Baby boomers in Japan are defined as the people born from 1947 to 1949 (Amano 2001). According to the statistics by the Japanese Ministry of Health, Labor, and Welfare, just over eight million people were born in these three years. It was projected this cohort would comprise about one-fourth of the elderly population in 2015. Having grown up in the zeitgeist of the postwar economic miracle, they are often characterized as self-expressive and individualistic consumers (Amano 2001). Influenced by the Western cultures at a mass level due to the diffusion of mass media, some baby boomers have revealed these new values through creolized gift-giving rituals such as Valentine's Day (Minowa et al. 2011) and Christmas (Kimura and Belk 2005). They are the cohort that has experienced the most drastic economic and sociocultural changes in Japan. Locating consumers in cohorts by approximately the same birth years (1947–1949) provides precise historical placement as this process links age to historical time. This helps our analysis to maintain the same cohort and period effects, both of which are evidence of historical influences, although the historical experience of consumers in a cohort may be significantly diverse (Elder et al. 2003; Moschis 2012).

Method

We conducted in-depth interviews that allowed each informant to retrospectively describe his or her life history and the private story of romantic gift-giving in his or her lived world and to articulate the network of meanings that constitutes their gift-giving practices (Belk, Fischer, and Kozinets 2013). Textual data were generated with 30 baby boom participants regarding their experiences of romantic gift-giving, gender socialization, memorable gift-giving from their youth, and intergenerational differences—a comparison with their parents' and children's gift-giving practices—in their romantic gift-giving. We encouraged the informants to narrate their memories of gift-giving experiences throughout their lives, although the trustworthiness of such personal oral history potentially suffers from forgetting, faulty memory, telescoping, and nostalgic glamorization (Belk 1992). Although these memories may not be entirely veridical, they give a good view of what is deemed significant; those memories which continue to be vivid at a later life stage are likely to be recalled rather accurately (Rodgers and Herzog 1987).

All participants were residents of Metropolitan Tokyo and were recruited by a marketing research agency. They consisted of 15 males and 15 females, ranging in age from 60 to 65. Occupations varied that included retired former office worker, taxi driver, business owner, college student, and housewives. Four native Japanese researchers conducted interviews with one informant at a time in a private office in downtown Tokyo. The length of the interviews ranged from 60 to 75 minutes. Each was audio recorded, translated, and transcribed in English. Anonymity was guaranteed, and a pseudonym assigned to each informant. The analysis of the verbatim interview transcripts involved a part-to-whole iterative strategy (Spiggle 1994; Thompson 1997). Repeated ideas and similarities across the transcripts were analyzed. We developed a holistic understanding of factors affecting the "storgic" later-in-life gift-giving orientations: mature, "perfect gift" experiences, distance of intimacy, and concern for well-being. We organized the emergent themes around their motives and relational processes (Lowrey, Otnes, and Ruth 2004). A summary is provided in Table 3.1. We will discuss how consumers use

Table 3.1 Aging Influences on Romantic Gift-Giving

	Aging Influence	Description	Giver's Motive	Underlying Relational Process
Mature "Perfect Gift" Experience	Appreciating	Giver conveys appreciation for being together many years	Maintains affectionate relationship by expressing appreciation	Enhancing relational significance
	Enriching everyday life	Giver enriches sensualities of everyday consumption experience	Extends the longevity of the partner with hedonic consumption experience	Developing new or better relational styles
	Simplifying	Giver reduces non-essential consumption	Maintains affectionate relationship while reducing consumption and possessions	Developing new or better relational styles

	Aging Influence	Description	Giver's Motive	Underlying Relational Process
Distance of Intimacy	Reflecting Meaning in Life	Giver redefines the meaning of human relationship	Develops and maintains affectionate relationship by improving communications	Adjusting to new relational rules
	Redefining relational closeness	Giver redefines the meaning of romance in later life	Maintains affectionate relationship after passion dies and transforms to Storge	Adjusting to new relational rules
	Reminiscing	Giver (partially) replicates the romantic gift-giving of youthful past	Maintains affectionate relationship after the Third Age economically made the sustenance of lifestyle of the youthful past infeasible	Adjusting to new relational rules
Concern for Well-being	Empathizing	Giver empathizes the partner's ailments and frailty	Maintains affectionate relationship by taking extra good care of the partner's physical diminution	Enhancing relational significance
	Anti-Ageing	Giver attempts to defy partner's aging process	To the recipient, confirms the recipient stays youthful	Adjusting mature identity to aging process
	Rejuvenating (as a magic gift)	Giver tries to reverse the partner's age or aging.	Pleases the partner by aiding his or her wish to stay youthful	Adjusting mature identity to aging process
	Preparing for aging	Giver instructs how to manage living in elderly	Maintains affectionate relationship by teaching the partner how to live a better senior life.	Adjusting mature identity to aging process

their mature identity—understood through positioning theory—to negotiate their past memories and the later-in-life romantic gift-giving practices.

The Emergent Storgic Love Model

Mature "Perfect Gift" Experience of Later Life

The premise of ideal romantic gift-giving formerly characterized with the "perfect gift" is based on a contemporary conception of courtly love (Belk 1996, 2005). It is altruistic and selfless, often antithetical to reason and will. One crucial aspect of agapic love in gift-giving, commonly taken as a sign of its irrationality, is the sacrifice lovers make for one another (Belk 1996). Rather than emphasizing the monetary value of the material gift, the symbolic meaning and associated extraordinary experiences, such as surprise and sacrifice, are intended to make the beloved happy. We consider these as extraordinary "perfect gift" experiences. The perfect gift-giver strives to create an extraordinary experience for the recipient. Existing studies have focused on extraordinary experiences, but primarily outside of a gift context (e.g., Tumbat and Belk 2011). Bhattacharjee and Mogilner (2014) found that age plays a critical role in eliciting greater happiness from ordinary experiences in our daily lives, while extraordinary, once-in-a-lifetime experiences continue to make us happy regardless of age. Ordinary experiences can include social relationships, indulgent treats, and romantic love, while extraordinary experiences entail rites of passage, travel, and significant cultural events. Our informants indicate that they use romantic gift-giving within ordinary mature "perfect gift" experiences to enhance relational significance and develop new relational styles in their old age, by expressing appreciation, enriching everyday life, and simplifying. Belk and Coon (1993) discuss evolutionary aspects of dating gifts as the relationship evolves: from economic exchange to social exchange to romantic love. In this regard, the mature "perfect gift" of storgic love can be considered to manifest after the end of romantic love associated with passion and excitement, when the giver feels the beloved as "not a lover any longer but an old friend" (Tolstoy 1965 [1859], 212). The basic differences between the agapic love paradigm and storgic love paradigm, as well as exchange paradigm, are summarized in Table 3.2.

Appreciating

Givers in later life become more reflexive about the total sum of their relationship. Romantic gift-giving is an opportunity to express their appreciation to the beloved. Makoto said "[My gift] is like saying 'Good job. Thank you so much for supporting me all our life.' I want

Table 3.2 A Comparison of Three Gift-Giving Paradigms

Extending exchange and agapic love paradigms (Belk and Coon 1993, 409)

Exchange paradigm	*Agapic love paradigm*	*Storgic love paradigm*
Instrumental (designed purposive)	Expressive (spontaneous and celebratory)	Appreciative (empathetic and caring)
Rational (dispassionate)	Emotional (passionate)	Prudent (considerate)
Pragmatic	Idealistic	Realistic
Masculine	Feminine	Androgenic
Reciprocal gifts	Nonbinding gifts	Sharing gifts (Gifts to share)
Egoistic	Altruistic	Companionate
Giver dominant (seeks control)	Giver submissive (abandons control)	Giver equitable (neutralizes or shares control)
Money is relevant (economically or symbolically)	Money is irrelevant	Money is relevant as the budget constraint
Gifts singularize objects	Gifts singularize recipient	Gifts singularize couple

it that way." Taro, who used to be a busy businessman and absent husband and father and who relied on his wife for everything about household matters, explained the transformation of their relationship in married life:

> I think that love is more like trust … a relationship of mutual trust more than romance. You know, I am 61 and my wife has become 55, so our life has been starting the countdown. Therefore, I'm thinking how we can manage rest of our life together with trust and not get involved in trouble. … Our relationship was just a man and a woman when we were young. We got married, got kids, became a father and a mother … then we were changed as children grew up. … We try to cooperate with each other. Husband and wife should stand by each other throughout their life. … I believe that it's beyond love.

Taro and his wife celebrated wedding anniversaries for the first 15 years of their marriage and stopped because "we got tired of it." He then changed his gifts to sending flowers and simply taking her out to restaurants. He explained what he wanted to express through gift-giving lately:

> Well, that is an appreciation, I think. When I was younger, I think I gave her gifts as my obligation … for instance, I thought I had to

> give her gifts for our wedding anniversary. But as we get older. . . . I can think of an appreciation to her. Thank her for washing my clothes, making meals and raising children … something like that. I think that gifts are showing my appreciation.

Taro used to give his wife designer brand bags and shoes at wedding anniversaries. But, he stopped treating anniversaries as extraordinary ritual events and transformed them to indulgent treats while reverting to nonmaterial gifts in a household full of stuff already. The material gifts to express their appreciation has transformed from extraordinary to something simpler such as flowers and experience-based events such as dining in less expensive restaurants. From a normative perspective on life course, one recognition is prominent in his narrative: his inter-locking roles as lover, husband, and father, and their transitions that affected adaptations to new identities and changing behaviors, including romantic gift-giving practices. His beloved has become his social partner who provides him with more affective rewards while her role to provide practical means (e.g., knowledge, information) has become less signifi-cant. Carstensen (1992) explains that because of the increased focus on the present potential for the quality of social contact with age (or a limited time horizon), deriving emotional meaning becomes more impor-tant social goal pursuit, and emotional closeness increases in significant relationships. Meanwhile, increased focus on emotion is the consequence of maturation: as people mature, they develop a more intricate under-standing of emotions, and are better able to regulate their emotions and emotional experiences compared to their younger counterparts (Drolet et al. 2010). Another former businessman, Haruki, who was obsessed with his work, used to take advantage of gifts to show his affec-tion to his wife and daughters as he could not help with the housekeeping or he was not at home during the weekend. But now he is enthralled by the feeling of appreciation.

> I would like to give [my wife] the condition of her skin and hair that she used to have when she was young. . . . After getting married and raising children, she was too occupied with housekeeping duties to take a good care of herself for decades, which made her get aged fast. I noticed that clearly because she was beautiful when she was young. I realized it was me who gave her gray hairs.

In our data, male informants made more earnest expressions of appreci-ation, with guilt-ridden remorse. Admittedly many male baby boomers served as "organization men" (Amano 2001, 11) prioritizing work over family. Realizing the long-term impact of their absence from family in later life, these men seemed to desire to please the beloved with more regular attention through simple gift experiences.

Enriching Everyday Life

The mature "perfect gift" experience in later life may involve exploring new relational styles, such as enriching sensualities of everyday consumption experiences and simplifying. Givers seem to believe that such a hedonic experiential gift extends the partner's longevity. For mature consumers, experiences have greater value, and hence experiential gifts are valued more as compared with gifts of material goods and possessions. Yutaka says, "Going on a trip, eating delicious food, giving a gift ... amid all of that, there is that sense of everyday life ... and there is that feeling that I want her to live a long life. ... When I go with my wife, eat something delicious and say 'this is great, isn't it?' and seeing her smile ... that's the best ... this sounds affected ... it's hard to express in words." It is not the passion, excitement, or sacrifice, but the rich, enduring fulfillment with affection that the giver is motivated to provide through the gift-giving experience. Furthermore, givers may pay attention to both the gift object and the accompanying service quality. For instance, Manabu used to like to give material things that remained, "but lately as [he is] getting older, [he] prefers a food gift," not because it is perishable, he says, but because everybody enjoys good food. In his youth, an expensive dinner gift was not affordable, and so the quality of food and the dining experience have improved over the time. Keiko cooks her husband a local cuisine that has a special memory for both of them. Various senses decline with age (Margrain and Boulton 2005). A decrease in sensitivity and an increased threshold could lead to loss of pleasure through association (e.g., taste- and odor-evoked memories), but, in turn, make felt, sensory experiences more valuable in old age compared to those in younger counterpart. Thus, the value of good-tasting food and the right atmosphere could be greater in old age compared with that in younger age. At the same time, food is a renewable pleasure since it disappears, and we will always be hungry again. And perhaps hunger is a metaphor indicating that desire has shifted from sexual to food, from one kind of carnal pleasure to another.

Simplifying

Givers may also choose certain gifts in order to reduce consumption and eliminate possessions: i.e., simplifying. They aim to maintain or enhance affectionate relationships through gift-giving while concurrently modifying mutually agreeable new relational and consumption styles. Kumiko recalls "when I was young. ... I thought [my husband] would be happier with fancy packages. But at our age, packages are not as important. We don't want to leave anything anymore; kind of we are preparing to go away. I think we are at the age that we should not leave anything behind." Thus, food is an excellent gift. Sounding rather overwhelmed, Kenji says he buys more food and more practical things: "It's not a change in my state of mind. It's just, we have too many things. We have everything we need." Kanako sees the change as a function of aging: "When I was young, I was happy with whatever I received. I didn't have a lot of stuff. But after a certain age, I have a lot of stuff and I don't want anything. ..." They imply that by late life their important developmental goals have changed from the acquisition and display of resources to the maintenance of basic resources or avoidance of loss (Freund and Blanchard-Fields 2014). On the other hand, none of our informants stated generative or ego-transcending altruistic goals, such as ecological concern as a negative effect of material waste, which may be expected in old age and moving closer to finitude (Brandtstädter et al. 2010). Informants indicated that giving a food gift is not meant to express detachment or purging of the relationship with perishables, but rather a result of (re)acting on material abundance.

The Distance for Intimacy

Reflecting Meaning in Life

In later life, relational closeness and romantic gift-giving become part of one's life review—an evaluation of one's life by integrating both positive and negative memories in the life story, or by utilizing positive memories to cope with present problems (Korte, Westerhof, and Bohlmeijer 2012). According to Erikson's (1993 [1950]) theory of psychosocial development, mature consumers are entering the stage of resolute crisis of ego integrity versus despair. Ego integrity is the "accrued assurance of its proclivity for order and meaning" (Erikson 1993 [1950], 268). Regret resolution and making sense of one's whole life becomes the central issue in later life. Meaning in life, or making sense of one's existence, is highly influential on one's well-being and contributes to greater life satisfaction in later life. We found that, for mature consumers, gift-giving may become an occasion to reflect on the sense of meaning in life and evaluate the value given to human relationships and the relational closeness with the intimate other. Givers use the reflexive evaluation for adjusting to new relational rules. For instance, once a successful businessperson, Kohei, who is now a part-time civil servant, reflects on his life course and describes the changing meaning of gift-giving in relation to his changing perspectives on human (including romantic) relationships:

> I think in the past, there wasn't [gift-giving] routine, but once life started to settle down, I started to care about doing it regularly ... whether it be a birthday or another occasion ... there has been that kind of change in heart ... up until then, I wasn't thinking much about things like that ... I think work was quite busy ... once you have pretty much lived your life, this might be a big

change too, but . . . mid-career retirement . . . at a time when corporate restructuring was a great boom, I retired due to that . . . since
then, I might have nurtured a feeling of paying attention to things
like that . . . and I want to value that type of thing . . . since then [pre-
sents] for my wife may have changed.

Kohei's induced early retirement—a non-normative transition in life—
and resultant loss of purpose led to his feeling an existential vacuum,
or the loss of feeling that his life has significance. Not being able to
find coherence and purpose in his own life experiences, reminiscing in
this case did not contribute to a sense of meaning in life. His goals
and purposes were unclear. He was not at peace with his past. Thus,
the values that guided his behavior changed. Instead of reminiscing, he
follows another way: finding meaning in life "by experiencing value in
life through interaction with other people" (Guttmann 1999; cited in
Koren and Lowenstein 2008, 142). Gift-giving as part of human relational experience thus imparts a heavier weight for meaning in his
later life. Older adults find social interaction rewarding as it promotes
the sense of self-worth and social competence, leading to positive self-
concept and greater life satisfaction (Dowd 1975; Mathur 1996).
Thus, they may be motivated for gift-giving as a form of social inter-
course. From the perspective of a life span theory of control, gift-
giving may also serve as a means of restoring one's control as his or
her sense of social loss increases and there is a greater need for control
over one's environment (Heckhausen and Schulz 1995).

Redefining Relational Closeness

Givers in later life also reflect and redefine relational closeness through
romantic gift-giving experiences. There is increasing closeness with
time and as love grows and matures. Relational closeness may be
defined as an interdependence with a relational partner by including
the intimate other into the self through sharing identities, perspectives,
and resources (Aron, Mashek, and Aron 2004). The more the innermost
self is being disclosed, validated, understood, and cared for, the more
the partners may feel each other as part of the self. Couples may feel
the self as a possession of the other. Thus, they feel the self as the aggre-
gate extended self with the beloved (Belk 1988). Our informants meta-
phorically expressed the cognitive and emotional closeness of the
partner as air (a common Japanese phrase): omnipresent and necessary
for existence. For example, Kanako describes the relationship with her
husband:

We have developed a relationship where we don't even have to say
anything but we understand each other. Like we are air for each
other; we don't feel each other, but we need each other.

Romantic gifts serve to build trust for the couple. After a certain age, however, Kanako and her husband became shy at expressing love through presents. Kohei, who also says, "[my wife] is rather like air to me now, so I'm not really conscious of being in love … it's like we give and receive naturally," would rather go out for a meal instead of exchanging material objects as gifts. In later life, these givers seem to consider material gifts as rather unnecessary and affected devices and prefer instead to invest more emphasis on the quality of emotional closeness through sharing experiential gifts.

Not everybody feels comfortable with the level of closeness his or her partner desires and may instead want more distance, especially when the partner is an emotional pursuer who copes with angst by seeking closeness. Threats to personal control and personal identity cause partners to prefer relational autonomy (Mashek and Sherman 2004). Such threats are experienced by married individuals much less than by young adults who are supposedly resolving the crisis of intimacy versus isolation in terms of Erikson's (1993 [1950]) psychosocial development. Some informants indicate they use gift-giving instrumentally to control and maintain a certain distance. Yasuko, a former musician and now a retired widower, prefers to use gifts to maintain close intimate relationship with her boyfriend on a regular basis: "Exchange of gifts such as these … when you reach my age, becomes a chance, or a timing to connect, so I think we do it pretty often." Another former businessman, Noboru, who retired due to corporate restructuring, uses gift-giving to specifically draw a line and define the distance of intimacy in the relationship with his girlfriend:

> We're both singles. … We're young at our heart, even [though] we're over [60], and we're friends … I can't put it in a good way, but there's something like a silent courtesy between us, which stimulates us. We do not want to be too familiar to each other.

The informants who indicate their sensitivity to issues of control and use gift-giving instrumentally to regulate the distance of intimacy are the ones with the strongest inclination to either avoid or seek fantasy in romantic gift-giving. They tend to report some kind of earlier-in-life traumatic or stressful experience in their family environments, such as early parental loss and exposure to domestic violence. In our data, they are the minority.

Reminiscing

Our informants also used instrumental reminiscing about romantic gift-giving experiences and the associated feelings from the past in order to resolve current problems. More specifically, givers partially replicate these intimate practices, but in an affordable way. For example, Haruki takes his wife to her favorite French restaurant in the neighborhood as its atmosphere reminds them of a small diner at countryside along the Loire, River Valley that they visited on their honeymoon. In their Third Age (Laslett 1996)—a time of freedom and fulfillment after retirement until the onset of physical dependency—their unexpectedly tight budget does not allow luxury vacations in Europe. Yutaka, a pensioner, says he feels financially strained and can afford neither vacation trips nor expensive jewelry gifts as in the past.

> About once a year. In the past, when we were young, it was more frequent, but now ... we have to think about our living ... we have to be careful. ... There were times I went to department stores in Tokyo [to purchase jewelry] in the past, but ... now, it's rather, ... we go to the local shop or look at [the souvenir], and can reminisce like, "this is from when we went to Hawaii."

They maintain intimacy by partially replicating gift-giving practices of the past and immersing themselves in nostalgic feelings, which serves as a successful coping strategy against economic hardships for the couple.

Concern for Well-Being

Prejudice toward older adults—known as negative ageism—does exist and has become a prevalent social problem particularly in the workplace (Yamada et al. 2005). However, originating from Buddhist and Confucian traditions, chronological age and aging are also considered positively in general as measures of relative social status and maturity (Karasawa et al. 2011; Kimmel 1988). As Levy, Ashman, and Slade (2010) and Karasawa et al. (2011) find older adults in Japan tend to make more direct age attributions without negative connotations and report higher levels of personal growth as they age in comparison to their US counterparts. On the other hand, Japan perceives itself as having more "bedridden" older adults than other developed nations, because they lagged behind in developing rehabilitation technologies and social welfare policies in the late 20th century (Long 2012). Medical care is supported by universal public insurance policy, and since 2000, long-term care insurance is mandatory. However, as longevity exceeds 80 years of age and since the nation expects to continue being a "super-aging society" with decreased social security in the future, a social fear of aging has emerged. Mature consumers are susceptible to the physical difficulties that may accompany aging while making efforts to improve "healthy life expectancy" with lowered medical costs and being responsible for self-maintenance without relying on public funding (Saito 2014; Shirahase 2014). Our informants indicate that they use gifts to express their empathy for the beloved's physical diminution and to help manage the beloved's aging process.

Empathizing

Some givers use simpler and more frequent gift-giving to maintain affectionate relationships by expressing empathy for the beloved's physical diminution. Atsuko's husband has problems with his teeth, so she wanted to give him good dentures that he could wear without pain, stating "If there were a miracle denture, he'd have been very much appreciative." Recently Atsuko herself feels she is getting old and becoming forgetful. As such, she feels that she conveys her empathy by expressing her concerns for his pain thoughtfully. Even if the giver is healthy and does not quite feel empathy, he or she may be sympathetic. For instance, Izumi, who goes to fitness classes, wishes her husband to be equally well and take care of his body. She expresses her sympathy for her husband's impairment:

> When I heard him saying that his knees were bothering him, I thought about something for his knees. Maybe it is a present for him. I bought him some Chinese medicine from TV shopping and said, "Take this medicine for your knees." Maybe it is sympathy.

Some informants combine empathy and fashion. Makoto realizes his wife is getting farsighted. "So [he] thought about one [a wrist watch] where she could read the time more easily and that had a nice rich tasteful design." For Kazuko, the role of gift-giving for the couple is the expression of such feeling as, "although there is not much more time left to live, please enjoy what is left in our lives," echoing a sense of her own mortality. Her taciturn, nine-year-older husband has been experiencing physical frailty. Through gifts, she wants to say, "you can understand your body best and please take care of your body" as she cannot constantly pay attention to his afflictions. Ultimately one is left responsible for taking care of the self. Kazuko thinks about life in such a way. Her gift-giving is not motivated to delight him with extraordinary experience. Rather, she tries to support him with warm feelings of empathy and affection.

Anti-Aging

Our informants indicate they sometimes use gifts to manage their susceptibility to aging in two ways. One is to defy aging: givers attempt to deter the aging process of the beloved with gifts or gift-giving experiences. Another is to take a proactive measure on possible frailty in elder age: givers use gift-giving to impart to the beloved how to manage late life independently. Either way, the goal is empowerment. To encourage a successful aging process, or staying youthful both physically and psychologically, Hideo received a necklace from his wife, as a charm that symbolically helps defy aging. "I thought I had to do something about [my feeling a lack of purpose], and thought that I had to have a goal to keep myself motivated. And I decided to go back to the Honolulu marathon again at the age of sixty five ... when I told my wife about my plan of trying the marathon again, she bought me this one." His wife suggested that they wear the same necklaces and go to the marathon together. This baby boom generation is known for being Americanized. They do things together as a couple, unlike their parents' generation. Here, the couple's attitudes also seem to partly reflect the long-standing American cultural ideals of individual responsibility, for "the course of old age is not predestined, but rather a condition that can be modified and controlled by individual choices" (Flatt et al. 2013, 944).

Rejuvenating

Informants indicate strong wishes to rejuvenate the beloved. Timeless living without the burden of dealing with signs of aging is a "postmodern life course" targeted to the ageless "seniors" market in a consumer society (Katz 2001/2002). Givers may wish to help their partners to restore a younger appearance or physique. Kenji, whose wife suffers from physical discomfort related to menopause, says: "I want her to be young again ... it would be the best if she could go back to her adolescence ... but at least 50 years old ... that's around the time when she was energetic. ... Being healthy is more important compared to being just young." On the other hand, Jiro, a successful entrepreneur, says "[my wife] is really concerned about looking older, not so much ageing." He wishes her appearance could stay at her 35 years of age until she dies:

> I'm not really concerned about other people's perception of "ugliness," but it's unforgivable to look at yourself and think "ugly," especially for women. It would be great if I could take away that suffering. Of course, it would be nice to have lots of money or to give her a huge mountainous diamond but they are objects ... at certain point, you part with things. You need magic to die in a physical form that you had at age 35. They all turn into figures who don't want to look at themselves in a mirror. That, by itself, leaves a mark as a magic of life, but you end up wanting to avoid their external appearances. This goes for men as well. And they end their life that way. So, it would be great if she could end her life with looks at her peak.

Female informants are also as concerned with the appearance of their male partners, as Yuriko, for instance, says of her husband:

I like to give him a hair growth-stimulating agent. He used to be slim and a pretty good-looking man. ... He's been bald for decades. He often checks his back of the head using two mirrors, saying "Wow, I lost this much." So, he would be so happy to see hair on his head getting up in the morning.

Yuriko does not mind her husband's bald head but thinks it affects his self-esteem. As for her, she says, "He's been bald for decades, and I got used to [it]." Givers would want to please partners by aiding his or her wish to stay youthful. Some informants, however, indicate an ulterior self-serving motive. Kohei describes his as follows:

Because my wife wants to dress up and go out ... and if you were to walk around together, it's better if she's in good shape. I'm sure it's better for her too ... and for the people around her. Not that I want to go back to the past, but if you're able to transform her into a slimmer figure ... if there's a magic present ... I think that would be the best.

Similarly, ulterior motives appear in female informants' narratives concerning their male partners' bald heads, as discussed by Kumiko, whose motive is similar to that of Kohei: "My husband is bald. So, I want him to grow his hair, like those men who have beautiful grey hair. ... It's more for me I guess. When I got married, I really didn't want to marry a bald man." While the Japanese are known for their respect for the elderly and positive aging, the cosmetic and cosmetic/pharmaceutical industry reports large consumer spending on anti-ageing skincare products in comparison with other Asian markets (MarketLine 2012), which seems to evidence their concern for preserving a youthful look without invasive means (i.e., cosmetic surgery, as is the case in South Korea). On the one hand, marketers emphatically reinforce the yearning for such a look. On the other, there is historically a cultural norm for Japanese women to preserve natural "flawless" white skin with daily regimes (Li et al. 2008).

Preparing for Aging

Givers may try to impart to the beloved how to manage later life independently. Such givers seem to have expansive time horizons, while considering the remainder more fragile and typical of the Fourth Age—characterized by impairment in late life (Grenier 2012)—as problematic. Thus, instead of focusing solely on current well-being by maximizing present emotional gains, they also focus on knowledge-related goals for the beloved, as postulated by socio-emotional selectivity theory (Carstensen 1992). Ichiro says, "It is my wife's point of view that I need to learn how to cook so that I wouldn't have a problem with housekeeping in case of living alone after getting older." Ichiro's wife supposes Ichiro would be a lone widower if he survives her. The gerontology literature suggests various coping strategies, such as active coping by improving social relationships and regulatory coping by lowering expectations about relationships and focusing on solitary activities such as reading and gardening (Schoenmakers, van Tilburg and Fokkema 2012).

The investment in the future, while becoming physically and perhaps mentally diminished, aims to provide the beloved with better control of his or her immediate environment that further enables him or her to sustain quality social networks and emotional rewards. In other words, some givers try to ensure that the beloved is capable of controlling their immediate external environment (i.e., primary control) by first making sure of his or her capability for controlling the self (i.e., secondary control), as posited by the life span theory of control (Heckhausen and Schulz 1995, 295): There is "stability in primary control striving throughout most of adult life; however, as one moves into old age, the maintenance of primary control increasingly depends on secondary control processes because of biological declines and sociocultural constraints." Mature consumers in reality shift between limited and expansive time horizon perspectives (Drolet et al. 2010). Thus, some givers rationally impart knowledge and skills for the beloved's elderly independence as gifts, which are concurrently a manifestation of caregiving and responsibility, the facets of Storgic love.

Discussion

Based on our in-depth interviews, we examined the different meanings of gift-giving for mature consumers in an aging cohort—the Baby Boomer in Japan—and their desire to give gifts to their partners and manage their individual emotions as mediated by the culture. The emergent storgic love model, characterized by caring, appreciative, and empathetic companionate love, illustrates that their gift-giving orientations are influenced by mature "perfect gift" experiences, the distance of intimacy, and the concern for well-being (see Table 3.1).

The current study is a response to Belk and Coon's (1993, 413) contention that "the agapic love paradigm includes not only romantic love, but also brotherly love, spiritual love, and parental or familial love. Each is as ripe for investigations that go beyond the exchange paradigm." We elucidated the unique place for mature, storgic love paradigm, which also stands apart from the utilitarian exchange paradigm. Belk and Coon (1993, 412) also postulated that older divorcing couples may use gift-giving "to produce pain rather than pleasure as partners attempt to deconstruct and negate their love and life together." On the contrary, our results demonstrate that older couples use romantic

gift-giving to maintain affectionate relationships by expressing appreciation for being together for many years. Hence, gift-giving serves to
enhance relational significance. Mature couples use gift-giving as they
try to extend their longevity by enriching sensualities of everyday consumption experiences with gifts. Or, they use gift-giving to suggest
new relational styles involving consumption, such as simplifying by
reducing non-essential consumption, as they face the countdown of
their lives. The results of our study also indicate that mature couples
may reflect on the meaning in life or the meaning of romance in later
life through romantic gift-giving. Mature couples may partially replicate
the romantic gift-giving practice of their youthful past in order to cope
with economic difficulty in the Third Age. They may use gift-giving to
express empathy over the partner's physical diminution or reduce susceptibility to aging by managing the partner's aging process, or by
imparting the partner with skills and wisdom for how to live independently in late elderly life if they were to become the surviving partner.
These are manifestation of giver's concern for partner's well-being.

Our study reveals that memories of "perfect gift" experience associated with youth (Belk 1996) manifest keenly in the narratives of "nostalgic indulgers," the discontented informants who are regressive so as to
avoid anxieties and hostilities stemming from painful conflict and disrup-
tion in their lives (Minowa et al. 2012). They strongly yearn for the
romantic gift-giving experiences of the long past, either as a giver or a
recipient. Bittersweet memories of sacrifice or surprise—e.g., making
or receiving a hand-knitted sweater—that ended as unrequited love
appear in the narratives of retirees without a sense of purpose and financially vulnerable strugglers. Nostalgia, or sentimental yearning for the
past, is functional and social emotion (Routledge et al. 2012) as well
as a predictor of consumer preferences and adult behaviors (Holbrook
and Schindler 1989, 1996, 2003; Holak 2014). Nostalgia is a positive
resource for the self that enables the consumer to maintain the perception that their lives are meaningful (Routledge et al. 2012; Vess et al.
2012). It mitigates threats to meaning in life and hence promotes well-
being across life spans, including in later life (Routledge et al. 2012).
In the nostalgic narrative of the momentous "perfect gift" events, the
self invariably figures as the protagonist and the experience takes place
in a specific setting (Wildschut et al. 2006): The gift is valorized as a
luxury in this interiority—a timeless tableau defined by particular time,
place, identity, and a way of life (Belk 1996; Stewart 1988).

Another finding is that the meaning of romantic gift-giving in later life
is as fluid as the subjective nature of aging for consumers. Mature consumers in the current study use various ways to identify their aging
state and process in their narratives conveyed to us. These included
"old," "older," "young at heart," "at 'my' age," and "retired." Such a
discursive construction of the subjective self is referred to the positioning

theory (Allen and Wiles 2013). The positioning is intrapersonal as well as interpersonal, and it shows the multivocality of postmodern reality—the subjective self unfolds dialogically. Then they confirm or negotiate to make sense of their actions and legitimatize their deviations from supposedly objective norms for their intimate practices and romantic gift-giving. In other words, the romantic gift-giving practices and experiences of mature consumers are, to some extent, shaped by the language they choose to constitute their autobiographic selves with earlier-in-life and their later-in-life gift-giving experiences. While language constitutes the consumer's emotions recalled from the past, autobiographical memory functions to preserve the self and give directions for their future romantic gift-giving practices (Bluck 2003). Positioning the self in such a manner seems to provide consumers with room for flexible practical reasoning for using a gift as a tool to strategize their actions and undulate the subjective meanings of their existence, practices of intimacy, romantic gift-giving, and aging.

The implication of the current study is that through the storgic love paradigm of gift-giving, mature consumers are not seeking to fulfill temporal satisfaction from dyadic exchange or altruistic giving. Their concerns such as the continued pursuit of meaning in their life implies that they are more interested in fulfillment, or well-being, through romantic gift-giving experiences in later life. Then the pertinent questions should include what is seen to constitute meaning in life, aside from the sense of purpose, the value of human relationships, and nostalgia as discussed in the present study, and how gift-giving experiences can contribute to reviving, enhancing, and exulting the consumer's sense of meaning—or well-being—in later life. How do spirituality and religion intertwine with storgic love and romantic gift-giving in later life, mediated by the consumer's search for meaning in life? How do cultural differences manifest in enduring romantic gift experiences, especially East versus West, where previous studies have found that people attain happiness and cope with unhappiness differently in these two parts of the world (Karasawa et al. 2011; Uchida and Kitayama 2009)? And how is the individual's emotional experience organized and interpreted within a frame of socio-historically constructed culture?

Finally, future studies should incorporate "existential love" into studying storgic love and romantic gift-giving in later life. Realizing the transient nature of human existence, "existential love" that cherishes the present moment is also considered as love for later life (Gibson 1997). Conceptual links between romantic gift-giving practice and socio-historically constructed emotions may be used to explain the deployment of cultural fantasies for aging consumers while the meanings of gift-giving rituals are renewed and evolve through cultural media (Bell 1997; Minowa et al. 2011). Romantic gift-giving is psychological manifestation as much as culturally constructed consumer practice. As such, the findings from Japanese Baby Boomers' discourse may not be necessarily unique to them. We adopted the life retrospective approach in order to understand the reasons for the meanings Baby Boomers attached to gift-giving, and our study, therefore, is hoped to provide rich implications for future studies of consumers over the course of their lives.

Acknowledgment

The authors gratefully acknowledge Professor Takeshi Matsui for his administrative and data collection efforts, and Professors Anil Mathur, George Moschis, and Cele Otnes for their constructive advice.

References

Allen, Ruth E. S. and Janine L. Wiles (2013), "How Older People Position Their Childlessness in Their Late Life: A Qualitative Study," *Journal of Marriage and Family*, 75 (February), 206–20.

Amano, Masako (2001), *Dankai sedai: Shinron* [The Baby Boom Generation: A New Theory], Tokyo: Yushindo kobunsha.

Aron, Arthur P., Debra J. Mashek, and Elaine N. Aron (2004), "Closeness as Including Other in the Self," in *Handbook of Closeness and Intimacy*, ed. Debra J. Mashek and Arthur Aron, Mahwah, NJ: Lawrence Erlbaum Associates, Inc., 27–42.

Baker, Andrew, George Moschis, Edward Rigdon, and Anil Mathur (2011), "Effects of Family Structure on Compulsive Buying: A Life Course Perspective," in *Advances in Consumer Research*, Vol. 39, ed. Rohini Ahluwalia, Tanya L. Chartrand, and Rebecca K. Ratner, Duluth, MN: Association for Consumer Research, 422.

Barak, Benny and Stephen J. Gould (1985), "Alternative Age Measures: A Research Agenda," in *Advances in Consumer Research*, Vol. 12, ed. Elizabeth C. Hirschman and Morris B. Holbrook, Provo, UT: Association for Consumer Research, 53–8.

Barak, Benny, Anil Mathur, Keun Lee, and Yong Zhang (2001), "Perceptions of Age-Identity: A Cross-Cultural Inner-Age Exploration," *Psychology and Marketing*, 18 (10), 1003–29.

Barak, Benny and Leon G. Schiffman (1981), "Cognitive Age: A Nonchronological Age Variable," in *Advances in Consumer Research*, Vol. 8, ed. Kent B. Monroe, Ann Arbor, MI: Association for Consumer Research, 602–6.

Barusch, Amanda Smith (2008), *Love Stories of Later Life*, New York: Oxford University Press.

Belk, Russell W. (1979), "Gift Giving Behavior," in *Research in Marketing*, Vol. 2, ed. Jagdish Sheth, Greenwich, CT: JAI Press, 95–126.

—— (1988), "Possessions and the Extended Self," *Journal of Consumer Research*, 15 (2), 139–68.

—— (1992), "Moving Possessions: An Analysis Based on Personal Documents from the 1847–1869 Mormon Migration," *Journal of Consumer Research*, 19 (3), 339–61.

────── (1996), "The Perfect Gift," in *Gift Giving: A Research Anthology*, ed. Cele Otnes and Richard F. Beltramini, Bowling Green, OH: Bowling Green State University Popular Press, 59–84.

────── (2005), "Exchange Taboos from an Interpretive Perspective," *Journal of Consumer Psychology*, 15 (1), 16–21.

Belk, Russell W. and Gregory Coon (1993), "Gift Giving as Agapic Love: An Alternative to the Exchange Paradigm Based on Dating Experiences," *Journal of Consumer Research*, 20 (December), 393–417.

Belk, Russell W., Eileen Fischer, and Robert V. Kozinets (eds.) (2013), "Depth Interview," in *Qualitative Consumer and Marketing Research*, London: Sage Publications, 31–57.

Bell, Catherine (1997), *Ritual: Perspectives and Dimensions*, New York: Oxford University Press.

Bhattacharjee, Amit and Cassie Mogilner (2014), "Happiness from Ordinary and Extraordinary Experiences," *Journal of Consumer Research*, 41 (1), 1–17.

Bluck, Susan (2003), "Autobiographical Memory: Exploring Its Functions in Daily Life," *Memory*, 11 (2), 113–23.

Bode, Matthias and Per Østergaard (2011), "From Age to Ageing: Consumer Identity Projects in a Sociology of Life Course Perspective," A Paper presented at the Consumer Culture Theory Conference at Northwestern University, Evanston, IL, USA, July.

Brandtstädter, Jochen, Klaus Rothermund, Dirk Kranz, and Waldemar Kuhn (2010), "Final Decentrations: Personal Goals, Rationality Perspectives, and the Awareness of Life's Finitude," *European Psychologist*, 15 (2), 152–63.

Carstensen, Laura L. (1992), "Social and Emotional Patterns in Adulthood: Support for Socioemotional Selectivity Theory," *Psychology and Aging*, 7 (3), 331–8.

Chéron, Emmanuel J. (2011), "Elderly Consumers in Japan: The Most Mature 'Silver Market' Worldwide," in *Japanese Consumer Dynamics*, ed. Parissa Haghirian, New York: Palgrave Macmillan, 65–90.

Creighton, Mille R. (1993), "'Sweet Love' and Women's Place: Valentine's Day, Japan Style," *Journal of Popular Culture*, 27 (3), 1–19.

Dowd, James J. (1975), "Aging as Exchange: A Preface to Theory," *Journal of Gerontology*, 30 (5), 584–94.

Drolet, Aimee, Loraine Lau-Gesk, Patti Williams, and Hyewook Genevieve Jeong (2010), "Socioemotional Selectivity Theory: Implications for Consumer Research," in *The Aging Consumer: Perspectives from Psychology and Economics*, ed. Aimee Drolet, Norbert Schwartz, and Carolyn Yoon, New York: Routledge, 51–72.

Elder, Glen H., Jr., Monica Kirkpatrick Johnson, and Robert Crosnoe (2003), "The Emergence and Development of Life Course Theory," in *Handbook of the Life Course*, ed. J. T. Mortimer and M. J. Shanahan, New York: Plenum, 3–19.

Erikson, Erik H. (1993 [1950]), *Childhood and Society*, New York: W. W. Norton & Company.

Fischer, Eileen and Stephen J. Arnold (1990), "More Than a Labor of Love: Gender Roles and Christmas Gift Shopping," *Journal of Consumer Research*, 17 (3), 333–45.

Flatt, Michael A., Richard A. Settersten, Jr., Roselle Ponsaran, and Jennifer R. Fishman (2013), "Are 'Anti-Aging Medicine' and 'Successful Aging' Two Sides of the Same Coin? Views of Anti-Aging Practitioners," *Journals of*

Gerontology, Series B: Psychological Sciences and Social Sciences, 68 (6), 944–55.

Francks, Penelope (2009), *The Japanese Consumer: An Alternative Economic History of Modern Japan*, Cambridge: Cambridge University Press.

Freund, Alexandra M. and Fredda Blanchard-Fields (2014), "Age-Related Differences in Altruism across Adulthood: Making Personal Financial Gain Versus Contributing to the Public Good," *Developmental Psychology*, 50 (4), 1125–36.

Fromm, Erich (1956), *The Art of Loving*, New York: HarperCollins.

George, Linda K. (1993), "Sociological Perspective on Life Transitions," *Annual Review of Sociology*, 19, 353–73.

Gibson, Hamilton Bertie (1997), *Love in Later Life*, London: Peter Owen Publishers.

Gould, Stephen J. and Claudia E. Weil (1991), "Gift-Giving Roles and Gender Self-Concepts," *Sex Roles*, 24 (9/10), 617–37.

Grenier, Amanda (2012), *Transitions and the Lifecourse: Challenging the Constructions of "Growing Old"*, Bristol, UK: Polity Press.

Guttmann, David (1999), *Logotherapy for the Therapist: Meaningful Social Work*, Tel-Aviv University, Tel Aviv: Dionon. (In Hebrew).

Hashimoto, Akiko (1996), *The Gift of Generations: Japanese and American Perspectives on Aging and the Social Contract*, Cambridge: Cambridge University Press.

Heaven, Patrick C. L., Tatiana Da Silva, Christine Carey, and Janet Holen (2004), "Loving Styles: Relationships with Personality and Attachment Styles," *European Journal of Personality*, 18 (2), 103–13.

Heckhausen, Jutta and Richard Schulz (1995), "A Life-Span Theory of Control," *Psychological Review*, 102 (2), 284–304.

Hendrick, Clyde and Susan Hendrick (1986), "A Theory and Method of Love," *Journal of Personality and Social Psychology*, 50 (2), 392–402.

Hetsroni, Amir (2012), "Associations between Television Viewing and Love Styles: An Interpretation Using Cultivation Theory," *Psychological Reports*, 110 (1), 35–50.

Holak, Susan L. (2014), "From Brighton Beach to Blogs: Exploring Food-Related Nostalgia in the Russian Diaspora," *Consumption Markets & Culture*, 17 (2), 185–207.

Holbrook, Morris B. and Robert M. Schindler (1989), "Some Exploratory Findings on the Development of Musical Tastes," *Journal of Consumer Research*, 16 (1), 119–24.

——— (1996), "Market Segmentation Based on Age and Attitude toward the Past: Concepts, Methods, and Findings Concerning Nostalgic Influences on Customer Tastes," *Journal of Business Research*, 37 (1), 27–39.

——— (2003), "Nostalgic Bonding: Exploring the Role of Nostalgia in the Consumption Experience," *Journal of Consumer Behaviour*, 3 (2), 107–27.

Hyde, Lewis (1983), *The Gift: Imagination and the Erotic Life of Property*, New York: Vintage Books.

Ito, Mikiharu (2011), *Zōtō no nihonbunka* [Japanese Culture with Gift Giving], Tokyo: Chikuma shobō.

Joy, Annamma (2001), "Gift Giving in Hong Kong and the Continuum of Social Ties," *Journal of Consumer Research*, 28 (September), 236–59.

Kanemasa, Yuji, Junichi Taniguchi, Ikuo Daibo, and Masanori Ishimori (2004), "Love Styles and Romantic Love Experiences in Japan," *Social Behavior and Personality*, 23 (3), 265–82.

Karasawa, Mayumi, Katherine B. Curhan, Hazel Rose Markus, Shinobu S. Kitayama, Gayle Dienberg Love, Barry T. Radler, and Carol D. Ryff (2011), "Cultural Perspectives on Aging and Well-Being: A Comparison of Japan and the United States," *International Journal of Aging and Human Development*, 73 (1), 73–98.

Katz, Stephen (2001/2002), "Growing Older without Aging? Positive Aging, Anti-Ageism, and Anti-Aging," *Generations*, 25 (4), 27–32.

Kimmel, Douglas C. (1988), "Ageism, Psychology, and Public Policy," *American Psychologist*, 43 (3), 175–8.

Kimura, Junko and Russell W. Belk (2005), "Christmas in Japan: Globalization Versus Localization," *Consumption, Markets and Culture*, 8 (September), 325–38.

Kohlbacher, Florian and Emmanuel Chéron (2012), "Understanding 'Silver' Consumers through Cognitive age, Health Condition Financial Status, and Personal Values: Empirical Evidence from the World's Most Mature Market Japan," *Journal of Consumer Behaviour*, 11 (3), 179–88.

Koren, Chaya and Ariela Lowenstein (2008), "Late-Life Widowhood and Meaning in Life," *Ageing International*, 32 (2), 140–55.

Korte, Jojanneke, Gerben J. Westerhof, and Ernst T. Bohlmeijer (2012), "Mediating Processes in an Effective Life-Review Intervention," *Psychology and Ageing*, 27 (4), 1172–81.

Laslett, Peter (1996), *A Fresh Map of Life: The Emergence of the Third Age*, Houndmills, Basingstoke, and Hampshire: Palgrave Macmillan.

Lee, John Alan (1973), *Colours of Love: An Exploration of the Ways of Loving*, Toronto: New Press.

Levy, Becca R., Ori Ashman, and Martin D. Slade (2010), "Age Attributions and Aging Health: Contrast between the United States and Japan," *Journal of Gerontology: Psychological Sciences*, 64B (3), 335–8.

Lewis, Clive Staples (1960), *The Four Loves*, New York: Harcourt, Brace & World, Inc.

Li, Eric P. H., Hyun Jeong Min, Russell W. Belk, Junko Kimura, and Shalini Bahl (2008), "Skin Lightening and Beauty in Four Asian Cultures," in *Advances in Consumer Research*, Vol. 35, ed. Angela Y. Lee and Dilip Soman, Duluth, MN: Association for Consumer Research, 444–9.

Long, Susan O. (2012), "Bodies, Technologies, and Aging in Japan: Thinking about Old People and Their Silver Products," *Journal of Cross-Cultural Gerontology*, 27 (2), 119–37.

Lowrey, Tina M., Cele C. Otnes, and Julie A. Ruth (2004), "Social Influences on Dyadic Giving over Time: A Taxonomy from the Giver's Perspective," *Journal of Consumer Research*, 30 (4), 547–58.

Margrain, Tom H. and Mike Boulton (2005), "Sensory Impairment," in *The Cambridge Handbook of Age and Ageing*, ed. Malcolm L. Johnson, New York: Cambridge University Press, 121–30.

MarketLine (2012), *Facial Care in Japan: MarketLine Industry Profile*, Reference Code: 0104–0093, November.

Mashek, Debra J. and Michelle D. Sherman (2004), "Desiring Less Closeness with Intimate Others" in *Handbook of Closeness and Intimacy*, ed. Debra J. Mashek and Arthur Aron, Mahwah, NJ: Lawrence Erlbaum Associates, Inc., 343–56.

Mathur, Anil (1996), "Older Adults' Motivations for Gift Giving to Charitable Organizations: An Exchange Theory Perspective," *Psychology and Marketing*, 13 (1), 107–23.

Mathur, Anil, George P. Moschis, and Euehun Lee (2008), "A Longitudinal Study of the Effects of Life Status Changes on Changes in Consumer Preferences," *Journal of the Academy of Marketing Science*, 36 (2), 234–46.

Mauss, Marcel (1990 [1925]), *The Gift: Forms and Functions of Exchange in Archaic Societies*, New York: W. W. Norton & Company.

Minowa, Yuko and Stephen J. Gould (1999), "Love My Gift, Love Me or Is It Love Me, Love My Gift: A Study of the Cultural Construction of Love and Gift-Giving among Japanese Couples," in *Advances in Consumer Research*, Vol. 26, ed. Eric J. Arnould and Linda M. Scott, Provo, UT: Association for Consumer Research, 119–24.

Minowa, Yuko, Olga Khomenko, and Russell W. Belk (2011), "Social Change and Gendered Gift-Giving Rituals: A Historical Analysis of Valentine's Day in Japan," *Journal of Macromarketing*, 31 (1), 41–56.

Minowa, Yuko, Takeshi Matsui, and Russell W. Belk (2012), "'I Would Want a Magic Gift': Desire for Romantic Gift Giving and the Cultural Fantasies of Baby Boomers in Japan," in *NA: Advances in Consumer Research*, Vol. 40, ed. Zeynep Gürhan-Canli, Cele Otnes, and Rui (Juliet) Zhu, Duluth, MN: Association for Consumer Research, 901–2.

——— (2013), "'Make Someone Happy': Romantic Gift Giving of Teenagers in Japan," in *European Advances for Consumer Research*, Vol. 10, ed. Gert Cornelissen, Elena Reutskaja, and Ana Valenzuela, Duluth, MN: Association for Consumer Research, 219–20.

Moschis, George P. (1991), "Approaches to the Study of Consumer Behavior in Late Life," in *Advances in Consumer Research*, Vol. 18, ed. Rebecca H. Holman and Michael R. Solomon, Provo, UT: Association for Consumer Research, 517–20.

——— (2007), "Life Course Perspectives on Consumer Behavior," *Journal of the Academy of Marketing Science*, 35 (2), 295–307.

——— (2012), "Consumer Behavior in Later Life: Current Knowledge, Issues, and New Directions for Research," *Psychology and Marketing*, 29 (2), 57–75.

Nguyen, Hung Vu, George P. Moschis, and Randall Shannon (2009), "Effects of Family Structure and Socialization on Materialism: A Life Course Study in Thailand," *International Journal of Consumer Studies*, 33 (4), 486–95.

Otnes, Cele and Richard F. Beltramini (eds.) (1996), *Gift Giving: A Research Anthology*, Bowling Green, OH: Bowling Green State University Popular Press.

Otnes, Cele, Julie A. Ruth, and C. Milbourne (1994), "The Pleasure and Pain of Being Close: Men's Mixed Feelings about Participation in Valentine's Day Gift Exchange," in *Advances in Consumer Research*, Vol. 21, ed. Chris T. Allen and Deborah R. John, Provo, UT: Association for Consumer Research, 159–64.

Otnes, Cele, Kyle Zolner, and Tina M. Lowrey (1994), "In-Laws and Outlaws: The Impact of Divorce and Remarriage upon Christmas Gift Exchange," in

Advances in Consumer Research, Vol. 21, ed. Chris T. Allen and Deborah Roedder John, Provo, UT: Association for Consumer Research, 25–9.

Rodgers, Willard and A. Regula Herzog (1987), "Interviewing Older Adults: The Accuracy of Factual Information," *Journal of Gerontology*, 42 (4), 387–94.

Rook, Dennis W. (1985), "The Ritual Dimension of Consumer Behavior," *Journal of Consumer Research*, 12 (December), 251–64.

Routledge, Clay, Tim Wildschut, Constantine Sedikides, Jacob Juhl, and Jamie Arndt (2012), "The Power of the Past: Nostalgia as A Meaning-Making Resource," *Memory*, 20 (5), 452–60.

Rugimbana, Robert, Brett Donahay, Christopher Neal, and Michael Jay Polonsky (2003), "The Role of Social Power Relations in Gift Giving in Valentine's Day," *Journal of Consumer Behaviour*, 3 (1), 63–73.

Rupp, Katherine (2003), *Gift-Giving in Japan: Cash, Connections, Cosmologies*, Stanford, CA: Stanford University Press.

Ruth, Julie A., Cele C. Otnes, and Frederic F. Brunel (1999), "Gift Receipt and the Reformulation of Interpersonal Relationships," *Journal of Consumer Research*, 25 (March), 385–402.

Saad, Gad and Tripat Gill (2003), "An Evolutionary Psychology Perspective to Romantic Gift Giving of Young Adults," *Psychology and Marketing*, 20 (9), 765–84.

Saito, Katsutoshi (2014), "Solving the Super-Ageing Challenge," *OECD Yearbook 2014*, 49.

Schau, Hope Jensen, Mary C. Gilly, and Mary Wolfinbarger (2009), "Consumer Identity Renaissance: The Resurgence of Identity-Inspired Consumption in Retirement," *Journal of Consumer Research*, 36 (2), 255–76.

Schoenmakers, Eric C., Theo G. van Tilburg, and Tineke Fokkema (2012), "Coping with Loneliness: What Do Older Adults Suggest?," *Aging and Mental Health*, 16 (3), 353–60.

Shakespeare, William (1997 [1602]), *The Merry Wives of Windsor*, New York: Cambridge University Press.

Sherry, John F., Jr. (1983), "Gift Giving in Anthropological Perspective," *Journal of Consumer Research*, 10 (2), 157–68.

Shirahase, Sawako (2014), *Social Inequality in Japan*, New York: Routledge.

Spiggle, Susan (1994), "Analysis and Interpretation of Qualitative Data in Consumer Research," *Journal of Consumer Research*, 21 (3), 491–503.

Stavropoulos, Dimitri N. (1995), *Oxford Greek-English Learner's Dictionary*, Oxford, UK: Oxford University Press.

Sternberg, Robert J. (1986), "A Triangular Theory of Love," *Psychological Review*, 93 (2), 119–35.

Stewart, Kathleen (1988), "Nostalgia: A Polemic," *Cultural Anthropology*, 3 (3), 227–41.

Tanizaki, Junichiro (2004 [1965]), *Diary of a Mad Old Man*, New York: Vintage Books.

Thompson, Craig J. (1997), "Interpreting Consumers: A Hermeneutical Framework for Deriving Marketing Insights from the Texts of Consumers' Consumption Stories," *Journal of Marketing Research*, 34 (November), 438–55.

Tolstoy, Leo (1965 [1859]), "Family Happiness," Trans. J. D. Duff, in *Leo Tolstoy Short Novels*, New York: The Modern Library, 127–213.

Tumbat, Gulnur and Russell W. Belk (2011), "Marketplace Tensions in Extraordinary Experiences," *Journal of Consumer Research*, 38 (June), 42–61.

Uchida, Yukiko and Shinobu Kitayama (2009), "Happiness and Unhappiness in East and West: Themes and Variations," *Emotion*, 9 (4), 441–56.

Vess, Mathew, Jamie Arndt, Clay Routledge, Tim Wildschut, and Constantine Sedikides (2012), "Nostalgia as a Resource for the Self," *Self and Identity*, 11 (3), 273–84.

Wildschut, Tim, Constantine Sedikides, Jamie Arndt, and Clay Routledge (2006), "Nostalgia: Content, Triggers, Functions," *Journal of Personality and Social Psychology*, 91 (5), 975–93.

Yamada, Yoshiko, Hidehiro Sugisawa, Yoko Sugihara, and Hiroshi Shibata (2005), "Factors Relating to Organizational Commitment of Older Male Employees in Japan," *Journal of Cross Cultural Gerontology*, 20 (3), 181–90.

Yamaguchi, Mutsumi (2012), *Zōtoh no kindai* [The Modernity of Japanese Gift-Exchange, Zoto], Sendai: Tohoku University Press.

Yancey, George and Sarah Berglass (1991), "Love Styles and Life Satisfaction," *Psychological Reports*, 68 (3), 883–90.

Zelizer, Viviana A. (2005), *Purchase of Intimacy*, Princeton, NJ: Princeton University Press.

4 If You Love Me, Surprise Me

Aditya Gupta and James W. Gentry

Is there anyone who can resist a rush of delight when presented with a thoughtful surprise from a loved one? It could be something as grand as getting prime tickets to a favorite Broadway show as an anniversary present or something as simple as being greeted at the end of a harrowing workday by a flower plucked from the roadside by your better half. The sheer delight of being the recipient of a surprise gift would wash away most worries and cares in its wake and replace it with a warm glow instead. Or, at the very least, it will make you smile.

Surprise has always been posited as an integral element of "the perfect gift." Belk (1996, 66) commented on the importance of surprise as being one of the six characteristics that the perfect gift should possess, noting that the unexpectedness of the gift was as important as its appropriateness for the recipient. What makes surprise even more interesting is its link to delight, which has surfaced time and again in academic research (and continues to do so), which forms yet another prerequisite for a gift to be perfect. In the context of romantic gift-giving, the ability to spring a delightful surprise on the object of one's affections could nudge a relationship further along a more optimistic trajectory while a negative surprise might well bring it to a grinding halt.

The transience of surprise makes the emotion an elusive one to study, something attested to by the fact that academic research on surprise gifting has only recently begun to gather steam. However, the emotion itself has been an object of enquiry for a fairly long time and continues to provide, well, *surprising* findings for researchers and practitioners alike. Consequently, in this chapter we take a closer look at surprise itself and explore the role it can play in sustaining the magic of romantic gift-giving.

The chapter is structured as follows: We first provide a brief overview about the emotion of surprise and then look at its conceptual and empirical link with customer delight. We then focus on how research has made several references to the role of surprise in the context of romantic gift-giving, and also provide a discussion on how surprise can backfire within relationships. This leads into our proposed framework that utilizes the notion of the shared self to illustrate how romantic surprises can be conceptualized for couples who are in a romantic relationship. We conclude with a brief discussion on some future directions for research.

On Surprise

Initial research on surprise can be said to have begun as part of an overall interest in the role of emotion in people's lives. Richins (1997) credits two scholars in particular whose work would eventually influence how consumer behavior research dealt with emotions—Robert Plutchik and Carroll Izard. Both psychologists approached human emotion from an evolutionary standpoint. They contended that there was a certain set of "basic" human emotions that had evolved to enhance an organism's chance of survival. Complex emotions were posited to result from a combination or mixture of these primary emotions. Plutchik (1980) listed eight primary emotions—fear, anger, joy, sadness, acceptance, disgust, expectancy, and surprise—while Izard (1977) included ten—interest, enjoyment, surprise, distress (sadness), anger, disgust, contempt, fear, shame/shyness, and guilt—in his Differential Emotions Scale (DES). The similarity in both lists cannot be ignored.

Serendipitously, it was around this time that consumer behavior research started questioning the prevailing information processing paradigm of consumer choice (Bettman 1979) that viewed the consumer as being, if anything, too logical and rational to be true. In what would go on to become seminal pieces in the history of consumer research, Elizabeth Hirschman and Morris Holbrook took the bull by the horns and outlined the beginnings of the hedonic/experiential approach toward consumption that would turn the spotlight on the "symbolic, hedonic, and esthetic [sic] nature of consumption" (Holbrook and Hirschman 1982, 132) and the "multisensory, fantasy, and emotive aspects of the product usage experience" (Hirschman and Holbrook 1982, 92). The ambit of consumer research had to be expanded, and one way to do that was to start looking at the emotional side of the consumer.

As should be the case in a programmatic scheme of research, initial work on consumption emotion focused on concerns with the measurement of emotions. While some articles looked at (or used) the existing approaches to emotion measurement, such as Havlena and Holbrook's (1986) comparative evaluation of Mehrabian and Russell's (1974) Pleasure, Arousal, and Dominance (PAD) paradigm with Plutchik's (1980) eight emotional categories, or Westbrook's (1987) use of Izard's (1977) DES-II scale to measure consumption-based affective responses, others focused on developing measures specific to consumption research such as Richins' (1997) studies that tested and validated the Consumption Emotion Set (CES). In all such studies, surprise continued to be included as part of the entire emotion spectrum but was not being singled out as a variable of interest.

The Link Between Surprise and Delight

Interest in the surprise construct started increasing around the beginning of the 90s when scholars started looking at the link between consumption emotion and satisfaction. Among the first studies to do so was Westbrook and Oliver's (1991) inquiry into the affective dimensions of emotional responses to consumption experiences. The scholars found five categories of affective responses, namely consumers who were happy/content (a combination of interest and joy), pleasantly surprised (a combination of joy and surprise), unemotional (below average levels of all consumption emotions), unpleasantly surprised (a combination of sadness and surprise), or angry/upset (disgust/contempt) in response to a consumption experience. The multi-valence of surprise was clearly illustrated by the presence of pleasantly surprised consumers and unpleasantly surprised consumers.

Oliver, Rust, and Varki (1997) brought into clearer focus the role surprise could play in the pursuit of customer delight, the holy grail of marketers. They conceptualized surprise in two distinct ways—as "disconfirmation" (by asking consumers their perception of the overall experience against expectations) and as "surprising consumption" (by asking consumers their satisfaction against expected satisfaction from the experience). Through two studies that looked at the experiences of visitors to a recreational wildlife theme park and symphony concert goers, they were able to demonstrate a pattern wherein surprise led to arousal that, in turn, created positive affect which finally resulted in delight. Thus, surprise was demonstrated to have a key starting role in the creation of delight. Soon after, Rust and Oliver (2000) urged firms to aim for customer delight (marking it as something distinct from mere satisfaction) in their marketing activities. Creating delight was, of course, not easy precisely because of the surprise element—if a given customer experience was delightful then it was posited to have the effect of raising repurchase expectations, i.e., the "threshold" of delight was raised for the next purchase occasion. Then why go to all this trouble? Because, as the authors put it, although "the delighting firm is injured by raised customer expectations, the (nondelighting) competition is hurt worse through customer attrition to the delighting firm" (Rust and Oliver 2000, 86).

Over the last decade or so, the body of work on surprise has continued to grow with initial exploratory work looking at the link between surprise and satisfaction (Vanhamme 2000) gradually branching out into more focused examination. Heilman, Nakamoto, and Rao (2002) found evidence to support the use of "surprise" in-store coupons as a means to increase the size of a consumer's shopping basket by increasing the number of unplanned purchases, while Vanhamme and Snelders (2003) showed that consumers liked "the surprising element" in a consumption experience. Even more interesting were findings that related to the inclusion of surprise in consumption contexts that were more hedonic in nature. In one study, Vanhamme (2008, 129) found that "positively surprising experiences are most often consumption or purchase episodes with a dominant experiential component" (a subsequent experimental study corroborated this finding though the effect was marginal). Laran and Tsiros (2013, 112) further strengthened this link by showing how, when a purchase decision is more affective than cognitive in nature, "people like to be surprised and appreciate uncertainty in the purchase process." Given that romantic gift-giving is largely a hedonic act (even after allowing for "utilitarian" cases where the gifting motivation stems more from an obligation or a dispassionately calculative cost-benefit approach), the role of surprise as an amplifier of satisfaction and delight now gains additional glamor.

Putting Surprise Into Romantic Gift-Giving

If, as we have seen, surprise is key to generating delight, then it's only befitting that it forms a crucial ingredient in the recipe of "the perfect gift," the other five being sacrifice on the part of the giver, the giver's wish to please the recipient, the luxuriousness of the gift, the uniquely appropriate nature of the gift for the recipient (i.e. suitability), and, finally, the recipient's desire for, and subsequent delight with, the gift (Belk 1996, 61).

Along with noting how surprise can be heightened by the simple act of gift-wrapping a present, Belk further noted that while a gift should be "the primary source of surprise on an occasion and in a relationship where a gift is expected, additional surprise comes from the spontaneous gift given for no occasion at all" (Belk 1996, 67). Indeed, the sheer spontaneity of the gift signals that the recipient was uppermost in one's mind. Otherwise, why buy a gift without a specific occasion in mind?

Does the conclusion hold when it comes specifically to romantic surprise gifts? Other than the fact that Belk (1996) chose nothing less than O. Henry's classic "The Gift of the Magi"—a story that is arguably one of the finest odes to romantic love—to illustrate his conception of the perfect gift, a re-look at Belk and Coon's (1993) conceptualization of romantic love (within the larger agapic love paradigm) might help answer that question, especially when coupled with recent findings from interpretivist research.

The authors highlight four aspects of gifting within agapic romantic love that sharply distinguish this model from the more instrumental and rational exchange paradigm of gifting—emotion, expressiveness, singularization of the recipient, and selfless sacrifice. The discussion on emotion focuses on the magical or mystical nature of love between two people which imbues the gifts given or received in such a relationship with an all-encompassing feeling of ecstasy, passion, magic, and self-transcendence. On a similar note, romantic gifts are seen to be expressions of feelings too deep to be put into words and emerge as conduits to convey one's deepest emotions to her/his romantic partner. They are also given without any expectation of getting a reciprocal gift, in sharp contrast to the instrumentalism of exchange models which necessitate reciprocity. The focus, therefore, is on the uniqueness of the recipient—the ideal gift being one which is as special and distinctive as the recipient herself/himself, the choice of which would illustrate the giver's almost intuitive understanding of the recipient's wishes and desires. Finally, there is the element of sacrifice inherent in such romantic gifts where the giver's personal pleasure is altruistically placed second to that of the recipient (whose happiness becomes the primary goal).

A surprise gift given within the ambit of a romantic relationship seems particularly well suited to the abovementioned ideas. The delight at receiving (and giving) a surprise gift is an emotional peak for both the giver and the recipient. Aren't we all familiar with the reaction of the (usually) female protagonist in movies when the (usually) male lover opens a little square box to reveal an engagement ring? Few emotional highs can compare with what is easily among the biggest and most significant surprise gifts one could get from one's loved one.

Moreover, if a romantic gift is meant to be a surprise, then it's clearly being done as an expressive act and not to elicit a reciprocal reaction from one's partner (a cynic might claim that it can set up an expectation that the recipient should also surprise the giver when a suitable occasion arises, but there would be few couples indeed who would indulge in such calculation and still manage to stay a couple of their own accord). The focus is on communicating the affection one feels for another if one goes to all the trouble of springing a surprise.

When it comes to recognizing the uniqueness of an individual, few things would be as indicative as a thoughtfully chosen surprise. It would be the easiest thing to ask someone what they want the most, tell them that you're going to buy it for them, and then proceed to do so. If we think of this logically, at first glance it seems to be the only way to give full credence to someone's uniquely distinctive tastes and preferences. However, including the element of surprise in such a gift would accentuate (remember the discussion of the amplifying nature of surprise?) the pleasure from the gift because it is that which would signal to someone that one's better half recognizes her/his unique desires so exceptionally well that the giver didn't need to ask the recipient about what to buy.

Lastly, given that a surprise always takes a modicum of effort—from the simple act of holding a present behind one's back before bringing it out with a flourish to the mammoth effort which can go into planning and staging a full-scale surprise birthday party—it embodies, in ways big or small, sacrifice on part of the giver, simply in order to delight the recipient even more.

References to surprise romantic gifts can be found sprinkled throughout research inquiries ranging across cultures and contexts. Respondents in Belk and Coon's (1993) study reflected on the symbolic value of a surprise gift, either in remarking on the delight in being presented with a surprising gift like a stuffed teddy bear from a boyfriend or noting how little presents or flowers on unexpected occasions mattered more to them than a deluge of gifts on more "expected" occasions such as birthdays or Christmas celebrations. In their study on the gifting experiences of married couples, Durgee and Sego (2001, 65) found that several "hits" (gifts that were reported to be special to each of the two) reflected a combination of high degrees of pleasure and surprise.

A rare (and much-needed) cross-cultural perspective on romantic gifting was provided by Minowa and Gould (1999) regarding Japanese couples. Looking at the gifting experience from both angles—giving as well as receiving—for both genders, the authors found "surprise" to be a recurring (and important) theme for three of the four cases, namely in the receiving experience of females, and the receiving as well as giving experiences of males. Among the female receiver accounts, for instance, pleasant gift-related memories were the result of an impeccably planned surprise birthday dinner at a restaurant or a muffler secretly bought by a girl's boyfriend, while one of the men reported that a surprise gift of a sweater from his partner was the most memorable, despite the fact that it did not fit and he could never wear it, simply because it was a reflection of the effort she had put into it. These emotional highs were corroborated to a degree in a later piece by Minowa, Matsui, and Belk (2012), which found that two segments of Japanese Baby Boomers, labeled by the authors as Fantasy Seekers and Nostalgia Inducers, expressed a desire for thoughtful gifts from their romantic partners.

Finally, in a spirit that marked a fitting return to the experiential and hedonic nature of gift-giving, Clarke (2006, 2013) advanced an argument that experience gifts—gifts that had a negligible material component and were primarily "experienced"—were superior to material gifts from the perspectives of both donors and receivers. The two studies conducted by her in the UK brought out the importance of gifts of travel and leisure because the list of memorable experience gifts mentioned by informants ranged from the more awe-inspiring Disneyland visits and helicopter flights to the relatively simpler spa days and evenings of theater and good food. One of the key themes, and one especially pertinent to this chapter, that emerged was the inherent "surprise" in such romantic experience gifts because one can never truly engineer all the aspects of a consumption experience. Thus, unlike material gifts, surprise extended beyond mere wrapping, and became a fundamental part of the experience itself because there would always be an element of something unexpected. Recent findings by Chan and Mogilner (2017) lend further credence to this as they show how experiential gifts improved relationship strength more than material gifts due to the higher intensity of emotion evoked by the former. Therefore, the element of surprise can be seen to intensify the feelings, fantasies, and fun that Holbrook and Hirschman (1982) had spoken of so many years ago.

Bad Surprises

Unlike other emotions, surprise is unique in its inherent bivalence—it can either be positive or negative. This distinctive characteristic imbues surprise romantic gifts with a similar polarity wherein a gift could result in a lovely surprise for the recipient but could also carry the risk of being a disappointment and, consequently, a "gift failure" (Rucker et al. 1991).

Given the complexity of the gift-giving process and the multitude of factors comprising it (Sherry 1983), it is no surprise that gift-giving can backfire. Research within the consumer behavior domain brought out the dark side of gifting fairly early on and was especially evident in the unhappiness accompanied with the return of unwanted or unsuitable gifts (Sherry, McGrath, and Levy 1992, 1993). No wonder, then, that gift-giving and receiving have been thought to "engender high levels of anxiety among consumers" (Sherry et al. 1993, 225). Even the purchase of a gift as simple as a birthday card could be fraught with the dangers of a "minefield" (Dodson and Belk 1996, 14) if one doesn't adequately personalize it and/or doesn't select a card that is age and gender appropriate. If we consider the case of surprise gifts in particular, then the following insight from Sherry et al. (1992, 53) rings harshly true: "The promise of the present is double-edged with the strong potential for either disappointment or delight. The gift contains the potential to bond recipients more tightly to each other or to reaffirm the other's secret suspicions of mistrust and personal inadequacy." Surprise gifts are also likely to take on a greater importance for relational implications of romantic partners given that the dynamic engenders a high intensity of sentiment involved in the gifting experience and an expectation that the gift will be something substantial (Sherry et al. 1993). Thus, romantic partners could be seen as "thrice" burdened when it comes to their search for the perfect gift—the gift must possess substance, it must match the depth of the sentiments that is (arguably) shared by the two people in love, and it must be a surprise.

And, as if that were not enough, gender (of both the giver and the recipient) also has to be factored into the gifting equation. Rucker et al. (1991, 246) found that people make differential judgments regarding what would comprise "good guy gifts" and "good gal gifts." A rose, as per their findings, was considered a suitable gift for a female but not so for a male. What also emerged from their studies was the "double jeopardy" (Rucker et al. 1991, 247) situation for males who were not only "relatively unattuned [sic] to female preferences" but were also "relatively unappreciative of what they [didn't] know." If men reading this right now are beginning to sweat profusely thinking back to their many "well meaning" gifting mistakes, they might well wonder why their relationships didn't disintegrate. An answer of sorts was provided by Dunn et al. (2008) who found that women and men reacted differently to bad gifts. Through their studies (in which the "gift" element was actually a surprise in that a respondent didn't know beforehand whether they would be getting a good gift or a bad gift), they found that men reported a dip in perceived similarity to their girlfriends and became pessimistic about the relationship's future outlook upon (ostensibly) receiving a bad gift from their girlfriends. However, women kept their relationship future outlook intact and, in fact, even reported *increased* feelings of similarity to their boyfriends upon receiving a bad gift supposedly chosen by them. Why did that happen? Dunn et al. (2008, 477) suggested that a possible key lay in how women "marshalled psychological defences in response to the threat posed by receiving a bad gift." Alternatively, women could also be more forgiving of bad gifts than men were. In any case, women seemed keener to insulate the relationship from gifting shocks than did men. So, men may breathe a tiny sigh of relief.

Cheal (1987), recognizing the possible pitfalls of gifting early on, observed how even close relationships did not, at times, furnish enough information that could ensure the selection of a good gift. This was corroborated by Ruth, Otnes, and Brunel (1999) who, in their study on gifting experiences, found that 58% of the gift contexts discussed by their informants were negative ones, and more recently by Chan and Mogilner (2017), who noted that gift-givers are often poor predictors of what recipients will like. The inescapable fact is that even when the giver has made an effortful attempt to provide a personalized gift, the success or failure of the gift is ultimately determined by the recipient (Dodson and Belk 1996). Further, the gift's magnitude may be seen as a threat if it exceeds the recipient's perception of the strength of the relationship, as noted by Belk and Coon (1993).

Indeed, given our earlier mention of the role of surprise as an amplifier of delight, the reverse effect could also operate wherein a badly chosen surprise gift ends up causing or widening a rift between two people currently in a romantic relationship. In their framework describing the possible relational effects of gift-receipt, Ruth et al. (1999, 389) delineate six possible consequences—three of them negative (Negative confirmation, Weakening, and Severing), two of them positive (Strengthening and Affirmation), and one termed Negligible effect (that doesn't have a significant impact on the relationship). Respondent accounts across most categories showed how surprise gifts could work differently in different cases. On the positive side were examples such as an expensive sleeping bag given by a man to his girlfriend "out of the blue" that led to the strengthening of the relationship by acting as an epiphanic "turning point" (Ruth et al. 1999, 388) and signaling a deepening of the relationship. However, a gift could also be an overkill (Ruth et al. 1999, 393)—an uncomfortable surprise (an expensive CD player) that was "too good for the current state of the relationship"—even though it may only have a negligible effect on the relationship. And then there is the rarest, though harshest, extreme— severing. This occurred when the negative surprise (or, more accurately, the shock) effectively led to the termination of the relationship, either by embodying a dramatic level of threat or by being intentionally chosen to expedite the dissolution (Ruth et al. 1999, 396).

The literature on husband and wife decision making does not provide evidence for strong understanding of spousal preferences (Commuri and Gentry 2000), especially given the implicit nature of most family communication. For instance, in their study of women dealing with breast cancer, Pavia and Mason (2004) discuss the negative reaction of a respondent to the purchase of a new consumer durable by her husband—she accused him of buying it for his next wife. One informant in Ruth et al. (1999) was unhappy that her husband gave her a gift on their tenth wedding anniversary, given that he had never given her anything on their previous nine anniversaries. Instead of reacting positively to what must have been a surprise, she was angry when she thought of the ungifted history.

Towards a Conceptual Framework for Surprise Romantic Gifts

Gift-giving within the context of romantic relationships acquires an additional layer of complexity once surprise is brought into the picture. This is best illustrated using the concept of the shared self that was recently articulated by Wong, Hogg, and Vanharanta (2017) in response to calls for a stronger understanding of sharing within consumer behavior (Belk 2010). Building on the central concept of how close relationships could be viewed as including the other in one's sense of self (Aron et al. 1992; Aron et al. 1991), Wong et al. (2017, 78) provide a temporal model of how two people in a romantic relationship share resources, perspectives, and identities to construct a "shared self" that transitions from a discrete "me" and "you" to a shared "we" over time. Thus, the existence of overlapping selves provides a common base from which consumption and possessions are perceived. Given the nature of Simon's (1957) bounded rationality, one might infer that the common base might provide limits to finding a gift outside the shared base that would be seen as a positive surprise. Figure 4.1 provides an illustration of our proposed framework for surprise gift-giving within the context of a romantic relationship.

The overlapping circles represent the shared self between a person (denoted as the circle labeled "Self") and her/his romantic partner (denoted as the circle labeled "Other"). This visualization borrows from the Inclusion of Other in Self (IOS) scale used by Aron et al. (1992, 597). Placing this concept of shared self in a space divided into two categories—positively perceived stimuli and negatively perceived stimuli—allows us to map the spaces of good gifts (which would correspond to positively perceived stimuli) and bad gifts (which would correspond to negatively perceived stimuli).

A good surprise gift, as shown by the area shaded with diagonal lines, would be one that would (a) utilize stimuli that is positively perceived by the recipient, (b) lie within her/his overall preference set, and (c) lie outside the shared self. Analogously, a bad surprise would be any gift that fails to meet any of the three criteria thus outlined. If the gift utilizes a negatively perceived stimulus, then it may well evoke a negative response from the recipient. If the gift does not lie within the recipient's preference set (her/his "circle"), then the recipient would be indifferent towards the gift because, even though it might utilize a positively perceived stimulus, it would not be something that the recipient actively wants. Finally, if the gift lies within the shared self of the two people in the romantic relationship, then it would no longer be a surprise (or at best a very weak one) for the recipient because she/he could almost have predicted receiving that

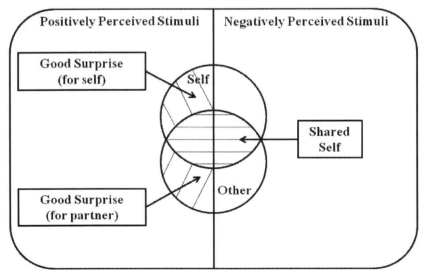

Figure 4.1 A Conceptual Framework for Surprise Romantic Gifts

from her/his partner. Moreover, the larger the common base of the shared self, the fewer would be the options open to a person's partner to select a good surprise gift for her/him. Thus, as can be seen, it is not always going to be easy to give the perfect romantic surprise to a loved one.

Surprise and Romantic Gift-Giving—The Road Ahead

As research continues to uncover newer facets in the domains of surprise, relationships, and gift-giving (e.g., Chan and Mogilner 2017; Laran and Tsiros 2013), it is worthwhile to think about a few possible directions which future research could explore, given the unique nature of surprise romantic gifts that this chapter aimed to illustrate.

While the need for cross-cultural research remains relevant, it might be useful to study the metamorphosis of gift-giving across the trajectory of different forms of romantic relationships. Given that surprises are perceived differently at different stages of a relationship, they carry differential risks and returns depending on the stage. A clearer understanding of this might also help tease out whether there are any transitional stages in the evolution of a relationship that mark one or more turning points during which a good or bad surprise gift might significantly affect the course of the relationship. Such an enquiry into the situational contexts of romantic relationships should also be supplemented by studying the role of individual differences in the preference for surprise gifts. While relationship partners who are, for instance, low on risk-aversion, high on curiosity and/or need for novelty, or are more open to experiences, surprise gifts might pose a lower risk for the giver. Similarly, it might also be interesting to investigate how personality differences *between* the relationship partners themselves can impact the experience of surprise romantic gift-giving. For instance, could one person's love for surprise be "cancelled" by their partner's aversion to uncertainty? Or could each person learn to appreciate the other's preferences? Finally, there is also the need to explore this phenomenon with different populations who have not been systematically considered in gift-giving literature, such as same-sex couples. Given the gender differences noted earlier in the chapter, a look at the giving and receiving of surprise romantic gifts among two people who identify with the same gender can provide a novel perspective to further understand the endlessly fascinating world of gift-giving itself.

Conclusion

It could be argued that the American market in particular needs to rediscover the joy of surprise given that it constitutes one of the biggest markets for gift cards, a gift item that is only a thinly disguised version of cash. While a gift card is a convenient purchase from the point of view of the giver, it is likely going to lack the element of surprise not just from the perspective of the product itself (an envelope that contains a gift card is unlikely to be mistaken for anything else), but also because the recipient makes the final purchase selection on her/his own. The only surprise in such a case is going to occur if the recipient chances upon a good "deal" while making the purchase, but it is unlikely that it will match the suspense of an actual surprise gift.

A key element in a romantic relationship is the quest for assurance on the part of each person that the other one "knows her/him" in a true sense. While telepathy remains outside the grasp of mere mortals, we always wish that our significant others would magically divine what we want and then proceed to give that to us. This is why, when we get a surprise present from that special someone (whether it is a budding romance or a stable relationship), it gives us that indefinable rush of delight. "Here," we think to ourselves, "is someone who finally understands what I want."

A pleasant surprise being as elusive as it is, the perfect surprise gift in a romance might not be an easy task to accomplish (and a badly chosen surprise could easily set back the relationship significantly). A thoughtful surprise, chosen by virtue of paying due attention to the preferences and tastes of the object of your affections, could well spin a touch of magic into the tapestry of your relationship and reassure her/him that you really do understand the unique, distinctive individual that she/he is.

Think back to the gifts that Della and Jim got each other in "The Gift of Magi." Even though Della couldn't use the tortoise-shell combs because she no longer had her beautiful hair and the platinum watch chain was also effectively useless for Jim as he had sold his watch, they were invaluable as markers of the love each had for the other. Despite their eventual lack of functional utility, the care which went into planning and procuring the perfect surprise made them the ideal gifts. Perhaps it is time that we take a leaf out of the book and infuse surprise into the gifts we buy for the ones we love.

And wouldn't that be delightful?

References

Aron, Arthur, Elain N. Aron, and Danny Smollan (1992), "Inclusion of Other in the Self Scale and the Structure of Interpersonal Closeness," *Journal of Personality and Social Psychology*, 63 (4), 596–612.

Aron, Arthur, Elaine N. Aron, Michael Tudor, and Greg Nelson (1991), "Close Relationships as Including Other in the Self," *Journal of Personality and Social Psychology*, 60 (2), 241–53.

Belk, Russell W. (1996), "The Perfect Gift," in *Gift Giving: A Research Anthology*, ed. Cele Otnes and Richard F. Beltramini, Bowling Green, OH: Bowling Green State University Popular Press, 59–84.

———— (2010), "Sharing," *Journal of Consumer Research*, 36 (5), 715–34.

Belk, Russell W. and Gregory Coon (1993), "Gift Giving as Agapic Love: An Alternative to the Exchange Paradigm Based on Dating Experiences," *Journal of Consumer Research*, 20 (3), 393–417.

Bettman, James R. (1979), *An Information Processing Theory of Consumer Choice*, Reading, MA: Addison-Wesley.

Chan, Cindy and Cassie Mogilner (2017), "Experiential Gifts Foster Stronger Social Relationships Than Material Gifts," *Journal of Consumer Research*, 43 (6), 913–31.

Cheal, David (1987), "'Showing Them You Love Them': Gift Giving and the Dialectic of Intimacy," *The Sociological Review*, 35 (1), 150–69.

Clarke, Jackie R. (2006), "Different to 'Dust Collectors'? The Giving and Receiving of Experience Gifts," *Journal of Consumer Behaviour*, 5 (6), 533–49.

———— (2013), "Experiential Aspects of Tourism Gift Consumption," *Journal of Vacation Marketing*, 19 (1), 75–87.

Commuri, Suraj and James W. Gentry (2000), "Opportunities for Family Research in Marketing," *Academy of Marketing Science Review*, 8, 1–34.

Dodson, Kimberly J. and Russell W. Belk (1996), "The Birthday Card Minefield," *NA: Advances in Consumer Research*, Vol. 23, ed. Kim P. Corfman and John G. Lynch, Jr., Provo, UT: Association for Consumer Research, 14–20.

Dunn, Elizabeth W., Jeff Huntsinger, Janetta Lun, and Stacey Sinclair (2008), "The Gift of Similarity: How Good and Bad Gifts Influence Relationships," *Social Cognition*, 26 (4), 469–81.

Durgee, Jeffrey F. and Trina Sego (2001), "Gift-Giving as a Metaphor for Understanding New Products That Delight," in *NA: Advances in Consumer Research*, Vol. 28, ed. Mary C. Gilly and Joan Meyers-Levy, Valdosta, GA: Association for Consumer Research, 64–9.

Havlena, William J. and Morris B. Holbrook (1986), "The Varieties of Consumption Experience: Comparing Two Typologies of Emotion in Consumer Behavior," *Journal of Consumer Research*, 13 (3), 394–404.

Heilman, Carrie M., Kent Nakamoto, and Ambar G. Rao (2002), "Pleasant Surprises: Consumer Response to Unexpected In-Store Coupons," *Journal of Marketing Research*, 39 (2), 242–52.

Hirschman, Elizabeth C. and Morris B. Holbrook (1982), "Hedonic Consumption: Emerging Concepts, Methods and Propositions," *The Journal of Marketing*, 46 (3), 92–101.

Holbrook, Morris B. and Elizabeth C. Hirschman (1982), "The Experiential Aspects of Consumption: Consumer Fantasies, Feelings, and Fun," *Journal of Consumer Research*, 9 (2), 132–40.

Izard, Carroll E. (1977), *Human Emotions*, New York: Plenum.

Laran, Juliano and Michael Tsiros (2013), "An Investigation of the Effectiveness of Uncertainty in Marketing Promotions Involving Free Gifts," *Journal of Marketing*, 77 (2), 112–23.

Mehrabian, Albert and James A. Russell (1974), *An Approach to Environmental Psychology*, Cambridge, MA: MIT Press.

Minowa, Yuko and Stephen J. Gould (1999), "Love My Gift, Love Me or Is It Love Me, Love My Gift: A Study of the Cultural Construction of Romantic Gift Giving among Japanese Couples," *NA: Advances in Consumer Research*,

Vol. 26, ed. Eric J. Arnould and Linda M. Scott, Provo, UT: Association for Consumer Research, 119–24.

Minowa, Yuko, Takeshi Matsui, and Russell Belk (2012), "I Would Want a Magic Gift: Desire For Romantic Gift Giving and the Cultural Fantasies of Baby Boomers in Japan," *NA: Advances in Consumer Research*, Vol. 40, ed. Zeynep Gurhan-Canli, Cele Otnes, and Rui (Juliet) Zhu, Duluth, MN: Association for Consumer Research, 901–2.

Oliver, Richard L., Roland T. Rust, and Sajeev Varki (1997), "Customer Delight: Foundations, Findings, and Managerial Insight," *Journal of Retailing*, 73 (3), 311–36.

Pavia, Teresa M. and Marlys J. Mason (2004), "The Reflexive Relationship between Consumer Behavior and Adaptive Coping," *Journal of Consumer Research*, 31 (2), 441–55.

Plutchik, Robert (1980), *Emotion: A Psychoevolutionary Synthesis*, New York: Harper & Row.

Richins, Marsha L. (1997), "Measuring Emotions in the Consumption Experience," *Journal of Consumer Research*, 24 (2), 127–46.

Rucker, Margaret, Anthony Freitas, Deborah Murray, and Harriet Prato (1991), "Gender Stereotypes and Gift Failures: When the Sweet Don't Want Sweets," *GCB: Gender and Consumer Behavior*, Vol. 1, ed. Dr. Janeen Arnold Costa, Salt Lake City, UT: Association for Consumer Research, 244–52.

Rust, Roland T. and Richard L. Oliver (2000), "Should We Delight the Customer?," *Journal of the Academy of Marketing Science*, 28 (1), 86–94.

Ruth, Julie A., Cele C. Otnes, and Frederic F. Brunel (1999), "Gift Receipt and the Reformulation of Interpersonal Relationships," *Journal of Consumer Research*, 25 (4), 385–402.

Sherry, John F. (1983), "Gift Giving in Anthropological Perspective," *Journal of Consumer Research*, 10 (2), 157–68.

Sherry, John F., Mary Ann McGrath, and Sidney J. Levy (1992), "The Disposition of the Gift and Many Unhappy Returns," *Journal of Retailing*, 68 (1), 40–65.

——— (1993), "The Dark Side of the Gift," *Journal of Business Research*, 28 (3), 225–44.

Simon, Herbert A. (1957), *Models of Man, Social and Rational: Mathematical Essays on Rational Human Behavior in a Social Setting*, New York: Wiley.

Vanhamme, Joelle (2000), "The Link between Surprise and Satisfaction: An Exploratory Research on How Best to Measure Surprise," *Journal of Marketing Management*, 16 (6), 565–82.

——— (2008), "The Surprise-Delight Relationship Revisited in the Management of Experience," *Recherche et Applications en Marketing (English Edition)*, 23 (3), 113–38.

Vanhamme, Joelle and Dirk Snelders (2003), "What if You Surprise Your Customers. …. Will They Be More Satisfied? Findings from a Pilot Experiment," in *NA: Advances in Consumer Research*, Vol. 30, ed. Punam Anand Keller and Dennis W. Rook, Valdosta, GA: Association for Consumer Research, 48–55.

Westbrook, Robert A. (1987), "Product/Consumption-Based Affective Responses and Postpurchase Processes," *Journal of Marketing Research*, 24 (3), 258–70.

Westbrook, Robert A. and Richard L. Oliver (1991), "The Dimensionality of Consumption Emotion Patterns and Consumer Satisfaction," *Journal of Consumer Research*, 18 (1), 84–91.

Wong, Phoebe, Margaret K. Hogg, and Markus Vanharanta (2017), "Couples' Narratives of Shared-Self, Possessions and Consumption," *Journal of Consumer Behaviour*, 16 (January/February), 72–81.

5 Characteristics and Meanings of Good and Bad Romantic Gifts Across Cultures

A Recipient's Perspective

Sydney Chinchanachokchai and Theeranuch Pusaksrikit

Introduction

Gift exchange between romantic partners is a type of ritual widely practiced throughout the world. Romantic gifts are generally used as a mechanism to enhance the romantic relationship (Belk and Coon 1993) and increase its chances of survival (Huang and Yu 2000). Different kinds of romantic gifts are often given on special occasions (e.g., birthdays, Valentine's Day, Christmas, and wedding anniversaries) and serve different purposes in a romantic relationship. The gifts that romantic partners exchange carry deep and subtle meanings for both givers and recipients (Tournier 1966). For example, gifts such as chocolate and roses are frequently exchanged on Valentine's Day as a form of symbolic communication to convey love to one another (Close and Zinkhan 2006). Other gifts such as matching clothes and couple necklaces are customarily shared to announce their relationship to the world (Huang and Yu 2000).

Prior research explored various aspects of romantic gift-giving to understand the attitudes and behaviors of both givers and recipients, including motives and intentions of romantic gift-giving (Rugimbana et al. 2002), the giver's perception of romantic gift-giving (Close and Zinkhan 2006; Otnes, Ruth, and Milbourne 1994), the effect of gifts on a romantic relationship (Huang and Yu 2000), and the cultural aspects of romantic gift-giving (Beichen and Murshed 2015; Minowa, Khomenko, and Belk 2011). To investigate romantic gift-giving in more detail, many researchers have paid more attention to Valentine's Day as it is a special day to celebrate romantic love through gift-giving. Valentine's Day has become extremely commercialized worldwide. In 2016, American consumers spent an average of $146.84 for gifts on Valentine's Day (Allen and Reynolds 2016), and Asian consumers spent an average of $100 (Sile 2016). In 2016, Mastercard Love Index in Asia Pacific region showed that Valentine's Day is more popular in markets such as Thailand, China, and Malaysia, than in Australia and New Zealand where Valentine's Day is considered the tradition (Sile 2016). In Thailand alone, Valentine's

Day's spending reached 3.21 billion baht (around $100 million) in 2016, according to Nation Multimedia (Pratruangkrai 2016).

While prior research on romantic gift-giving has focused on Valentine's Day, romantic couples practice gift-giving behavior on various other occasions. Therefore, it is worthwhile to investigate the cross-cultural romantic gift-giving in terms of the characteristics and meanings of romantic gifts on various occasions, as knowledge on this topic is limited.

Literature Review

Romantic Gift-Giving Model

Romantic love is a universal emotion experienced by people around the world (Jankowiak and Fischer 1992). It is defined as the strong affection and preoccupation with love, unrealistic and idealistic attitude toward a partner, and the feeling that love never ends (Karandashev 2015), which could be reflected in an attachment process (Hazan and Shaver 1987). To understand romantic gift-giving as an expression of romantic love, Belk and Coon (1993) introduced the agapic love paradigm. Unlike an economic gift exchange, the agapic love paradigm emphasizes the passion, altruism, and submissiveness of the giver; the idealization and singularization of the recipient; an expressive, non-reciprocal obligation; and the monetary irrelevance of the gift. Whilst there is some evidence suggesting that romantic gift-giving has been practiced worldwide, it is possible that such practices may differ across cultures because people from different cultures consider how to express their love through gift-giving differently (Beichen and Murshed 2015). Comparing individuals in the US and China in the expression of romantic love, Beichen and Murshed (2015) found that East Asians were more likely to practice gift-giving to express their love than Westerners. They also found that the frequency of gift-giving decreases as age increases, particularly among East Asians. As their income increases, East Asians purchase gifts more often than Westerners. In addition, Westerners often buy gifts for specific occasions and their gift selections are more varied, whereas East Asians often buy gifts for random occasions and the gift selections are typical and traditional ones. These findings expand our understanding of romantic love expression in the cross-cultural context. However, prior research limited its focus to the giver's perspective. To understand whether the gifts successfully convey the meaning of love expression, the recipient's perspective needs to be considered.

The Good, the Bad, and the Perfect Gifts

Gifts are signals of information to show the intentions of partners in a personal relationship (Camerer 1988). For a romantic couple, gifts are tokens of affection (Close and Zinkhan 2006). Thus, many givers are willing to search for perfect gifts to please their recipients. Belk (1996, 61) defines six characteristics of perfect gifts for couples in Western societies: sacrifice, altruism, luxury, appropriateness, surprise, and delight. These characteristics involve the giver, the gift, and the recipient. The giver needs to make an extraordinary sacrifice and wishes solely to please the recipient. The gift should be something luxurious and uniquely appropriate to the recipient. Additionally, the recipient desires the gift and is surprised and delighted by it. Failing to achieve one or more of these characteristics, the gift becomes imperfect. Givi and Galak (2017) also found that perfect gifts are relevant to the preferences of the recipients and can be reminders of the relationship on special occasions.

Cultural Differences in Gift-Giving

Since the characteristics of perfect gifts have been studied primarily in Western cultures, Belk (1996) suggested that some characteristics may vary in other cultures. For example, the characteristics of appropriateness and surprise may be much more salient in Western than in Eastern cultures, perhaps because the gift-giving process is laden with cultural meanings (Beichen and Murshed 2015). An individual's reaction to a gift may vary from one culture to another, particularly with cross-cultural differences between Eastern and Western cultures. The differences between Eastern and Western individuals in social motivation and behavior are reflected in the manner in which individuals view themselves and their relationship to others (Markus and Kitayama 1991). In Western cultures, individuals are inclined to think of themselves as independent of others and believe that distinct individuals are inherently separate. They tend to place emphasis on the inner self (preferences, tastes, and abilities) in regulating behavior. In contrast, Easterners emphasize their connectedness with others. Their identity lies in familial, cultural, professional, and social relationships (Wong and Ahuvia 1998). The differences in self-concept between Westerners and Easterners may have implications for the types of gifts they seek. Tse, Belk, and Zhou (1989) found that advertisements in a Western-influenced country (Hong Kong) focus on the inner self and the hedonic experience compared with ads in Eastern cultures such as those in China and Taiwan. Therefore, it is possible that Westerners will focus on gifts that are unique and represent hedonic experiences compared with Easterners.

In contrast, Easterners emphasize the roles and public perceptions of their identity, which refers to the concept of "face" (Ho 1976). The face concept is particularly strong in Confucian cultures and is used to explain the behaviors of Easterners (Wong and Ahuvia 1998). Due to the face concept, individuals in Eastern cultures are more concerned with other people's perceptions of them and are likely to perform actions to maintain their status (e.g., use luxurious products). Thus, individuals in Eastern cultures may prefer publicly visible possessions that signify their social self-worth to earn respect from others in society.

To understand cultural differences in the characteristics of perfect gifts, Rucker, Freitas, and Kangas (1996) examined these characteristics through the models of Belk's (1996) perfect gifts and Rucker et al.'s (1992) good and bad gifts. They compared White and Asian students' perceptions of the best and the worst gifts to give and receive. In terms of perfect gifts, their findings confirmed Belk's (1996) suggestions that the characteristics of appropriateness are much more salient for White than Asian students, whereas the characteristics of surprise were found to be similar in both cultural groups. For sacrifice, Rucker et al. (1996) found that they were similar in terms of financial sacrifice as both cultural groups preferred expensive products. However, Whites preferred handmade products that required a sacrifice of more time and effort than Asians did.

In terms of good and bad gifts, Rucker et al. (1996) found that Asians mentioned money as a gift more often than Whites. In addition, Asians were more likely to mention being with others as a good gift, whereas Whites were more likely to mention doing something for the recipient as a good gift. Asians were found to be more likely than Whites to report best and worst gifts being given to and received from people outside their kinship network. Due to insufficient data, the research could not determine whether there are cultural differences of bad gifts as additions to a collection. Whilst Rucker et al. (1996) provide very insightful findings, their study examined gift-giving in all types of relationships (family, romantic partner, friends, etc.), as opposed to only romantic relationships.

Similar to other Asian cultures (Minowa et al. 2011), Thais practice gift-giving in various occasions; for example, casual visits to someone's home, celebrating a new home or new job, returning from a trip abroad, and meeting new people. As observed in other Asian countries (e.g., Japan, China, and Korea), Thais have also adopted Western traditions of gift-giving behavior such as celebrating Valentine's Day and Christmas in the postmodern marketplace (Moeran and Skov 1993; Minowa et al. 2011). Whilst Americans tend to exchange gifts on special occasions such as anniversaries, birthdays, and Christmas, gift-giving in Thailand is less special-occasion centric. There is no set pattern in Thai gift-giving behavior. Generally, Thais use gifts to represent their good intention and respect to others.

To further our understanding of the good, bad, and perfect romantic gifts in a cross-cultural context, this research aims to compare the characteristics and meanings from the recipient's perspective in Thailand and the U.S. It is extremely important to understand gift-receiving behaviors across societies and cultures because the recipient's perception and interpretation of the gift and gift-receipt experience can determine positive and negative relationships (Ruth, Otnes, and Brunel 1999).

Methods

To capture the recipient's perspective of romantic gifts, this study used the critical incident technique to collect information from the respondents. The benefit of this technique is to provide a flexible format for respondents to freely express themselves. It also allows the researchers to distribute surveys across a broad sample, thus providing more access to the gift-receiving experience in a variety of contexts (Ruth et al. 1999). The drawback is that it relies heavily on content analysis, which has been criticized based on the validity and reliability of the categories (Kolbe and Burnett 1991). Nevertheless, this technique can successfully extract rich and specific accounts of phenomena (Grove and Fisk 1997). When the research objective is to enhance knowledge of a phenomenon and/or to describe a real-world phenomenon based on thorough understanding, the critical incident technique is particularly well suited to the task (Bitner, Booms, and Tetreault 1990). This study's purpose is to explore the characteristics and meanings of romantic gifts in Eastern (Thailand) and Western societies (the US).

Samples

The US and Thailand were selected for conducting this study of cross-cultural romantic gift-giving behavior because each country represents typical individualistic and collectivistic cultures. The US has been characterized as an individualistic culture emphasizing independence, personal autonomy, and self-interest (Hofstede, Hofstede, and Minkov 2010). In contrast, Thailand has been pointed out as a collectivistic culture emphasizing interdependence, loyalty to a group, and conformity to group norms (Hofstede et al. 2010).

The researchers recruited student and non-student respondents to participate. Recruited through classroom announcements, the student respondents comprised undergraduate and graduate students at a university in Thailand and a Midwestern university in the US. The students received extra credit in exchange for their participation. The non-student respondents were recruited through announcements posted on the researchers' social media. These respondents received a chance to enter a drawing for $25 gift cards in exchange for their participation. At the end of the data collection period, two respondents (one in Thailand and one in the US) were randomly selected to win the gift cards. One hundred and eighty-five people provided critical incident reports. The composition of the respondents was 48% Thais (N = 89) and 52% Americans (N = 96). Of the total respondents, 62% were female

(N = 114), 37% (N = 69) were male, and 1% was not reported (N = 2). The age of the respondents ranged from 17 to 60 years old.

Critical Incident Survey and Procedure

A critical incident survey was used to collect data. After the respondents signed up, they were sent a link to the survey. The questionnaire began with the definition of a romantic gift: "A romantic gift is a gift that you receive from your significant others or loved ones (boyfriend/girlfriend/ fiancé/husband/wife/partner) in any occasion such as anniversary, birthday, Valentine's, Christmas, etc." The survey followed with open-ended questions to prompt the respondents to describe a perfect romantic gift that they would like to receive and to explain the reasons. The next section asked the respondents to recall a gift from a current or former romantic partner that they especially liked (good gift) and provide a description of the gift, the occasion, their feeling when receiving the gift, and the reason they liked the gift or found it special. The following section asked about their experience with a bad gift. Similar to the previous section, the respondents recalled a gift they disliked (bad gift), described it in detail, the occasion for the gift, the reason they disliked it, and what they did with it after receiving it. The researchers asked the respondents to provide the reasons they liked/disliked the gifts to obtain a deeper understanding of each participant's meaning. This question permitted the researchers to fully explore the respondents' feelings, behavior or experience that helped to underpin their answers (Legard, Keegan, and Ward 2003). The survey ended with demographic questions about their age and gender.

Content analysis was performed by coding the reported circumstances, types of gifts, occasions, feelings, and reasons why the respondents liked or disliked their gifts. Both authors read separate copies of the survey data and coded them with respect to the themes of interest in the study. Any disagreements were resolved through discussion. The authors also went through the data and counted the types of gifts mentioned as perfect gifts, good gifts, and bad gifts. The results were finalized and checked by the authors.

Results

Common Characteristics of a Perfect Romantic Gift Across Western and Eastern Cultures

From the content analysis, two common themes for the characteristics of a perfect romantic gift across both cultures—relationship representation and sacrifice—were found based on the number of times they were mentioned among the respondents from both countries.

Relationship Representation

The main emergent theme regarding a perfect romantic gift is using a gift to represent a relationship. This theme is similar to the characteristics of good gifts as defined by Rucker et al. (1992). The majority of respondents across both cultures reported that the perfect romantic gift for them must represent their relationship, that is, to represent the memory that reminds them of the relationship with their romantic partners. To some, the gift may be a liaison between both parties that fulfills the relationship. The gift should reflect the recipient's preferences and remind both partners of a special-occasion (Givi and Galak 2017). Below are examples of statements showing that the gift must represent the relationship.

> *Photo books or a card or something that he puts a lot of thought into makes me feel like he is reflecting on us and loves the idea of us.*
>
> (Female, 26, American)

> *(A perfect romantic gift is) something that the giver (my partner) makes himself and has personal value to me. It reminds me of our relationship.*
>
> (Female, 34, Thai)

Sacrifice

Similar to the characteristics defined by Belk (1996), sacrifice was found to be an important aspect of a perfect romantic gift. In the romantic love model, sacrifices are made because givers, emotionally swept up in the feeling of love, wish to express an overwhelming magnitude of love toward their recipients (Belk 1996). Sacrifice can refer to the time and effort expended into making or finding a gift or even the financial resources one invests in the gift (Rucker et al. 1996; Katz 1976). The perfect gift does not need to be of great monetary value, but it must represent the work and intention of the giver as the following statements illustrate.

> *A romantic gift is one that someone put time and effort into, or even made. A gift that they deliberated over, and if it were a physical gift, even wrapped it themselves. I would consider a gift like this the most romantic because it came from the heart.*
>
> (Female, 21, American)

> *(A perfect romantic gift is) something that my partner makes for me— something that shows the intention and effort. It doesn't have to be expensive like cooking dinner or baking a cake for me.*
>
> (Female, 35, Thai)

Differences Between Perfect Romantic Gifts in Western and Eastern Cultures

Surprise

As Rucker et al. (1996, 151) wrote, "surprise can occur as a result of a particular gift being unexpected or from any kind of gift being unexpected on a particular occasion." The element of surprise in gift-giving is much more salient in Western cultures than in Eastern cultures (Beichen and Murshed 2015). We coded the gifts that people would consider a perfect gift and found a difference between Westerners and Easterners. While American respondents highly emphasized that the perfect romantic gift must be a surprise gift or something they did not expect to receive, none of the Eastern respondents did so. On the contrary, one Thai respondent even mentioned that, for her, the perfect gift does not have to be a surprise gift, but she would prefer a gift that she could use in her daily life. Easterners would view surprise as a less positive aspect of the gift-giving experience compared with Westerners due to a strong cultural emphasis on predictability and reciprocity (Rucker et al. 1996). Moreover, Easterners were less surprised when they were given an unexpected gift because they wanted to maintain balance and emotional control (Valenzuela, Mellers, and Strebel 2010).

> *My favorite physical objects are "surprise flowers" for no reason and a well picked out piece of jewelry because I can wear it and I like knowing someone bought it for me and thinks I'm worthy of it.*
> (Female, 21, American)

> *The most romantic gift I received was a CD of songs that were special to us as a couple or songs that made him think of me. I don't expect them, but they are wonderful surprises when they come. The "romance" is reduced when it's expected. Conversely, it is increased when it is a genuine surprise.*
> (Female, 48, American)

Experiential Versus Material Gifts

Interestingly, another difference of a perfect gift between the two cultures is the emphasis on experiential versus material gifts. Experiential gifts are events that the recipient lives through (e.g., dinner, concert tickets, and vacation), whereas material gifts are objects to be kept in the recipient's possession (e.g., jewelry, flowers, and clothes) (Chan and Mogilner 2017). Experiential gifts produce greater improvements in the relationship compared with material gifts (Chan and Mogilner 2017). They also lead to higher satisfaction (Carter and Gilovich 2010) because experiences are likely to be shared with others (Caprariello and Reis 2013).

The findings showed that the majority of American respondents consider experiential gifts (40.7%) or DIY (do it yourself) gifts (29.7%) as perfect gifts, whereas most Thai respondents place more emphasis on material gifts such as jewelry (26.1%) or other usable gifts (not specified) (18.2%). Westerners place greater importance on hedonic experience and emphasize uniqueness (Wong and Ahuvia 1998). Therefore, they prefer experiential gifts more than material gifts because each experience is unique to each individual. Experience also relates to the higher emotional and hedonic qualities of the consumption (Jantzen et al. 2012). Rucker et al. (1996) also found that Western respondents mentioned handmade creations more than Eastern respondents at a rate of approximately four to one. In contrast, material gifts, especially luxury products or accessories, can represent social status in society (Han, Nunes, and Drèze 2010). In Asian cultures, status, and the idea of not losing social face are important to maintain one's status in society and social groups (Ho 1976). Therefore, Easterners may be more interested in material gifts due to the desire to have favorable social worth and to be respected by others in society. See Table 5.1 for the three highest-ranked perfect romantic gifts mentioned across cultures.

Common Characteristics of Good Romantic Gifts Across Western and Eastern Cultures

When asked about their real experience with romantic gifts that they liked and the reasons why they liked those gifts, two main themes emerged from the data—thoughtfulness and functionality.

Table 5.1 Top Three Perfect Gifts, Good Gifts, and Bad Gifts

Westerners (Americans)			Easterners (Thais)		
	N	%		N	%
Type of perfect gifts			*Type of perfect gifts*		
Experience (dinner, date night, vacation, concert)	37	40.7	Jewelry	23	26.1
DIY gift	27	29.7	Usable gift (not specified)	16	18.2
Jewelry	12	13.2	Experience (dinner, trip)	13	14.8
Type of good gifts			*Type of good gifts*		
Jewelry	24	26.1	Jewelry	26	29.2
Experience (vacation, dinner, trip, concert)	19	20.7	Doll	9	10.1
DIY gift	15	16.3	DIY gift	8	9
Type of bad gifts			*Type of bad gifts*		
Clothes	25	30	N/A (liked everything)	26	32
Jewelry	16	19	Snacks, candy, chocolate	11	13
N/A (liked everything)	10	12	Jewelry	10	12

Thoughtfulness

The key emergent theme of the characteristics of good romantic gifts that recipients receive is thoughtfulness. The majority of respondents in both cultures liked a gift when it showed that the giver put some thought into making or finding it. Thoughtfulness can be a reflection of time and effort invested in a gift such as DIY or handmade gifts. Some respondents perceived a gift as thoughtful when it demonstrated that the givers listened to them, paid attention, and cared about them as shown in the following statements. When the giver puts careful thought into a gift, it is an effortful process, which serves as a signal to the quality of the relationship for the giver. A thoughtful gift has been shown to increase relational bonds (Zhang and Epley 2012).

> (*It was) a jar full of popsicle sticks with ideas of things we can do for dates. (The total cost was) probably three dollars. It was a homemade craft. (I liked it) because she put thought and time into it and I could tell she cared.*
>
> (Male, 21, American)

> *My ex-boyfriend bought me a smartphone because the old one got overheated when we talked for a long time. I told him that I had to hang up because my cellphone was too hot to carry on the conversation. Not long after that he bought the new phone for me. He said it's not safe to use my old phone. I liked it because it showed that he cared about me and was very thoughtful.*
>
> (Female, 33, Thai)

Unlike the expensiveness characteristics of good gifts as defined by Rucker et al. (1992), some recipients do not care much about monetary value. They, however, like a gift when it has some meaning or reminds them of the good times they spent together as a couple.

> (*It was) the picture collage (that) had pictures dating back to different times during our relationship. It didn't cost any money but the meaning it held was priceless. I found it special because it was handmade and well thought out.*
>
> (Male, 21, American)

Functionality

The usefulness or functionality of a gift is shown as important characteristics of good gifts in both cultures. It is one of the most sought-after attributes from the recipient's perspective (DeVere, Scott, and Shulby 1983). This finding is very surprising as it is opposite of what Rucker et al. (1992) found to be the characteristics of good gifts; they found that practical items possessed the characteristics of a bad gift. Some of our respondents paid attention to the functionality of a product rather than its esthetics. When recipients use these gifts, they will then think of the givers and their relationships. The gift may not need to be expensive or luxurious. It can be an everyday item that is useful to the recipients. One respondent mentioned that she received a Swiss Army knife from her husband on her birthday and she carried it with her at all times. Below are examples of romantic gifts that focus on functionality.

> (*The gift was a*) *remote starter for my car. It allowed me to start my car up and get it nice and toasty all winter long without having to go out in the cold to start it ahead of time. It was also great to leave work and at most I'd just have to brush off some snow. It was really thoughtful to have a gift I can use for as long as I owned the car and made every day easier (at least in the winter!) . . . . It made winter days less obnoxious! And it showed he really put thought into what would be useful and I would enjoy, not just a trinket.*
>
> (Female, 35, American)

> (*The gift was*) *a pocket-sized planner book with multiple colors inside. It also came with cute stickers that I liked. I liked it because I normally use a planner. When he bought one for me as a gift, it showed that he cared about me. He knew what was important to me without me telling him what I liked.*
>
> (Female, 34, Thai)

Differences Between Good Romantic Gifts in Western and Eastern Cultures

For both American and Thai respondents, most people considered jewelry as a good gift. However, the reasons why they liked jewelry differed widely. American respondents mentioned jewelry as something to represent the relationship or remind them of the experience they shared with their romantic partners. However, Thai respondents placed more emphasis on the value of the gifts. For Thai respondents, a good gift must be something that looks expensive or luxurious.

> (*The gift was*) *jewelry made with an item reminiscent of a vacation to Hawaii. The necklace made with native seed pods from Hawaii. I had admired them on our trip. He found a similar artist online and bought. (It) very thoughtful.*
>
> (Female, 42, American)

> (*They were*) *golden earrings. I liked them because they were valuable and looked expensive.*
>
> (Female, 42, Thai)

Another interesting result was that when they were asked to think about good gifts they received from their romantic partners, American respondents mentioned experiential gifts more than Thai respondents. Examples of experiential gifts mentioned were a trip or vacation, tickets to a concert or sporting event, dinner at a restaurant, or a class. Some gifts were also given as a surprise (Rucker et al. 1996).

> *(I received) a surprise trip to Virginia Beach. I'd never been to the ocean at that point. He planned a long weekend away in Virginia Beach. He booked a hotel and planned a fancy dinner. ... He knew how badly I wanted to see the beach and he made the whole thing a surprise until we left.*
>
> (Female, 31, American)

Common Characteristics of Bad Romantic Gifts Across Western and Eastern Culture

Uselessness

Although some gifts enhance the relationship between the giver and the recipient, some can worsen the relationship (Otnes, Lowrey, and Kim 1993). The gift exchange process could engender high levels of anxiety among consumers because a gift can create interpersonal conflict (Sherry, McGrath, and Levy 1993). Through our data, we found that in a romantic relationship both Westerners and Easterners considered useless gifts as bad gifts. Useless gifts either refer to a gift that the recipient cannot use or one that reflects thoughtlessness by the giver.

> *The gift was a black watch. Good quality, but simple. I don't like wearing anything on my wrists, and never wear a watch. It seemed like a last-minute purchase just to give a gift for the fact of giving one.*
>
> (Male, 24, American)

> *My boyfriend bought me an expensive bouquet of roses on Valentine's Day. I did not like it because roses are useless. I just left them sit on a table and they died.*
>
> (Female, 36, Thai)

Differences Between Bad Romantic Gifts in Western and Eastern Cultures

We found differences in the perception of bad gifts between Western and Eastern respondents. For Westerners (Americans), a bad gift is one that does not represent the recipient's self-identity. Consumers express their identities through the products/gifts they purchase or consume (Ward and Broniarczyk 2011). They link such products to particular social identities (Kleine, Kleine, and Kernan 1993). Therefore, receiving a disliked gift may create an identity threat for the recipient. American respondents reported that they did not like those gifts because the gifts did not represent themselves or their lifestyles while using the gifts.

> *(The gift was) a necklace (which) was a cheap, gaudy, piece. . . . It was nothing special and something I would have never picked out for myself. It wasn't my style, looked a little childish, proving that he didn't know much about me. I felt embarrassed to wear it around, and only really wore it on weekends or when I wasn't going out. It didn't go with anything and was way too casual for my style.*
>
> (Female, 21, American)

In some cases, the gift does not represent the recipient's perception of his/her self-identity but rather reflects the identity that the giver desires of the recipient.

> *It was clothing that was his style and taste. Mostly very skater or edgy styled-distressed looking, very reminiscent of what you'd see in a tattoo shop or on biker chicks. It was not my style AT ALL!*
>
> (Female, 35, American)

Surprisingly, when asked about the gifts that they disliked, many Thai respondents reported that they always liked the gifts they received from their romantic partners and could not think of anything they disliked. They focused more on the giver than the gift itself. If the gift is from a romantic partner, it usually means something to the recipient or the gift implies that the giver has already put some thought into finding it.

> *I've never received any gift that I did not like from my husband. Usually, receiving a gift from our loved one is already something to be grateful for. In my opinion, one generally avoids giving a gift that their romantic partner does not like. On the other hand, if the gift was from a friend, the bad gift situation might have occurred.*
>
> (Female, 39, Thai)

Occasions for the Gifts

The results show that birthdays are an occasion for which people in both cultures give the most gifts (both good and bad). Religion affects the gift-giving occasion in Western cultures more than in Eastern cultures. Christmas is the second-highest occasion on which Western consumers exchange gifts and, interestingly, the occasion when most romantic partners receive gifts they do not like. In Eastern cultures such as that in

Thailand, where Buddhists comprise the majority of the population, gifts are given on New Year's Day. Similar to Christmas, many people also receive bad gifts on New Year's Day. That may be because traditionally people exchange gifts during these two occasions. However, they are not specific to the couple or the relationship itself. Therefore, most people do not spend much time and effort to find a gift for their partners. On the other hand, an anniversary is an occasion that is more specific to a couple. Therefore, most partners tend to invest more time and effort in finding gifts for their romantic partners.

Discussion and Conclusion

Gift exchange between romantic couples is widely practiced around the world. It is used as a mechanism to enhance the romantic relationship (Belk and Coon 1993). Belk (1996) described the notion of a perfect gift in Western culture and suggested that some characteristics may vary in other cultures. In this research, we extend the body of research on romantic gifts and study the perfect gift in the Eastern context. In this research, a perfect gift refers to an ideal gift that people would like to receive from their romantic partners. We determined the characteristics and meanings of romantic gifts in an Eastern society (Thailand's) and compared them with those in a Western society (the USA's) (see the summary of the main findings in Table 5.2).

Regarding the characteristics of perfect gifts, the study revealed two themes that both cultures have in common—relationship representation and sacrifice. Relationship representation means that a gift must represent the romantic relationship and remind the couple of the memories they share. To some, the gift can be the liaison between both parties and fulfill the relationship. Sacrifice means that the gift must show that the giver has invested considerable time and effort in making or finding it. The key differences in the characteristics of the perfect gift between Western and Eastern cultures are that 1) Westerners highly emphasize that the perfect gift must be a surprise gift, whereas Easterners pay less attention to surprise because they want to maintain balance and emotional control. For Easterners, a surprise gift may prophesize fortune (Valenzuela et al. 2010). And, 2) Westerners prefer experiential gifts, while Easterners focus on material gifts. That may be because Westerners live in individualistic cultures that place emphases on oneself, independence, freedom, and pleasure. They also look for uniqueness and the hedonic aspect of a gift. Since experiential gifts are more specific to an individual and cannot be compared with others, these gifts would attract more interest from Westerners. The sense of uniqueness is important to Westerners. It is also why they prefer DIY or personalized gifts. Moreover, experiences deliver higher emotional and hedonic qualities, which Westerners look for in their consumption. On the other hand,

Table 5.2 Summary of the Cross-Cultural Comparison of Three Types of Gifts

	Westerners (Americans)	*Easterners (Thais)*
Perfect gift: Similarities	*Relationship representation:* the gift must represent the relationship. It needs to represent the memory that reminds them of the relationship with their romantic partners.	
	Sacrifice: the gift does not need to be of a great monetary value, but it must represent the work and intention of the giver.	
Perfect gift: Differences	Emphasis on surprise. Prefer experiential gifts.	No emphasis on surprise. Prefer material gifts.
Good gift: Similarities	*Thoughtfulness:* the gift shows that the giver put some thought into making or finding it. It can be a reflection of time and effort invested in the gift.	
	Functionality: the gift is useful to the receiver. It can be an everyday item that the receiver uses on a daily basis.	
Good gift: Differences	Focus on the relationship representation aspect of the gift. Prefer experiential gifts.	Focus on the value of the gift. Prefer material gifts.
Bad gift: Similarities	*Uselessness:* the gift that the recipient cannot use or show that the giver did not put any thought into them.	
Bad gift: Differences	The gift does not represent the recipient's self-identity.	Nothing the recipient disliked. The recipient showed appreciation toward the gift.

Easterners focus on the interdependent relationship between themselves and their in-groups. These people usually possess brand names or luxurious products because their desire to have favorable social worth and to be respected by others in society (social face). These factors could lead to the desire to receive luxurious material gifts.

Regarding what people consider as good gifts based on their experience, both cultures indicated that a good gift must be something that is thoughtful and functional. A thoughtful gift is a gift that the giver has put some thought into. The recipients also like gifts that are useful to them (functionality). However, for the same type of gift (jewelry), Westerners pay more attention to the meaning of gift toward their relationship, while Easterners pay attention to the value of the gift.

Some gifts, however, can worsen a relationship if they are useless or show that the givers put little or no thought or effort into selecting them. This is true among both Westerners and Easterners, but with some differences. Westerners dislike a gift that does not represent their self-identity ("This gift is not me.") or one that reflects the identity that the giver desires of the recipient, perhaps because Westerners represent individualistic cultures that focus on the concept of self and self-expression. Thus, when recipients received such gifts, they felt disappointed as they thought that the givers should have known their needs or interests. The findings extend that of Ward and Broniarczyk (2011), who suggested an investigation into how a recipient felt an identity threat when receiving something incongruous with his/her own self-identity. Interestingly, many Easterners said that they always liked and appreciated gifts they received from their romantic partners, perhaps because Easterners live in collectivistic cultures that try to maintain harmony in relationships and, as such, they may tend to focus on the positive side of gift-giving and feel more appreciative of gifts.

In terms of theoretical contributions, we extend Rucker et al. (1996) by looking particularly at cross-cultural gift-giving in romantic relationships. In a romantic relationship, the concept of self is important in gift-giving among Westerners (Americans) because of their independent self-concept (Markus and Kitayama 1991). The gift must represent the recipient's self-identity as well as focus on uniqueness, which can be found in experiential gifts (e.g., a romantic dinner or concert) or DIY gifts (Wong and Ahuvia 1998). In contrast, Easterners (Thais) generally prefer material gifts that have value because they focus on the public perception of their social identity (Ho 1976; Joy 2001), which is strong in Confucian cultures. Additionally, Joy (2001) found that the gift-giving patterns among lovers in Easterners (Hong Kongers) are similar to those of Westerners. We argue that although the behavioral patterns are the same, the content and meaning of the gifts that recipients prefer differs between Easterners and Westerners.

Our recommendations to consumers around the world are that they should listen to their romantic partners before choosing gifts. Gifts are more appreciated when they show that the givers have invested either time or effort in it (sacrifice). One way to show that the givers put some thought into gifts is to personalize the gifts or make the gifts themselves. For consumers in Western cultures (e.g., the USA and Europe), it is important that they also find gifts that represent a partner's self-identity (who they are). For consumers in Eastern cultures (e.g., China, Thailand), a gift should be a material gift that focuses on its usefulness and value, in contrast to an experiential gift.

As companies become more multinational, understanding the characteristics and meanings of romantic gifts in different cultures will help marketers devise strategies to promote their products and services, especially during romantic occasions worldwide such as anniversaries, Valentine's Day, and White Day in Japan and South Korea.

References

Allen, Kathy Grannis and Treacy Reynolds (2016), "Dinner and a Movie, Flowers and Jewelry Bring Valentine's Day Spending to Record High,"

National Retail Federation: Consumer Trends. Available at https://nrf.com/media/press-releases/dinner-and-movie-flowers-and-jewelry-bring-valentines-day-spending-record-high

Beichen, Liang and Feisal Murshed (2015), "Culture, Expressions of Romantic Love, and Gift-Giving," *Journal of International Business Research*, 14 (1), 68–84.

Belk, Russell W. (1996), "The Perfect Gift," in *Gift Giving: A Research Anthology*, ed. Cele Otnes and Richard F. Beltramini, Bowling Green, OH: Bowling Green State University Popular Press, 59–84.

Belk, Russell W. and Gregory S. Coon (1993), "Gift Giving as Agapic Love: An Alternative to the Exchange Paradigm Based on Dating Experiences," *Journal of Consumer Research*, 20 (December), 393–417.

Bitner, Mary J. and Bernard H. Booms, and Mary S. Tetreault (1990), "The Service Encounter: Diagnosing Favorable and Unfavorable Incidents," *Journal of Marketing*, 54 (1), 71–84.

Camerer, Colin (1988), "Gifts as Economic Signals and Social Symbols," *The American Journal of Sociology*, 94, Supplement: Organizations and Institutions: Sociological and Economic Approaches to the Analysis of Social Structure, 180–214.

Caprariello, Peter A. and Harry T. Reis (2013), "To Do, to Have, or to Share? Valuing Experiences over Material Possessions Depends on the Involvement of Others," *Journal of Personality and Social Psychology*, 104 (2), 199–215.

Carter, Travis J. and Thomas Gilovich (2010), "The Relative Relativity of Material and Experiential Purchases," *Journal of Personality and Social Psychology*, 98 (1), 146–59.

Chan, Cindy and Cassie Mogilner (2017), "Experiential Gifts Foster Stronger Social Relationships Than Material Gifts," *Journal of Consumer Research*, 43 (6), 913–31.

Close, Angeline and George Zinkhan (2006), "A Holiday Loved and Loathed: A Consumer Perspective of Valentine's Day," in *Advances in Consumer Research*, Vol. 33, ed. Connie Pechmann and Linda Price, Duluth, MN: Association for Consumer Research, 356–65.

DeVere, Stephen P., Clifford D. Scott, and William L. Shulby (1983), "Consumer Perceptions of Gift-Giving Occasions: Attribute Saliency and Structure," in *Advances in Consumer Research*, Vol. 10, ed. Richard P. Bagozzi and Alice M. Tybout, Ann Arbor, MI: Association for Consumer Research, 185–90.

Givi, Julian and Jeff Galak (2017), "Sentimental Value and Gift Giving: Givers' Fears of Getting It Wrong Prevents Them from Getting It Right," *Journal of Consumer Psychology*, 27 (4), 473–9.

Grove, Stephen J. and Raymond P. Fisk (1997), "The Impact of Other Customers on Service Experiences: A Critical Incident Examination of 'Getting Along'," *Journal of Retailing*, 73 (1), 63–85.

Han, Young Jee, Joseph C. Nunes, and Xavier Drèze (2010), "Signaling Status with Luxury Goods: The Role of Brand Prominence," *Journal of Marketing*, 74 (4), 15–30.

Hazan, Cindy and Phillip Shaver (1987), "Romantic Love Conceptualized as an Attachment Process," *Journal of Personality and Social Psychology*, 52 (3), 511–24.

Ho, David Yua-Fai (1976), "On the Concept of Face," *American Journal of Sociology*, 81 (4), 867–84.

Hofstede, Geert, Gert J. Hofstede, and Michael Minkov (2010), *Cultures and Organizations: Software of the Mind*, 3rd edition, Berkshire: McGraw-Hill Education.

Huang, Ming-Hui and Shihti Yu (2000), "Gifts in a Romantic Relationship: A Survival Analysis," *Journal of Consumer Psychology*, 9 (3), 179–88.

Jankowiak, William R. and Edward F. Fischer (1992), "A Cross-Cultural Perspective on Romantic Love," *Ethnology*, 31 (2), 149–55.

Jantzen, Christian, James Fitchett, Per Østergaard, and Mikael Vetner (2012), "Just for Fun? The Emotional Regime of Experiential Consumption," *Marketing Theory*, 12 (2), 137–54.

Joy, Annamma (2001), "Gift Giving in Hong Kong and the Continuum of Social Ties," *Journal of Consumer Research*, 28 (2), 239–56.

Karandashev, Victor (2015), "A Cultural Perspective on Romantic Love," *Online Readings in Psychology and Culture*, 5 (4). https://doi.org/10.9707/2307-0919.1135

Katz, Judith Milstein (1976), "How Do You Love Me? Let Me Count the Ways (The Phenomenology of Being Loved)," *Sociological Inquiry*, 46 (1), 17–22.

Kleine, Robert E., III, Susan S. Kleine, and Jerome B. Kernan (1993), "Mundane Consumption and the Self: A Social Identity Perspective," *Journal of Consumer Psychology*, 2 (3), 209–35.

Kolbe, Richard H. and Melissa S. Burnett (1991), "Content-Analysis Research: An Examination of Applications with Directives for Improving Research Reliability and Objectivity," *Journal of Consumer Research*, 18 (September), 243–50.

Legard, Robin, Jill Keegan, and Kit Ward (2003), "In-Depth Interview," in *Qualitative Research Practice: A Guide for Social Science Students and Researchers*, 1st edition, ed. Jane Ritchie and Jane Lewis, London: Sage Publications, 138–69.

Markus, Hazel R. and Shinobu Kitayama (1991), "Culture and the Self: Implications for Cognition, Emotion, and Motivation," *Psychological Review*, 98 (2), 224–53.

Minowa, Yuko, Olga Khomenko, and Russell W. Belk (2011), "Social Change and Gendered Gift-Giving Rituals: A Historical Analysis of Valentine's Day in Japan," *Journal of Macromarketing*, 3 (1), 44–56.

Moeran, Brian and Lise Skov (1993), "Cinderella Christmas: Kitsch, Consumerism, and Youth Culture in Japan," in *Unwrapping Christmas*, ed. Daniel Miller, Oxford: Oxford University Press, 105–33.

Otnes, Cele C., Tina M. Lowrey, and Young Chan Kim (1993), "Gift Selection for Easy and Difficult Recipients: A Social Roles Interpretation," *Journal of Consumer Research*, 20 (2), 229–44.

Otnes, Cele, C., Julie A. Ruth, and Constance C. Milbourne (1994), "The Pleasure and Pain of Being Close: Men's Mixed Feelings about Participation in Valentine's Day Gift Exchange," in *Advances in Consumer Research*, Vol. 21, ed. Chris T. Allen and Deborah Roedder John, Provo, UT: Association for Consumer Research, 159–64.

Pratruangkrai, Petchanet (2016), "Valentine's Day Spending to See Lowest Growth in Nine Years Amid Economic Woes," *The Nation: Economics Section*. Available at www.nationmultimedia.com/business/Valentines-Day-spending-to-see-lowest-growth-in-ni-30253730.html

Rucker, Margaret H., Tamara Balch, Fiona Higham, and Kimberly Schenter (1992), "Thanks But No Thanks: Rejection, Possession and Disposition of the Failed Gift," in *Advances in Consumer Research*, Vol. 19, ed. John F. Sherry, Jr. and Brian Sternthal, Provo, UT: Association for Consumer Research, 488.

Rucker, Margaret H., Anthony Freitas, and April Kangas (1996), "The Role of Ethnic Identity in Gift Giving," in *Gift Giving: A Research Anthology*, ed. Cele Otness and Richard F. Beltramini, Bowling Green, OH: Bowling Green State University Popular Press, 143–62.

Rugimbana, Robert, Brett Donahay, Christopher Neal, and Michael Jay Polonsky (2002), "The Role of Social Power Relations in Gift Giving on Valentine's Day," *Journal of Consumer Behaviour*, 3 (1), 63–73.

Ruth, Julie A., Cele C. Otnes, and Frédéric F. Brunel (1999), "Gift Receipt and the Reformulation of Interpersonal Relationship," *Journal of Consumer Research*, 25 (4), 385–402.

Sherry, John F., Jr., Mary A. McGrath, and Sidney J. Levy (1993), "The Dark Side of the Gift," *Journal of Business Research*, 28 (3), 225–44.

Sile, Aza Wee (2016), "Hong Kong Men are Region's Biggest Valentine's Day Spenders, Love Index Survey Shows," *CNBC: Life*. Available at www.cnbc. com/2016/02/12/hong-kong-men-are-regions-biggest-valentines-day-spenders-love-index-survey-shows.html

Tournier, Paul (1966), *The Meaning of Gifts*, Trans. John S. Gilmour, 4th printing, Richmond, VA: John Knox Press.

Tse, David K., Russell W. Belk, and Nan Zhou (1989), "Becoming a Consumer Society: A Longitudinal and Cross-Cultural Content Analysis of Print Ads from Hong Kong, the People's Republic of China, and Taiwan," *Journal of Consumer Research*, 15 (4), 457–72.

Valenzuela, Ana, Barbara Mellers, and Judi Strebel (2010), "Pleasurable Surprises: A Cross-Cultural Study of Consumer Responses to Unexpected Incentives," *Journal of Consumer Research*, 36 (February), 792–805.

Ward, Morgan K. and Susan M. Broniarczyk (2011), "It's Not Me, It's You: How Gift Giving Creates Giver Identity Threat as a Function of Social Closeness," *Journal of Consumer Research*, 38 (1), 164–81.

Wong, Nancy Y. and Aaron C. Ahuvia (1998), "Personal Taste and Family Face: Luxury Consumption in Confucian and Western Societies," *Psychology and Marketing*, 15 (5), 423–41.

Zhang, Yan and Nicholas Epley (2012), "Exaggerated, Mispredicted, and Misplaced: When 'It's the Thought That Counts' in Gift Exchanges," *Journal of Experimental Psychology: General*, 141 (4), 667–81.

Section III

Romantic Gift-Giving Contexts

6 Practicing Masculinity and Reciprocation in Gendered Gift-Giving Rituals

White Day in Japan, 1980–2009

Yuko Minowa, Russell W. Belk, and Takeshi Matsui

One of the fundamental tenets of post-structuralism is the role of history in diachronically constructing idiosyncratic culture and multiple truths in social reality. In discussing the corpus of his accomplishments, Foucault (1988, 17–18) stated that his objective was to analyze "a history of the different ways in our culture that humans develop knowledge about themselves." Such cultivation of self-knowledge, Foucault contended, should be regarded as "truth games," which are constituted within relations of power. At the same time, he emphasized engaging in genealogy, or the effective history, that readily admits biases in totalizing history and embraces the disparity in perspectives through interpreting the multiple truths of history. This chapter concerns how male consumers develop knowledge about themselves and construct masculinities through gendered rituals. In particular, we are interested in understanding the role that reciprocation and gendered power negotiation in gift-giving rituals play in constituting these masculinities. We investigate these problematics in the context of White Day in Japan.

White Day is a commercially constructed consumer holiday that began in 1980. It takes place on March 14. It is the day on which men who have received gifts from women on Valentine's Day on February 14 reciprocate by giving return gifts to these women. While gifts are supposed to be opposite of commodities, the act of giving and reciprocating requires much rational calculation about value, symbolism, and equivalence (Bourdieu 1989; Slater 1997). Infused with capitalist, pluralistic masculinity discourses, White Day provides an exemplary context for investigating the complex ways in which male consumers negotiate understandings of their masculinities. Although romantic gift-giving has been widely practiced by both genders in Japan (Minowa and Gould 1999; Rupp 2003), Valentine's Day and White Day are characteristically gender asymmetric gift-giving rituals that have been strategically used as tools for the gender power negotiation inside and outside of social institutions (Creighton 1993; Minowa, Khomenko, and Belk 2011; Ogasawara 1998).

Because of the heightened sociocultural importance Japan has historically assigned to gift-giving occasions and rituals (Rupp 2003; Minowa and Belk 2017; Minowa and Gould 1999; Minowa et al. 2011), White Day has come to achieve growing importance in the minds of consumers, aided by its frequent presence in the dominant media. Regardless of whether Japanese men celebrate, resist, or are ambiguous about the legitimacy of this commercial holiday, the symbolic exchange and the negotiation of power involved in this ritual is an inescapable social reality in their lives. Despite the significance of White Day as a signifier of masculinity in Japan, there has been a void of research examining how reciprocation in this gendered gift-giving ritual inflects male consumers' understandings of what it means to be a man. At the same time, there has been a paucity of consumer research in general which investigates the role of gender and the meanings of masculinity in gift-giving rituals, with some exceptions (Newman and Nelson 1996; Otnes, Ruth, and Milbourne 1994; Rucker, Freitas, and Dolstra 1994; Rucker et al. 1991; Rugimbana et al. 2003).

The current chapter seeks to compensate for shortcomings by examining the utterances and discourses on White Day manifested in the media within a historical framework. The organization of the paper is as follows: First, we discuss the historical transformations of masculinities in Japan. Our intention is not to narrate the past but to identify the contingencies or principal features in epochal moments that have constituted our "episteme" (Foucault 1994 [1966]) regarding masculinity. Second, we surface the polemics surrounding consumption, rituals, and masculinity literatures. This leads to a discussion of reciprocation in gift-giving rituals, masculinities, and power relations peculiar to Japanese culture. We then discuss our findings based on discourses and "found" visual information in the media in an effort to understand the socially constructed realities of masculinity which manifest in White Day in Japan.

Transformations of Masculinity in Japan

Japanese culture has been discussed as masculine and patriarchal—i.e., male dominant. This is based on the gender dichotomy visibility, the explicit duality of gender roles, and the polarized binary gender value systems. Characterized by male assertiveness and female nurturance, the traditional hegemonic gender system has led to male dominance in public domains. The varying magnitudes of masculinity in a culture may be attributable to specific historical influences of a region (Bourdieu 2001). It is enacted and perpetuated by family gender role socialization and media indoctrination reinforcing these learned behaviors. Gender practices have historic trajectories that are contingent upon time, space, and social context (Warde 2005). Hence, rather than synchronically examining the system of gender dichotomy and masculinity, diachronic examinations of the "historical unconscious" of the time and the conditions necessary for given things, phenomena, or people to occur, are essential for understanding the meaning of discourses on masculinity today (Downing 2008).

Men's roles in the society and the meaning of masculinity have been transformed throughout the history of Japan, reflecting the nation's socioeconomic and political systems. Recently, the nation's demographic changes—declining birthrate and super-aging population—led the Japanese government to enforce the Basic Law for Gender-equal Society which was passed in 1998. It extended the Law for Equal Opportunity for Employment passed in 1986 and has affected the broad meaning of masculinity and men's place in society in relation to that of women.

A common misconception about Japanese society is that it is historically masculine. The masculinization of the society began notably during the rise and control of samurai warriors in the Medieval Period. Then, masculine domination flourished during the Edo Period (1603–1868). The Confucianist Kaibara Ekiken (1630–1714) indoctrinated society about the supremacy of men through his writing of *Onna Daigaku*, a moral precept for women, drawing from androcratic Confucian ideology. *Danson johi*, the Japanese term for male chauvinism, which literally means "respect men, despise women," became the prevalent norm since this time. Women were instructed to deny their self-interests because their lives were to be devoted to their father, husband, and sons (Sugii 2008).

During the Fifteen-Year War (1931–1945) in the twentieth century, the ideal Japanese portrayal of masculinity was the war hero. They were called *Nihon-danji*, or sons of Japan, and were characterized as stouthearted, heroic, and brave, filled with the traditional Japanese spirit, which was implicated with ultranationalist ideology (Obinata 2006). The destruction of the national economy in postwar Japan necessitated a new type of male warrior: Businessmen, or salarymen, who were to fight on the battle field of the economic war. They were now called corporate fighters. The norm constituted the core of the work ethos and had implications for family and gender norms as well (Amano 2006). Meanwhile, to legitimatize the aim of these male corporate fighters, and to legitimatize their wives' domestic assistance, the government instituted a tax deduction for married people in 1961 and enhanced the gendered curricula at school.

Studies by Amano (2001, 2006) show that men's beliefs about "masculinity" are changing and depend on their social class and generation: Corporate fighter (postwar generation: –1945); Company-oriented person (baby boom generation: 1946–1950); and Post-company-oriented person (moratorium generation: 1951–present). In postwar Japanese society, ideal hegemonic masculinity was constructed through salaried men's lives: breadwinners for their families and committed worker in the corporate environment. "True masculinity" was equated with "control over self and others, including women and children" (Ishii-Kuntz 2003, 199).

However, the younger generation has indicated their emancipation from the traditional notion of masculinity that is characterized by decisiveness, and competitiveness. A study by Kitakata et al. (2012) suggests the influence of men's fashion and lifestyle magazines, which became popular since 1980s, on their meaning of masculinity that is closely related to their appearance. Rather than playing the conventional gender role, Japanese males came to be concerned with expressing and performing "masculine" character—in a Goffmanian sense—prescribed by the members of the network to which they belong (Miyadai et al. 2009). Such expressions are hyper-ritualized in advertising (Kohyama 1999). During the same period, thoughtfulness and kindness also became traits of being masculine (Kitakata et al. 2012).

This means both the variety and modes of masculinity diversified. For instance, obsessive enthusiasts, or so-called otaku, may use private, secretive consumption as an appropriate expression of masculinity (Condry 2013). Unlike their mainstream counterpart salarymen, otaku masculinity is judged by consumption, and not productivity. Concurrently, there has been a shift in the importance from being masculine to being an individual self. Thus, vulnerable, sensitive, and insecure men each came to have their own fuzzy realm of masculinity, as evidenced by, for example, the emergence of "herbivorous men," or gentle men who lack traditional virility. Miyadai et al. (2009) postulate that anomie and repressive collectivism in contemporary Japanese society are the problematics of emergent masculinities. Media and popular culture, as well as social psychological and socio-political factors, have played a critical role in constructing multivalent masculinities.

The genealogy of masculinities presented here is admittedly incomplete. We believe, however, that the above episodes show that the changes in the ideology of masculinities in Japan occurred in a contingent and disruptive manner rather than evolving continuously.

Masculinities, Consumption, and Rituals

There is a long history of gendered consumption (e.g., Forty 1986; de Grazia 1996; Spark 1995). Men seek and practice masculine identities through their everyday consumption (Holt and Thompson 2004). Hegemonic masculinity (Connell and Messerschmidt 2005) has been studied in consumer behavior contexts involving enactment of masculinity and sexuality by men (Brubaker and Johnson 2008), consumption of "masculine products" by women (McGinnis, Gentry, and McQuillan 2009), and gendered consumption-based manipulation of identities and roles (Alexander 2003; Buerkle 2009). Consumption that enhances masculine appearance and sexual potency seems to be a principal current interest, and the problematic of male bodies has been attributed to "the ever-widening vortex of late-twentieth-century consumerism" (Bordo 1999, 18). Here consumption is used to avoid feeling "emasculated" by virulent scrutiny in a display culture (Faludi 1999) and to compensate for insecurities about men's masculinities (Schouten and McAlexander 1995). At the same time, alternative male lifestyles have emerged embracing degendered domestic devotion (Aarseth 2009).

Men use collective consumption in ritualized contexts to explore and practice masculinities. For example, consumption of alcohol is a central activity within male-dominated subcultures (Driessen 1983; Muir and Seitz 2004), and there are male-only rites of passage, such as bachelor parties (Williams 1994). While consumption practices of male-dominated rituals, such as the mountain man rendezvous (Belk and Costa 1998), can serve as the realization of romanticized fantasy experiences, other rituals, such as regular visits to bars (Driessen 1983), strip clubs (Frank 2003), girl hunts (Grazian 2007), and macho activities (Schouten and McAlexander 1995; Scott, Cayla, and Arnould 2017) also enact performances of masculine behavior, reinforce dominant sexual myths, and enhance confidence in men's performance of heterosexual prowess.

Gift-giving is another gendered ritual—pivotal in society and consumer behavior (Belk 1979; Belk and Coon 1993; Sherry 1983)—in which the meaning of masculinity may be explored. The gift-giving ritual may serve either utilitarian or romantic purposes: The gift may be employed for instrumental reasons or used as an expression of altruistic love (Belk 1996). Gift-giving can be assessed from the tripartite paradigm of economic exchange, social exchange, and agapic love (Belk and Coon 1993). The agapic love paradigm involves non-reciprocal altruistic gifts, idealization, and singularization of the beloved, and submissiveness by the giver (Belk 1995). The singularity of gifts from loved ones sacralizes these gifts (Belk, Wallendorf, and Sherry 1989).

The ritual process tends to be gender asymmetric and dependent on the context of the gift-giving (Fischer and Arnold 1990; Mortelmans and Sinardet 2004). The asymmetry seems to arise based on the masculine or feminine traits the giver assigns to a gift according to the gender of the recipient (Gould and Weil 1991), the affective response to giving and receiving experiences (Areni, Kiecher, and Palan 1998), and the accuracy of guessing the giver's thoughts and feelings by the recipient (Minowa and Gould 1999). Although reciprocation is an integral part of the exchange process and is often regarded as part of the dark side of the exchange (Marcoux 2009; Ruth, Otnes, and Brunel 1999; Sherry, McGrath, and Levy 1993), the literature specifically focusing on the relationship between masculinity and reciprocation in the gendered power negotiation of gift-giving rituals is scarce.

In Japan, gift-giving rituals and occasions, both voluntary and obligatory, occupy an indispensable part of society (Rupp 2003). Annual events, rites of passage, accidents, religious rituals, and signs of appreciation, apology, friendship, and romantic feeling, all involve giving and repayment of gifts. The large number of Japanese gift-giving occasions hints at the dispositions of Japanese consumers: They value *wa*, or harmony, in society; they cannot say "no" and thus cannot refuse receiving gifts; and they have a strong sense of obligation to reciprocate.

The Japanese term for gift-giving, *zōtoh*, which literally means present and reply, implies that *okaeshi*, or gift repayment, is integral part of the entire ritual process. What constitutes an appropriate (and more importantly inappropriate) gift, and repayment gift, depends on the occasion and the relationship between the giver and the recipient. The norms regarding the ritual protocol are prescribed, and their importance is witnessed by the popularity of reference books on etiquette at ceremonial occasions. Although the prescribed rules for gift-giving are for traditional customs, reference books make some suggestions for gifts exchanged between men and women for expressing personal (romantic) feelings. These gifts are commonly called *purezento*, or present, by consumers and are distinguished from traditional obligatory *zōtoh* (Minowa and Gould 1999).

Among the Japanese, gift-receipt generates the feeling of *giri*, or obligation, *on*, or indebtedness, and *oime*, or guilt. The importance assigned to reciprocating with a return gift reflects the Japanese norm that one has to fulfill a social obligation, which may be thought as if having to pay off a debt (Befu 1968). Also, the relationship between the giver and recipient is balanced by generally reciprocating a gift of equal value (Ito 1995), although this may depend on the nature of the relationship (Rupp 2003). It seems that this feeling of indebtedness is gendered. Males are inclined to say "*katajikenai*,"—"I feel a heavy debt of gratitude," when they receive a gift. The etymology of the Chinese character used in the phrase implies that recipients are being insulted. Thus, the feelings of gratitude and indignity seems to be inseparable when receiving a gift and the weight of indignity is often heavier for men than for women in cross-gender giving. While Valentine's Day and White Day are foreign or imposed (versus indigenous) consumer holidays, they were both well accepted in Japanese society. One of the reasons for the adoption of the latter was that it gave an opportunity for male recipients to reciprocate and to fulfill an obligation a month after Valentine's Day, the time frame that is also most appropriate for traditional gift-giving occasions (Ito 1984). Thus, Japanese consumer behavior, even in contemporary society, is deeply influenced by a historically rooted culture.

Methods

Underpinned by Foucault's studies of histories (Kendall and Wickham 1999), our research employs discourse analysis as its method, a strategy that involves "analysis of representations of knowledge as found in historical documents" (Marvasti 2004, 110). Discourse is a body of statements—in writing and speaking—whose organization is regular and systematic. It is considered to create reality and construct a particular type of knowledge with practical and rhetorical implications. Because of his interest in the reflexive relationship between knowledge and power, Foucault analyzed historical documents to demonstrate how the exercise of power and ways of knowing change over time. His main concern was to "locate the forms of power, the channel it takes, and discourses it permeates" (1990 [1976], 11). According to Foucault, the self is constructed through discourses that produce certain ways of understanding who we should be and what we should do (Foucault 1990 [1976]). Discourse not only restricts but empowers certain agents to create representations and to proclaim the "truth" of the world, or the nature of a given phenomenon (Prior 1997).

We aimed to relate textual and sociological levels by examining formal features of statements and visuals, such as metaphors, and social practice, while eliciting the hidden and chauvinistic presumptions of discourses encompassed in discursive mechanisms: editorials and advertisements in print media, such as newspapers, magazines, and brochures, dating from 1980 to 2009. We collected 1,550 articles and 45 advertisements from nationally circulated newspapers, such as *Yomiuri Shinbun* and *Asahi Shinbun*, and male and female magazines, such as *Shukan posto* and *non-no*. Our archive includes statements and discourses of the trade association in catalogs, brochures, and on the Internet, which demonstrate practice, and 882 articles from industry newspapers that contain tables, charts, and summaries of surveys—scientific statements—all of which represent knowledge through particular schemes of classification. In this paper, we selected seven texts for detailed analyses: These represent instantiations of discursive struggles from epochal moments. The advertisements in our archive indicate typical White Day gifts as confectionery and handkerchief for reciprocating obligatory (*giri*) Valentine chocolate, and jewelry, accessories, cosmetics, apparels, and dining out for reciprocating true love (*honmei*) Valentine gifts. Editorials suggest other possibilities, however, that are discussed in the discourse analysis section.

While reading the range of discourses in these sources, we tried to focus on the authority of the text rather than the authorship. We tried to understand how political, legislative, and economic factors produced the power to affect gender practice in potential scripts for White Day ritual gift-giving. At the same time, instead of dichotomizing discourse as something that exists between the dominant and the dominated, or accepted and excluded, we looked into the polyvalent elements in the masculinity discourse. Hence our focus was to investigate what realities are made possible through the text. We could not merely accept outcomes but had to reconstruct the discourses with "things said and those concealed" (Foucault 1990 [1976], 100).

In order to assure the validity of our findings, we triangulated our interpretations (Belk, Fischer, and Kozinets 2013). We also interviewed the advisory director of the National Candy Confectionery Manufacturers' Cooperative Union that invented White Day in 1980. The confectioners wanted candy to complement every White Day gift, like *noshi*, an auspicious symbol attached to the gift wrap. Their early promotional campaigns were influential in ingraining White Day gift-giving in consumer psyches as a legitimate consumption ritual and gender practices. Furthermore, we visited the Ad Museum started by Dentsu in Tokyo where we interviewed the curator about the history of advertising in Japan.

Discourse Analysis

Our analysis of the discourses in the media revealed the four major findings. One is that White Day is used as an event for both men and women to search, practice, and perform gender through the act of giving and receiving a reciprocal gift. Second, White Day is a rite of institution in corporations in which male and female coworkers shape and reshape institutionalized collective masculinity through a gendered practice enacting the protocols prescribed for gift-giving rituals. Third, White Day is used as an occasion for male consumers to explore the meaning of masculinity through the negotiation of power with their female counterparts. Lastly, White Day is an opportunity to disclose a man's emasculated self through consumption practices. The first two findings are in the context of workplace gift-giving, while the latter two entail romantic gift-giving. Thus, the nature of the gifts is social for the former and personal for the other. Aside from workplace, school is another typical sphere of practicing White Day gift-giving.

White Day as an Event for Gender Performance

White Day provides a discursive context in which male consumers may come to understand, assure, and reconfirm masculinities, masculine behaviors, and gender role expectations by accepting and performing the role prescribed by the media and framed by the culture. Practice as performance refers to the enactment of practices, or the performance of actions and sayings which together actualize and sustain practices (Warde 2005). Regarding identity as a practice and gender as a performance is profoundly Foucauldian. While there are no universally fixed rules for gender performance that women and men play interactively and contingently in society (Butler 1999 [1990]), any culture has its own rules for the gender game. Furthermore, such rules may be challenged and subverted by consumers when gender roles and displays change (Holt and Thompson 2004; Thompson and Haytko 1997).

In a purportedly post-androcentric society, masculinity is fragmented, and it changes depending on the role that the male consumer must perform on a particular social stage (Ito 1993; Miyadai et al. 2009). For example, the advertisement (see Figure 6.1) by the National Candy Confectionary Manufacturers' Cooperative Union published in a weekly male magazine *Shukan Sankei* in 1984 presents an alternative masculinity appropriated for middle-aged men in a particular place in the social hierarchy. The headline "Hiroko-chan, it seems *ojisan* is getting excited" is followed by the copy on the left:

> March14. On White Day, send candies to her from him. Do you recall Hiroko-chan at the reception, Seiko-chan in the general affairs section, Yoshie-chan at the coffee shop, and Hidemi-chan in the bar ...? White Day is the answer-day for Valentine's Day. For someone you want to treasure, for someone you want to be always together [with], for someone who suddenly crosses your mind. ... Send candies to those you love on this day.

First of all, what does it mean to address the self as *ojisan*, or middle-aged man, to Hiroko-chan, the diminutive of a woman named Hiroko? According to Nakamura (2007), the way to address the self, or the designation of first-person pronoun, is a learned behavior often copied from fiction. Traditionally, *ojisan* is supposed to be a moral middle-aged man who is a role model of the behavioral code for children. However, in corporations, *ojisan* has come to mean "older salaryman who always gets drunk and talks about sex" (Mathews 2003, 123). The ad discussed above also has an erotic tone as *ojisan* admits that he seems to be excited (aroused). The women's names in the ad coincide those of the contemporary young idol singers, implying his yearning for those unattainable as sexual objects.

But the eros is not induced by the corporeality of the adult woman: her body itself is nonmaterial in this discourse. Rather, the desire is incited by the candies that adorn the woman's neck which seem to symbolize sweet childishness. Hence it is decorating her with a wreath of candies that makes her body discursive. On the other hand, the women in the ad copy are all addressed in a diminutive form which eliminates their adult sexuality. None of these women holds a corporate managerial position. They are not a threat to middle-aged men. For a generation of men whose *ikigai*, or "that which most makes life worth living" (Mathews

Figure 6.1 An Ad with the "White Day as an Event for Gender Performance" Theme (*Shukan Sankei* March 2, 1984)

2003, 109), is work, they might have had more human communication with the young girls in their office than they resort to with their own families.

By publicly identifying themselves as *ojisan* and addressing young women in a diminutive manner, the men addressed are not only consciously creating a distance from the young women in the social hierarchy but also attempting to justify their position for exercising the power without having virility. The middle-aged man may be uncertain about his power; he lacks confidence to physically challenge adult women. His fantasy to deviate from the adult masculine self is projected onto the illusion of the woman with similarly anomalous kitschy candies on her neck. His fantasy for enticing multiple women with material gifts suggests his fear of commitment. So the gender performance instructed here for the middle-aged men is to admit their position in a declining stage of the "gendered lifecycle" (Taga 2006b), and perform, defy, and enact a persona anomalous to the disciplined masculine corporate self. The ad edifies the reader that, in performing masculinity and multiple roles in society concurrently, the White Day ritual can aid in alleviating dilemmas of unmet sexual desires through fantasy, can justify this anomaly, and may reconcile current identity with a self adrift in the ambiguity of multivalent masculinities at this particular stage of the gendered lifecycle.

White Day as a Rite of Institution

Various institutions construct masculinities. In Japan, the workplace is a key arena in which gender is enacted. Workplace culture may mirror the organization's collective masculinities. Groups and institutions enact masculinities as patterns of gender practice (Connell 1998). Through collective practice, masculinities are constituted and reconstituted while gender meanings are reshaped within the institutional contexts of practice. Such collective practice further constitutes gendered institutions that circulate definitions of masculinity (and femininity) and of gender roles. Rites and rituals are key conditions in the social practice of gender performance. Economic behavior, including gift-giving, is often embedded in the ongoing, concrete system of social relations, which shape and are shaped by the institutional culture for strategic reasons (Granovetter 1985). While it appears that the performer, here the individual male consumer, is an atomized individual acting in a dyadic gift-giving situation, his behavior is in fact constrained by the broader, oversocialized institutional context, especially in a collectivistic culture such as Japan.

From a Durkheimian perspective, rituals serve to maintain a focus on ideology and provide a sense of commonality among group members (Durkheim 2008 [1912]). While rites of passage (van Gennep 1960) describe the phases of ritual, anthropological theory has paid less attention to the social functions of ritual. Rites of institution (Bourdieu 1991) legitimize and perpetuate the difference between those who participate and those who do not. In other words, rites and rituals, including White Day, create "magical boundaries" (Bourdieu 1991, 122) between masculine and feminine, giver and recipient, and impose these distinctions on the practice of gender and as barriers to transgressing the boundaries of gendered behavior in the intuitional realm. The symbolic efficacy of these rites, which is the power they possess to act on reality through representation, consecrates the difference. It follows that men possess and practice symbolic power as givers on White Day, as much as women do as givers on Valentine's Day, in order to affirm gender and gift-giving boundaries while practicing gender in the organization.

White Day is a rite of institution that consecrates the boundary between men and women, and shapes and reshapes institutionalized collective masculinity through gendered practice. It reinforces the power structure and the unspoken rules of the power game within and across genders within the institution. The copy of a newspaper advertisement published in 1991 reads:

> There must be many of you who received a gift on Valentine's Day from women in the office. By all means, please give them a thank-you gift. Women are sensitive about scrupulous consideration, and above all, it creates a vibrant office atmosphere. ... It is a struggle to buy gifts for all the women in the office because there are a large number. ... They will be troubled if they receive a number of the same or similar items. Because it is the White Day gift exchange at the office, you need to give some thought to avoid duplicating with your male colleagues in the same office.

This ad states that many men must have received a gift on Valentine's Day, implying that there are also males who did not receive a gift. This means that males in organizations are stratified into two classes: those who are "given" and "not given" a gift by women. Because the decision to give men obligatory *giri-choko* [obligatory chocolate] gifts—for a pragmatic purpose (Kohyama 2001)—is often made collectively, it is women's collective privilege to thereby empower some men and marginalize the others (those not given *giri-choko*), thus bestowing different statuses within the institution (Ogasawara 1998). The ad hints at the potential consequences if men fail to practice the legitimate masculine behavior in the institution: women will not be indifferent if men fail to reciprocate. The outcome may manifest in an unpleasant incident, such as ostracism. Men are taught, or they learn by experience, that women do not welcome a mere token return: The gift has to be individuated even if the Valentine's Day *giri-choko* were given by a group of women collectively.

Presentations of knowledge about women's collective coercive power teach male consumers in the organization the importance of reciprocation as a rite of institution. The advertisement entitled "I'm not going to let you go unpunished, if you forget" (see Figure 6.2) explicitly reminds men of the potential retaliation of female workers. The visual image of handkerchiefs dominates the ad in the center. Each handkerchief is meticulously folded into a polygonal shape with sharp edges and pointing corners, as if to allude to something dangerous, like office ladies being in charge. They appear uniformly lovely on the surface and their politeness is spotless, paralleling the characteristics of the handkerchief. The women are depicted as cohesive and tacitly exercising power in solidarity. On the right, the young woman in a business suit holds her arms across her chest to create an aura of authority. She looks down at the male reader and her posture rejects any argument against her commands, and demands. She is not a mature woman. In fact, there is a stuffed animal, a cat named "nekorobi nyan-nyan," priced at 950 yen on the bottom of the ad. She is still of an age to call a cat using its onomatopoeic nyan-nyan (meow-meow). The ad suggests that a young immature woman like her is dangerous as she will quickly acquire knowledge of how to perform collective femininity. She is also implacable. Thus, the rite of institution, White Day, not only consecrates the difference between the masculine and the feminine but also didactically propagandizes to men the dispositions of women as evil beings who are immature yet demanding consumers beyond the organizational context. The same model of fragile male dependency is depicted in the Nintendo DS and 3DS portable game *LovePlus* (Galbraith 2011, 2014; Taylor 2007), in which men must continue to give gifts to, take on vacations, and otherwise please their virtual girlfriends.

White Day and the Negotiation of Power

The predicament of modern men manifested in contemporary social discourses is that of masculinity crises caused by social changes (Ashe 2007). Equality legislation and challenges by feminists have altered perspectives on traditional male gender roles in the Japanese workplace and family. Not every man is pro-feminist. Women's equality gains have been seen as men's losses by many, especially conservative men who often proclaim that "in the workplace men are losing their jobs because 'mediocre women' are being promoted at the expense of able men" (Ashe 2007, 59). Women and men of the same or similar rank also compete to remain equal. There exist non (and anti) -feminist men's gender politics to resist changes in gendered power relationships and attempt to sustain traditional male gender roles and masculine identities. This may entail

Figure 6.2 An Ad With the "White Day as a Rite of Institution" Theme (*Asahi Shinbun* March 4, 1993)
Reproduced with permission of Seiyu GK.

implicitly as well as explicitly communicating this manifesto to women through campaigns for re-establishing male power in social arenas. The implicit communication is partly waged by symbolic exchanges of gifts in gendered gift-giving rituals. A gift exchange is a message; it can spoil human relationships inadvertently or purposefully. Thus, reciprocating with an inappropriate gift can convey challenge and competition (Bailey 1971).

Male consumers use White Day as an opportunity to negotiate and renegotiate power relations with women through their language, gestures, bodies, and the material objects involved in the gift-giving process. For example, giving the woman, the giver of Valentine's gift, white panties as the White Day repayment gift can entail symbolically violent meanings and tacit negotiation of power. It became a popular practice in the mid-80s when women started to gain power in the workplace and society as a result of the enforcement of the Equal Employment Opportunity Act of 1986. The judicial intervention as well as everyday gender practice affects the interplay between intimate interpersonal relations and economic activity (Zelizer 2005). While the law potentially has the power to subvert identity politics, from a Foucauldian perspective, the real negotiation of power exists as it is exercised outside the traditional juridico-discursive framework (Schrift 1994).

The cultural meaning of receiving a gift from Japanese women involves a feeling of indignity on the part of male recipients, as discussed previously. Valentine's gifts can be interpreted as woman's emancipation from their traditional gender role as a care receiver. It allows her to assert her economic independence; it is her tactic for negotiating gender power and allows her to exercise her dominance over men under the guise of giving a "romantic" gift. The woman's challenge is taken as unequivocal humiliation of men who are, in turn, obliged to offer the women a return gift of a material object that would equally serve as his admission of humiliation from receipt of a romantic gift. White panties are neither romantic nor sexual. The plain, colorless underwear of the white panty can even be interpreted as symbolic of a desexualized woman. Giving such an item as a return gift in a supposedly romantic ritual signifies the male giver's silent anger and his unconscious desire to reduce the female recipient into a piece of under-clothing, or a powerless infantile object of sexual desire, so that he can exercise power. So, the campaign by the Body Fashion Association was successful partly because it translated for men, particularly businessmen, that "competent businessmen" could stand up against women and show their pride by giving them white panties on White Day.

The gender power negotiation with a gift of underwear was thus a battle that involved the exercise of power over the body. According to Foucault (1977, 26), "the power exercised on the body is conceived not as a property, but as a strategy, that its effects of domination are attributed not to 'appropriation,' but to dispositions, maneuvers, tactics, techniques, functionings; that one should decipher it in a network of relations, constantly in tension, in activity ... one should take as its model a perpetual battle." An editorial in the March 11, 1988 issue of the male magazine, *Shūkan Posuto*, is dialectic on love and strategy:

> White Day: The stratagems of love, finalized on White Day. This is a special day to convey honest feelings from men to women. The problem is what to present on White Day. Because you want the woman you love to become more beautiful. Because you want that she cultivates her femininity more. Let's be brave and send her underwear. The fine lingerie is the object of adoration for all the women.

This monolog is didactic, first because it explicates gift-giving rituals and love in terms of stratagems. A stratagem is a ruse for deceiving an enemy. So the male reader is presented with the knowledge that this gift-giving ritual is implicated in scheming against a woman. Although she is supposedly an object of adoration, she is at the same time his foe against whom he has to design a clever scheme. The male reader is instructed to convey his honest feelings to women. But the problem is how to convey them without insulting her. Refusal is power, and it may be her strategy: Resistance to power is the exercise of power. The ritual is problematized due to the importance of the material gift to be presented to the woman in order to accomplish his mission of getting the upper hand. Further, it imposes the normative value that beauty is a criterion for appeasing a woman. The reader is taught that a woman who strives for developing femininity is desirable. Sending underwear to his intimate partner requires brevity, as it is not honorable behavior and may cause her embarrassment that leads to resentment. Why should he care whether she would be embarrassed or not, if he is the one who can control her? In order to triumph over the woman whose body and mind he wants to control, the man has to utilize this carefully crafted gift-giving tactic by bombarding her with underwear. In reality, it is often he who adores fine lingerie, more than the woman who is made to wear it. But, there has to be a rationale to conceal his real motive and to appear tactful. So the ad presents a mind-relieving solution by concluding with the propagandizing generalization: All women are universally the same in their preferences; they, like men themselves, should all like fine lingerie. In this way, conflicting ideas—love and war strategies—become a unified whole, and the new knowledge is synthesized while the power relations between the man and the woman, or the giver and the recipient of fine lingerie, is schematized.

White Day as a Confession for the Emasculated Self

Masculinities have come to bear psychic pressures, such as mid-life crises and anxieties about reciprocation, which in turn may cause feelings of depression, loss of virility, and emasculation. Talking about these anxieties may unburden men and provide a sense of relief. Hence confession may serve as a cathartic "act of therapy" for a man who undergoes distressing life events, while the Foucauldian perspective posits that confession discursively fixes identities. Taylor (2009, 6) notes that "there is a transhistorical human need or psychological compulsion to confess," and this need is attested to by the popularity of psychotherapy and confessional memoirs in the marketplace. While men function as the confessors—the judges of women's confessions—in the Valentine's Day ritual in which they determine the consequence of the gifts received, their own confession takes place in the torturous experience of White Day. The cost of this cathartic release of psychic pressures is an admission of their emasculation. While women's confessions of love on Valentine's Day burst outward, men's confessions on White Day seem to implode inward. Whereas the white panties rebellion of the 1980s and 1990s was an aggressive tactic resisting such emasculation, the now more common compliance with female expectations for a more lavish return gift is experienced as a confession of defeat in the battle of the sexes.

The Heisei recession in the 1990s was a factor that contributed to the masculinity crisis in Japan. Men's loss of economic authority with the restructuring and downsizing of corporations together with the dissolving of their traditional gender roles as breadwinners, caused a dilemma in the eyes of many Japanese men (Taga 2006a; Miyadai et al. 2009). Loyalty to his company, sense of obligation to his fellow men, and other old virtues that honored selfless dedication to the collective self of the corporation now seem quaint. Facing a super-aged society with a declining birthrate, men were preached by the Ministry of Health, Labor, and Welfare which called for gender role change in 1999: "A man who doesn't raise his children can't be called father" (Ishii-Kuntz 2003). This slogan was aimed to reconfigure ideal hegemonic masculinity by emphasizing the man's familial involvement as part of responsible masculine behavior. With the proclamation of such authority, phallic masculinity, or the quest for patriarchal authority seemed officially invalidated. Thus, men have lost compelling reasons to become psychologically mature, economically independent, and socially able to prove their masculinity under these socioeconomic conditions (Taga 2006a). At the same time, rapid social change and the resulting loss of masculine identity was for many a painful experience that caused stress, anxiety, and low self-esteem.

The White Day gift-giving ritual that involves reluctant spending for a reciprocal gift object can be seen as analogous to the penal ritual in both senses of the term. There is, first, a woman's preliminary investigation into the worthiness of the man who will be marked and targeted in the power negotiation. Then, the sentence is given in the form of a Valentines gift, the value of which symbolizes the worthiness of the man. The penalty is the White Day gift to be reciprocated; it may well be the focus of psychological as well as financial torture for the man. Finally, the effects of the penalty can be lasting psychic distress, resentment toward the Valentine's Day gift-giver, and feelings of humiliation and emasculation.

The media play an important role in interpreting men's psyches and acting as their voice. For instance, the editorial in the male magazine *Bart* published in 1995 had the title, "The Shivering White Day." The subtitle says, "I convey my condolences from the bottom of my heart to those men who were proud of receiving Valentine's Day chocolate a month ago. What you strived for was really an absurdly expensive bill from worldly wise women." The copy begins, "You will be cursed if you receive chocolate." Thus, the reader is presented with the view that the Japanese woman is dangerous, and their proclivity is greed and deceit. Aside from panties, male consumers use other material objects to negotiate their power with women. With the stagnant Japanese economy, inexpensive items served as gift items while negotiating gender power. The following article appeared in the male magazine *Spa!* in 1996:

> White Day is nothing to be afraid of if you deflect it with a joke. March 14 is White Day. You were in seventh heaven when you received Valentines gift, but it is about the time that you start to feel that you are being looked at by those women who wait for a return gift. If you just receive and leave the matter as it is, you will be sorry for the dangerous consequences, but selecting a return gift is also quite a struggle. Even if the Valentines gift is a bundle of cheap chocolates bought in the convenience store, it's the psychology of a woman that she expects to receive an expensive return gift

This passage is presented as a male consumer's conscience, a reverberation of his inner voice, and is addressed to him. In this editorial, as his conscience speaks, the torturous aspects of the confessional discourse become apparent in recounting the turmoil of gift-giving rituals. The male consumer recollects the felicitous disruptions on Valentine's Day that tickled his manhood with a surfeit of rank, prurient pleasure. All of a sudden, the feeling of happiness fades away as he remembers that the White Day gift-giving ritual is approaching. Now he bleakly recalls that the Valentines gifts he received were a bundle of cheap bargain items from a convenience store, as if to imply his lack of worthiness in the eyes of women. Obsessive thoughts about the dangerous outcome of failing to give an appropriate return gift and compulsive illusions about the woman's anger stirred by the unappreciated gift make him feel emasculated. Shivering with fear, he feels White Day is a horror. He realizes that she wants an expensive return gift. Yet, he cannot afford one under his current impecunious circumstances. A perpetual cycle of imaginings about possible consequences of gift-giving faux pas haunts him and worsens his anxiety. So he seeks a solution in the media to alleviate his anxiety by suggesting recourses with unique affordable gift items. The knowledge presented here is that the anxiety is not uncommon; in fact, it is collectively experienced among male consumers who undergo the torturous experiences of the gift-giving ritual.

Discussion and Conclusion

In the current study, the practice of masculinities and reciprocation in gendered gift-giving rituals was investigated in the context of White Day in Japan. We attempted to answer the question, how do male consumers develop knowledge about themselves and masculinities through gendered rituals. We investigated the role that reciprocation and gender power negotiation play in constituting masculinities through these gift-giving rituals. We examined these problematics using discourse analysis, an approach influenced by Michel Foucault. We educed the hidden presumptions of discourses encompassed in editorials and advertisements in print media dating from 1980 to 2009. We analyzed representations of knowledge in these visual images. Unlike previous research on romantic gift-giving rituals in Japan (Minowa and Gould 1999; Minowa et al. 2011), the present study investigated how masculinity and reciprocation are intertwined in negotiating power in the gendered gift-giving ritual of White Day.

Our discourse analysis produced four major findings. One is that gendered gift-giving rituals, such as White Day, function as events for gender performance. White Day provides a discursive context in which male consumers may come to understand, assure, and reconfirm masculinities, masculine behaviors, and gender role expectations, by accepting and performing the role prescribed by the media and framed by the culture. Second, White Day is a rite of institution that consecrates the boundary between men and women, and shapes and reshapes institutionalized collective masculinity through gendered practice. It reinforces the power structure and the unspoken rules of the power game within and across genders within the institution. Third, White Day is used as an opportunity for male consumers to negotiate and renegotiate power relations with women through the material objects involved in the gift-giving process. Men's gender politics to resist changes in gendered power relationships and to sustain traditional male gender roles and masculine identities lead to a declaration of their response to the messages communicated implicitly by the gifts they received from women a month earlier.

Lastly, White Day is an opportunity to examine and admit the vulnerable self, facing masculinity crises and anxieties about gift-giving faux pas. The White Day gift to be reciprocated may induce psychological and financial torture for the man, which may result in lasting psychic distress, resentment toward the recipient, loss of confidence and self dignity, and feelings of humiliation and emasculation.

The results of our study show complex, pluralistic masculinities manifest in the discourse of gendered gift-giving rituals. Generations and positions in the social hierarchy influence men's perspectives toward female gender roles, as well as their own normative masculine performances in the twin-holiday ritual. Social changes over the 30 years of White Day, along with legislative enforcement to promote gender equality, have produced multivocal masculinities and have helped shape the meanings of reciprocation, incising the feelings of emasculation on the men who found themselves losers at the expense of women's equality gains in society. Media constituted and presented knowledge about their collective masculine and emasculated selves. These selves were constructed through discourses that produced certain ways of understanding how Japanese men should be and what they should think and do. At the same time, they were indoctrinated about the proclivity and dispositions of Japanese women in the gendered gift-giving rituals. These women were described as dangerous, greedy, and deceitful. However, these discourses are polyvalent, reflecting the lack of a singular culturally dominant masculinity as well as the reinforced dichotomy between dominant and the dominated in gender relationships in present day Japan.

References

Aarseth, Helene (2009), "From Modernized Masculinity to Degendered Lifestyle Projects Changes in Men's Narratives on Domestic Participation 1990–2005," *Men and Masculinities*, 11 (4), 424–40.

Alexander, Susan M. (2003), "Stylish Hard Bodies: Branded Masculinity in 'Men's Health' Magazine," *Sociological Perspectives*, 46 (4), 535–54.

Amano, Masako (2001), "Dankai sedai no 'mou hitotsu no' yomikata" ["Another" Way to Read the Baby Boom Generation], in *Dankai sedai: Shinron* [The Baby Boom Generation: A New Theory], ed. Masako Amano, Tokyo: Yūshindō, 3–37.

——— (2006), "Sōron: 'Otoko de arukoto' no sengoshi" [Introduction: The Postwar History of "Being a Man"], in *"Otoko rashisa" no gendaishi* [Contemporary History of "Masculinity"], ed. T. Abe, S. Obinata, and M. Amano, Tokyo: Nihon keizai hyōronsha, 1–32.

Areni, Charles S., Pamela Kiecher, and Kay M. Palan (1998), "Is It Better to Give Than to Receive? Exploring Gender Differences in the Meaning of Memorable Gifts," *Psychology and Marketing*, 15 (January), 81–109.

Ashe, Fidelma (2007), *The New Politics of Masculinity: Men, Power and Resistance*, New York: Routledge.

Bailey, Frederick George (1971), "Gifts and Poison," in *Gifts and Poison: The Politics of Reputation*, ed. F. G. Bailey, New York: Schocken Books, 1–25.

Befu, Harumi (1968), "Gift-Giving in a Modernizing Japan," *Monumenta Nipponica*, 23 (3–4), 445–56.

Belk, Russell W. (1979), "Gift-Giving Behavior," in *Research in Marketing*, Vol. 2, ed. J. Sheth, Greenwich, CT: JAI Press, 95–126.

——— (1995), "Studies in the New Consumer Behaviour," in *Acknowledging Consumption*, ed. D. Miller, New York: Routledge, 53–93.

——— (1996), "The Perfect Gift," in *Gift Giving: A Research Anthology*, ed. C. Otnes and R. Beltramini, Bowling Green, OH: Bowling Green State University Popular Press, 59–84.

Belk, Russell W. and Gregory Coon (1993), "Gift Giving as Agapic Love: An Alternative to the Exchange Paradigm Based on Dating Experiences," *Journal of Consumer Research*, 20 (3), 393–417.

Belk, Russell W. and Janean Costa (1998), "The Mountain Man Myth: A Contemporary Consuming Fantasy," *Journal of Consumer Research*, 25 (3), 218–40.

Belk, Russell W., Eileen Fischer, and Robert V. Kozinets (2013), *Qualitative Consumer and Marketing Research*, Thousand Oaks, CA: Sage Publications.

Belk, Russell W., Melanie Wallendorf, and John F. Sherry (1989), "The Sacred and the Profane in Consumer Behavior: Theodicy on the Odyssey," *Journal of Consumer Research*, 16 (June), 1–38.

Bordo, Susan (1999), *The Male Body: A New Look at Men in Public and in Private*, New York: Farrar, Straus and Giroux.

Bourdieu, Pierre (1989), *Outline of a Theory of Practice*, Cambridge: Cambridge University Press.

——— (1991), "Rites of Institution," in *Language and Symbolic Power*, ed. J. Thompson, Cambridge: Polity Press, 117–26.

——— (2001), *Masculine Domination*, Stanford, CA: Stanford University Press.

Brubaker, Sarah Jane and Jennifer J. Johnson (2008), "'Pack a More Powerful Punch' and 'Lay the Pipe': Erectile Enhancement Discourse as a Body Project for Masculinity," *Journal of Gender Studies*, 17 (2), 131–46.

Buerkle, C. Wesley (2009), "Metrosexuality Can Stuff It: Beef Consumption as (Heteromasculine) Fortification," *Text and Performance Quarterly*, 29 (1), 77–93.

Butler, Judith (1999 [1990]), *Gender Trouble: Feminism and the Subversion of Identity*, New York: Routledge.

Condry, Ian (2013), "Love Revolution: Anime, Masculinity, and the Future," in *Recreating Japanese Men*, ed. Sabine Frühstück and Anne Walthall, Los Angeles, CA: University of California Press.

Connell, Robert W. (1998), "Masculinities and Globalization," in *Men's Lives*, 5th edition, ed. M. Kimmel and M. Messner, Boston, MA: Allyn and Bacon, 56–70.

Connell, Robert W. and James W. Messerschmidt (2005), "Hegemonic Masculinity: Rethinking the Concept," *Gender and Society*, 19 (6), 829–59.

Creighton, Mille R. (1993), "Sweet Love" and Women's Place: Valentine's Day, Japan Style," *Journal of Popular Culture*, 27 (3), 1–19.

De Grazia, Victoria (1996), *The Sex of Things: Gender and Consumption in Historical Perspective*, Berkeley, CA: University of California Press.

Downing, Lisa (2008), *The Cambridge Introduction to Michel Foucault*, New York: Cambridge University Press.

Driessen, Henk (1983), "Male Sociability and Rituals of Masculinity in Rural Andalusia," *Anthropological Quarterly*, 56 (3), 125–33.

Durkheim, Émile (2008 [1912]), *The Elementary Forms of Religious Life*, Oxford: Oxford University Press.

Faludi, Susan (1999), *Stiffed: The Betrayal of the American Man*, New York: Williams Morrow.

Fischer, Eileen and Stephen J. Arnold (1990), "More Than a Labor of Love: Gender Roles and Christmas Gift Shopping," *Journal of Consumer Research*, 17 (3), 333–45.

Forty, Adrian (1986), *Objects of Desire: Design and Society from Wedgwood to IMB*, New York: Pantheon Books.

Foucault, Michel (1977), *Discipline and Punish: The Birth of the Prison*, New York: Pantheon Books.

——— (1988), "Technologies of the Self," in *Technologies of the Self: A Seminar with Michel Foucault*, ed. L. Martin, H. Gutman, and P. Hutton, Amherst, MA: University of Massachusetts Press, 14–49.

——— (1990 [1976]), *The History of Sexuality, Volume I: An Introduction*, New York: Vintage Books.

——— (1994 [1966]), *The Order of Things: An Archaeology of the Human Sciences*, New York: Vintage Books.

Frank, Katherine (2003), "'Just Trying to Relax': Masculinity, Masculinizing Practices, and Strip Club Regulars," *The Journal of Sex Research*, 40 (1), 61–75.

Galbraith, Patrick (2011), "Bishōjo Games: 'Techno-Intimacy' and the Virtually Human in Japan," *International Journal of Computer Game Research*, 11 (2), online edition.

——— (2014), *The Moé Manifesto: An Insider's Look at the Worlds of Manga, Anime, and Gaming*, Hong Kong: Peripus Editions.

Gennep, Arnold van (1960), *Rites of Passage*, Chicago: University of Chicago Press.

Gould, Stephen J. and Claudia Weil (1991), "Gift-Giving Roles and Gender Self-Concepts," *Sex Roles*, 24 (9/10), 617–37.

Granovetter, Mark (1985), "Economic Action and Social Structure: The Problem of Embeddedness," *The American Journal of Sociology*, 91 (3), 481–510.

Grazian, David (2007), "The Girl Hunt: Urban Nightlife and the Performance of Masculinity as Collective Activity," *Symbolic Interaction*, 30 (2), 221–43.

Holt, Douglas and Craig J. Thompson (2004), "Man-of-Action Heroes: The Pursuit of Heroic Masculinity in Everyday Consumption," *Journal of Consumer Research*, 31 (2), 425–40.

Ishii-Kuntz, Masako (2003), "Balancing Fatherhood and Work: Emergence of Diverse Masculinities in Contemporary Japan," in *Men and Masculinities in Contemporary Japan: Dislocating the Salaryman Doxa*, ed. J. Roberson and N. Suzuki, New York: Routledge Curzon, 198–216.

Ito, Kimio (1993), *"Otokorashisa" no yukue: Dansei bunka no bunka shakai-gaku* [The Traces of "Masculinity": Cultural Sociology of Men's Culture], Tokyo: Shinyōsha.

Ito, Mikio (1984), "Josetsu: Nihon ni okeru zōtoh no kenkyu" [Introduction: Studies on Gift Giving in Japanese Society], in *Nihon jin no zōtoh* [Gift Giving of Japanese], ed. M. Ito and Y. Kurita, Kyoto: Mineruva shobō, 1–16.

———— (1995), *Zōtoh kōkan no jinruigaku* [Anthropology of Gift Exchange], Tokyo: Chikuma shobō.

Kendall, Gavin and Gary Wickham (1999), *Using Foucault's Methods*, Thousand Oaks, CA: Sage Publications.

Kitakata, Haruko, Saori Oishi, Takuya Kimura, Takuya Kikuta, and Yum hae jung (2012), "A Contemporary Image of 'Masculinity' and the Role of Japanese Men's Magazines since 1980s with a Focus on Men's NON-NO," *Fukushoku Bunka Kyodo Kenkyu Saishu Hokoku*, (2013–03), 78–85.

Kohyama, Susumu (1999), "Sei no shohinka to shohin kachi: jenda wo shoten ni shite" [Commercialization of Sexuality and Commercial Value: A Focus on Gender], *Hikone Ronso*, 317, 153–77.

———— (2001), "Sei no shohin ka to shohin kachi: romanchikku rabu wo shoten ni shite" [Commercialization of Sexuality and Commercial Value: A Focus on Romantic Love], *Hikone Ronso*, 333, 43–67.

Marcoux, Jean-Sebastien (2009), "Escaping the Gift Economy," *Journal of Consumer Research*, 36 (December), 671–85.

Marvasti, Amir B. (2004), *Qualitative Research in Sociology*, Thousand Oaks, CA: Sage Publications.

Mathews, Gordon (2003), "Can 'a Real Man' Live for His Family? *Ikigai* and Masculinity in Today's Japan," in *Men and Masculinities in Contemporary Japan: Dislocating the Salaryman Doxa*, ed. J. Roberson and N. Suzuki, New York: Routledge Curzon, 108–25.

McGinnis, Lee Phillip, James Gentry, and Julia McQuillan (2009), "Ritual-Based Behavior That Reinforces Hegemonic Masculinity in Golf: Variations in Women Golfers' Responses," *Leisure Sciences*, 31 (1), 19–36.

Minowa, Yuko and Russell W. Belk (2017), "Ad Hoc Japonisme: How National Rhetorics Work in Japanese Advertising," *Consumption, Markets and Culture*, 20 (2), 1–21.

Minowa, Yuko and Stephen J. Gould (1999), "Love My Gift, Love Me or Is It Love Me, Love My Gift: A Study of the Cultural Construction of Romantic Gift Giving among Japanese Couples," in *Advances in Consumer Research*, Vol. 26, ed. E. Arnould and L. Scott, Provo, UT: Association for Consumer Research, 119–24.

Minowa, Yuko, Olga Khomenko, and Russell W. Belk (2011), "Social Change and Gendered Gift-Giving Rituals: A Historical Analysis of Valentine's Day in Japan," *Journal of Macromarketing*, 31 (1), 41–56.

Miyadai, Shinji, Izumi Tsuji, and Takayuki Okai (eds.) (2009), *"Otokorashisa" no kairaku: popura karucha kara mita jittai* [Pleasure of "Manhood": The True State from the Perspective of Popular Culture], Tokyo: Keisō shobō.

Mortelmans, Dimitri and Dave Sinardet (2004), "The Role of Gender in Gift Buying in Belgium," *Journal of Family and Consumer Sciences*, 96 (2), 34–9.

Muir, Kenneth B. and Trina Seitz (2004), "Machismo, Misogyny, and Homophobia in a Male Athletic Subculture: A Participant-Observation Study of Deviant Rituals in Collegiate Rugby," *Deviant Behavior*, 25 (4), 303–27.

Nakamura, Momoko (2007), *"Sei" to Nihongo: Kotoba ga tsukuru otoko to onna* [Gender and Japanese: Men and Women Constructed by Language], Tokyo: Nihon hōsō shuppan kyōkai.

Newman, Peter J. and Michelle Nelson (1996), "Mainstream Legitimization of Homosexual Men through Valentine's Day Gift-Giving and Consumption Rituals," *Journal of Homosexuality*, 31 (1/2), 57–69.

Obinata, Sumio (2006), "Sōron: Tsukurareta otoko no kiseki" [Introduction: The Locus of Well-Wrought Men], in *Dansei-shi II: Modanizumu kara sosenryokue* [History of Men, Volume 2: From Modernism to Full War Potential], ed. T. Abe, S. Obinata, and M. Amano, Tokyo: Nihon keizai hyōronsha, 1–23.

Ogasawara, Yoko (1998), *Office Ladies and Salaried Men: Power, Gender, and Works in Japanese Companies*, Berkeley, CA: University of California Press.

Otnes, Cele, Judy A. Ruth, and Constance C. Milbourne (1994), "The Pleasure and Pain of Being Close: Men's Mixed Feelings about Participation in Valentine's Day Gift Exchange," in *Advances in Consumer Research*, Vol. 21, ed. C. Allen and D. John, Provo, UT: Association for Consumer Research, 159–64.

Prior, Lindsay (1997), "Following in Foucault's Footsteps: Text and Context in Qualitative Research," in *Qualitative Research: Theory, Method and Practice*, ed. D. Silverman, Thousand Oaks, CA: Sage Publications, 63–79.

Rucker, Margaret, Anthony Freitas, and Jamie Dolstra (1994), "A Toast for the Host? The Male Perspective on Gifts That Say Thank You," *Advances in Consumer Research*, 21, 165–8.

Rucker, Margaret, Anthony Freitas, Deborah Murray, and Harriet Parto (1991), "Gender Stereotypes and Gift Failures: When the Sweets Don't Want Sweets," *Gender and Consumer Behavior*, Vol. 1, ed. Janeen Costa, Salt Lake City, UT: University of Utah, 244–52.

Rugimbana, Robert, Brett Donahay, Christopher Neal, and Michael J. Polonski (2003), "The Role of Social Power Relations in Gift Giving in Valentine's Day," *Journal of Consumer Behaviour*, 3 (September), 63–73.

Rupp, Katherine (2003), *Gift-Giving in Japan: Cash, Connections, Cosmologies*, Stanford, CA: Stanford University Press.

Ruth, Judy A., Cele Otnes, and Frédéric F. Brunel (1999), "Gift Receipt and Reformulation of Interpersonal Relationships," *Journal of Consumer Research*, 25 (4), 385–402.

Schouten, John and James H. McAlexander (1995), "Subcultures of Consumption: An Ethnography of New Bikers," *Journal of Consumer Research*, 22 (June), 43–61.

Schrift, Alan D. (1994), "Reconfiguring the Subject: Foucault's Analytics of Power," in *Reconstructing Foucault: Essays in the Wake of the 80s*, ed. R. Miguel-Alfonso and S. Caporale-Bizzini, Atlanta, GA: Rodopi, 185–99.

Scott, Rebecca, Julien Cayla, and Eric Arnould (2017), "Selling Pain to the Saturated Self," *Journal of Consumer Research*, 41 (1), 22–43.

Sherry, John F. (1983), "Gift Giving in Anthropological Perspective," *Journal of Consumer Research*, 10 (September), 157–68.

Sherry, John F., Mary Ann McGrath, and Sidney Levy (1993), "The Dark Side of the Gift," *Journal of Business Research*, 28 (3), 225–44.

Slater, Don (1997), *Consumer Culture & Modernity*, Cambridge: Polity Press.

Spark, Penny (1995), *As Long as It's Pink: The Sexual Politics of Taste*, London: Pandora.

Sugii, Shizuko (2008), *Kakusa shakai wo ikiru: Otoko to onna no shin jendā-ron* [Living the Society with Disparity: New Gender Theory for Men and Women], Kyoto: Kamogawa shuppan.

Taga, Futoshi (2006a), *Otokorashisa no shakaigaku* [Sociology of Masculinity], Kyoto: Sekai shisōsha.

———— (2006b), "Tsukurareru otoko no raifusaikuru" [The Lifecycle of Gendered Men], in *"Otokorashisa" no gendaishi* [Contemporary History of "Masculinity"], ed. T. Abe, S. Obinata, and M. Amano, Tokyo: Nihon keizai hyōronsha, 158–90.

Taylor, Chloë (2009), *The Culture of Confession from Augustine to Foucault: A Genealogy of the "Confessing Animal,"* New York: Routledge.

Taylor, Emily (2007), "Dating-Simulation Games: Leisure and Gaming of Japanese Youth Culture," *Southeast Review of Asian Studies*, 29, 192–208.

Thompson, Craig J. and Daniel L. Haytko (1997), "Speaking of Fashion: Consumers' Uses of Fashion Discourses and the Appropriation of Countervailing Cultural Meanings," *Journal of Consumer Research*, 24 (June), 15–42.

Warde, Alan (2005), "Consumption and Theories of Practice," *Journal of Consumer Culture*, 5 (2), 131–53.

Williams, Clover Nolan (1994), "The Bachelor's Transgression," *Journal of American Folklore*, 107 (423), 106–20.

Zelizer, Vivian (2005), *Purchase of Intimacy*, Princeton, NJ: Princeton University Press.

7 Romantic Gifts as an Expression of Masculinity Amongst Young Men With Disabilities in Zimbabwe

Tafadzwa Rugoho

Introduction

The World Bank (2011) estimated that 15% of the global population are people with disabilities. It further estimates that disabled youths are between 180 and 200 million. The majority of people with disabilities are in developing countries (Bogart, Tickle-Degnen, and Ambady 2012; Naami 2015). Youths with disabilities endure psychological and emotional pain as they are bullied, discriminated, and ill-treated by many communities (Lindsay and McPherson 2012). Thus, they are shunned and isolated (Green et al. 2005). In other parts of the world such as Southern Africa, communities were socialized to discriminate against people with disabilities. This is largely expressed in their language, proverbs, culture, and beliefs. People with disabilities are seen as cursed or useless. To compound this discrimination on people with disabilities, the colonial government established institutions for the care of people with disabilities. This reinforced the belief that people with disabilities are sick. They were now treated as people without agency. When isolated from their families and community, their rights were also limited. Institutions made them follow a rigid routine of living.

One area in which institutions disadvantaged people with disabilities was socialization especially in issues to do with love. Most institutions caring for people with disabilities were run by missionaries (White 2014). These missionaries, who in most cases were running institutions for people with disabilities, were monks and nuns. Monks and nuns are people who are believed to have taken a sacred oath and are seen as clean. They shun any romantic relationship and sexual activity. Literature is mute on how people with disabilities indulged in sexual and romantic relationships under the watchful eyes of nuns and monks. The area has received little academic attention as to how people with disabilities quenched their sexual desires under these institutions. Historically, people with disabilities were seen as broken objects. Ellis (2014) observed that they were never treated as normal and ordinary beings by their families and communities. Furthermore, Rugoho and Siziba

(2014) noted that they were treated as second-class citizens. People with disabilities were regarded as asexual (Milligan and Neufeldt 2001). They were seen as lacking the mental stamina to engage in any sexual and romantic relationship. This view of treating people with disabilities has hence hampered the global fight against HIV and AIDS, as observed by Bankole and Malarcher (2010).

With the general increasing protection of people with disabilities and their rights, the world was forced to introduce a number of laws for the promotions of rights of people with disabilities. Recently, the United Nations adopted the Convention on the Rights of Persons with Disabilities. This Convention is now part of the international human rights law (Hoffman, Sritharan, and Tejpar 2016; Szmukler, Daw, and Callard 2014). The Convention on the Rights of Persons with Disabilities (CRPD) gives elaborate rights on the areas of marriage and sexuality of people with disabilities. The convention does not see sex as a secondary issue but as a primary issue. Thus, people with disabilities should be given the opportunity to access their civil and social rights. Shakespeare (2006) argued that when people have access to their civil and social rights they have confidence, self-esteem and desirability that make relationships possible. Just like their able-bodied counterparts, the Convention explicitly emphasizes that sexual and reproductive rights of people with disabilities be promoted and guaranteed. As the rights of people are improving, they now have access to self-independence and control through employment and education. It is of great importance to understand the context and outcomes of demands for choice and agency over sexuality and relationships. There have been worldwide campaigns, lobbying, and debates focused on recognizing people with disabilities as sexual beings with equal rights to aspirations for romance, sexual pleasure, love, friendship, intimacy, relationships, and sexual and reproductive choices (Addlakha, Price, and Heidari 2017).

People with disabilities who are in sexual relationships have different experiences just like their non-disabled fellows. According to Rugoho and Maphosa (2017), in their study on challenges faced by women with disabilities in accessing sexual and reproductive health in Zimbabwe, each type of disability has got its own challenges. Some people with disabilities are involved in romantic relationships with non-disabled people, while some have chosen their fellows with disabilities. The choice of a partner with or without disability largely depends on personal experiences or perceptions. Salehi et al. (2015) argued that self-esteem is important for people with disabilities to enter into any sexual relationship. Some disabilities make men less comfortable to express their sexual feelings (Janus 2009). Other people with disabilities are demotivated to enter into romantic relationships because they fear they would not be able to cope with the demands of sex.

People with disabilities face a number of challenges, especially in developing countries. Those with mobility challenges face challenges from moving from one place to another. Nosek et al. (2001) observed that having a physical disability which inhibits your mobility limits the opportunity for sexual adventure and activity. Some people with physical disabilities require the assistance of others in mobility and communication. This weighs on their privacy hence becoming hard to maintain sexual relations (Gartrell, Baesel, and Becker 2017). Issues of unfriendly or inaccessible houses and transport also discourage people with disabilities to engage in romantic relationships. In Southern Africa, where the current study is located, marriage is greatly valued. For those who failed to enter into marriage, marriages were arranged. Rugoho (2017a) observed that communities used to arrange marriages for their members with disabilities. However, parents of women with disabilities were reluctant to let their children get married for they feared that they would be abused (Gartrell et al. 2017).

The present chapter seeks to understand how young men with disabilities express their masculinity when they are in romantic relationships. Could gift buying be an expression of masculinity? If so, where do they buy such gifts? Communities get anxious when they see young men with disabilities buying romantic gifts (Rugoho 2017b). How do men with disabilities deal with such negative perceptions? It is of paramount importance in this chapter to seek to understand how such gifts are sustained by taking into consideration that they face marginalization in employment and entrepreneurship opportunities. In drawing data, the author will relate to his personal experience as a family young man with disability and also his experience as a family therapist having worked with young people with disabilities over the last ten years. Data will also be drawn from five focus group discussions the author conducted with young men with disabilities.

The Convention on the Rights of Persons With Disabilities

On December 13, 2006, the Convention on the Rights of Persons with Disabilities and its optional protocol was adopted by the United Nations. There were 82 signatories to the Convention, 44 signatories to the Optional Protocol, and ratification of the Convention. The Convention on the Rights of Persons with Disabilities brought a paradigm shift in disability issues. The convention took a rights-based approach to disability issues (Rugoho and Maphosa 2017; Skempes and Bickenbach 2015). The convention called for governments to outlaw all cultural, political, and religious practices which discriminated against people with disabilities. This include allowing people with disabilities to enter into romantic relationships and marriages. Nations were mandated to protect people with disabilities from all forms of abuse including forced marriages and domestic violence.

Zimbabwe ratified the CRPD and its Optional Protocol on September 23, 2013, but it has not yet domesticated it as required by its constitution (Rugoho and Maphosa 2015). While sexual and reproductive issues have become of importance in the twenty-first century, very little has been done for people with disabilities (Rugoho and Maphosa 2017). People with disabilities still face challenges the world over in accessing issues of sexual and reproductive health (Burke et al. 2017). Rugoho and Maphosa (2017) in a study on sexual and reproductive health for women with disabilities, noted that accessing information and discrimination are some of challenges that are faced by women with disabilities.

Masculinity and Gift Buying

A substantial number of scholars have written about the intersection of disability and masculinity (Lipenga 2014). While masculinity is a contested term, Shuttleworth, Wedgwood, and Wilson (2012) noted that there is conflict where disability and masculinity intersect because disability is associated with being dependent and helpless whereas masculinity is associated with being powerful and autonomous, thus creating a lived and embodied dilemma for disabled men. Shah (2017) observed that disability potentially negates sexuality, and this results in communities perceiving disabled people as asexual or not having the capacity of engaging in sexual or romantic relationships with another person. As Porter (1997) notes,

> a disabled body seems to be lacking something essential, something to make it identifiable and something to identify with; a body that is deficiently itself, not quite a body in the full sense of the word, not real enough," and in turn "potentially absent of sexual identity."
>
> [P12]

Gordon (1995) has argued against the use of the term masculinity after he observed that there are a lot of masculinities that are exhibited by men from different cultures and classes. He argued that not all males can be grouped in one category. There are competing masculinities. Some are hegemonically marginalized and stigmatized. Each of these masculinities have different structural, psychosocial, and cultural moorings as noted by Gordon (1995). However, this multiplicity of masculinities is partially informed by "a system of internal dominance in which a minority of men dominates the masses of men." The desire to dominate forms what Connell and Messerschmidt (2005) labeled as hegemonic masculinity. Scholars and researchers of disability have analyzed the relationship between gender identity and ability. Gender has remained as one of the major first social categories that socialize children in today's societies about issues of gender (Steffens and Viladot 2015) and into adulthood, with both adolescents and college students construing their self-concepts in line with the gender stereotypes they have internalized (Nosek et al. 2001; Steffens, Kirschbaum, and Glados 2008). Murnen and Kohlman (2007) favor calling it hegemonic masculinity. Hegemonic masculinity forms a hierarchy of different types of masculinity and those few men that embody the most archaic forms of masculinity are seen as leaders (Connell and Messerschmidt 2005).

Gifts are exchanged in romantic relationships for a variety of reasons. Ertimur and Sandikci (2005) noted that gift-giving is a topic that has received significant attention from consumer behavior researchers. Sherry (1983) has looked at the process of gift-giving; Belk (1982) and Otnes, Lowrey, and Kim (1993) focused on search time and the effort of givers, while Belk and Coon (1993) looked at gift-giving and dating behavior. In a nutshell, different authors have looked at a wide variety of issues concerning gifts (Sherry 1983). Sherry and McGrath (1989) have looked the agenda used in giving gifts. What motivates individual or groups to give gifts? Belk (1976) found that the major reason why people give gifts is to fulfill the cultural norms or general expectations. Ruth, Otnes, and Brunel (1999) also noted that giving gifts may be a way of communicating social relationships. Ertimur and Sandikci (2005) assert that gifts provide symbolic value in the sense that thought and effort were put into their selection, and that gifts of cash or gift certificates appear inappropriate, impersonal, and too materialistic unless they are given in certain context such as romantic relationships. Gifts can also be seen as a demonstration power or masculinity.

Men with disabilities in sexual and romantic relationships have taken the breadwinner role as a way of expressing their masculinities. As noted by Willer (2005), masculinity can be demonstrated by the notion of "bread winning." Men are expected to be providers when in romantic relationships. Men with disabilities have understood this and have always tried to impress their women. Not only do they buy romantic gifts, but they should be seen as occupying the role of the breadwinner in the relationship. They provide their women with accommodation, food, and other amenities. By playing the breadwinning role, males with disabilities feel that they are in charge of the relationship and they are "man enough." As noted by Willer (2005) the failure to provide the breadwinning role unsettles men. Phoenix and Frosh (2001) have demonstrated that men in different situations and different societies demonstrate their masculinities differently. Those who are in poverty or staying in slums also have their own way of showing their masculinities. In this study men with disabilities showed that breadwinner hood was a common denominator. Although they are struggling economically, without jobs and reliable sources of income, men with disabilities I studied celebrated and clung doggedly to provider masculinity, pursuing it in different ways. They frequently mentioned how "real men" provided adequately for themselves and their lovers. For them, a real man are those who are able to spoil their lovers; and buying romantic gifts shows the women that their men are capable. The ability to buy gifts distinguishes "real" men from others. Real men are defined by their capacity to provide.

> One respondent put it like this, "if you are a man and you are unable to provide for your woman or to buy her romantic gifts, you are useless. You are a woman. Remember that these gifts will also give the woman some sort of confidence in you. How will a woman take you seriously when you are unable even to buy flowers, chocolates, and other gifts on special occasions such as her birthdays or Valentine's Day?"

Evidence from these young men with disabilities clearly suggested that the belief in breadwinner manliness was incredibly strong. Being a breadwinner separates real men from other men. For young men with disabilities, the time to demonstrate that you are a man by your physical appearance has since lapsed. Women are no longer interested by masculine bodies. At the global level, as noted by Amuyunzu-Nyamongo and Francis (2006); Coughlin and Wade (2012); Gavanas (2004); and Silberschmidt (2001), men are still defined in terms of provision, family headship, marriage, and community leadership. Even poor men would also want to define themselves as providers for their families, wives, and community. The masculinities that are being expressed by men with disabilities are therefore not unique from global trends and tendencies. What could be noted was the difference in the kinds of strategic cultural materials, resources, practices, norms, and values that men with disabilities relied on to achieve their masculine identities and breadwinner hood.

Narratives by young men with disabilities demonstrate that "real" men are those who are able to have lovers and provide them with material goods. Others may have families or marriages as a way of demonstrating masculinity. Men with disabilities think that marriages can be arranged for people with disabilities hence marriages are not a true reflection of masculinity. Groce et al. (2014) observed that in many societies, people with disabilities are entering arranged marriages. These arranged marriages are usually influenced by family members. Hence, men with disabilities consider marriage important in demonstrating masculinities but they do not see it superseding the capacity to provide or play the breadwinning role.

> *You can't claim to be a real man because you have a marriage. That one is debatable. Many of people with disabilities have arranged marriages. The church or family may arrange a marriage for you.*

All things like bride price paid by the family. And such a man who is being provided for by his family cannot claim to be a man. A man is the one who is able to stand on his own. A man will be seen buying romantic gifts for his girlfriend. In arranged relationships, it's hard to buy those romantic gifts because you will know quite well that's it's not because of your effort to be in that romantic relationship. It is the effort of others. Any man who relies on the effort of others cannot claim to be a "real" man.

Another participant added "When I buy her romantic gifts, I feel man enough. A man should be able to provide for his lover. When I buy gifts to my girlfriend I feel complete. I feel that I am a real man."

Men with disabilities have also expressed their masculinity by having several girlfriends just like other men without disabilities. Zulu, Dodoo, and Chika-Ezeh (2002) in their studies in Nairobi among men who stay in slums also noted a similar trend of having multiple girlfriends, extramarital affairs and multiple sexual partnerships, found that poor women are lured into transactional sex. However, when having multiple partners, these men still have to play the breadwinner's role to demonstrate their ability. Men with disabilities believe that women are like a battle field were the fittest will win the most beautiful women. For any man to win in this game, he had to demonstrate possession of a fat pocket, which is shown by buying romantic gifts.

In an unpublished research by Rugoho (2017b) on the expression of masculinity by men with disabilities, he noted that some demonstrate their masculinity in engaging in different sexual positions. Sex is not only an act of procreation but also one of dominance that demonstrates the ability to tame one another. To young men with disabilities, the ability to engage in certain sexual positions demonstrates that they are macho. Practising the missionary position shows that you are a subdued man. Men with disabilities have been practising many sexual positions which demonstrates their endurance, hence showing their masculinity.

Types of Romantic Gifts

Many gifts that are bought by men with disabilities have some gold component within them. Some may not be pure gold but will resemble gold. Gold is highly valued in Zimbabwe (Kanyenze et al. 2011). Historically, it was one of the minerals which demonstrated wealth and men who had access to gold had access to many women. It is a major investment, adornment, and gift item in Zimbabwean and African communities. In fact, Zimbabwe has quite a number of gold mines. Gold confers some status. Those who are seen with gold products are admired and respected in the community. For a man to give such a gift shows his ability to provide. Gold watches, bangles, necklaces, and earrings are some of the golden gifts that are bought by men with disabilities in order to impress their women.

Flowers and romance are linked and traditionally have been seen as a way to the woman's heart. Different flowers have different meanings. Most commonly, they're tied to romance, prosperity, and bashfulness. Men with disabilities are seen buying flowers on different occasions. During Valentines they also buy a lot of red roses. For them, buying this flowers is a sign of ability, as one of my participants pointed out,

> We all know that there are two types of flowers. There are the artificial ones and the genuine ones. If you see a man buying the artificial one, he is not a genuine man. He is fake. Personally, I buy original flowers. Fresh from the garden. When you buy those ones women will see that you value them. They will not only appreciate them, but they will regard you as a man. Usually, original flowers do not last long, so you will be communicating the message that "I can afford it." Unlike the artificial ones which can be kept for years. If you see a man giving his woman an artificial flower, that person is not worth being called a man.

Some people see Valentine's Day as a special time to express their love and admiration of each other. This is the time to buy each other romantic gifts. It's the correct season of expressing love. On Valentine's Day, flowers are some of the gifts that are purchased by men with disabilities to impress their women. For them, a flower symbolizes the understanding of what it means to love someone. Men with disabilities buy different gifts which range in cost. However, they usually tried to buy expensive gifts. Expensive gifts are associated with the ability to access the means of production. It is men of status who are able to access money. Another participant said,

> For me, buying my girlfriends these romantic gifts separates me from other men with disabilities. Some men with disabilities are always crying, that they are not being loved and that they are being scolded by women. But for me, I can compete even with able-bodied men. Actually, all the ladies that I have dated have always complimented me that I am a hustler.

The Role of Social Media

Social media has transformed communities in terms of accessing informations. Jackson (2010) observed that social media had both negative and positive impacts on romantic relationships. It has destroyed some relationships while cementing others. Social media greatly help people with disabilities to get access to information, especially on love and romantic issues. In Africa, people rarely talk of romantic relationships with people with disabilities. There are a number of reasons why communities or families are not comfortable with discussing love and romantic relationship with their members with disabilities. One of the reasons is that disability is viewed as a sickness. Sick people are often assumed not to have the mental or physical strength to cope with the demands of a sexual relationship. Historically people with disabilities were forbidden to enter into any sexual relationship. Some communities and families will do anything in their power to destroy such relationships. In schools, people with disabilities were excluded when there was a discussion on issues of sexuality, as noted in Rugoho and Maphosa (2017).This arrangement made it difficult for people with disabilities to access information on sexuality.

Social media has also allowed men with disabilities to join dating sites. In Zimbabwe, dating sites are still in their infant stages. However, quite a number of them have been established. The majority of these sites are found in two large cities of Zimbabwe (Harare and Bulawayo). Dating sites such as Chachaya Dating, DatingBuzz Zimbabwe, Zim Hookup, and Topface are patronized by males with disabilities. Those with Christian backgrounds will also visit a dating site called Zimbabwe Christian Dating Site. These sites have played a critical role in linking people who are in search of partners. Besides linking partners, the sites also offer valuable tips on how to be romantic. They teach on the type of gifts that women would want their partners to buy for them. Social media has enabled access to information. A participant said,

> It's hard to ask people what type of romantic gifts you can buy for your girlfriend. The do not expect me as a disabled person to have a girlfriend. It's hard to ask even my siblings. If I ask them, they will make a mountain out of an anthill. So for me, the social media has been my source of information. I belong to many social groups. During special occasions such as Valentine's people advertise romantic gifts that they are selling. Some even offer advice on how to make your partner happy.

Another added,

> I once had this relationship with a beautiful girl. She was from affluent family and I am from a humble background. At first I was clueless on what type of romantic gifts I could buy for her. Even places where we could have romantic dinners and lunches. I could sense that she was not happy with the type of gifts that I was buying. I then started joining some social media groups. At first I was afraid to ask but eventually I presented my scenario. I started getting

some tips. And it worked. Eventfully she was happy and appreciated the presents I gave her. Social media has made love life easier for us people with disabilities. Sometimes you are stuck when you don't know romantic messages to write on your presents, it is easy now. It's there on social media. People are willing to help. I don't know if they knew I was on a wheelchair.

Sustainability

Zimbabwe's economy has been declining over the past 15 years. Industries are closing on a yearly basis. Prices are going up as business people struggle to remain in business. There is no reliable estimate of the unemployment percentage for people with disabilities. The country's unemployment levels are estimated to be over 90%. With such national unemployment, one can only conclude that the percentages are even higher for people with disabilities. Zimbabwe does not have a policy on the employment of people with disabilities. People with disabilities struggle to get employed. As noted by Rugoho and Siziba (2014), even degreed people with disabilities are not hired by employers. The majority of people with disabilities with qualifications have started begging and vending as a way of getting livelihoods. Employers have negative attitudes. A participant said,

> I am a hustler. I may be disabled but I know how to look for money. I may have not have education and a good paying job, but I know how to spoil girlfriends. This makes it hard for women to ditch me.

Buying romantic gifts has resulted in some young people with disabilities getting into debt. They borrow money from friends and family in order to impress their women. This phenomenon had led some of these youth into a cycle of debt. When they get money, instead of investing the money, it is used to pay the debts. Due to the fact that many of them are not formally employed and rely on part-time jobs and vending, they are unable to save money to invest in productive enterprises for they are always preoccupied by buying these romantic gifts. Romantic relationships need to be sustained.

The Compensatory Behavior

People with disabilities had been found to indulge in compensatory behavior, Bogart et al. (2012). When people with disabilities realize that their impairments have been identified, many of them feel the necessity to overcompensate in order to cope with the notion of being disabled. Stocker (2001) described her experience as a disabled person by saying she felt the need to work harder to outperform her able-bodied peers. In Rugoho and Jeffress (2018), Rugoho describes his teaching experience as a disabled lecturer. He worked hard in research and publishing as a way of showing that he is able to do things better than non-disabled lecturers. To him, he had to overcompensate so that he would suffer less discrimination from his students. Cook (2001) discusses the occurrence of people with psychological impairments taking the identity of "survivor" to cope with their disabling conditions, pushing themselves to overcome obstacles. These experiences are also similar to young men in romantic relationships. They are buying romantic gifts as compensatory materials. One participant said,

> I have no option, if I don't buy she will see the disability in me. I have to push myself to perform. I buy these romantic gifts so that she does not see me as a disabled person.

Public Perception

The public is fascinated when they see people with disabilities buying romantic gifts. Men with disabilities have confirmed that they are often stared at when they buy romantic gifts in shops, and at gardens when buying flowers. Some people will go as far as whistling when they see men with disabilities buying these gifts. One of my participants put it clearly as,

> People will stare at you when they see you buying romantic gifts. Some will ask you if you have managed to get love. I felt embarrassed at first but with time I have developed a thick skin. I am no longer afraid of being stared at. People will talk in whispers. But do we have any options? Not if you are stopped from buying romantic gifts for your women.

Conclusion

The issue of masculinity expression is strong within young, disabled men in Zimbabwe. Society feels pity for them but also discriminates them. Men with disabilities have the desire to show their masculinity. However, they have limited space to show their masculinity. The love world presented the opportunity for them to demonstrate and exercise their masculinity. Just like men without disabilities, they enjoy being in charge of the relationship. They enjoy dominance in a relationship. For those in love, this has presented them with an opportunity to show their masculinity. They do so through buying romantic gifts. The buying of gifts gives them the assurance that they are still men and have the capacity to look after their loved ones. However, in buying these gifts, they face discomfort when buying from traditional shops. Sales people and other members of the public become fascinated and anxious when they see people with disabilities buying romantic gifts. A lot of questions are posed to them. Some members of the public would even want to know if they are engaging in any sexual relationship. Social media has helped people with disabilities to avoid being asked such embarrassing questions, as they are now able to purchase such gifts via social media. Social media has thus provided them with a lot of opportunities, ranging from access to information on types of gifts to buy and places where one can get such presents. Presents are tied to expenditures and these expenditures need to be financed and sustained, which causes more difficulties due to the higher levels of unemployment prevailing amongst people with disabilities.

References

Addlakha, Renu, Janet Price, and Shirin Heidari (2017), "Disability and Sexuality: Claiming Sexual and Reproductive Rights," *Reproductive Health Matters*, 50 (May), 4–9.

Amuyunzu-Nyamongo, Mary, and Paul Francis (2006), "Collapsing Livelihoods and the Crisis of Masculinity in Rural Kenya," in *The Other Half of Gender: Men's Issues in Development*, ed. I. Bannon and M. Correia, Washington, DC: World Bank, 219–44.

Bankole, Akinrinola and Shawn Malarcher (2010), "Removing Barriers to Adolescents' Access to Contraceptive Information and Service," *Studies in Family Planning*, 41 (June), 117–23.

Belk, Russell W. (1976), "It's the Thought That Counts: A Signed Digraph Analysis of Gift-Giving," *Journal of Consumer Research*, 3 (December), 155–62.

——— (1982), "Effects of Gift-Giving Involvement on Gift Selection Strategies," in *Advances in Consumer Research*, ed. M. Andrew and A. Ann, London: Association for Consumer Research, 408–12.

Belk, Russell W. and Gregory S. Coon (1993), "Gift Giving as Agapic Love: An Alternative to the Exchange Paradigm Based on Dating Experiences," *Journal of Consumer Research*, 3 (December), 393–417.

Bogart, Kathleen R., Linda Tickle-Degnen, and Nalini Ambady (2012), "Compensatory Expressive Behavior for Facial Paralysis: Adaptation to Congenital or Acquired Disability," *Rehabilitation Psychology*, 54 (February), 43–51.

Burke, Eva, Kébé Fatau, Iise Flink, Miranda van Reeuwijk, and M. Alex le May (2017), "A Qualitative Study to Explore the Barriers and Enablers for Young People with Disabilities to Access Sexual and Reproductive Health Services in Senegal," *Reproduction Health Matters*, 25 (May), 43–54.

Connell, Raewyn W. and James W. Messerschmidt (2005), "Hegemonic Masculinity Rethinking the Concept," *Gender and Society*, 57 (February), 829–59.

Cook, B. G. (2001), "A Comparison of Teachers' Attitudes Towards Their Included Students with Mild and Severe Disabilities," *The Journal of Special Education*, 34, 203–13.

Coughlin, Patrick and Jay C. Wade (2012), "Masculinity Ideology, Income Disparity, and Romantic Relationship Quality among Men with Higher Earning Female Partners," *Sex Roles*, 67 (June), 311–22.

Ellis, Katie M. (2014), "Cripples, Bastards and Broken Things: Disability in Game of Thrones," *Journal of Media and Culture*, 17 (5), 34–48.

Ertimur, Burcak and Ozlem Sandikci (2005), "Giving Gold Jewellery and Coins as Gifts: The Interplay of Utilitarianism and Symbolism," *Advances in Consumer Research*, 32 (May), 322–7.

Gartrell, Alexandra, Klaus Baesel, and Cornelia Becker (2017), "We Do Not Dare to Love: Women with Disabilities' Sexual and Reproductive Health and Rights in Rural Cambodia," *Journal of Reproductive Health Matter*, 25 (May), 32–42.

Gavanas, Anna (2004), "Domesticating Masculinity and Masculinizing Domesticity in Contemporary U.S. Fatherhood Politics," *Social Politics*, 11 (August), 247–66.

Gordon, David F. (1995), "Testicular Cancer and Masculinity," in *Men's Health and Illness: Gender, Power and the Body*, ed. D. Sabo and D. F. Gordon, London: Sage Publications, 123–40.

Green, Sara, Christine Davis, Elana Karshmer, Pete Marsh, and Benjamin Straight (2005), "Living Stigma: The Impact of Labeling, Stereotyping, Separation, Status Loss, and Discrimination in the Lives of Individuals with Disabilities and Their Families," *Sociological Inquiry*, 75 (2), 197–215.

Groce, Nora, Barbara Murray, Marie Loeb, Carlo Tramontano, Jean F. Trani, and Asfaw Mekonnen (2014), *Disabled Beggars in Addis Ababa: Current Situation and Prospects for Change*, Geneva: International Labour Organization, United Nations.

Hoffman, Steven J., Lathika Sritharan, and Ali Tejpar (2016), "Is the UN Convention on the Rights of Persons with Disabilities Impacting Mental Health Laws and Policies in High-Income Countries? A Case Study of Implementation in Canada," *BMC International Health and Human Rights*, 11 (November), 1–18.

Jackson, Jeffrey B. (2010), "Premarital Couple Predictors of Marital Relationship Quality and Stability: A Meta-Analytic Study," *Dissertation Abstracts International Section*, 9 (December), 33–6.

Janus, Alexander L. (2009), "Disability and the Rransition to Adulthood," *Social Forces*, 88 (September), 99–120.

Kanyenze, Godfrey, Timothy Kondo, Prosper Chitambara, and James Martens (2011), *Beyond the Enclave: Towards a Pro-Poor and Inclusive Development Strategy for Zimbabwe*, Harare: Labour and Economic Research Institute of Zimbabwe and Alternatives to Neo-Liberalism in Southern Africa.

Lindsay, Sally I. and Amy C. McPherson (2012), "Experiences of Social Exclusion and Bullying at School among Children and Youth with Cerebral Palsy," *Disability Rehabilitation*, 34 (May), 101–9.

Lipenga, Ken J. (2014), "Disability and Masculinity in South African Autosomatography," *African Journal of Disability*, 3 (April), 1–11.

Milligan, Maureen S. and Alfred H. Neufeldt (2001), "The Myth of Asexuality: A Survey of Social and Empirical Evidence," *Sexuality and Disability*, 14 (August), 91–109.

Murnen, Sarah K. and Marla H. Kohlman (2007), "Athletic Participation, Fraternity Membership, and Sexual Aggression among College Men: A Meta-Analytic Review," *Sex Roles*, 57 (April), 145–57.

Naami, Augustina (2015), "Disability, Gender, and Employment Relationships in Africa: The Case of Ghana," *African Journal of Disability*, 4 (October), 1–13.

Nosek, Margaret A., Carol Howland, Diana H. Rintala, Mary E. Young, and Gail F. Chanpong (2001), "National Study of Women with Physical Disabilities," *Sexuality and Disability*, 78 (December), 5–40.

Otnes, Cele, Tina M. Lowrey, and Young Chan Kim (1993), "Gift Selection for Easy and Difficult Recipients: A Social Roles Interpretation," *Journal of Consumer Research*, 20 (September), 229–44.

Phoenix, Ann and Stephen Frosh (2001), "Positioned by 'Hegemonic' Masculinities: A Study of London Boys' Narratives of Identity," *Australian Psychologist*, 36 (September), 27–35.

Porter, Jill I. (1997), "Forward to the Body and Physical Difference: Discourses of Disability," in *The Body and Physical Difference: Discourses of Disability*, ed. T. Mitchell and L. Synder, Ann Arbor, MI: University of Michigan Press, 207–30.

Rugoho, Tafadzwa (2017a), "Fishing in Deep Waters: Sex Workers with Disabilities in Harare, Zimbabwe," *International Journal of Gender Studies in Developing Societies*, 2 (February), 76–91.

——— (2017b), "Our Marriages, Our Prisons, the Experience of Married Women with Albinism in Zimbabwe," Social Work, Education and Social Development 2017 Conference (p. 23), Association of Schools of Social Work in Africa (ASSWA), the International Federation of Social Workers (IFSW, Africa), and Social Workers' Association of Zambia (SWAZ), Livingstone.

Rugoho, Tafadzwa and Michael Jeffress (2018), "My Class, My Disability, My Struggle," in *International Perspectives on Teaching with Disability: Overcoming Obstacles and Enriching Lives*, ed. M. Jeffress, Oxford: Routledge, 50–61.

Rugoho, Tafadzwa and France Maphosa (2015), "Gender-Based Violence amongst Women with Disabilities: A Case Study of Mwenezi District, Zimbabwe," *Gender Questions*, 3 (December), 12–27.

——— (2017), "Challenges Faced by Women with Disabilities in Accessing Sexual and Reproductive Health in Zimbabwe: The Case of Chitungwiza Town," *African Journal of Disability*, 6 (May), 1–8.

Rugoho, Tafadzwa and Bekezela Siziba (2014), "Rejected People: Beggars with Disabilities in the City of Harare," *Developing Country Studies*, 4 (November), 51–6.

Ruth, Julie A., Cele C. Otnes, and Frédéric F. Brunel (1999), "Gift Receipt and the Reformulation of Interpersonal Relationships," *Journal of Consumer Research*, 25 (March), 385–402.

Salehi, Mehrdad, Tavako H. Kharaz, Maede Shabani, and Tayebe Ziaei (2015), "The Relationship between Self-Esteem and Sexual Self-Concept in People with Physical-Motor Disabilities," *Iranian Red Crescent Medical Journal*, 1 (January), 1–15.

Shah, Sonali (2017), "Disabled People Are Sexual Citizens Too, Supporting Sexual Identity, Well-Being, and Safety for Disabled Young People," *Frontiers in Education*, 1 (September), 14–31.

Shakespeare, Tom W. (2006), *Disability Rights and Wrongs*, London: Routledge.

Sherry, John F. (1983), "Gift Giving in Anthropological Perspective," *Journal of Consumer Research*, 32 (September), 157–67.

Sherry, John F. and Mary Ann McGrath (1989), "Unpacking the Holiday Presence: A Comparative Ethnography of the Gift Store," In *SV-Interpretive Consumer Research*, ed. Elizabeth C. Hirschman, Provo, UT: Association for Consumer Research, 148–67.

Shuttleworth, Russel, Nikki Wedgwood, and Nathan J. Wilson (2012), "The Dilemma of Disabled Masculinity," *Men and Masculinities*, 15 (June), 174–94.

Silberschmidt, Margrethe (2001), "Disempowerment of Men in Rural and East Africa: Implications for Male Identity and Sexual Behaviour," *World Development*, 657–71.

Skempes, Dimitrios and Jerome Bickenbach (2015), "Developing Human Rights Based Indicators to Support Country Monitoring of Rehabilitation Services and Programmes for People with Disabilities: A Study Protocol," *International Health and Human Rights*, 15 (September), 1–10.

Steffens, Melanie C., Mark Kirschbaum, and Paul Glados (2008), "Avoiding Stimulus Confounds in Implicit Association Tests by Using the Concepts as Stimuli," *British Journal of Social Psychology*, 47 (June), 217–43.

Steffens, Melanie C. and Vilado, M. A. (2015), *Gender at Work: A Social Psychological Perspective*, New York: Peter Lang.

Stocker, Susan S. (2001), "Disability and Identity: Overcoming Perfectionism," *Frontiers*, 22 (January), 154–73.

Szmukler, George, Rowena Daw and Felicity Callard (2014), "Mental Health Law and the UN Convention on the Rights of Persons with Disabilities," *International Journal of Law and Psychiatry*, 37 (May), 245–52.

White, George F. (2014), "People with Disabilities in Christian Community," *Journal of the Christian Institute on Disability*, 10 (November), 11–35.

Willer, Robb (2005), "Overdoing Gender: A Test of the Masculine Overcompensation Thesis," in *American Sociological Association Meetings*, Philadelphia: American Sociological Association Meetings, 12.

World Health Organisation and The World Bank. 2011. World report on disability. Geneva: WHO.

Zulu, Eliya M., Nii-Amoo F. Dodoo, and Alex Chika-Ezeh (2002), "Sexual Risk-Taking in the Slums of Nairobi, Kenya," *Population Studies*, 30 (November), 311–23.

8 Gift-Giving Within Adult Daughter-Mother Dyads

Chihling Liu, Xin Zhao, and Margaret K. Hogg

Introduction

Extant consumer research about gift exchange emphasizes that gifts in modern societies are intended to be desired by the recipient, otherwise there is a risk of damaging the relationship (Bradford 2009; Joy 2001; Lowrey, Otnes, and Ruth 2004). Gift-giving has been conceptualized as a system of desirable or competitive transactions in which reciprocation and obligation play important roles in creating, sustaining, reproducing, and reinforcing social ties (Cheal 1988; Mauss 1954; Sherry 1983). This perspective highlights the importance of gifting as a means of reinforcing the recipient's desired self in a (mutually) beneficial, harmonious relationship, especially in gift exchange motivated by agapic love (Belk and Coon 1993). Gifts symbolize one's intentions, and gifts from our loved ones are most likely to be incorporated into a definition of who we are (Belk and Coon 1993; Bradford 2009; Joy 2001). However, gifts may also challenge and represent a potential threat to the recipient's sense of self, and they are used to seek a change of state in the recipient, especially when social relations cannot be easily severed or abandoned (e.g., mothers and daughters). In this essay, we build on the study by Otnes et al. (1993) about the gift-giver's social roles and explore: 1) the different social roles gift-givers express within the mother-daughter dyad, and 2) how gift-givers, in expressing their different social roles, might influence the dynamics of mother-daughter relationships.

The adult daughter-mother dyad provides a unique context to examine instances where gifts are intended not only to please but are also used as a mechanism to change the recipient for the better. When daughters are young, the mother-daughter relationship revolves around nurturing and socializing the child. As the daughter grows up, she assumes filial responsibilities to preserve her aging mother's life and foster her growth (Allen and Walker 1992). "Mutual mothering" takes place as the daughters enter adulthood and start to realize their mothers as situated women who also struggle in life and can be vulnerable at times (Gilligan and Rogers 1993). Both rely on each other for support and guidance (Fingerman 2001; Fischer 1986). Yet, they also struggle with finding ways of supervising each other to become or remain a valuable member of society (Allen and Walker 1992; Ruddick 1989). This obligation of supervision may conflict with Western norms for autonomy in adulthood (Allen and Walker 1992). The conflict leads to a continuous struggle between balancing the desire for intimacy with their needs for autonomy (De Kanter 1993). Tensions arise when parents and children have different developmental needs (Birditt and Fingerman 2013). Gifts play an important role in mitigating such tensions.

In the love and power relationship between mothers and daughters, intimacy, and irritation often go hand-in-hand (Boyd 1989). As both mothers and daughters age, they simultaneously struggle and compete for the acknowledgement of their own subjectivity (De Kanter 1993). It becomes unclear whose needs and opinions should be prioritized (Fingerman 2001). This is particularly true for the daughters as they begin to undertake the developmental tasks of separation and individuation in seeking to develop an identity of their own, distinct from their mothers (Flax 1978; Ruddick 1989; Smith, Mullis, and Hill 1995). While separation means "establishing a firm sense of differentiation from the mother, of possessing one's own physical and mental boundaries," individuation refers to "the development of a range of characteristics, skills, and personality traits which are uniquely one's own" (Flax 1978, 172). Daughters thus often try hard to magnify how different they are from their mothers and dis-identify signs of similarities, especially in the Western context in which the cultural message emphasizes "don't be like your mother" (Fischer 1986; Surrey 1993). Nevertheless, differences are also feared as they symbolize a source of potential disconnections that could undermine the relationship (Surrey 1993). Responding to the daughters' developmental tasks, the mothers undergo internal conflicts as they continue to identify strongly with a girl child and hope the child will be just like themselves (Flax 1978). Gift exchange between the adult daughter and mother can be reframed as a space in which they negotiate separation and attachment, differentiation, and identification, and continuity and discontinuation (van Mens-Verhulst 1993). While gift-giving often represents the givers' wishes to merge with the recipient, gift rejection can signal a breakaway from these wishes. We explore such dynamics of gift exchange between mothers and daughters, and report some of our initial findings in this essay.

Previous Consumer Research on Gift-Giving

Gift-giving can be motivated by both reciprocity (Gouldner 1960; Mauss 1954; Sahlins 1972) and agapic love (Belk and Coon 1993). Gifts that celebrate agapic love may include goods or service such as the giver's time, activities, and ideas offered to the gift-recipient. We found that gifts between mothers and daughters often take the form of nonmaterial gifts and emphasize on shared experiences. Reciprocity is a key conceptual element in the gift exchange process. A sense of obligation (informal or formal), and a sense of indebtedness are often created when a gift is not reciprocated. However, such obligated reciprocity is often absent for continued gift-giving in mother-daughter dyads. Neither party seeks to quickly repay the gift given by the other. The gives and takes are often different in kind and only balance over time (Sahlins 1972). In many cases, gifting in this context reinforces a bond of kinship and goodwill rather than creating social indebtedness. However, extant works of intergenerational gift-giving tend to focus on valued assets, cherished possessions, and heirlooms rather than on more mundane gifting and everyday experiences (Bradford 2009; Curasi, Price, and Arnould 2004; Price, Arnould, and Curasi 2000). We examine gift-giving within the mother-daughter dyad and highlight how mundane gifts may also constitute an important means of intergenerational influence (Miller 1998).

Focusing on the emotional experiences of gift recipients, Ruth, Otnes, and Brunel (1999) studied the relational effects of gifts and discovered six ways in which the giver-recipient relationships can be reformulated. The gift is conceptualized as an important tool through which relationships can be realigned based on the assessment of gift-receipt experiences (Sherry 1983) and the expectations for future interactions (Ruth et al. 1999). Through gifting, the social bonds between the giver and the recipient could be strengthened, affirmed, attenuated, unchanged, negatively confirmed, weakened, or severed. However, such findings did not take into account how the giver might view the reformulated relationship, and hence potentially change her ways of giving with the recipient over time. Gift-giving within the mother-daughter dyad is usually continued over a lifetime and gifts, however, negatively viewed, are very unlikely to sever such an enduring and close relationship. We examine how the nature of gift-giving can change over time as the mothers and daughters learn more about each other. We also examine whether or not negative emotions will always lead to an attenuated relationship as noted by Ruth et al. (1999).

The nature of the relationship between gift-giver and recipient in Otnes et al.'s (1993) study ranges from casual acquaintance to extreme intimacy. Consumers adopt different gifting strategies to express their social roles in these relationships. Otnes et al.'s (1993) study identified six social roles expressed by givers to gift recipients: the pleaser, the provider, the socializer, the compensator, the avoider and the acknowledger. Here, the pleaser gives gifts to please the recipient, even when the gifts might violate the giver's own taste. The provider typically offers utilitarian gifts to take care of the recipient's needs. The socializer utilizes gifts as an instrument to educate and instill new values or knowledge into the recipient, even when such gifts may not be desired. The compensator is a hybrid of both pleaser and provider, with a focus on helping the recipient cope with a loss she has experienced. The avoider seeks to not enter into or to minimize relationship building by not engaging in any actual gift exchange. Finally, the acknowledger engages in gift-giving because it is perceived as obligatory. In this exploratory study, we examine how the particular context of adult daughter-mother dyads may help provide important variations on Otnes et al.'s (1993) findings about gift selection and gift-receipt.

Methods

In addressing our research questions, we focused on the gifting behavior within adult daughter-mother dyads (eight mother-daughter dyads which resulted in 16 in-depth interviews in total). The mother-daughter dyad constitutes a central socialization structure throughout family life (Fingerman 2003; Moore, Wilkie, and Lutz 2002). The daughters who participated in this study were all aged 18 years old and above, and had all achieved financial independence from their family. They varied in education level and social class. Similar to Belk and Coon (1993), our informants define gifting behaviors as including both material and nonmaterial gift-giving (e.g., advice, time, service, etc.).

Data were collected in the UK by the first author either via video calls or at informants' homes or in local pubs and coffee shops chosen by the informants. Informants were initially recruited through personal networks and through a snowballing process (Joy 2001). The interviews lasted between 50 minutes and 2.5 hours, and the interviewer started with general questions regarding everyday mother-daughter shopping experiences that eventually led to conversations about gift exchanges between mother and daughter over the years (McCracken 1988). The interviewer was nondirective and allowed informants to share their most memorable gift exchange memories that were judged to be important by the informants (Ruth et al. 1999). Data collection continued until no new theoretical insights could be obtained. Interviews were audio recorded and transcribed for joint analysis.

The analysis was iterative between interview data and prior theories on gift exchange and mother-daughter relationships. Analysis was also both intra-textual and intertextual, moving from individual interview transcripts to the entire set of interview data (Thompson, Locander, and Pollio 1989). The first author also reflected upon her own experiences as a daughter who regularly exchanges gifts with her mother. Such introspective analysis also helps to enrich our understanding of the phenomenon (Wallendorf and Brucks 1993).

Analysis and Findings

Ruth et al. (1999) called for an investigation into the relational effects of gifts and the impact of time on giver/recipient relationships. Our study takes this, along with Otnes et al.'s (1993) work, as a starting point to organize our findings on gift exchanges within adult daughter-mother dyads. In their seminal work, Otnes et al. (1993) found that gift-givers may express the social roles of a pleaser, provider, socializer, compensator, avoider, and acknowledger, when they select gifts for different recipients ranging from acquaintances to kin. Gift-givers may also shift among these social roles depending on the gifting situation. In the following analysis, we present the similarities and differences that exist between our own findings and Otnes et al.'s (1993) findings on the social roles of gift-givers.

Our findings show that the social roles a gift-giver expresses might change over time as a result of her growing understanding of the gift-recipient. Below, Aurora's gift-giver role changed from being a socializer to being a pleaser (Otnes et al. 1993) when interacting with her mother over the years:

> I paid for my parents to go away for a weekend. They hated the drive and when they were back, they kept saying how awful it was and how my mum would never want to do it again. I felt very frustrated. ... I'd like my mum to do more but at the end of the day, I need to know that's not my life. I realized this about 6–7 years ago after the horrible weekend away gift. ... It's now just about us spending time together. It needs to be in her comfort zone ... like the India and Sri Lanka trip I took them on, mum enjoyed it because I was there to organize everything.

Here, the weekend away gift was not appreciated by the parents, who found it "awful" and would "never want to do it again." However, unlike empathy, which involves understanding and working with the recipient to facilitate empowerment, "compulsive care-taking" may lead to anger or frustration if the giver fails to "fix" the other, resulting in overt or covert "other-blaming" (see Surrey 1993). Parents often use gifts to mold, educate, and morally improve their offspring, or at least to make their children more amenable to the image they desire them to have (Belk 1979; Miller 1998; Schwartz 1967). Yet, as both children and parents grow older, it becomes increasingly likely that children also seek to socialize their parents into someone who they can continue to value and appreciate (Allen and Walker 1992). Here Aurora sought a change of state in her mother by giving her mother gifts that Aurora perceived would help her mother with confidence building. Aurora's weekend away gift to her mother reflected what she believed her mother should become rather than what her mother would see as pleasing, despite knowing that such a gift might lead to tensions in their relationship.

Although a sense of appreciation is considered essential in earlier conceptualizations of gifting (Godbout and Caille 1998), the lack of gratitude does not always deter continuous gift-exchanges of potentially undesirable gifts between mothers and daughters. It was only after about 6–7 years, Aurora started to become more tolerant about the differences between her and her mother: "My husband told me to stop getting so angry ... I should give them what they would want and not something I would want them to have." The strong bond between mothers and daughters allows the giver to keep giving undesirable gifts (Ruth et al. 1999) without the fear of losing the relationship (Gilligan and Rogers 1993). As Anna, Aurora's mother, reflected on the gifts she had been receiving from Aurora, that were intended to care for her, Anna said: "Oh I hated the weekend away ... but Aurora thinks for me and tells me the right things to do. She just doesn't give up! She cares for me like my mother." In line with past studies (Fingerman 2001; Fischer 1981), our findings indicate that as both aged, the mother-daughter relationship often became more positive over time. They learned to tolerate and appreciate each other's individuality, facilitating a change in the gift-giver from being a socializer to a pleaser in her act of giving to the recipient over time.

In addition, Otnes et al.'s (1993) original theorization of the avoider is conceptualized as someone who pursues relationship dissolution through the absence of any actual gift exchange. We add to this notion by showing that the avoider's anti-gift endeavor can also be aimed at relationship maintenance, especially when the relationship has been undergoing stress or difficulties. Nora talks about how her desire for and frustration around connection and mutuality in the mother-daughter relationship shape her anti-gift behavior:

> Meeting less helps maintain the relationship ... when I tried to invite her and arrange something, afternoon tea etc. it's like she doesn't want to be there. I was always left feeling angry and annoyed. ... I obviously love her because she is my mum, but she is very hard work.

Likewise, Nora's mother states, "we just always argued whenever we spend prolonged time together, no afternoon teas. I've never wanted to go to lunch with her, but we would speak on the phone." Kinships are intimate and binding (Fischer 1986). As seen here, mothers and daughters may strive to stay on good terms by adopting the role of an avoider in gift exchange. Experiential gifts such as shared activities foster close relationships (Chan and Mogilner 2017). Yet, Nora and her mother avoid exchanging gifts to prevent relationship dissolution.

Our findings also provide a conceptual variation on Otnes et al.'s (1993) concept of the socializer. In their work, givers who expressed this role were parents giving to children with the intention to inculcate appropriate values in their children. We show that daughters also often take on this role to "mother" their mothers through gift exchange. But their gift-giving motives to socialize their mothers may not always be about being altruistic, as is illustrated by the following remarks by Cristina:

> I think the thing that she (my mum) probably influenced me most was what not to wear. Like, very bright blusher or really bright lipstick. I always remember, like, both me and my sister at the time would be sat in the back of the car going, "Oh, my God. This is awful.".... I just find it embarrassing because it's just so much. I know she wouldn't think it's too much at all. ... I always buy her like ... quite neutral colors to suit lots of skin tones. I try to stop her from doing that [heavy, thick make-up] ... it sounds quite bad, but I think, especially mom, people think, "That's what you're going to be like when you're older."

Daughters often have no sense where they end and their mothers begin, even in a literal, physical way (Flax 1978). Belk and Coon (1993) called for an investigation into understanding the way in which overlapping extended selves affect gift-giving in established relationships. Here we see how Cristina was motivated to express her giver role as the socializer at least in part because of her sense of embarrassment about the perceived inappropriateness of her mother's self-presentation. It seems that the inappropriateness violates Cristina's self-definition that is experienced in relation to her mother. Interestingly, we found that only daughters have mentioned this sense of embarrassment, not the mothers in our study. This could be because mothers are commonly regarded as the parent with the ultimate responsibility for bringing up the child successfully rather than vice-versa (Anderson and Eifert 1989; Gray 2002).

Finally, we found three new social roles that were not previously discussed in Otnes et al.'s (1993) study—the guardian, the mender and the keeper. These social roles are perhaps more unique to intimate relationships as in a case like the mother-daughter dyad.

The Guardian

The guardian seeks to maintain relationship stability with the recipient by upholding past gifting rituals. This is especially when the giver fears losing connection with the recipient whom she sees as going through a major period of transition in life. Helen describes the importance of continuing to give gifts when she felt her daughter started to break away from home:

> For the first time Maya withdrew from the family. She had a relationship she knows we don't agree with. ... It was hard to watch but we knew things would fall apart, so we carried on buying her flowers and groceries etc. We kept everything as normal as possible. ... I thought if everything went wrong and it did, we'd have at least been one constant in her life, showing that we have stood with her.

Lowrey et al. (2004) suggested the involvement of third parties in influencing dyadic giving over time. For daughters, if mothers do not approve of their relationship partners, there is strain in the mother-daughter bond—partly because it is the daughters' developmental task to leave their natal families and establish their own (Fischer 1986). Many mothers in our interviews appeared helpless to interfere in daughters' love relationships. By taking the role of the guardian, mothers are able to communicate their continued care and concern for their daughters, even though the gifts may not be appreciated (at the time). We found that the perceived quality of the mother-daughter relationship often improved for both parties once the recipient came to recognize that the main message behind the guardian's gift-giving was: "*I will always be there for you during ups and downs.*" As Maya says, "she (my mum) was there for me ... we often clashed but we're very close now." And Helen concludes: "since they broke up, I think it strengthened our relationship. She came home more and I was more relaxed with her more than ever before."

The Mender

The mender is a combination of the pleaser (Otnes et al. 1993) and the guardian, with a focus on repairing the relationship and reconnecting with an intimate other. Debbie was on a mission to win her daughter back:

> Evelyn turned against me because I initiated the divorce with her dad. We split up when she was about 11. I met someone else and tried to introduce him to the family. I would buy her game consoles etc. to try to make her feel better about the situation, to make her feel more comfortable. I tried to buy her affection. I felt as though I am trying to help her get out of a bad mood. You gotta do it as a mother when your daughter is going through a difficult time, you try to carry on as normal as possible with buying her things. ... It worked eventually. She just realized mum was better!

Here the mender's gift reflects an effort to utilize desirable gifts in exchange for affection through which the troubled mother-daughter relationship can be restored. When asked about the game console she received at the time, Evelyn was fully aware of such an exchange taking place: "Mum had an affair. She and her new boyfriend bought me PlayStation and got me a native Indian doll I really liked and kept till today. ... I guess dad got depressed and I felt bad for dad. But the gifts worked." In addition to the efforts to mend the mother-daughter relationship, Debbie's gifts were also driven by her perceived duties of safeguarding her child's sense of well-being. In this regard, the child was singularized as unique and special and the mother was not only willing but also anxious to bring happiness to the child.

The Keeper

The keeper engages in gift-giving to keep their own possessions/resources within the family or within an intimate relationship. Studies of intergenerational gifting show how individuals' cherished possessions become families' inalienable wealth and the importance of heirlooms in sustaining a family's collective identity (Bradford 2009; Curasi et al. 2004). We found that mothers often gifted daughters cherished possessions, ranging from jewelry to stuffed animals and personally meaningful collections. Both parties described these possessions as gifts that are of high sentimental value, facilitating a joint definition of self with each other. However, our findings also suggest a more mundane aspect of being the keeper, in that mothers and daughters often give each other things that they no longer use. Gaynor said, "These handbags were not cheap. ... I bought them on impulse ... too expensive to give away [to someone not my daughter]." In many cases, it is because they feel used items do not constitute as appropriate gifts to others, or these are things that the giver perceived as too expensive to gift to others.

Discussion and Conclusion

We highlighted the potentially negative emotions (e.g., frustration, ambivalence, and a sense of embarrassment) that might underpin gifting activities within mother-daughter dyads. These negative emotions underline the struggle mothers and daughters often face when negotiating between separation and attachment, between differentiation and identification, and between autonomy and dependence. Our findings also suggest variations to Otnes et al.'s (1993) study about the social roles gift-givers express across various types of social relationship. These variations, we argue, might be more unique to intimate relationships (e.g., the socializer/sense of embarrassment, the avoider/relationship maintenance, the guardian, the mender and the keeper). Cheal (1996) suggested that gift-giving within families in the Western context is characterized by non-practical and non-utilitarian goods—since the basic needs are often already fulfilled in routine and impersonal ways. We found that mothers and daughters still often focused on offering mundane gifts to each other based on their perceptions of what the self and/or the other might need. Mundane gifts may be perceived as a way of bringing stability to the recipient and demonstrating the giver's continued commitment to the relationship as in the case of the guardian. Our notion of the gift-giver as the mender also underlines the perceived obligation of safeguarding and reaching out to an intimate other when the relationship is strained. The keeper engages in gifting to keep resources within the "household" or the "extended" self.

In addition, we contribute to previous studies that focused on the relationship between gift exchange and self-identity. Gifts constitute a particular type of social bond between different people (Mauss 1954). Through the ritual of gift exchange, a sense of the givers' extended self is retained by the gift-recipient (Belk 1988). In the mother-daughter dyad, in which there is already an impregnated extended self, refusal or acceptance of gifts may reveal severance or overlaps of the joint self-definition. Giving and receiving gifts can be an important means through which mothers and daughters (re-)negotiate perceived independence and what constitutes their desired and undesired selves over time as in relation to the intimate other. The success or failure of such negotiations could have important implications for how the mother-daughter relationship may develop over time. Gift-givers in our study often perceive gift rejection by the recipient as an unwelcomed extended self or a loss of their desired extended self. Whereas previous works have focused on self-extension through gift exchange, we find instances of self-severance when an intimate other rejects a self-extending gift.

References

Allen, Katherine R. and Alexis J. Walker (1992), "Attentive Love: A Feminist Perspective on the Caregiving of Adult Daughters," *Family Relations*, 41 (3), 284–9.

Anderson, Joan M. and Helen Eifert (1989), "Managing Chronic Illness in the Family: Women as Caretakers," *Journal of Advanced Nursing*, 14 (9), 735–43.

Belk, Rusell W. (1979), "Gift Giving Behavior," in *Research in Marketing*, ed. Jagdish N. Sheth, Greenwich, CT: JAI Press, 96–126.

———— (1988), "Possessions and the Extended Self," *Journal of Consumer Research*, 15 (2), 139–68.

Belk, Rusell W. and Gregory S. Coon (1993), "Gift Giving as Agapic Love: An Alternative to the Exchange Paradigm Based on Dating Experiences," *Journal of Consumer Research*, 20 (3), 393–417.

Birditt, Kira A. and Karen L. Fingerman (2013), "Parent-Child Intergenerational Relationships in Adulthood," in *Handbook of Family Theories: A Content-Based Approach*, ed. Mark A. Fine and Frank D. Fincham, New York and London: Routledge.

Boyd, Carol J. (1989), "Mothers and Daughters: A Discussion of Theory and Research," *Journal of Marriage and the Family*, 51 (2), 291–301.

Bradford, Tonya Williams (2009), "Intergenerationally Gifted Asset Dispositions," *Journal of Consumer Research*, 36 (1), 93–111.

Chan, Cindy and Cassie Mogilner (2017), "Experiential Gifts Foster Stronger Relationships Than Material Gifts," *Journal of Consumer Research*, 43 (6), 913–31.

Cheal, David (1988), *The Gift Economy*, New York: Routledge.

—— (1996), "Gift in Contemporary North America," in *Gift Giving*, ed. Cele Otnes and Richard Beltramini, Bowling Green, OH: Bowling Green State University Popular Press, 85–99.

Curasi, Carolyn Folkman, Linda L. Price, and Eric J. Arnould (2004), "How Individuals' Cherished Possessions become Families' Inalienable Wealth," *Journal of Consumer Research*, 31 (3), 609–22.

De Kanter, Ruth (1993), "Becoming a Situated Daughter," in *Daughtering and Mothering: Female Subjectivity Reanalyzed*, ed. Janneke van Mens-Verhulst, Karlein Schreurs, and Liesbeth Woertman, London and New York: Routledge, 26–34.

Fingerman, Karen L. (2001), *Aging Mothers and Their Adult Daughters: A Study in Mixed Emotions*, New York, NY: Springer.

—— (2003), *Mothers and Their Adult Daughters: Mixed Emotions, Enduring Bonds*, Amherst, NY: Prometheus Books.

Fischer, Lucy Rose (1981), "Transitions in the Mother-Daughter Relationship," *Journal of Marriage and the Family*, 43 (3), 613–22.

—— (1986), *Linked Lives: Adult Daughters and Their Mothers*, New York: Harper & Row.

Flax, Jane (1978), "The Conflict between Nurturance and Autonomy in Mother-Daughter Relationships and within Feminism," *Feminist Studies*, 4 (2), 171–89.

Gilligan, Caro and Annie Rogers (1993), "Reframing Daughtering and Mothering a Paradigm Shift in Psychology," in *Daughtering and Mothering: Female Subjectivity Reanalysed*, ed. Janneke van Mens-Verhulst, Karlein Schreurs, and Liesbeth Woertman, London and New York: Routledge, 125–34.

Godbout, Jacques T. and Alain C. Caille (1998), *World of the Gift*, Trans. D. Winkler, Montreal, Canada: McGill-Queen's University Press.

Gouldner, Alvin Ward (1960), "The Norm of Reciprocity: A Preliminary Statement," *American Sociological Review*, 25 (2), 161–78.

Gray, David E. (2002), "'Everybody Just Freezes: Everybody Is Just Embarrassed': Felt and Enacted Stigma among Parents of Children with High Functioning Autism," *Sociology of Health & Illness*, 24 (6), 734–49.

Joy, Annamma (2001), "Gift Giving in Hong Kong and the Continuum of Social Ties," *Journal of Consumer Research*, 28 (2), 239–56.

Lowrey, Tina M., Cele C. Otnes, and Julie A. Ruth (2004), "Social Influences on Dyadic Giving over Time: A Taxonomy from the Giver's Perspective," *Journal of Consumer Research*, 30 (4), 547–58.

Mauss, Marcel (1954), *The Gift: Forms and Functions of Exchange in Archaic Society*. Trans. Ian Cunnison, London: Cohen & West.

McCracken, Grant (1988), *The Long Interview*, Newbury Park, CA: Sage Publications.

Miller, Daniel (1998), *A Theory of Shopping*, Cambridge: Polity Press.

Moore, Elizabeth S., William L. Wilkie, and Richard J. Lutz (2002), "Passing the Torch: Intergenerational Influences as a Source of Brand Equity," *Journal of Marketing*, 66 (2), 17–37.

Otnes, Cele, Tina M. Lowrey, and Young Chan Kim (1993), "Gift Selection for Easy and Difficult Recipients: A Social Roles Interpretation," *Journal of Consumer Research*, 20 (2), 229–44.

Price, Linda L., Eric J. Arnould, and Carolyn Folkman Curasi (2000), "Older Consumers' Disposition of Special Possessions," *Journal of Consumer Research*, 27 (2), 179–201.

Ruddick, Sara (1989), *Maternal Thinking: Toward a Politics of Peace*, New York: Beacon.

Ruth, Julie A., Cele C. Otnes, and Frederic F. Brunel (1999), "Gift Receipt and the Reformulation of Interpersonal Relationships," *Journal of Consumer Research*, 25 (4), 385–402.

Sahlins, Marshall (1972), *Stone Age Economics*, Chicago: Aldine de Gruyter.

Schwartz, Barry (1967), "The Social Psychology of the Gift," *American Journal of Sociology*, 73 (1), 1–11.

Sherry, John F. (1983), "Gift Giving in Anthropological Perspective," *Journal of Consumer Research*, 10 (2), 157–68.

Smith, Linda M., Ronald L. Mullis, and E. Wayne Hill (1995), "Identity Strivings within the Mother-Daughter Relationship," *Psychological Reports*, 76 (2), 495–503.

Surrey, Janet (1993), "The Mother-Daughter Relationship: Themes in Psychotherapy," in *Daughtering and Mothering: Female Subjectivity Reanalysed*, ed. Janneke van Mens-Verhulst, Karlein Schreurs, and Liesbeth Woertman, London and New York: Routledge.

Thompson, Craig J., William B. Locander, and Howard R. Pollio (1989), "Putting Consumer Experience Back into Consumer Research: The Philosophy and Method of Existential-Phenomenology," *Journal of Consumer Research*, 16 (2), 133–46.

van Mens-Verhulst, Janneke (1993), "Beyond Daughtering and Mothering," in *Daughtering and Mothering: Female Subjectivity Reanalysed*, ed. Janneke van Mens-Verhulst, Karlein Schreurs, and Liesbeth Woertman, London and New York: Routledge, 159–64.

Wallendorf, Melanie and Merrie Brucks (1993), "Introspection in Consumer Research: Implementation and Implications," *Journal of Consumer Research*, 20 (3), 339–59.

9 Crunch My Heart! It Falls for You

Carnal-Singularity and Chocolate Gift-Giving Across Language Contexts

Marjaana Mäkelä, Shona Bettany, and Lorna Stevens

Introduction

"Go ahead, it's your favorite ..." tempts the main character Vianne (Juliette Binoche) to her lover-to-be Roux (Johnny Depp), who soon sensually licks his fingers after having tasted the magical chocolate praline concocted by Vianne. What Roux doesn't know is that Vianne perpetuates an ancient Mayan tradition of recognizing a person's secret desires and translating them into a piece of chocolate of exactly the right flavor, either to seduce, or to make people discover their innermost aspirations. The scene is from Lasse Hallström's film *Chocolat*, based on Joanne Harris' eponymous novel, where chocolate becomes the currency for love, envy, passion, fear—and religious censure. Most of all, it is a fairy-tale that binds together myths and emotions around *Theobroma cacao*, the food of the gods, which represented life and fertility to ancient Aztecs and Mayas, and has been associated with aphrodisiac qualities ever since, thus establishing a powerful bond between chocolate and the body.

Is it the slightly phallic shape of the cacao tree pod, growing in mysteriously humid and hot tropical climates, hence combining masculine and feminine features, or the reputation of the derived substances that have forged the myth? Or is it the taste, as bittersweet as love itself, and so easy to combine innumerable flavors and aromas, which is apt to accentuate the sensation and the message? We are now told that chocolate is a seductive product because of the alleged love molecule, phenylethylamine, it contains, which gives chocolate the ability to simulate the euphoria and quickening of the pulse associated with being in love. Whatever may be the reasons for the legend of chocolate as a love drug, it has been developing since those ancient civilizations in Central America first discovered the virtues of the fruit of the cacao tree. It is a stimulant, relaxant, and euphoriant—a perfect combination to become an aphrodisiac, and the element of mystery has been accentuated by its use in rituals, as well as its controversial medicinal effects which were particularly sought after in the seventeenth to nineteenth centuries (Grivetti 2005) and which continue to be investigated. It is a product which is both a food and a drug, without being exactly either of them (Morris and Taren 2005).

Mayas believed that cacao had been donated to mankind by the god Xmucane, as one of the divine beverages from which man was constituted (Grivetti 2005), and in their nuptial rites chocolate was an element for assuring fertility. Aztecs, however, considered chocolate, in the form of a beverage, so intoxicating and stimulating that it had to be prohibited from women and children. Hence, consumption of chocolate was permitted only for high-ranked males such as noblemen, priests, and distinguished warriors. Nevertheless, the pleasure of eating chocolate on each other's skin may not have been unfamiliar to them (Fahim 2010). The Aztec king Montezuma is said to have drunk *xocolatl* from cups of pure gold before entering his harem, believing that the potion enhanced a sovereign's wisdom and power as well as his virility and sexual stamina. A text on Montezuma's court by Bernal Díaz from 1560 is presumably the first in a European language to document chocolate's associations with sexual potency (Grivetti 2005).

The Spanish brought chocolate to Europe in the seventeenth century, and it was rapidly introduced from King Philip's Spain to Western courts, where concubines and mistresses like Madame de Pompadour and Madame du Barry used it to provide access to royal beds, and for maintaining those hazardous positions. Naturally, the Marquis de Sade, Giacomo Casanova, and Mata Hari were aware of its miraculous powers.

Into the dessert he slipped chocolate pastilles so good that a number of people devoured them. There were lots of them, and no one failed to eat some, but he had mixed in some Spanish fly. The virtue of the medication is well known. It proved to be so potent that those who ate the pastilles began to burn with unchaste ardor and to carry on as if in the grip of the most amorous frenzy.

(Marquis de Sade)

Chocolate as a Gift

The tradition of offering chocolates to sweethearts may have started in the Royal courts, when Maria Theresa of Spain gave her fiancé Louis XIV of France a beautifully decorated box of chocolates for their engagement. The sensual and emotional characteristics of chocolate were henceforth associated with the ceremonial tradition of gift-giving. Since then, the scenery has shifted toward the opposite gender: Nowadays, it is most often the man who makes a gift of chocolates to his beloved one as a token of love. Mary Douglas writes in the foreword to "The Gift" by Marcel Mauss (Douglas 2002, XII): *"There are no free gifts; gift cycles engage persons in permanent commitments that articulate the dominant institutions."* This view is developed further by Diane Barthel, who argues that a gift of chocolate implies an act of patronage (1989). Nevertheless, romantic gift-giving is a skillful reciprocal game, and women have used chocolate for romantic and erotic purposes as well as men; indeed they represent the vast majority of chocolate consumption (Belk and Costa 1998).

As chocolate became commercialized for ordinary consumers, it maintained its reputation as a romantic gift *par excellence*; it is not an ordinary food, but an affordable luxury, which is laden with a thick layer of associations (Belk and Costa 1998). It is said to be addictive. This is a fact that hasn't however been proved scientifically, although popular culture is rich with connections made between chocolate and craving, which is a state easily associated with carnality and female desire (Fahim 2010). Chocolate leverages the everyday experience and uplifts one's spirits when consumed alone, and is reputably efficient against heartache or feeling depressed or down, hence assuming the role of a perfect self-gift which is oftentimes emphasized in romantic movies and chick-lit. First and foremost, chocolate enhances a romantic relationship by its physiological and above all emotional effects. Askegaard and Bengtsson (2005) characterize chocolate as the most important seduction present, rivaled only by flowers in the imagery of romance.

It is noteworthy that chocolate is a gift that is accessible in some form to almost everyone, which has contributed to its democratization in becoming an all-round tool of seduction: It is a versatile product which can be purchased for a very affordable price, or it may represent an extremely costly gift, when crafted into a luxurious selection of exclusively handmade pralines and truffles. Raw ingredients can be of bulk or of meticulously hand-picked, prime-quality beans and fruit, and the same applies to the rest of the brand construction: packaging, promotion, and distribution. The expenditure and effort a suitor has invested in purchasing the gift reveals a lot about his commitment to the relationship: a tiny selection of gold-packaged Leonidas, Godiva pralines, or a mass-produced box from Tesco? According to Diane Barthel (1989, 434), there is a direct relationship between the amount of money spent by a man on chocolate and the "sexually generous response" expected from the woman. Regardless of the expenditure, it is an interesting argument to suggest that a luxury status for food is achieved only when communicated by social relations (Barthel 1989). This makes gifts of chocolate a particularly intriguing phenomenon. For Alan Beardsworth and Teresa Keil (1997), this capacity is based on the dual nature of confectionaries like chocolate: their status as an in-between food and a non-food allows for a wide variety of social meanings, especially as a gift. In fact, Zarantonello and Luomala (2011) have identified seven categories for contextual chocolate consumption:

physiological need, sensorial gratification, memories, and nostalgia, escapism, materialism, chocoholism (addictive consumption of chocolate), and interpersonal and self-gifts. These are interconnected in the fetish role of chocolate as a romantic gift: it fulfills sensorial, physiological, and material needs, provides occasions for nostalgic emotions, and translates dissimulated or expressed feelings into an action of gift-giving.

Chocoholic consumption may be associated with what is often culturally viewed as an essentially female tendency for physical and gustatory self-pleasure, although it is entwined in a fascinating way to the imagery of sweet-loving women who yearn to surrender to temptation, hence calling for seduction (Barthel 1989). Interestingly enough, the locution *chocolate-boxy* in English tends to be associated with kitschy, mostly female features and characteristics: over-sentimental, over-sweet, and luscious (Barthel 1989). Indeed, we may argue that no product reflects the erotic power of food more than chocolate, and no food is so strongly associated with women's carnal desires and weaknesses. Chocolate is coded as a feminine food, with women being constantly tempted to give in to their desires, and men encouraged to buy women the gift of chocolate as an expression of love, with the promise of erotic rewards.

Locating Carnal-Singularity in Consumer Culture Theory

The corner of a mouth (dark chocolate/red fruits),
a piece of a nose (dark chocolate/chestnut honey),
an eyelid (dark chocolate/fleur de sel, sichuan pepper),
a bellybutton (dark chocolate/pimento pepper, red pepper),
and a delicious nipple (dark chocolate/the fragrance of flowers).
Small pieces of an edible body

(www.gastronomista.com 2010)

In this chapter, we seek to draw on existing consumer culture ontologies of gift-giving (Sherry 1983) in the context of chocolate consumption. We aim to re-theorize this unique form of gift-giving using a material-semiotic approach, which we call *carnal-singularity*, adapting the concept of singularity (Kopytoff 1986; Miller 1987; Belk and Coon 1993; Epp and Price 2010) which has been used to understand the agency of material (predominantly nonhuman, non-sentient) objects within consumer culture research. Prior theorizing of gift-giving *per se*, following largely the work of Mauss (1925), as theoretically focused on semiotics and meaning, symbolism, social, and personal exchange, reciprocity, and social and personal bonds. We suggest that the specificity of chocolate as a gift, as explained above, requires a theory which explicitly deals with not only meaning but also materiality. Sociomateriality is *"the relation and co-creation of subjects and objects"* (Borgerson 2005, 439; see also Bettany 2018), and as agentic and consuming subjects we interact with material objects which are also agentic; this perpetual interaction occurs in a co-creative and transformative manner. This emphasis fits well with our intentions in this chapter.

In terms of gift-giving, Belk and Coon's use of the concept of singularity hints at this in their discussion of Arjun Appadurai (1986, 16), who describes singularity *vis-à-vis* material objects: "It … seems worthwhile to distinguish 'singular' from 'homogeneous' commodities in order to discriminate between commodities whose candidacy for the commodity state is precisely a matter of their class characteristics (a perfectly standardized steel bar, indistinguishable in practical terms from any other steel bar) and those whose candidacy is precisely their uniqueness within some class" (Appadurai 1986, 16 as cited in Belk and Coon 1993, 408). In this vein, singularity means that the material object has a personal meaning, and is imbued with value and symbolism that de-commoditizes it (Epp and Price 2010).

Kopytoff (1986) shifts this concept usage from the material object (inanimate) to the human subject, making the analogy between the slave and the free man, with the free man being singularized, de-commodified or unique, and the slave being commodified or interchangeable. As Belk and Coon (1993, 408) argue, *"whereas gift-giving rituals generally transform the object given into a singularized non-commodity* (Kopytoff 1986), *in the romantic love model the gift recipient is also singularized."* Picking up from this idea, that within romantic gift-giving it is not only the gift but also the recipient that is being singularized, provides us with a starting point for our development of this concept, and our theoretical contribution. In order to do this, we bring in another concept, carnality, adapting the singularity concept to understand how the gift, in this case, chocolate, not only becomes de-commodified due to becoming laden with meaning and symbolism but effectively also becomes imbued with the body of the recipient (and giver), and hence with their sexual agency.

According to the OED, carnal means "of the body or flesh; worldly." Its secondary meaning is "worldly, sensual, sexual." Carnal is from the Latin *carnalis*, from *caro carnis* meaning "flesh." Traditionally, women were identified with the body and nature, and men with the mind and culture. (Paglia 1992; Schiebinger 2000). Whilst the binary opposites of man/woman, mind/body, culture/nature, subject/object, and so on have been challenged by postmodern thought, nevertheless, these Cartesian opposites persist and continue to provide a reference for contemporary cultural texts, many of which juxtapose womanhood with the body's appetites and the exquisite (natural and instinctive) torture of "narcissistic desire" on the one hand and (cultural and moral) self-control and self-denial on the other. Indeed Cronin et al. (2014) write, in their study of women, food preparation and eating, that the feminine subject is *"a negotiator, or* performatist *of contrary spaces"* (Cronin et al. 2014, 387).

Braidotti (1994) writes that embodiment of the subject should be understood as *"a point of overlapping between the physical, the symbolic, and the sociological"* (1994, 4), and in similar vein, McNay (1999) notes that the body *"is the threshold through which the subject's lived experience of the world is incorporated and realized and, as such, is neither pure object nor pure subject"* (1999, 4). Whilst embodiment and embodied theory strike a chord with many feminist scholars (Probyn 2000), the domain of food is particularly interesting, in that *"the realm of the alimentary brings these considerations down to earth and extends them ... tracing out the connections between bodies that, in eating, open up and connect in different ways."* (Probyn 2000, 3). Probyn suggests that eating provides a useful lens to consider issues of identities, and the interactions between sex, gender, and power which are always being negotiated. Above all, Probyn seeks to explore the "interminglings" of the cultural, the culinary and the corporeal (2000, 4). This has also been the intention of Martin (2005) who in her interdisciplinary study of food, literature, and art, considers, drawing on Curtin's (1992) work, a *"food-centred philosophy of human being"* as a means of reconciling the self-other dualism and mind-body split in Western culture, in particular by considering the *"nexus of food, sexuality, and language ... in relation to border crossings and cultural negotiations of food-based identity"* (2005, 30).

Joy and Venkatesh (1994) argue that traditionally, consumption was conceptualized and described as a disembodied phenomenon in our discipline. However, alongside this neglect of the body, there was a preoccupation with the spectacularized and colonized female body. This view was challenged by postmodernism, drawing from an increasing commodification and scrutinization of the male body; a development which entwines this growing interest in the body with more general postmodernist views. Accordingly, traditional binary opposites such as mind/body or man/woman have been questioned (Joy and Venkatesh 1994; Firat and Venkatesh 1995), but the image of women as "consummate consumers," who are ruled by their bodies and thus unable to resist carnal temptations, has continued to persist (Belk 1998; Belk and Costa 1998; Stevens and Maclaran 2007, 2012). In this powerful trope, the symbolic connotations of sex and food (Stratton 2003), are typically conflated into one powerful, irresistible urge, so that women's consumption of food is associated with the seductive, the erotic and/or auto-erotic; anticipating the ultimate orgasmic culmination of sensory bliss and complete satisfaction. This erotic narrative is bound up with women's weak flesh, which makes them particularly susceptible to temptation and sin (Paglia 1992). Women, we argue, continue to be culturally coded as more vulnerable to their bodily appetites than men, being the eternal "carnal feminine" who cannot resist temptation (Grosz 1994; Maclaran and Stevens 2004, Stevens and Maclaran 2007).

Dejmanee (2016), in the context of "food porn," suggests that such carnal embeddedness *vis-à-vis* woman consumers resonates less with marketers' gendered positioning of women, but more with the *"agency and digital identity play of postfeminist subjects."* Postfeminism, she suggests, marked an ideological shift emerging in the 1990s *"largely expressed through consumption practices and the neoliberal focus upon individualism, choice, and empowerment"* (Gill 2007, 149), where women increasingly used digital tools to negotiate contradictory postfeminist politics, rendering them both exploited *and* resistant. It should also be noted in this context that the female body and its pleasures were foregrounded in the postfeminist (or third-wave feminist) phase, framed within a discourse of liberatory play and empowerment, and that the problematics of women's identification with the body are now revisited in the current fourth wave of feminism.

The concept of carnal-singularity allows us to map the shifting relation to gender/ed and sexualized structures of empowerment and resistance over time and space, as chocolate shifts in its carnal-singularity, heating up or cooling down together with the body of the female recipient or gifter (Epp and Price 2010). Prior work on singularization has tended to focus on the study of things or nonhuman objects. We argue that this reifies the subject-object and body-mind dualisms and, as such, the rendering of the female and feminine as 'other' within marketing and consumer discourse. The concept of carnal-singularity makes explicit the idea that the body is invoked in the analysis as a significant materiality, inextricably linked with the meaning processes of singularization. It is here we make a feminist intervention into the theory. Following this, by tracing the carnal-singularization of chocolate consumption *vis-à-vis* gift-giving across language contexts, we demonstrate a further critical intervention, extrapolating the notion that by tracing these differences we challenge the naturalization and normalization of womens' subordination to the body (and bodily impulses) as an uncontested, universal taken-for-granted.

Method and Data

The primary researcher collected online data in the English, French, and Finnish language, through a multi-sited netnography (Kozinets 2002), with the aim of seeking a cross section of opinion. Blogs, advertising, commentaries, posts, and threads relating to chocolate consumption were retrieved, by using the key words "chocolate" and "gift" in their respective languages, in order to analyze the gendered nature and the underlying assumptions of chocolate discourse. The netnography was conducted by lurking, hence with no participation in the interaction

across researched online communities (Kozinets 2002), and it was pre-
ceded by a long period of intensive observation of various food-related
online communities, aligning partly with the research by Kozinets, Patterson, and Ashman (2017) on online food contexts, and the increased
desire of consumption stemming from technological affordances. Kozinets et al. (2017) argue that digital technologies, far from extinguishing
our desire to consume, have increased these desires by creating powerful
networks that have a "free-flowing productive energy" (2017, 661).
These networks of desire are complex and open systems of technologies,
consumers, and energized passion, where the virtual and the physical
mingle (2017). In our study, we also hope to capture the energy and
desire that flourishes in the context of our research site: online foodie
blogs and forums.

The corpus was constituted of four major parts: the most voluminous
one originates from prior research on foodie blogs in French and Finnish
(Mäkelä 2016). There, data were gathered from two online sources: the
most popular foodie community in French, *Marmiton* (www.marmiton.
org), and a similar, albeit smaller, community in Finnish, *Maku* (www.
maku.fi.) Both are linked to a printed magazine and also include blogs
written by the journalists of the publishing company. The foodie blog
corpus consists of 128 pages in total and it reflects the consumptive orientation of foodies, seen in the wider context of omnivorous and trans-
national consumption trends.

In order to complement the first data set, and for the purpose of the
present chapter in the context of gift-giving, additional data were retrieved
in 2017. A search from the discussion section "Coin salon" of the *Marmiton* website, with search words *chocolat* and *cadeau* (gift) provided altogether an astonishing amount of 29,718 feeds (January 2017), with
recipes, reflections, and comments, written either by journalists or by
users. Out of these, a sample of 38 feeds was analyzed in detail.

The third constituent of the corpus is in Finnish. It was formed by
streams on a popular Finnish conversation forum, *Suomi24*, and by
feeds from a trendy foodie blog, *52 weeks of deliciousness*, created in
Finnish, despite the name. The section Food and drink, and its sub-
section Delicacies, with the keyword *Suklaa* (Chocolate) were analysed
in *Suomi24*. *Suomi24* is a site with a wide array of user profiles, and it
is characterized as representing the views of average Finns. Purposefully,
the discussion forum data represented a context where no specific user
profiles can be identified, and the blog sample a context where the
blogger and her followers are consumers interested in food and
baking, hence having an emotional relationship with food. Therein, all
recipes and comment feeds with chocolate were analyzed. This resulted
in 94 feeds, including the blog posting, the recipe and the readers' comments, altogether totaling 32 pages. The *Suomi24* data consist of 123
feeds on 35 pages, of the 2,723 pages under the section Chocolate.
Both sets of data were retrieved in February 2017.

Corporate-generated online discourse on chocolate in English constitutes the fourth section of the multi-sited netnography. It was retrieved for the purpose of having a wider array of genres in the corpus, and for incorporating English data to enhance the comparative aspect. These excerpts were retrieved in 2016–2017 from commercial websites related to chocolate consumption and gift-giving. Due to the nature of this data and the structure of the sites, the volume of pages was not measured.

The primary researcher analyzed all texts in their original language by manual coding, which resulted in three themes, Romance of St. Valentine's Day, An Emotionally Charged Gift and Self-Gift, and Baking with Chocolate. These are highlighted in the section on findings, with interlinguistic comparison. Notwithstanding the volume and width of the data, inconsistencies remain, hence the analysis presented below is indicative, and requires thorough further investigation.

Findings

Romance of St. Valentine's Day

The gender-reinforcing capacity of St. Valentine's Day and its rituals associated with chocolate, have been emphasized in prior research by Minowa, Khomenko, and Belk (2011) and by Close (2012). An overview of websites that specialized in chocolate gifts shows a tendency that in the French-speaking world it is more common to offer chocolate to men and women, whereas sites in English are more focused on confectionary gifts designed primarily for women. Despite corporate attempts to commercialize chocolate as a gift to both women and men, the market for St. Valentine's Day targets essentially female recipients. It is abundant, which reveals the importance of chocolate as the ultimate romantic gift. The website Hotel Chocolat (www.hotelchocolat.com) displays a collection of chocolate gifts for St. Valentine's Day, with an interesting array of themes that go from a discreet "Straight from the heart" to strictly "Naughty," both embodying the central theme of offering chocolate in exchange of something else:

> *If Valentine's Day was a black and white movie, this is what our big love would be holding when they turned up on our doorstep at the end: the classic huge, heart-shaped box of chocolates with a ribbon. Sweep them off their feet the old-fashioned way this February 14th with 35 breathtaking caramels, cocktails, fruities, pralines, and more.*
> *One thing on your mind this Valentine's Day? Make sure your other half is on the same page with these five solid 40% milk chocolate hearts. Irresistibly mellow, they're perfect for leaving on pillows, sneaking into pockets or slipping across dinner tables.*
> (www.hotelchocolat.com/uk/shop/valentines-day-gifts/
> straight-from-the-heart-valentine-chocolates/21.12.2016)

An interesting feature is that the romantic version costs £39.00 and the naughty one only £2.50. When the case is almost closed, why spend more? Indeed, an overarching meta-discourse in the English data on chocolate gifts is that of playfulness and humor, combined with layers of seduction and eroticism. Another famous chocolate manufacturer, Neuhaus, has chosen straightforward but elegant denominations for its chocolate gift selections. Even on the English version of the site, names are in French, the language of romance, and even more: Caprice, Plaisir, Désir, Tentation, Irrésistibles, or Séduction (www.neuhaus.fi).

Naturally, gift-giving on Valentine's Day is a tradition consolidating established relationships and does not restrict itself to seducing a new partner. In both contexts, the gift of chocolate is seen to be a prerequisite and an essential first step towards sexual conquest, melting away a woman's sexual resistance (Barthel 1989). Obviously, chocolate is also a product that women buy for themselves, a small treat that provides pleasure and perhaps engenders "jouissance" (joyful loving of oneself, even orgasm as in its signification in French), its auto-erotic and sensual power arguably making it the perfect monadic gift. Consuming chocolate, like love, is to be swept away by longing; both bring about euphoria, relaxation, and ecstasy, and both bring about strong emotional and physiological responses. The pleasure may be transitory, but intense while it lasts, with phrases such as "melting moments" conjuring up the highly sensual and embodied aspects of letting go and giving in to desire (Lupton 1996).

An Emotionally Charged Gift and Self-Gift

> He showed the words "chocolate cake" to a group of Americans and recorded their word associations. "Guilt" was the top response. If that strikes you as unexceptional, consider the response of French eaters to the same prompt: "celebration."
>
> —Michael Pollan, *In Defense of Food: An Eater's Manifesto* (2008)

Chocolate seems to hold an especial role in engendering positive feelings due to its link with indulgence, comfort, and pleasure, as well as negative emotions, weight gain and the loss of self-control (Lupton 1996). In their study of women's chocolate consumption, Belk (1998) and Belk and Costa (1998, 189) refer to the "emotionally charged" environment within which women consume chocolate, with ambivalence an integral part of women's consumption of such products. Bloggers express this clearly: "*Good thing about it is I can have it on my SW diet, while only being a little bit naughty. And being on a diet and a chocolate lover is a real killer!!!!*" (chocablog.com). Belk, Ger, and Askegaard (1996) also address this tension, when they write that "*the state of wanting itself is simultaneously exciting, pleasurable, and frustrating: an exquisite torture."* (1996, 370).

The theme of seduction is a key feature in the emotional process when a product associated with innocent indulgence and romance may become decadent and sinful. Here, we suggest a reading of this process by the notion of carnal objectification by and through food. This development of food and sex drives via chocolate remains a matter of interpretation and is highly dependent on the context of gift-giving, of the extant relationships, and the expectations of those involved. Nevertheless, the associational web of sweetness, sensuality, and sin is age-old and robust, and it can be reinforced by the physical substance of chocolate which makes it so versatile in cooking and baking.

The Finnish online discourse on chocolate reveal considerable differences with the English and French data. On Finnish conversation forums, the emotional index connected to chocolate is primarily that of an everyday pleasure, which is nevertheless somewhat stigmatized as easily leading to overeating and excessive self-indulgence, especially when one is in a blue mood. Chocolate is discussed for its nutritional faculties; taste differences are argued with vehemence, and ethical aspects of chocolate production, for example, child labor, are found in the discussion threads. However, emotionality is seldom found in Finnish chocolate discourse in the same way as in the overtly eroticized French discourse, or in the playful English chocolate talk. There are some allusions made to eating chocolate with sweethearts, but interestingly enough, these may be dealt with in a straightforward, practically oriented style: "*J. Tule käymään ja tuo suklaata mukanasi ... tekee niin paljon mieli!*" [J. Come over and bring chocolate with you. I am craving it so much!] (Suomi24). This discourse is far from chocolate-boxy poetics; quite the contrary. It is about need.

However, it is noteworthy that an objectification of men — to an extent of illustrating carnal-singularity similar to that of women — is found in several feeds in Finnish, especially in the highly racialized context of associating white and dark chocolate with the skin color of men: "*Tykkään tummasta suklaasta enemmän kuin vaaleasta :) Mutta kaipaan vaaleaa miestä.*" [I prefer dark chocolate to white :) But I miss a white man.] (Suomi24). Both men and women express themselves with this metaphor, which fits adequately the context of Finnish gender equality and imbues the male body with the chocolate gift. In this instance we see the conflation of the body and chocolate, between eating and sex, but here, it is the male body that is objectified as something delicious to consume. This example reinforces a cultural norm that women are driven by their carnal desires. Nevertheless, men tend to use this locution with a depreciative and somewhat jealous tone. Given the relatively late internationalization of Finnish society, skin color and the presumed high potency of non-white men are still an issue in colloquial and popular discourse. Examples of the metaphoric use of chocolate associated with female skin color were not found in this sample.

In blogs of Finnish foodies, chocolate occurred as an ingredient like any other, and it was not mystified nor ascribed any specific role. A number of allusions were made, however, to sin: not as in the sin of the flesh in an erotic sense, but in the sense of a highly calorific commodity, which is dangerous for one's figure. "*Syntisen hyvä*" [Sinfully good] was the epithet to chocolate creations in several blog feeds. Comments by readers accentuated this discourse: "*Oi oi. Kun puolen vuoden herkkulakko on tammikuussa ohitse, tiedän mitä sitten leivon!*" [Oh, when my six-month sweets strike is over in January, I know what I'm going to bake!] The more indulgent the cake, the more comments there were, with indexes of prohibition (I shouldn't), desire (I just have to start baking immediately) and pure delight (It's just so gooood). Pleasures of baking and especially of sharing the creations are present in the Finnish foodie talk, which appears almost denuded of sensual connotations, establishing a difference with the average Finns talking about chocolate on the discussion forum. The narrative of striving towards healthy eating is pre-eminent, although one can give in to sweet temptations every now and then.

Baking With Chocolate: A Pleasure for the Gifter and the Recipient

If chocolate in the form of confectionary products is most often offered by men to women (when in a heterosexual context of relationship building), baking with chocolate is a traditionally female way of conquering a heart and making a gift. Locher et al. (2005) claim that when women offer self-made gifts such as chocolate cookies or cakes, these are often associated by men with the comfort foods of their childhood. A clever woman plays the card of warm memories of a mother baking chocolate chip cookies, which is a safe and subtle way to start the seduction process. Making a mouthwatering, rich, and voluptuous chocolate cake might be the next step, and it reinforces the old adage that the way to a man's heart is through his stomach! Indeed, in our interpretation of carnal-singularity, anticipation of sex may constitute a continuum—from more de-carnal-singularized gifts such as chocolate cookies towards highly carnal-singularized products such as a luscious, promise-laden chocolate cake. The carnally evocative power of chocolate gifts shifts according to the relationship and the expectations of counterparts.

Most examples on carnal-singularity in the context of baking with chocolate were found in the French data. An analysis of the *Marmiton* discussion forum sheds light on the carnal associations cherished by French consumers: out of the 38 feeds analyzed, 18 contained an index of indulgence, self-pleasure or seduction: expressions, locutions or other types of discursive tools such as ellipses, which were used to enhance the association between chocolate and sensuality, to accentuate the sense of mystery or prohibition, and to emphasize the uniqueness of chocolate as an ingredient. Not only this, but the characterization of chocolate as a gift demonstrates that the chocolate gift becomes imbued with the body of the woman in the act of gift-giving:

> *Croque mon coeur, il craque pour toi ! Réalisez pas à pas un coeur en chocolat, marqué de votre plus beau message d'amour."* [Crunch my heart, it falls for you! Step by step, make a heart in chocolate, marked with your most beautiful message of love.]
>
> *S'il y a bien une chose à laquelle on ne résiste jamais, c'est le chocolat. Allez, ne prenez pas cet air innocent ! Qui n'a jamais ressenti une grande émotion en laissant fondre un carré de chocolat sous le palais, en respirant la bonne odeur du gâteau en train de cuire, en trempant son doigt dans la pâte encore crue ?"* [If there is one thing one never resists, it's chocolate. Come on, don't take that innocent look! Who has never felt a grand emotion while having a piece of chocolate melting in the palate, while sniffing the lovely scent of a cake baking, while dipping one's finger in the dough, still uncooked?]
>
> *(Attention, vous avez un peu de chocolat au coin des lèvres). Et, à notre grande surprise, l'opération est simplissime, divinement régressive ..."* [(Attention, you have a bit of chocolate on your lips.) And, to our big surprise, the operation is most simple, divinely regressive ...] (Marmiton)

Allusions to touching and the physical effects of chocolate are abundant in French baking scenes: licking, salivating, dipping fingers. This creates discursively a context which is as pleasurable for the baker as the result will be for the receiver of the chocolatey gift. The metaphor of succumbing is found in five feeds, where the image of melting chocolate can be interpreted as giving in to temptation. Interestingly, in our corpus, the more intimate context of a discussion forum provides more liberty to writers than the blog format.

French culinary discourse is prone to sensuality, which fits the stereotype of French culture with a constantly ongoing, subtle or overtly seductive play. The treasured culinary heritage is deeply embedded in national culture and heralded as one of the icons of Frenchness. When chocolate comes into the picture, the language becomes even more laden with allusions to seduction, temptation, giving up or resisting (but why should we? as one thread of the meta-discourse of bakers seems to ask). Chocolate truly is an iconic element for French bakers who wish to provide pleasure for themselves or for others, and the carnal connotations become more frequent within a context of the free, associative genre of online writing such as a conversation forum.

This discursive strategy weaves beautifully together the levels of tempting, hence constructing a setting for seduction: one is enchanted by the sweetness of the culinary result (sometimes also by the baking process, as it is so hard to resist tasting) and by the person to whom it is given. It is not surprising that one of the most beloved chocolate desserts in France is called *fondant au chocolat*, literally "chocolate melting." To be able to enjoy the voluptuous, almost liquid chocolate within, one needs to break the crust hiding it and let the sensual dark chocolate flow onto the plate. Tempting, and irrevocable—a deep metaphor of a seductive play.

In the Finnish data, we found an eloquent example of carnal-singularity by chocolate, which provoked interesting indignation and cyber-rage, as it disrupted the dominant discourse by associating baking with eroticism. A Finnish bake-off/beauty contestant/Instagram celebrity provoked a small storm online in January 2017 with her video feeds and Instagram photos, presenting scenes of baking tempting chocolate cakes and brownies flagged with "Eat me!" signs. Her looks and self-styling owe a great deal to Nigella Lawson, who is widely regarded as the celebrity cook who brought "gastroporn" into mainstream cookery TV programs (Hewer and Brownlie 2009; Stevens, Cappellini, and Smith 2015). Perhaps in a less sophisticated way than Nigella, she dressed in red satin and revealed her overgenerous décolleté (www.iltasanomat.fi).

Contrasting to French culinary discourse, baking in Finland has traditionally had scant carnal or erotic connotations, and Finnish women expressed outrage for this provocative intrusion into their domestic, nurturing domain: "*No need to go crying in yellow press after these kind of pics. ...*" The exasperation may result from the fact that this self-made, male-appealing media personality attempts to eroticize something which traditionally isn't erotic in Finland (resentment for the loss of innocence around eating chocolate cake) or, more intriguingly, in the Finnish context, since she wants to make public some of the ancient feminine tricks of baking (jealousy for complicity?). Empowering comments from both men *("Who's the lucky guy??")* and women *("Don't worry, go on!")* kept on coming, however, after the incident was made public in the national press, demonstrating a polarization of views around sexualizing chocolate.

Discussion and Conclusion

In this chapter, we have used cross-linguistic data to illustrate how chocolate as a gift shifts across national boundaries in the way the body of a woman (and, sometimes, of a man) is linked to the consuming and loving of chocolate. We have introduced the concept of carnal-singularity to progress the ideas around materiality in consumer culture, in particular "*the relation and co-creation of subjects and objects*" (Borgerson 2005,

439), and issues of agency, suggesting a way that might be used to map the shifting values and meanings of chocolate *vis-à-vis* womens' bodies in popular discourse. In doing so we have sought to demonstrate the inherent ambiguities of contemporary womanhood, where the female body is the contested site of liberation and is imbued with all the postmodern "paradoxical juxtapositions" that inhere in the concept and construction of ideal femininities (Cronin et al. 2014, 387). On these foodie internet sites, the woman is at once free to express her sexuality and at the same time, checked for "unfeminine" excesses of sexuality or (food) consumption—two aspects inextricably linked in the discourse, and recalling Probyn's (2000) work on the relationship between the culinary, the corporeal and the cultural.

When compared, English, Finnish, and French chocolate discourses seem to fulfill diversified functions for consumers. Where Finns adopt mostly a practical orientation with, for example, ethical, nutritious or caregiving concerns in the context of home life and women's responsibility to nurture others, the French tend to use chocolate more as a narrative for seduction, and the English express guilty pleasures, kitsch, and humor, reflecting the paradoxes highlighted by Cronin et al. (2014) in their study. Moreover, they are tempted by these attributes across commercial online discourse in English. There is a layer of mystery and invitation for chocolate in French, which manifests itself in Finnish as a prohibitive element, due to nutritional and calorific concerns.

Online discourse on chocolate gifts and self-gifts in all these languages construe a culturally embraced narrative where women may adopt various roles, shifting from carnal-singularized active gifters towards passive objects, expecting gifts, whereas the roles assigned for men tend to be narrowed down as gift-givers. Across the different language contexts, the carnal-singularity of the chocolate gift shifts, from the almost desexualized, humorous, and kitsch, with guilty pleasure of the self-gift in English, to the overtly sexualized, seduction in French, and the more serious, evaluative, and critical discourse in Finnish.

The concept of carnal-singularity thus demonstrates how conceptualizations of consumption, women, the body and sexuality, are culturally specific and nuanced, indicating a challenge to the carnal feminine in popular and academic Western discourse. Furthermore, they show, in their varied representations of women's relationship with food in online foodie blogs, how complex, open, and passionate these "networks of desire" can be, and the importance of food as a means of collapsing the self-other, subject-object, and material-virtual in the context of cultural negotiations about food and what it signifies between people. In relation to the gift and the recipient, when object and subject melt away in a mouthwatering moment of reciprocal exchange, one can begin to understand what Deleuze means when he writes that food is *"the mediator between discourse and the body,"* or doubt Curtin's

(1992) observation (in Martin 2005, 28) that food is *"one of the most common and pervasive sources of value in human experience,"* particularly, we would add, when it is offered to others as a gift.

References

Appadurai, Arjun (1986), *The Social Life of Things*, Cambridge: Cambridge University Press.

Askegaard, Søren and Anders Bengtsson (2005), "When Hershey met Betty: Love, Lust and Co-Branding," *Journal of Product & Brand Management*, 14 (5), 322–9.

Barthel, Diane (1989), "Modernism and Marketing: The Chocolate Box Revisited," *Theory, Culture and Society*, 6, 429–38.

Beardsworth, Alan and Teresa Keil (1997), *Sociology on the Menu: An Invitation to the Study of Food and Society*, London: Routledge.

Belk, Russell W. (1998), "In the Arms of the Overcoat: On Luxury, Romanticism, and Consumer Desire," in *Romancing the Market*, ed. Stephen Brown, Anne-Marie Doherty, and Bill Clarke, London: Routledge, 41–55.

Belk, Russell W. and Gregory S. Coon (1993), "Gift Giving as Agapic Love: An Alternative to the Exchange Paradigm Based on Dating Experiences," *Journal of Consumer Research*, 20 (3), 393–417.

Belk, Russell W. and Janeen A. Costa (1998), "Chocolate Delights: Gender and Consumer Indulgence," in *GCB: Gender and Consumer Behavior*, Vol. 4, ed. Eileen Fischer, San Francisco, CA: Association for Consumer Research, 179–94.

Belk, Russell W., Guliz Ger, and Søren Askegaard (1996), "Metaphors of Consumer Desire," in *Advances in Consumer Research*, Vol. 23, ed. Kim P. Corfman and John G. Lynch, Jr., Provo: UT: Association for Consumer Research, 369–73.

Borgerson, Janet (2005), "Materiality, Agency, and the Constitution of Consuming Subjects: Insights for Consumer Research," in *Advances in Consumer Research*, Vol. 32, ed. Geeta Menon and Akshay R. Rao, Duluth, MN: Association for Consumer Research, 439–43.

Braidotti, Rosi (1994), *Nomadic Subjects: Embodiment and Sexual Difference in Contemporary Feminist Theory*, New York: Columbia University Press.

Close, Angeline (2012), "Escalated Expectations and Expanded Gender Roles: Womens' Gift-Giving Rituals and Resistance for Valentine's Day Events," in *Gender, Culture and Consumer Behaviour*, ed. Cele Otnes and Linda Tuncay, Abingdon, UK: Routledge.

Cronin, James M., Mary B. McCarthy, Mary A. Newcombe, and Sinéad N. McCarthy (2014), "Paradox, Performance and Food: Managing Difference in the Construction of Femininity," *Consumption, Markets & Culture*, 17 (4), 367–91.

Curtin, Deane W. (1992), "Food/body/person," in *Cooking, Eating, Thinking: Transformative Philosophies of Food*, ed. D. Curtin and L. Heldke, Bloomington, IN: Indiana University Press, 3–22.

Dejmanee, Tisha (2016), "Food Porn' as Postfeminist Play: Digital Femininity and the Female Body on Food Blogs," *Television & New Media*, 17 (5), 429–48.

Douglas, Mary (2002), Foreword to *The Gift*, ed. Marcel Mauss, London: Routledge and Taylor & Francis e-Library.

Epp, Amber M. and Linda L. Price (2010), "The Storied Life of Singularized Objects: Forces of Agency and Network Transformation," *Journal of Consumer Research*, 36 (5), 820–37.

Fahim, Jamal (2010), *Beyond Cravings: Gender and Class Desires in Chocolate Marketing*, Sociology Student Scholarship. Available at http://scholar.oxy.edu/ sociology_student/3. Accessed on 15th December 2016.

Firat, A. Fuat and Alladi Venkatesh (1995), "Liberatory Postmodernism and the Reenchantment of Consumption," *Journal of Consumer Research*, 22 (3), 239–67.

Gill, Rosalind (2007), "Postfeminist Media Culture: Elements of a Sensibility," *European Journal of Cultural Studies*, 10 (2), 147–66.

Grivetti, Louis E. (2005), "From Aphrodisiac to Health Food: A Cultural History of Chocolate," *Karger Gazette* no. 68. Available at http://misc.karger.com/ gazette/68/grivetti/art_1.htm. Accessed on 2nd January 2017.

Grosz, Elizabeth (1994), *Volatile Bodies: Towards a Corporeal Feminism*, St Leonards: Allen and Unwin.

Hewer, Paul and Douglas Brownlie (2009), "Culinary Culture, Gastrobrands and Identity Myths: 'Nigella', an Iconic Brand in the Baking," in *NA: Advances in Consumer Research*, Vol. 36, ed. Ann L. McGill and Sharon Shavitt, Duluth, MN: Association for Consumer Research, 482–7.

Joy, Annamma and Alladi Venkatesh (1994), "Postmodernism, Feminism, and the Body: The Visible and the Invisible in Consumer Research," *International Journal of Research in Marketing*, 11 (4), 333–57.

Kopytoff, Igor (1986), "The Cultural Biography of Things: Commoditization as Process," in *The Social Life of Things: Commodities in Cultural Perspective*, ed. Arjun Appadurai, Cambridge: Cambridge University Press, 64–94.

Kozinets, Robert V. (2002), "The Field behind the Screen: Using Netnography for Marketing Research in Online Communities," *Journal of Marketing Research*, 39 (1), 61–72.

Kozinets, Robert V., Anthony Patterson, and Rachel Ashman (2017), "Networks of Desire: How Technology Increases Our Passion to Consume," *Journal of Consumer Research*, 43 (5), 659–82.

Locher, Julie L., William C. Yoels, Donna Maurer, and Jillian van Ells (2005), "Comfort Foods: An Exploratory Journey into the Social and Emotional Significance of Food," *Food and Foodways*, 13 (4), 273–97.

Lupton, Deborah (1996), *Food, the Body and the Self*, London: Sage Publications.

Maclaran, Pauline and Lorna Stevens (2004), "Gender and the Erotics of Consumption," Association for Consumer Research Conference on Gender, Marketing and Consumer Behavior, Madison, USA, June 2004.

Mäkelä, Marjaana (2016), "Suomalaista ja ranskalaista ruokadiskurssia etsimässä—Maku ja Marmiton," An Unpublished Master's thesis in Sociology, University of Jyväskylä, Jyväskylä.

Martin, Elaine (2005), "Food, Literature, Art, and the Demise of Dualistic Thought," *Consumption, Markets & Culture*, 8 (1), 27–48.

Mauss, Marcel (1925), *The Gift*. Trans. I. Cunnison, London: Cohen & West.

McNay, Lois (1999), "Gender, Habitus and the Field: Pierre Bourdieu and the Limits of Reflexivity," *Theory, Culture and Society*, 16 (1), 95–117.

Miller, Daniel (1987), *Material Culture and Mass Consumption*, Oxford: Basil Blackwell.

Minowa, Yuko, Olga Khomenko, and Russell W. Belk (2011), "Social Change and Gendered Gift-Giving Rituals: A Historical Analysis of Valentine's Day in Japan," *Journal of Macromarketing*, 31 (1), 44–56.

Morris, Kristen and Douglas Taren (2005), "Eating Your Way to Happiness: Chocolate, Brain Metabolism, and Mood," *Karger Gazette* no. 68. Available at http://misc.karger.com/gazette/68/morristaren/art_3.htm. Accessed on 6th January 2017.

Paglia, Camille (1992), *Sexual Personnae: Art and Decadence from Nefertiti to Emily Dickinson*, Harmondsworth: Penguin.

Pollan, Michael (2008), *In Defense of Food: An Eater's Manifesto*, New York: Penguin.

Probyn, Elspeth (2000), *Carnal Appetites: Food Sex Identities*, London: Routledge.

Schiebinger, Londa L. (ed.) (2000), *Feminism and the Body*, Oxford: Oxford University Press.

Sherry, John F. (1983), "Gift Giving in Anthropological Perspective," *Journal of Consumer Research*, 10 (2), 157–68.

Stevens, Lorna, Benedetta Cappellini, and Gilly Smith (May 2015), "Nigellissima: A Study of Glamour, Performativity and Embodiment," *Journal of Marketing Management*, 31 (5–6), 577–98.

Stevens, Lorna and Pauline Maclaran (2007), "The Carnal Feminine: Womanhood, Advertising and Consumption," in *European Advances in Consumer Research*, Vol. 8, ed. Stefania Borghini, Mary Ann McGrath, and Cele Otnes, Duluth, MN: Association for Consumer Research, 169–74.

—— (2012), "The Carnal Feminine: Consuming Representations of Womanhood in a Contemporary Media Text," in *Gender, Culture and Consumer Behavior*, ed. Cele Otnes and Linda Tuncay-Zayer, London: Routledge, 63–84.

Stratton, Jon (2003), *The Desirable Body: Cultural Fetishism and the Erotics of Consumption*, Urbana, IL: University of Illinois Press.

Zarantonello, Lia and Harri T. Luomala (2011), "Dear Mr Chocolate: Constructing a Typology of Contextualized Chocolate Consumption Experiences through Qualitative Diary Research," *Qualitative Marketing Research: An International Journal*, 14 (1), 55–82.

Websites and Blogs

52 Weeks of Deliciousness. www.52weeksofdeliciousness.com

Chocablog. The Chocolate Blog. www.chocablog.com

The Chocolate of the Month Club. www.chocolatemonthclub.com/chocolate-history.html

Gastronomista. Mangez-moi. www.gastronomista.com/2010/06/mangez-moi.html

Hotel Chocolat. Luxury Chocolates and Chocolate Gifts. www.hotelchocolat.com

Ilta-Sanomat. www.iltasanomat.fi/viihde/

Suomi24. http://keskustelu.suomi24.fi/ruoka-ja-juoma/herkut

Maku. www.maku.fi

Marmiton.www.marmiton.org

Neuhaus. www.neuhaus.fi/seduction

Planète Chocolat. www.planetechocolat.co

Section IV

Romantic Gift-Giving

Unselfishness and Self-Interest

10 The Romantic Potential of Money

When Credit Becomes a Gift

Domen Bajde and
Pilar Rojas Gaviria

After school on Monday, 9-year-old Amara Kirkpatrick did a little online shopping on her dad's laptop computer. But the San Marcos fourth-grader wasn't buying lollipop hammers for Candy Crush. She was making microloans to women in Lebanon, Peru and Tajikistan. ... After reading a few dozen profiles, Amara picked three women for new loans. ... With her father watching silently by her side, she popped their profiles into a "shopping cart," then with a few clicks she pledged $25 to each of their loan requests. ... "I could spend my money on clothes or fun stuff," she said, "but I like knowing I'm helping people all over the world."

("A Fourth-Grader Becomes a Global Micro-Lender,"
San Diego Union Tribune, 2016)

Introduction

The rapid development of microfinance over the past four decades (Mader 2015) begs the question of how finance, and monetary loans in particular, came to be construed as a highly meaningful form of gift-giving and a popular complement to, or substitute for, charitable giving. During the last decade individual lenders have lent hundreds of millions of dollars through online microlending platforms in the hope of helping the poor to improve their lives. Various explanations have been offered to account for the popularity of microlending. While these accounts commonly emphasize the importance of ideological meanings and sentiments (chiefly Bajde 2013a; Schwittay 2014), they do not systematically question the role that romantic construals of money, credit, and capital play in the popularization of microlending.

Extant literature rarely investigates the romantic meanings surrounding monetary exchanges and finance. To paraphrase Campbell's (1987) characterization of the romantic, we know little about how money and finance galvanize romantic experiences of detachment from the constraining realities of daily life, how they fuel imagination and passion, or how they are idealized and involved in the idealization of other aspects of life. Inspired by Simmel's work, Varul (2009) proposes that money is a structurally romantic force that opens a broad horizon of imagination and opportunity (i.e. the possibility of virtually unlimited uses of money). The actual spending of money typically diminishes this horizon (Varul 2009). However, we argue that this relationship is inverted when money is "spent" as productive capital or as credit endowed with endless future potentialities (Gregory 2012).

In the case of microcredit, concepts of capital and credit are joined into capital-credit, that is, credit endowed with the potential to serve as capital for future investments. Loans that in the hands of a hard-working micro-entrepreneurs will generate progress amidst poverty.

Lenders, such as the nine-year-old Amara in the opening vignette, see in microlending a double potentiality. A microloan not only sponsors the specific business endeavor of the borrower, it is also an investment that catalyzes further investments. Once the micro-entrepreneur reimburses the loan, the lender can re-assign that capital to another microloan. In this sense, for lenders the microloans are gifts that keeps giving. Microlending thus partakes in the romantic realm of "eternal becoming and possibilities that are never consummated" (Schmitt 1986, 66). In this way, money spent on a loan opens a broad spectrum of possibilities for both those receiving the credit and those sponsoring it.

The case of microlending indicates that the romanticization processes typically linked to modern-day consumer culture (Campbell 1987) might also be at work in capitalist finance. It suggests that the romantic ethic explicated by Campbell (1987) might not be as antithetical to the instrumental/calculative rationality of capitalism as commonly assumed. If anything, the case of microlending illustrates how the processes of romantic imagination and longing, which underpin microfinance and possibly many other financial practices, become strategically cultivated to mobilize a growing army of (social) investors, who experience their loans as a perfect gift to society (e.g., a perfect gift to the poor).

In the sections that follow, we further contextualize microlending in the broader setting that gave rise to microfinance as a popular development tool and a blossoming global industry. Next, we outline how these developments lead to the mass popularization of microcredit, evidenced by the growing popularity of online microlending platforms. We then situate zero-interest microlending to the poor within the spectrum ranging from charitable giving (i.e., monetary donations) to commercial lending (profit-driven loans), considering microlending both as a gift and a commodity exchange. We then consider the "dark side" of microlending by elaborating on the structural inequalities embedded within the system. In the last part of the chapter we show how the appeal of microlending as a popular form of giving to the poor is linked to the romantic qualities of money reconstituted as credit-capital. The chapter concludes by speculating on the broader relevance of the romantic aspects revealed in the chosen case to capitalist practices and the role that romanticization of credit-capital plays in the ongoing processes of financialization of development aid and humanitarianism (Roy 2010; Mader 2015).

Contextualizing Microlending

According to Mader's (2015) historical-institutionalist account, microfinance is a distinct product of the late twentieth century. This period provided the material, ideological, and political preconditions required for the institution of microfinance as a popular social policy tool and a flourishing global industry. Microcredit, a central microfinancial tool, has a long history as a social policy tool for poverty reduction. In South Asia, the cradle of modern microfinance, the history of microcredit stretches at least to the early 1900s, when British colonial powers began to institute cooperative credit as a social policy aimed at counteracting the exploitation of peasants by local moneylenders. The British authorities saw in microcredit a tool for economic development by way of liberating the poor from the shackles of exploitative debt.

A similar framing of poverty and development in terms of toxic debt and self-empowering credit, can be found in Muhammad Yunus's experiments with microcredit in Bangladesh, often lauded as the birth of modern microfinance. In the 1970s and 80s, Yunus's Grameen and other early MFIs successfully established microcredit as a powerful development tool that could unleash the untapped potential of the poor and the marginalized (e.g., women in developing countries). These efforts and the subsequent growth of the microfinance industry across the globe were significantly spurred by the neoliberal turn in development policy. This turn steered development policy away from large-scale, government-subsidized projects and toward market liberalization and the promotion of small-scale economic activities, often conducted in the informal sector. This neoliberal shift was headed by powerful international organizations such as the International Monetary Fund and the World Bank, as well as influential development agencies such as USAID (Roy 2010; Mader 2015).

Somewhat paradoxically, throughout the past four decades, microfinance institutions have benefited not only from the neoliberal push for market liberalization and market-driven development, but also from the substantial donations and subsidies supplied by governments, international organizations and individual donors. Yunus's Grameen, for example, received subsidies in the range of $175 million in the period between 1985 and 1996 (Morduch 1999). Despite the intensive commercialization of microfinance over the past decades, non-market support remains endemic in the microfinance sector (Mader 2015).

Moreover, the surprising marriage of neoliberalist free-market and self-reliance logic as well as the logic of giving and solidarity (Bajde 2013a, 2013b) has played a pivotal role in the recent mass popularization of microfinance. Take Kiva, the world's premiere microlending platform, where potential lenders can browse through online postings of loan requests and choose the borrowers they wish to support with interest-free loans. The founders of the platform had initially planned to motivate lenders with interest earnings, but instead had to settle for interest-free loans in order to avoid the manifold regulatory obstacles (Flannery 2009). Interest-free lending was initially seen as undesirable because it does not financially motivate lenders and, even more importantly, because with an absence of interest rates lending becomes too similar to donations (Flannery 2009).

To Matt Flannery and Jessica Fletcher, co-founders of Kiva, the conflation of loans and donations is very problematic. They argue that donations perpetuate a destructive, neo-colonial mentality that paints the poor as helpless recipients of charitable gifts. In other words, gifts that are difficult to repay subjugate and breed dependence. Interest rates, on the other hand, "turn a charitable relationship into a business relationship, empower[ing] the poor by making them business partners" (Flannery 2007, 54). Hence, loans with interest rates "convey a sense of dignity between lender and borrower in a relationship based on business, not charity" (Flannery 2009, 37). This paradoxical sentiment is well expressed by a lender and Kiva volunteer who argues that the difference between a microloan and a donation is that donations "create a paternalistic culture where the people become dependent on the assistance of outsiders," whereas a microloan "creates financial independence, instills responsibility, and helps others help themselves."

Yet, as it turned out, most of the lenders did not really want to receive interest rates. As recounted in Flannery's story of Kiva, interest-free loans unexpectedly added to the attractiveness of Kiva and differentiated it from other similar startups, such as the Lending Club or Prosper:

> *All the while, our popularity was soaring. Our user base was growing faster than we expected and we saw little evidence that our users wanted to earn interest on their loans. In fact, many considered themselves donors. Only a small percentage would withdraw their cash from the system once it was repaid. ... Our user base didn't want the interest. ... In 2008, our "decision" to stay at zero percent started to look brilliant. In the U.S., the SEC began to regulate the world of person-to-person (P2P) lending. Lending Club registered as a securities broker and so did Prosper—under a cease-and-desist order from the SEC. The securities model changed the P2P space, and dramatically. It significantly changed the type of borrowing and reduced the personal touch of a product that is*

supposed to be very personal. If we were to use it, we could not pursue our mission. So, instead of becoming an investment company, we decided to continue as a nonprofit offering zero percent loans to the public.

(Flannery 2009, 37)

Kiva discovered that instead of interest, lenders wanted to experience their loans as gifts with a "personal touch." What lenders find in microloans is a form of giving that allows them to help the poor while at the same time avoid the negative connotations of either charity or of profit-making (Bajde 2013a). If we are to contrast both Flannery's testimony and the testimony of the Kiva volunteer cited earlier, one can see how the absence of interest charges guarantees microloans the status of a benevolent gift without diminishing the self-responsibility and pride of micro-entrepreneurs. Thus, the microloan is neither a patronizing gift of charity, nor an exploitative profit-driven loan, but rather a combination of the best qualities that the worlds of commerce and giving can offer.

Neither a Gift of Charity Nor a Profit-Driven Loan

According to Premal Shah, current CEO of Kiva, it "is the space between a donation and a commercial investment that we're trying to pioneer." Interest-free microloans fall in-between the extreme poles of the spectrum between charitable donations and profit-driven lending. Unilateral gifts of charity (i.e., unilateral donations) cannot be reciprocated and thereby result in an inherently unequal exchange and asymmetric relation between benefactor and beneficiary. Loans with interest rates represent a form of commodity exchange, where the commodity in question is money (i.e., the right to usufruct rights to money, to be more precise) and the interest rate is the price. Interest-free loans fall in between the two positions and exhibit several qualities of commodity exchange and gift-giving (Bajde 2013b).

Similar to gift-giving (Gregory 1982), microlending reproduces social relations between lenders and borrowers. These social relations cannot be reduced to the mere financial obligations imposed by the loan contract. Past research, for instance, shows that the popularity of microlending among lenders is closely linked to lender experiences of connection to borrowers (Bajde 2013a). As bluntly stated in Kiva's "Product Philosophy": "Lending is connecting." Put differently, the platform encourages lenders to experience loans as a relation and ongoing communication with borrowers, a relation that is stronger and more enduring than those experienced when donating money (Flannery 2007).

However, unlike what one typically finds in gift-giving contexts, the communicative and relational capacity of microlending does not stem from the inalienable nature of the gifts exchanged (Gregory 1982).

Namely, there is nothing particularly personal about the (usufruct rights to) money exchanged. Quite the contrary, the money exchanged functions as a discrete, transactable commodity that can be contractually passed on as property (Slater 2002). The lenders and the borrowers are constituted as autonomous social and legal entities who can transact and balance out their contractual obligations after the loan period is completed. In other words, there are no lingering obligations between the parties after the loan is repaid (or defaulted). Whereas gifts typically reproduce social relationships between transactors by increasing (rather than balancing out) their mutual obligations, microloans set various limits on the social relationship between transactors in a manner comparable to commodity exchange (Belk 2009; Gregory 1982; Slater 2002). The mutual obligations between the lender and borrower are internalized in the loan contract.

However, by refusing to contractually internalize (and capitalize) on the opportunity costs/gains of the capital, lenders come to construe their loan as a gift to the poor. As further explored below, when money is turned into microcredit it obtains added communicational and relational value. What is more, microcredit is not merely money be spent, but rather a gifted opportunity to create a better future. The lenders commonly assume that every loan repayment confirms that gifted "seed-money" has been successfully multiplied by the borrower (Bajde 2013a). A highly problematic assumption, given that borrowers sometimes take extra loans to repay previous loans, or given that microfinancial institutions sometimes repay the borrowers' debts themselves in order to avoid the chilling effect that loan defaults have on lenders willingness to invest money in interest-free loans (Sinclair 2012).

The "Darker" Side of Microlending

In contrast to the lenders, the borrowers rarely experience the loan as a gift. They typically have very limited information regarding where the money comes from, and they have to pay interest rates to cover the costs of intermediary microfinance institutions (Bajde 2017). Therefore, the fact that lenders forgo interest rates does not significantly impact the manner in which borrowers experience the loan. The relational value of the loan is largely limited to lender experiences while the borrowers tend to experience the loan as a commodity transaction. Borrowers are asked to cooperate in providing their stories and pictures for the benefit of lenders, who are the ones that ultimately benefit from the captivating stories and photographs of borrowers, the reassuring repayment updates, etc. produced and circulated by microfinance institutions and lending platforms. The main goal of these activities is to enable lenders to experience their loans as a form of meaningful involvement and emotional connection with the poor (Schwittay 2014).

In sum, microloans are experienced differently by borrowers and lenders. From the lender perspective microloans are experienced as gifts of "free" money (i.e., not charging the commercial price of money), that are different from patronizing charitable gifts by incorporating certain elements of contractual commodity exchange (i.e., repayment of the loan in accord to contractual terms). Paradoxically, the lenders can experience their microloans to the poor as gifts that open endless possibilities for a better life thanks to borrowers' entrepreneurship. Thanks to the discipline and organization of processes for credit approval, disbursal, and repayment, the loans get reimbursed in almost all cases. At the time of writing this chapter, Kiva, for instance, had an overall repayment rate of 96.9%. High repayment rates instill hope for lenders, reinforcing their experience of being part of something that works. In a similar vein to Marcoux's (2009) reflections on the gift economy, this context also exhibits a turn to the market in order to control and limit the perceived limitations of the (charitable) gift. Lenders get enough detail to experience the loan as real and personal, while at the same time the lenders' information is limited enough to protect the lenders' romantic conceptions of quick progress and connection with the poor.

Past research has unpacked the emotional and relational capacity of microloans, yet largely missed the vital role that the romantic quality of money, or to be more precise, capital-credit, plays in microlending. We further address this gap by way of Simmel's work on the romantic potential of money (Varul 2009).

Credit Romanticized as Capital

Inspired by Simmel's work, Varul (2009) reminds us that money is structurally romantic inasmuch as it affords "a freedom from direct concern with things and from a direct relationship to them" (Simmel 1990, 469). Money serves as a mediator that enables people to distance themselves from the immediacy of traditional relations to things and nature. For example, for Simmel romantic experiences of nature are predicated on a remoteness from nature that is reinforced by the modern money economy (and the urban way of life tied to it). On the one hand, money affords distance and alienation, on the other it entices a longing to connect and obtain, it animates dreams that everything is possible, that everything is obtainable. In other words, money creates an impression of a horizon of opportunity, thus stimulating romantic longing (Varul 2009).

Simmel believed that the manifold opportunities and potentialities that money opens endow money with a certain kind of restlessness, the urge to be used. However, romantic yearnings and urges are rarely fulfilled. In the moment of choice and realization (i.e., the actual spending of money), all of the other infinite possibilities are forgone and the expansive potentiality of money is lost to the narrow reality of choice (Varul 2009). The reality of spending thus conflicts with the romantic taste for "eternal becoming and possibilities that are never consummated to the confines of concrete reality" (Schmitt 1986, 66).

This conflict is averted when money takes the form of capital or credit. Capital refers to a stock of resources that can *in the future* be employed in a productive manner (Schmitt et al. 2017). Although money often needs to be spent to accumulate capital, the spending of money on capital does not diminish the potentiality of money in the same way as consumptive spending does. To translate money into capital is to highlight the productive potentialities of money. That is, spending on capital is inherently future-oriented, invested with imagination of a better future, and with aspiration towards this better future. Hence, money is structurally romantic not only in its capacity to afford a freedom from direct relationship to things and nature (Simmel 1990). Money also mediates our relationship to the immediate present, encouraging us to imagine and long for a different future. The notion of financial capital encapsulates this romantic capacity of money.

Likewise, the notion of credit comes to exist "as a potentiality, as something belonging to the future" (Gregory 2012, 383). It is essentially a prospective claim on, or a promise directed towards, an imagined future. This promise/claim conjoins the futures of the creditor and the debtor, for better or for worse. We propose that microcredit combines the two concepts of capital and credit into capital-credit, that is, credit intended to serve as capital for future investments. This credit-capital opens up a future potentiality (for the lender) that leads to other future potentialities (for the borrower). Through their loans, lenders invest in borrowers so that the latter can in turn invest in their future. Put differently, for the lenders credit-capital creates an opportunity to create new opportunities.

As stated on Kiva.org, microloans "celebrate and support people looking to create a better future for themselves, their families and their communities." Accordingly, to lend is to "back a dream," to help borrowers start or grow a business, to go to school, to "realize their potential." This exceptional ability to unleash the potentiality of the poor (Yunus 2007) makes microlending a uniquely powerful and sustainable way to fight poverty and ensure development (Kiva.org). In contrast to the momentary, palliative effects of charity, microlending enables lenders to have an enduring impact. By giving people the "power to create opportunity for themselves" microcredit is said to garner genuine development and growth. Due to the extraordinarily high repayment rates, lenders can recuperate their money and perpetually reinvest it, thus in principle keeping the horizon of opportunity forever open. Further, Kiva suggests that when a loan "enables someone to grow a business and create opportunity for themselves, it creates opportunities for others as well. That ripple effect can shape the future for a family or an entire community." Lenders can thus "touch more lives with the same dollar" (Kiva.org).

As a result, microloans obtain a romantic quality that is seldom present in charitable giving. While charitable gifts are no strangers to romantic imagination and romanticized distancing from the daily realities of the poor (Chouliaraki 2013), they seldom inspire romantic visions of boundless potentiality and perpetual reinvestment. Recent polemics regarding the actual impact of microcredit and the dark side of micro-debt (Bateman 2010; Banerjee and Jackson 2017; Roodman 2011; Sinclair 2012) further highlight the romantic nature of the proposed visions and expectations regarding microlending. Existing studies show that the crediting of small-scale economic activity does not lead to substantial economic development (Bateman 2010). Microlending is not only less potent than commonly advertised. There are multiple recorded cases of microcredit hurting the poor by locking them into vicious cycles of debt (Banerjee and Jackson 2017; Mader 2015). Finally, doubts have been repeatedly cast on the accuracy of information presented to lenders by microfinance institutions and online lending platforms (Bajde 2017; Roodman 2009; Sinclair 2012).

Our intention here is not to debate the true merits of microcredit, but simply to highlight the romanticized character of mainstream renditions of microcredit, and their tendency to overshadow the realities of daily life in poverty, and the strains of bringing about development. While many lenders, and even the most ardent promotors of microcredit, do recognize various limitations to the power of credit, microlending nonetheless continues to enjoy the status of an almost magical cure to poverty (Giesler and Veresiu 2014) that has a powerful ripple effect (e.g., into the future, across the community) and never runs out (i.e., can be perpetually recuperated and reinvested). Romanticization of money and credit is thus a fundamental element of microlending's rise to popularity.

Concluding Thoughts on the Romantic Ethos of (Humanitarian) Capitalism

The conceptual outline of the romantic nature of credit-capital indicates that some of the romanticization processes linked to modern-day consumer culture (Campbell 1987) might also be at work as capitalist finance enters into domains of development policy and humanitarianism. Following the path set by Weber in his classic theory of Protestant ethic and the spirit of capitalism, Campbell identifies and describes a parallel Romantic ethic that drove, and arguably continues to drive, consumerism (Boden and Williams 2002). According to Campbell (1987), this ethic was instrumental in facilitating the shift from traditional hedonism of the senses to the contemporary hedonism of imagination.

The Romantic ethos of inwardly oriented, pleasurable imagination is commonly conceived as an antithetical reaction to the stifling instrumental rationality of the modern world (Boden and Williams 2002) dominated by capitalist calculation. Yet, a Simmelian reading of credit-capital, indicates that the Romantic ethos also plays a role in driving the expansions of capitalist finance into previously non-marketized realms, such as development aid. More fundamentally, such a reading reveals that capitalist practices of instrumental calculation and optimization might predicate on romanticized imaginations of potentiality and the romantic yearning for perpetual becoming, development, and growth. By galvanizing the future-oriented, romantic features of credit-capital, microfinance institutions elevate the power of microlending and sublimate it for lenders. Romanticized depictions of microlending stimulate lenders' imaginations and help them believe that small loans can make a remarkable difference and provide the basis for personal connection and solidarity with the poor.

Romantic meanings thus represent a fundamental asset for the expansion of capitalist practices such as finance and entrepreneurship into the terrain of development and humanitarian aid. These romantic meanings transform a mundane financial practice (i.e., lending) into an exciting way to bring people together and pave the way to a better future. In the words of Novalis (1997), "by endowing the commonplace with a higher meaning, the ordinary with mysterious respect, ... the finite with the appearance of the infinity, I am making it Romantic."

References

Bajde, Domen (2013a), "Marketized Philanthropy: Kiva's Utopian Ideology of Entrepreneurial Philanthropy," *Marketing Theory*, 13 (19), 3–18.

——— (2013b), "(Micro) Financing to Give: Kiva as a Gift-Market Hybrid," in *Consumer Culture Theory (Research in Consumer Behavior)*, Vol. 15, ed. Russell W. Belk, Linda Price, and Lisa Peñaloza, Bingley, UK: Emerald Group Publishing Limited, 209–23.

——— (2017), "Kiva's Staging of 'Peer-to-Peer' Charitable Lending: Innovative Marketing or Egregious Deception?," in *Seduced and Betrayed: Exposing the Contemporary Microfinance Phenomenon*, ed. Milford Bateman and Kate Mclean, Albuquerque: School for Advanced Research Advanced Seminar Series, 87–102.

Banerjee, S. Bobby and Laurel Jackson (2017), "Microfinance and the Business of Poverty Reduction: Critical Perspectives from Rural Bangladesh," *Human Relations*, 70 (1), 63–91.

Bateman, Milford (2010), *Why Doesn't Microfinance Work? The DestructiveRrise of Local Neoliberalism*, London: Zed Books Ltd.

Belk, Russell W. (2009), "Sharing," *Journal of Consumer Research*, 36 (5), 715–34.

Boden, Sharon and Simon, J. Williams (2002), "Consumption and Emotion: The Romantic Ethic Revisited," *Sociology*, 36 (3), 493–512.

Campbell, Colin (1987), *The Romantic Ethic and the Spirit of Modern Consumerism*, Oxford: Blackwell.

Chouliaraki, Lilie (2013), *The Ironic Spectator: Solidarity in the Age of Post-Humanitarianism*, Cambridge: John Wiley & Sons, Inc.

Flannery, Matt (2007), "Kiva and the Birth of Person-to-Person Microfinance," *Innovations*, 2 (1–2), 31–56.

—— (2009), "Kiva at Four (Innovations Case Narrative: Kiva)," *Innovations*, 4 (2), 31–49.

Giesler, Markus and Ela Veresiu (2014), "Creating the Responsible Consumer: Moralistic Governance Regimes and Consumer Subjectivity," *Journal of Consumer Research*, 41 (3), 840–57.

Gregory, Chris A. (1982), *Gifts and Commodities*, London: Academic Press.

—— (2012), "On Money Debt and Morality: Some Reflections on the Contribution of Economic Anthropology," *Social Anthropology*, 20 (4), 380–96.

Kragen, Pam (2016), "A Fourth-Grader becomes a Global Micro-Lender," *San Diego Union Tribune*, January 27.

Mader, Philip (2015), *The Political Economy of Microfinance: Financializing Poverty*, London: Palgrave Macmillan.

Marcoux, Jean-Sébastien (2009), "Escaping the Gift Economy," *Journal of Consumer Research*, 36 (4), 671–85.

Morduch, Jonathan J. (1999), "The Role of Subsidies in Microfinance: Evidence from the Grameen Bank," *Journal of Development Economics*, 60 (1), 229–48.

Novalis (1997), *Philosophical Writings*, Trans. Margaret Mahony Stoljar, Albany: State University of New York Press, 60.

Roodman, David (2009), "Kiva Is Not Quite What It Seems." Available at www.cgdev.org/blog/kiva-not-quite-what-it-seems

—— (2011), *Due Diligence: An Impertinent Inquiry into Microfinance*, Baltimore: Centre for Global Development.

Roy, Ananya (2010), *Poverty Capital: Microfinance and the Making of Development*, New York: Routledge.

Schmitt, Carl (1986), *Political Romanticism*, Cambridge, MA: MIT Press.

Schmitt, Hans Otto, Paul Lincoln, Kenneth E. Kleinsorge, and Jan Pen Boulding (2017), "Capital and Interest," *Encyclopaedia Britannica*. Available at www.britannica.com/topic/capital-economics

Schwittay, Anke (2014), *New Media and International Development: Representation and Affect in Microfinance*, London: Routledge.

Simmel, Georg (1990), *The Philosophy of Money*, London: Routledge.

Sinclair, Hugh (2012), *Confessions of a Microfinance Heretic: How Microlending Lost Its Way and Betrayed the Poor*, San Francisco, CA: Berrett-Koehler Publishers.

Slater, Don (2002), "From Calculation to Alienation: Disentangling Economic Abstractions," *Economy and Society*, 31 (2), 234–49.

Varul, Matthias Z. (2009), "The Eccentricity of the Romantic Consumer: Campbell, Simmel and Plessner," Paper presented at the 4th International Plessner Conference, Rotterdam, Netherlands, 16 to 18 September.

Yunus, Muhammad (2007), *Banker to the Poor: Micro-Lending and the Battle against World Poverty*, New Delhi, India: Penguin Books.

11 From Strangers to Family

How Material and Nonmaterial Gift-Giving Strategies Create Agapic Relationships Over Time

Lydia Ottlewski

Introduction

This book chapter contributes to our understanding of the social ontology of gifts, and gift-giving as a practice of giving and reciprocation in intimate relationships. The social framework in which I explore the gifting dynamics and relationship progression is the context "Housing for help"- a nonprofit home share arrangement between an elderly person (the homeowner) and a student (the tenant). This special arrangement is not organized as a typical rent contract. Support, in terms of assistance and activities for the elderly, is exchanged for low-cost/free lodging.

The "Housing for help" initiative is an interesting and illustrative case that addresses the increasing loneliness of elderly and the alienation of individuals in our society. It places two persons of different generations together in the same household, such that they begin to share their lives together. This is similar to former living arrangements of extended families that were characterized by different generations under one roof—with the major difference that the elderly person and the student are not related. They are, in fact, complete strangers.

Sahlins' (1972) model of kinship distance and reciprocity as well as Belk and Coon's (1993) relationship paradigms are central concepts of this chapter to understand the types, dynamics, and reciprocity of the relationships. Building upon these frameworks, I provide a processual model that discusses the progression of market-gift relationships.

Sahlins' (1972) model assumes an a priori condition that determines what kinds of reciprocity will occur among people- ranging from family at the closest to enemies at the most distant. Sahlins (1972) uses the term "kinship distance" to describe the kinship relations among people in terms of social distance. A high kinship distance exists between strangers and enemies, whereas we can find a low kinship distance between friends and family, "closest kin." According to Sahlins, this kinship distance defines the type of reciprocity one may expect. Negative reciprocity occurs among strangers and enemies in unbalanced transfers that are characterized by theft or underhanded dealings.

Balanced reciprocity occurs in a market exchange among people who are not close kin but rely on each other's trust and cooperation in a communal setting. Generalized reciprocity occurs among the closest kin, such as family. They are acts of kindness and generosity that do not assume a quid pro quo. I use Sahlins' framework of kinship distance and reciprocity to characterize the progression of the relationship dynamics among the "Housing for Help" participants.

The second theoretical building block for this chapter is Belk and Coon's (1993) agapic love paradigm that I use to specify the various types of relationships in the "Housing for help" context. According to Belk and Coon (1993), economic exchange and social exchange are not the only two models within the broader exchange paradigm. Building on that they present "agapic love" as an alternative paradigm of gift-giving. Agapic love is characterized by "altruistic gifts that celebrate powerful emotions" (Belk and Coon 1993, 393). The term "agapic" refers to altruism and selflessness (Oxford University Press 2018). It is important to note that the term "agapic" does not just refer to romantic love but also includes brotherly love, spiritual love, and parental or familial love (Belk and Coon 1993, 406). For simplification purposes, I extend this definition of "agapic love" by including friendships and quasi-family relations.

This chapter does not refer to the concepts of romance and intimacy as an emotional, sexual, or passionate attachment between lovers. Instead, the word intimacy is used to refer to a very close relationship, that is personal and private in nature and connotes familiarity, bonding, and belonging. In Sahlins' (1972) terms, it would be a relationship with a minimal kinship distance and only little or no expectation for reciprocity.

This book chapter presents the development from strangers in an economic exchange model into intimate relationships within an agapic love model. The starting point is a dyadic relationship between two strangers of different generations engaged in a balanced quid-pro-quo exchange, in which there exists no expectation of additional gifts or reciprocity. The ending point is an agapic bond (family-like relations and friendships) characterized by familiarity and closeness. Addressing Belk and Coon's (1993, 412) claim that "gift giving may reveal the move from economic exchange to romantic love," I explore the transformation of relationships by analyzing strategies of material and nonmaterial gifting, the dynamic development of the exchange types, and the relationship outcomes that flow from them.

The Establishment of Social Bonds Through Gift-Giving

The literature on gift-giving has a long history and started with classics like Mauss's (1967) work on the forms and functions of exchange and Sahlins' (1972) seminal theory on kinship distance and reciprocity. Since then, literature on gift-giving has been further explored throughout various disciplines such as anthropology, sociology, marketing, family studies, economics, and consumer behavior.

In these disciplines, studies consider different contexts of gift-giving such as dating (Belk and Coon 1993), festive occasions (Clarke 2006; Rugimbana et al. 2003; Lowrey, Otnes, and Ruth 2004; Fischer et al. 1990), business situations (D'Souza 2003; Lambsdorff and Frank 2010; Bellemare and Shearer 2009), online gifting (Hollenbeck, Peters, and Zinkhan 2010; Skågeby 2010), surrogacy and organ donation (Raymond 2014), meanings, values, and feelings associated with gift-giving (Chan, Denton, and Tsang 2003; McGrath, Sherry, and Levy 1993), charitable giving, volunteerism (Eckstein 2001; Bajde 2009, 2012; Mathur 1996), etc.

Most of these studies investigate relational aspects of gift-giving. We learn about different relational constructs, ranging from interpersonal, dyadic gifting to whole gift systems, and also negative influences of gifting on relationships (Marcoux 2009). More specifically, relational gift-giving studies cover gifting oneself (Mick and Demoss 1990), dyadic gifting (Lowrey et al. 2004; Raymond 2014; Saad and Gill 2003; Rugimbana et al. 2003), household/familial gifting (Joy 2001; Tumama Cowley, Paterson, and Williams 2004; Bradford 2009; Clarke 2006), business/ work gifting (Lambsdorff and Frank 2010; D'Souza 2003; Bellemare and Shearer 2009), community gifting (Eckstein 2001; Weinberger and Wallendorf 2012; Hollenbeck et al. 2010; Skågeby 2010), to whole gift systems (Giesler 2006; Weinberger 2017; Sherry 1983).

One common characteristic that we find in most of these relational gift-giving studies is that gift-giving strategies are applied to strengthen an existing personal connection between people: "to reproduce a social bond between people" (Mauss 1967), "to communicate and solidify intimate relationships" (Weinberger and Wallendorf 2012, 74), "strengthen and maintain relationships" (Joy 2001, 240), "demonstrate ones feelings through gifts" (Csikszentmihalyi 2000, 269), "promote ties and bonding between individuals" (Joy 2001, 239), and "gifts as expressions of the desire for connection ... and intimacy with others" (Belk 2010, 716).

For example, gift-giving is used to improve the relationship between people in various situations, such as dating (Belk and Coon 1993, 393), between lovers (Rugimbana et al. 2003), in between generations (Bradford 2009; Price, Arnould, and Curasi 2000), within a community rather than interpersonal relationship work (Weinberger and Wallendorf 2012), between employee and co-worker (Bellemare and Shearer 2009), or between family members (Cheal 1987), and business partners (Chan et al. 2003; D'Souza 2003).

Based on the common finding that gifts strengthen and maintain existing relationships, some studies further extend this knowledge by exploring the relational dynamics in more detail. Joy (2001) broadens our understanding about relational dynamics and presents a gift continuum that calibrates relationships from most effective to least. According to her study, gift-giving differs among the different relationship types. Sherry's foundational anthropological perspective (1983) about the relational dynamics of the gifting process provide an understanding about the gift-giving cycle itself. His work offers a detailed examination of a single gift-giving phase, consisting of three stages: gestation, prestation, and reformulation. Gestation is the behavior antecedent to the exchange on donor's side and his/her motivation (Giesler 2006, 284). Prestation is the substance of gift transaction and involves the recipient's response and donor's evaluation of the response (Giesler 2006, 284). The reformulation concerns the disposition of the gift, such as display, storage, or rejection (Giesler 2006, 284). Sherry's (1983) work covers a single gift-giving phase and assumes that gifting partners reciprocate the gift transaction continuously like a cycle.

Two important findings from prior research set the foundation for my research approach. First, gift giving is a means to transform relationships. Belk and Coon (1993, 403) provoke a new direction of thought by claiming that gifts do not just strengthen existing relationships — "gifts can be the symbolic ritual medium through which strangers are transformed into kin" (Belk and Coon 1993, 403). This statement claims that gift-giving can be used as means to establish a relationship between strangers. Second, market relationships can develop into family-like relationships. In their study on paid caregivers, Barnhart, Huff, and Cotte (2014) show that market relationships can get blurred, become more intimate, and even evolve into family-like relationships. These two perspectives serve as the starting point for my research.

In line with Belk and Coon's (1993) assumption, as well as Barnhart, Huff, and Cotte's (2014) finding, this book chapter explores the progression of a transactional market relationship to an agapic family-like bond and provides insights about how strangers can become quasi-family by applying material and nonmaterial strategies of gift-giving. In contrast to Sherry's work (1983) that covers a single gift-giving phase, I provide a temporally extended model that considers both the longitudinal emergence and reformulation of relations between alternating givers and recipients.

The "Housing for help" initiative provides the ideal context to study this research question. Starting off as strangers, the participants describe their relationships as friendship, mentorship, and family over time. This book chapter explains how they transformed their relationships by engaging in practices of gift-giving. A processual model provides the framework for discussing the progression of market-gift relationships.

Context and Methodology

Vast growth in elderly populations is disrupting existing social systems, health care approaches, markets, and public policy, leading to various challenges that existing institutions can barely cope with (Ulrich 2005; Mai 2008; World Health Organization 2008; Pavalko 2011; European Commission 2015; European Commission 2017). One condition that researchers identify as enhancing elderly consumers' well-being is the ability to grow old in the familiarity of their own homes, something that is often difficult to achieve given declining health, current economic conditions, and family structures (Aceros, Pols, and Domènech 2015; Ewen et al. 2014; Black, Dobbs, and Young 2015; Vasunilashorn et al. 2012; Granbom et al. 2014; Wiles et al. 2012). A possible initiative to address and overcome these challenges is the context of this study, the initiative "Housing for Help."

This nonprofit initiative arranges home sharing between an elderly homeowner and a student in need of lodging. Elderly persons act as landlords, providing students with low-cost or free rooms in their apartments or houses. In return, student tenants assist the elders with such things as household chores, gardening, technical matters, social activities, or basic consumption activities such as doctor visits and grocery shopping. Nursing-care activities (e.g., medication, bathing, assisting to go to the restroom, etc.) are forbidden by the organization. The arrangements allow the elderly to remain living in their homes more easily and safely than they otherwise could, and the students receive substantial housing benefits. "Housing for Help" developed independently in many countries in the world. It is institutionalized in different cities through sponsorship by various organizations, such as student unions, city governments, universities, federal ministries, volunteer organizations, senior, and social services, private sponsors, churches, the job center, the Red Cross, or Caritas. In facilitating service exchanges between elders and students, "Housing for Help" effectively offers a market-based approach to addressing the changing emotional, material, and health-related needs of older consumers desiring to age in place.

This research utilized an ethnographic approach (Weinberger and Wallendorf 2012; Marcoux 2009; Scaraboto 2015; Giesler 2006; Sherry 1983; Sherry and Kozinets 2001; McGrath et al. 1993) to advance our understanding about these elderly student home sharing arrangements in Germany and Switzerland. I visited the six pairs, consisting of six elderly women and the six corresponding student tenants, in their homes and spend a few hours with them. This allowed me to engage in in-situ observations of their private sphere. Moreover, in-depth, semi-structured interviews together as pairs and separately, took place ranging from two to four hours. It is important interviewing both, the elderly and the student, together to understand the interactions and dynamics of their relationships. Additionally, separate interviews were conducted to create a trustful atmosphere for the individual, making them feel comfortable to also talk about possible challenges and worries of the home share. A total of 18 participant interviews was recorded and transcribed verbatim, resulting in 200 pages of single spaced transcriptions.

The detailed emic perspective of the participants was enriched by formal interviews with four project coordinators. The interviews with the project coordinators lasted 1–1.5 hours resulting in 85 single-spaced pages. Further informal interviews with other project coordinators transpired in the course of the data collection. Enriching the 285 pages of transcribed interviews are 14 pages of field notes from 15 hours of in-situ observation, a researcher diary (11 single spaced pages), and 15 photo-graphs. Media data (180 items) in the form of newspaper articles, docu-mentaries, videos, and governmental reports about the "Housing for Help" initiative helped to triangulate my findings (Rothbauer 2008). An online blog (weekly posts over a two-year period) of one of the elderly participants allowed for a longitudinal perspective of her daily life with the student.

The data analysis was conducted in iterative steps, continuously moving between empirical data and theoretical background, using open, selective, and axial coding, until "subcategories, perspectives, and themes" evolved from the multidimensional data (Spiggle 1994, 492). Recurring patterns led to more abstract conceptualizations.

Transforming Strangers Into Quasi-Family and Friends

The "Housing for help" initiative illustrates that strangers in a balanced quid-pro-quo exchange use gift-giving practices as a strategy to create inti-macy and transform their relationships into agapic bonds. The dynamic changes in forms of reciprocity and kinship distance are in line with this transformation of exchange practices. The first section provides an under-standing about the economic exchange between strangers as a starting point. The second section demonstrates the type of relationships that developed over time in the home share arrangements. The concluding section explores material and nonmaterial gift-giving practices the that the pairs engaged in in order to move from strangers to quasi-family and friends. The findings will be discussed under the light of the spiral of reciprocity.

Starting Point: Quid Pro Quid Exchange Between Strangers

The "Housing for help" initiative serves as an intermediary to match the needs of students and those of the elderly. The volunteer-run project introduces potential participants and provides them with a contractual basis for home sharing. The contract specifies that the homeowner grants a certain amount of living space, measured in square meters, to the student in exchange for a certain amount of labor, measured in hours. The contract can be personalized to so that the living space is free or greatly reduced in price, with the labor hours adjusted accordingly. Other practical rules or expectations also are agreed upon in advance as well. The arrangement is beneficial for both sides, a tit-for-tat. This means that the elderly and the student enter the agreement in a balanced quid-pro-quo exchange as two strangers. The project coordinator describes it the following way:

> It is a clear and smart idea. Both parties have something that the other party needs or wishes for. It's mutual. So they just get together and the scale is balanced, and that is a very simple idea. That's why it fits. The one has 100% space and 0% strength, whereas the other brings strength and flexibility but no room to live. So the two sides just come together and exchange where they have a shortages and contribute from their abundance. It's a win-win situation. Maybe even win-win-win, because I also benefit from it. Because I am satisfied with my work since the student and older person are both happy. And that is just wonderful!
>
> (Project Coordinator, 45)

We find various market-like elements in the project coordinator's quote: balance, mutuality, reciprocity, and exchange. One of the seniors describes the market exchange character of the project in a similar way:

> This project is great, because it provides me the opportunity to do both, stay independent and continue living in my house. I worked hard to finance this home, so it means even more to me. There was a point last year when my health deteriorated drastically I certainly did not want to move to an elderly home. Luckily, I have the help of Nadine. Thanks to her, I can stay in my home receiving her help and she has a nice and spacious place to live in.
>
> (Anna, 82)

In this statement, Anna highlights the tangible advantages of the market-like arrangement that she has with the student Nadine. The elderly receives help and security to age in place, and the student benefits from a large place to live during the studies at minimal costs. Both the elderly and the student receive benefits from their arrangement and balance what they give and receive.

To describe this starting point of the arrangement in theoretical terms, it can be characterized as "commodity exchange" (Belk 2010) due to the involvement of strangers, who engage in an economic market-like exchange with a reciprocal transaction (Belk 2010, 718–20). A market transaction normally expects high reciprocity (Marcoux 2009, 681). In Sahlins' (1972) terms, considering the model of kinship distance and reciprocity, this case is characterized as balanced reciprocity- the closest equivalent to a market exchange. It occurs among people that are not close kin, but who rely on each other's trust and cooperation in a communal setting.

Development of Close Agapic Bonds: Establishing Quasi-Family Relations and Friendships

Over time, emotional dimensions develop in the dyads. One aspect that influences this emotional aspect is certainly the close collaboration and living conditions of the participants. However, this cannot be the sole reason, as we also find some dyads whose relations are kept to material and economic dimensions. In this work, I focus on the majority of dyads, which started to trade in nonmaterial aspects as well and developed into non-market types of relationships. An example of this is the pair Johanna (student, 25) and Elisabeth (homeowner, 73). Elisabeth, the elderly homeowner, describes their relationship the following way:

> Friendship! We maintain our independence but just with pleasure. It's a very warm relationship. When I'm in the kitchen she comes out of her room and we talk, and it is just so nice. Or when she comes home, she knocks and asks if I need something and tells me about her day. It is very kind. A very friendly communication. Recently, we went to the city together, because I needed to do some shopping, and it was very entertaining. She also tells me about herself and her mother, I appreciate that.
>
> (Elisabeth, 73)

Also Johanna, the student, describes their relationship as friendship:

> We are at least friends. We live very well together. And we talk about things, we help each other and I also receive important help. This is a very positive situation for me.
>
> (Johanna, 25)

The pair- Sophie (student, 21) and Inge (homeowner, 75) even describe their developed relationship as family.

> We also go out for a coffee. It's nice, because I don't live in a shared housing with other students any more, and sometimes I feel lonely. And also because she is a grandma for me here, since mine are back home. ... I think we just get along really well. And I am about the same age as her grandchildren. And yes, we also talk a lot. I don't know, we always have something to talk about. And that's really nice, not to just sit next to each other silently. We talk about anything. She tells me about her past—for example

about her husband and how they met—and I tell her about my family, my grandparents. It's really nice, she's my grandma here.

(Sophie, 21)

The development of close agapic and even family-like relationships is a non-planned side effect of the initiative. In Sahlins' (1972) terms, the pairs decreased their kinship distance and established kinship relations. Close kin, such as family, engage in generalized reciprocity, which includes acts of kindness and generosity with no expectation for quid pro quo. The age difference between the students and the homeowners points us towards grandmother/grandchild relations, as the "Housing for help" participants also refer to. I use Belk and Coon's (1993) terminology of "agapic" to describe non-romantic, but close family-like relationships and friendship bonds. The next section shows how the participants of the "Housing for help" initiative engaged in gift-giving strategies to transform their relationship from strangers to agapic relations.

Spiral of Reciprocity: Engaging in Material and Nonmaterial Practices of Gift-Giving

In the first section of the findings, we learn that the "Housing for help" participants enter their arrangement as strangers. Over time they develop close agapic bonds. This section explores how gifting as a practice of giving and reciprocation transformed these relationships. The formal exchange is already balanced and fulfilled, so the participants freely engage in material and nonmaterial gifting. Especially the nonmaterial "gifts" do not happen based on contractual obligations, but out of care, interest, generosity, and the willingness to bond with the other.

Material Gifts

Louisa (student, 22) regularly receives little gifts from Erna (79) when they go shopping.

When we are out in the city, she always invites me for something or pays for me. I always tell her that it is really not necessary and that she does not need to do that, but she insists on doing so. When we are grocery shopping for example, I take care of the shopping cart, she adds her things and I help her to find stuff. Simple as that, just like grandma and grandchild.

(Louisa, 22)

Louisa describes that she often receives little presents from Erna, when they are shopping together. Even though Louisa does not expect a gift and even tries to reject it, Erna constantly insists. Erna uses gift-giving as a strategy to thank Louisa for her companionship, even though Louisa already receives a cheap lodging to balance the exchange. Both developed a very close relationship, that Louisa describes as grandma and grandchild in the quote above.

Material gifts also play a role in the case of Judith (26) and Bettina (81). Judith describes that Bettina would like to pass along the furniture to her:

> I have my room and bathroom in the upper part of the house. Bettina got it refurbished before I moved in. The room was also furnished with really nice, wooden pieces so I didn't have to bring all the stuff from my hometown. Bettina told me a while ago that I could keep the furniture in the future if I'd like to, since she does not have any relatives.
>
> (Judith, 26)

This example draws a parallel to Price et al.'s study (2000, 180) about older consumers' disposition of special possessions. In their case, older consumers passed along their belongings to other family members. In the case of Judith and Bettina, the elderly does not have any extended family anymore and therefore decided to gift the student with the antique wooden furniture. The giving of material gifts is just one strategy applied by the participants to transform their relationships. Nonmaterial gifting plays a more important role in developing family-like relationships.

Nonmaterial Gifts

According to Belk and Coon (1993, 403), examples for nonmaterial gifts are time, ideas, feelings, and experiences. They are considered even more important than material gifts. The participants of "Housing for help" engage in strategies of sharing the same interests, learning from another, telling & listening, shared experiences, and caring about each other.

A) SHARING OF INTERESTS

A very basic form of nonmaterial gifting is to share the same interests. Marie (student, 24) describes how much Susan (homeowner, 68) and her have in common:

> Well, we share the same religious faith. And what else? So many things! We listen to music, because we both like Schlager music. (laughs). Other things—we talk about educational topics, because she used to be a teacher and I am becoming one. She is very interested in what has changed within the educational structures of universities, what is being taught. And also about parties of younger

people. She used to go out to dance as well. We both like the French language and we like to talk about our families.

(Marie, 24)

This quote illustrates that the both create a common bond through the same interests in music, education, dancing, and religion. Interests of other pairs include cooking and baking, theater plays, novels, and current politics.

B) TELLING AND LISTENING

An essential type of giving is to pay attention to and appreciate each other's interests, lives, and histories. The participants of the initiative engage in genuine conversations and share their thoughts, emotions, and stories with one another. The different pairs report about their profound conversations:

We also have a lot of long conversations, for example when I am eating downstairs, sometimes I am eating up here when Anna is on the phone, but otherwise, I learned a lot about her life and we talk about many things. It is really nice to talk to her. She also likes to talk a lot, that is good.

(Nadine, 28)

Nadine reports that most of their conversations happen in the course of joint dinner. The student enjoys the conversations with the senior. It is important to note that both sides value the common, non-contractually obliged time. Also, Sophie point out their special relationship and describes how much they contribute to each other's lives:

I think we just get along really well. And I am about the same age as her grandchildren. And yes, we can also talk a lot. I don't know. We always have something to talk about. And that is really nice, not to just sit next to each other silently. We talk about anything. She tells me about her past, for example from her husband and how they met—and I tell her from my family, my grandparents. It is really nice.

(Sophie, 21)

Also the elderly reports how much they share with one another, even very private matters:

She already told me about her life and these are things that you don't tell just anyone, it was very private. I perceived that as a big credit of trust towards me. And I also tell her about my family and my worries and that is very nice, because you spend more time together than with the own children.

(Inge, 75)

Inge feels honored that the student shares those details with her. She perceives this as a sign of trust, which makes her relationship very special. She also emphasizes that she spends even more time with the student, than with her own children, which creates a closeness and strong attachment among them. What we learn in all these quotes is that they do not just engage in deep conversations, but rather spend time together appreciating and respecting each other, and caring for another.

C) LEARNING FROM ANOTHER

Another gifting practice that pairs engage in is to teach each other and learn from another. Learning in this respect may have various facets. Anna (homeowner, 82) describes that she taught the student to appreciate the nature:

And Nadine certainly learns from me how to deal with the nature. Now she feeds the birds and the dog, and she really enjoys it.

(Anna, 82)

Erna describes that she learns from Louisa on a very personal level:

I learn from Louisa to be constantly friendly, always being willing to be responsive to others. And absolutely her understanding for the situation. I learn that from her. To settle into this situation without any egoism.

(Erna, 79)

Erna suffered from a stroke and it took her some time to recover and to be able to live a normal life again. Louisa supported her in this situation. What Erna values is not just the physical support, but also the emotional attitude that Louisa brought towards her. Furthermore, the participants mentioned to learn about tidiness, different cultural and religious beliefs, political perspectives, specialized medical knowledge, languages, about other generations, technical know-how, and discipline during their arrangements. Both sides give and receive in the process of learning and teaching, since it requires the willingness and goodwill of both.

D) SHARED EXPERIENCES

Another fundamental type of gifting is shared experiences. Both parties are simultaneously giving, or contributing, to the experience. It is important to note, that these common experiences are non-contractual and outside of the obligatory exchange dimension. Both sides engage in the common experiences freely. Shared experiences can be various activities, such as enjoying a coffee together, attending church services, or sharing meals. The following quotes describe the feelings of the participants:

> It is always so nice together. Sometimes we go for a coffee together, and it is really cozy. I really like that, and I think she is also happy to have someone to drink a coffee with, without any time-restrictions, without being hectic to have a proper exchange.
>
> (Marie, 24)

Marie emphasizes how much both enjoy being together without any stress. She appreciates the exchange they engage in, in a comfortable atmosphere. Susan (68) values the church visits with the student.

> Sometimes, we also go to church together. We share the same faith. Even though I can get there quite easily without her help- but if she has time and no other plans, she joins me.
>
> (Susan, 68)

Going to church together is a very private and family-like activity, similar to sharing meals as described by Elisabeth (homeowner, 73):

> I always wake up early and directly have to eat breakfast, but she usually joins later. And when she is having breakfast I join her with the newspaper and we start to talk. And also in the evening, we often talk a lot and sit together comfortably.
>
> (Elisabeth, 73)

Elisabeth emphasizes her ability to relax with the student and enjoy the time together. Sharing these experiences together is a central element that contributes to developing these close relationships. This takes place outside of the contractual exchange. Instead, the participants build closer connections through their shared experiences.

E) CARING ABOUT EACH OTHER

Gifting takes also place by expressing how much one cares for the other and the wish to contribute to facilitating each other's lives. Bettina, who sits in a wheelchair, describes how the student Judith takes care of her and surprises her with little favors:

> And I would really like to add that Judith spoils me. I am really spoiled! I just put all my dishes somewhere in the kitchen and she

just cleans everything, puts it into the dishwasher, unloads the dish-washer etc. I always realize that when she is not here, and I have to do it myself.

(Bettina, 81)

Claudia emphasizes how much she appreciates the extra effort Marina is doing for her and that she does not take it for granted. Also Nadine, the student, freely takes on additional chores, when Anna's cleaning lady is sick:

She has a cleaning lady who comes once a week to clean downstairs, I clean my room and the bathroom up here myself. And if the lady is sick, I clean downstairs as well—that is not a problem for me at all. I also do the dishes right after the meal, even though we did not set that in the contract. Anna normally just leaves the dishes during the day to do it all at once. But I just do all our dishes right away. She tells me that I don't have to do that, but I still do it.

(Nadine)

All these activities are examples for showing affection and care for the other person. To summarize, gifting occurs in various instances and facets. It can take place in a material and nonmaterial way. In the preceding sections, we learned that various facets of gifting are applied by the participants of the "Housing for help" initiative to transform their relationships from strangers to close agapic bonds.

The Gift-Giving Spiral

The participants of the initiative engage in spirals of reciprocity to establish trust and increasing care. The gift-giving spiral is characterized by non-circular movements that do not return to its original point: e.g., some of the gifts are not directly reciprocated and the relationships are progressively developed. In contrast to Sherry's work (1983) that covers only a single gift-giving phase, I provide a temporally extended model that considers both the longitudinal emergence and reformulation of relations between alternating givers and recipients. The following illustration (Figure 11.1) demonstrates the connections between the various elements of gift-giving in more detail.

The gift continuum (Joy 2001) represents the spectrum of gifting relationships. Economic exchange and romantic love lie at opposite ends of the continuum (Malinowski's (1922) cited in Belk and Coon 1993, 407).

The findings showed that the study's participants moved from one side of the continuum to the other as they engaged in practices of gift-giving and thus transformed their relationships from stranger on the left to family-like relations and friendships on the right. In Sahlins' (1972)

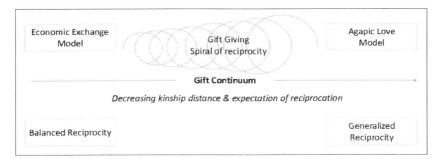

Figure 11.1 Gift-Giving Spiral Based on Sahlins (1972) and Belk and Coon (1993)

terms, balanced reciprocity lies at the very left and develops into generalized reciprocity on the right. In between, the expectation of reciprocity and the kinship distance, both decrease.

The spiral of reciprocity constitutes the center of the illustration. The "continuous cycle of reciprocities" (Giesler 2006, 284) consists of three distinct phases: giving, receiving, and reciprocating (Joy 2001, 239). Within the spiral, reciprocal giving repeats continuously. With each "turn of the circle" the levels of trust and caring increase. Throughout these rotations, the participants build up trust and increase their generosity and gift-giving.

The gifting can either be material or nonmaterial, as we have seen in the findings. Material gifting is more traditional and hence more akin to Sahlins's (1972) generalized reciprocity. Nonmaterial gifting has various facets. The sharing of interests and the shared experiences are special and important cases. Every shared experience represents a full rotation of the spiral, because both parties are simultaneously giving, or contributing, to the experience.

The pair starts off with a formalized, balanced, and contractual quid-pro-quo exchange (lodging in exchange for support) of two strangers. The kinship distance is high, and each side fulfills their obligations with a high expectation for reciprocity. Over time, a non-transactional relationship type develops. In alignment with this transformation of exchange practices are the dynamic changes in forms of reciprocity and kinship distance. Kinship distance as well as the expectation for reciprocity both decreased. Instead of contractual arrangements, the social aspect becomes the central element of the pair. They engage in material and nonmaterial strategies of gift-giving to create intimacy/closeness.

However, not all "Housing for help" pairs experienced the positive spiral of reciprocity. One of the couples described their relationship as negative. Their living arrangement started like all others as a contractual formalized home share agreement. The elderly loosened the formal rules of the home share agreement to grant trust to the student and improve their relationship. Instead of reciprocating this gift, the student (ab)used the freedom and increasingly stopped to fulfill his formalized obligations of the contract. In contrast to the elderly's expectation, the student did not seek a close relationship with the co-living partner. This unbalanced state of giving and receiving led to a broken gift spiral and to increasing conflicts between the elderly and the student. Sahlins' (1972) model describes this type of unbalanced transfers as negative reciprocity. Once the senior realized that the student gained more at her expense, she introduced formal control measures (e.g., bookkeeping of the student's tasks, reminder notes, timing the student's household activities, etc.). The student did not understand this drastic step out of the gift spiral, leading to further misunderstandings of the pair. Marcoux' "dark side of the gift" discusses these negative feelings and dangers of gift-giving like social indebtedness, embarrassment, emotional oppression, and a sense of dependence (Marcoux 2009, 671). As described in Marcoux' work, the senior turned to market logics and measures as a result of the broken reciprocity spiral to avoid further disadvantages and dangers of the gift economy.

This study contributes to the gift-giving literature by exploring the progression of a transactional market relationship to an agapic bond and provides insights about how strangers can become quasi-family and close friends by applying material and nonmaterial strategies of gift-giving. In contrast to Sherry's work (1983) that covers a single gift-giving phase, I provide a temporally extended model that considers both the longitudinal emergence and reformulation of relations between alternating givers and recipients.

It is important to discuss these findings in their broader context of aging populations. The data for this study was gathered in Switzerland and Germany. One might well wonder why elderly consumers in these two countries, being among the wealthiest countries in the world, with established social security and care systems, would choose to participate in the "Housing for help" initiative. The findings of this study clearly point to the fact, that the elderly are not primarily part of this initiative to receive support in the household or to receive assistance with any other activities. Instead, by transforming the transactional service arrangement into a family-like cohabitation constellation, the close relationships become the central element and raison d'être of the initiative.

The study is of high importance since elderly generations are the fastest-growing population groups in most countries. Population estimates predict that by 2050, every third German and every fifth person in the world will be aged 60 and over (The Boston Consulting Group 2012). Large percentages of elderly in a population place strains on social systems including but not limited to pensions and health care. Existing institutions struggle to meet these challenges. Many elderly people desire to continue living in their own homes, even as their abilities to maintain those homes are becoming compromised by declining strength and health. In preindustrial times, or even in many non-Western cultures, the situation of elderly isolation in their own homes would be rare because of the orientation to extended families. Members of multiple generations living in the same households naturally took care of each other. What "Housing for Help" has managed to do is to address the real needs of elderly consumers and craft a solution to the problems of elderly citizens in need of assistance, comfort, and companionship.

References

Aceros, Juan C., Jeannette Pols, and Miquel Domènech (2015), "Where Is Grandma? Home Telecare, Good Aging and the Domestication of Later Life," *Technological Forecasting and Social Change*, 93.

Bajde, Domen (2009), "Rethinking the Social and Cultural Dimensions of Charitable Giving," *Consumption Markets & Culture*, 12 (1), 65–84.

——— (2012), "Mapping the Imaginary of Charitable Giving," *Consumption Markets & Culture*, 15 (4), 358–73.

Barnhart, Michelle, Huff, Aimee D., and Cotte, June (2014), "Like a Member of the Family: Including and Excluding Paid Caregivers in Performances of Family," *Journal of Marketing Management. Routledge*, 30 (15–16), 1680–702.

Belk, Russell W. (2010), "Sharing," *Journal of Consumer Research*, 36 (5), 715–34.

Belk, Russell W. and Gregory S. Coon (1993), "Gift Giving as Agapic Love: An Alternative to the Exchange Paradigm Based on Dating Experiences," *Journal of Consumer Research*, 20 (3), 393–417.

Bellemare, Charles and Bruce Shearer (2009), "Gift Giving and Worker Productivity: Evidence from a Firm-Level Experiment," *Games and Economic Behavior*, 67 (1), 233–44.

Black, Kathy, Debra Dobbs, and Tiffany L. Young (2015), "Aging in Community: Mobilizing a New Paradigm of Older Adults as a Core Social Resource," *Journal of Applied Gerontology*, 34 (2), 219–43.

The Boston Consulting Group (2012), "Global Aging: How Companies Can Adapt to the New Reality." Available at www.bcgperspectives.com/content/articles/financial_institutions_insurance_global_aging_how_companies_can_adapt_new_reality/?chapter=6

Bradford, Tonya Williams (2009), "Intergenerationally Gifted Asset Dispositions," *Journal of Consumer Research*, 36 (1), 93–111.

Chan, Allan K. K., Luther Trey Denton, and Alex S. L. Tsang (2003), "The Art of Gift Giving in China," *Business Horizons*, 46 (4), 47–52.

Cheal, David (1987), "Showing Them You Love Them: Gift-Giving and the Dialectic of Intimacy," *Sociological Review*, 35 (1), 150–69.

Clarke, Peter (2006), "Christmas Gift Giving Involvement," *Journal of Consumer Marketing*, 23 (5), 283–91.

Csikszentmihalyi, Mihály (2000), "Reflections and Reviews: The Costs and Benefits of Consuming," *Journal of Consumer Research*, 27 (2), 267–72.

D'Souza, Clare (2003), "An Inference of Gift-Giving within Asian Business Culture," *Asia Pacific Journal of Marketing and Logistics*, 15 (1/2), 27–38.

Eckstein, Susan (2001), "Community as Gift-Giving: Collectivistic Roots of Volunteerism," *American Sociological Review*, 66 (6), 829–51.

European Commission (2015), "The 2015 Ageing Report." Available at: http://ec.europa.eu/economy_finance/publications/european_economy/2015/pdf/ee3_en.pdf

———— (2017), "The 2018 Ageing Report: State-of-Play." Available at: https://circabc.europa.eu/webdav/CircaBC/ESTAT/nationalaccountspublic/Library/Pensions%20in%20National%20accounts/Pensions%20meeting%202017/PENS_Item_1_AWG_ECFIN.PDF

Ewen, Heidi H., Sarah J. Hahn, Mary Ann Erickson, and John A. Krout (2014), "Aging in Place or Relocation? Plans of Community-Dwelling Older Adults," *Journal of Housing for the Elderly*, 28 (3), 288–309.

Fischer, Eileen, Stephen J. Arnold, Eileen Fischer, and Stephen J. Arnold (1990), "More Than a Labor of Love: Gender Roles and Christmas Gift Shopping," *Journal of Consumer Research*, 17 (3), 333–45.

Giesler, Markus (2006), "Consumer Gift Systems," *Journal of Consumer Research*, 33 (September), 283–90.

Granbom, Marianne, Ines Himmelsbach, Maria Haak, Charlotte Löfqvist, Frank Oswald, and Susanne Iwarsson (2014), "Residential Normalcy and Environmental Experiences of Very Old People: Changes in Residential Reasoning over Time," *Journal of Aging Studies*, 29 (1).

Hollenbeck, Candice R., Cara Peters, and George M. Zinkhan (2010), "Gift Giving: A Community Paradigm," *Psychology & Marketing*, 23 (7), 573–95.

Joy, Annamma (2001), "Gift Giving in Hong Kong and the Continuum of Social Ties," *Journal of Consumer Research*, 28 (2), 239–56.

Lambsdorff, Johann Graf, and Björn Frank (2010), "Bribing versus Gift-Giving: An Experiment," *Journal of Economic Psychology*, 31 (3), 347–57.

Lowrey, Tina M., Cele C. Otnes, and Julie A. Ruth (2004), "Social Influences on Dyadic Giving over Time: A Taxonomy from the Giver's Perspective," *Journal of Consumer Research*, 30 (4), 547–58.

Mai, Ralf (2008), "Demographic Change in Germany," *European View*, 7, 287–96.

Malinowski, Bronislaw (1922), Argonauts of the Western Pacific, London: Routledge & Sons.

Marcoux, Jean-Sébastien (2009), "Escaping the Gift Economy," *Journal of Consumer Research*, 36 (4), 671–85.

Mathur, Anil (1996), "Older Adults' Motivations for Gift Giving to Charitable Organizations: An Exchange Theory Perspective," *Psychology and Marketing*, 13 (1), 107–23.

Mauss, Marcel (1967), *The Gift: Forms and Functions of Exchange in Archaic Societies*, ed. I. Cunnison, New York: W. W. Norton & Company.

McGrath, Mary Ann, John F. Sherry, and Sidney J. Levy (1993), "Giving Voice to the Gift," *Journal of Consumer Psychology*, 2 (2), 171–91.

202 *Lydia Ottlewski*

Mick, David Glen and Michelle Demoss (1990), "Self-Gifts: Phenomenological Insights from Four Contexts," *Journal of Consumer Research*, 17 (3), 322–32.

Oxford University Press (2018), *Oxford Reference*. Available at www.oxfordreference.com/view/10.1093/oi/authority.20110803095355293

Pavalko, Eliza K. (2011), "Caregiving and the Life Course: Connecting the Personal and the Public," in *Handbook of Sociology of Ageing*, ed. R. A. Settersten, Jr. and J. L. Angel, [e-book], New York: Springer Science+Business Media. Available at http://link.springer.com.proxy1-bib.sdu.dk:2048/book/10.1007/978-1-4419-7374-0/page/1. Accessed on 3rd February 2015. Ch. 37.

Price, Linda L., Eric J. Arnould, and Carolyn F. Curasi (2000), "Older Consumers' Disposition of Special Possessions," *Journal of Consumer Research*, 27 (2), 179–201.

Raymond, Janice G. (2014), "Gifts and Reproductive Gift Giving: The Altruistic Woman," *The Hastings Center Report*, 20 (6), 7–11.

Rothbauer, Paulette (2008), "Triangulation," in *The Sage Encyclopedia of Qualitative Research Methods*, ed. L. M. Given, Thousand Oaks, CA: Sage Publications Inc, 893–5.

Rugimbana, Robert, Brett Donahay, Christopher Neal, and Michael Jay Polonsky (2003), "The Role of Social Power Relations in Gift Giving on Valentine's Day," *Journal of Consumer Behaviour*, 3 (1), 63.

Saad, Gad and Tripat Gill (2003), "An Evolutionary Psychology Perspective on Gift Giving among Young Adults," *Psychology and Marketing*, 20 (9), 765–84.

Sahlins, Marshall (1972), *Stone Age Economics*, New York: Aldine de Gruyter.

Scaraboto, Daiane (2015), "Selling, Sharing, and Everything in between: The Hybrid Economies of Collaborative Networks," *Journal of Consumer Research*, 42 (1), 152–76.

Sherry, John F., Jr. (1983), "Gift-Giving in Anthropological Perspective," *Journal of Consumer Research*, 10 (2), 157–68.

Sherry, John F. and Robert V. Kozinets (2001), "Qualitative Inquiry in Marketing and Consumer Research," in *Kellogg on Marketing*, ed. Dawn Iacobucci and Lakshman Krishnamurthi, New York: John Wiley & Sons, Inc., 165–94.

Skågeby, Jörgen (2010), "Gift-Giving as a Conceptual Framework: Framing Social Behavior in Online Networks," *Journal of Information Technology*, 25 (2), 170–7.

Spiggle, Susan (1994), "Analysis and Interpretation of Qualitative Data in Consumer Research," *Journal of Consumer Research*, 21 (3), 491–503.

Tumama Cowley, Esther, Janis Paterson, and Maynard Williams (2004), "Traditional Gift Giving among Pacific Families in New Zealand," *Journal of Family and Economic Issues*, 25 (3), 431–44.

Ulrich, Ralf E. (2005), "Demographic Change in Germany and Implications for the Health System," *Journal of Public Health*, 13 (1), 10–15.

Vasunilashorn, Sarinnapha, Bernard A. Steinman, Phoebe S. Liebig, and Jon Pynoos (2012), "Aging in Place: Evolution of a Research Topic Whose Time Has Come," *Journal of Aging Research*, 1–6.

Weinberger, Michelle F. (2017), "Gifts: Intertwining Market and Moral Economies and the Rise of Store Bought Gifts," *Consumption Markets and Culture*, 20 (3), 245–57.

Weinberger, Michelle F. and Melanie Wallendorf (2012), "Intracommunity Gifting at the Intersection of Contemporary Moral and Market Economies," *Journal of Consumer Research*, 39 (1), 74–92.

Wiles, Janine L., Annette Leibing, Nancy Guberman, Jeanne Reeve, and Ruth E. S. Allen (2012), "The Meaning of 'Aging in Place' to Older People," *Gerontologist*, 52 (3), 357–66.

World Health Organization (2008), "The World Health Report 2008: Primary Health Care (Now More Than Ever)." Available at www.who.int/whr/2008/en/

12 Romantic Self-Gifts to the "Hidden True Self"

Self-Gifting and Multiple Selves

Saori Kanno and Satoko Suzuki

Self-gifting is conceptualized as "personally symbolic self-communication through special indulgences that tend to be premeditated and highly context bound" (Mick and DeMoss 1990a, 328). As demonstrated by its name and definition, one of the predominant aspects of self-gifting consumer behavior (SGCB) is its focus on the self. The self has long been regarded as singular; however, it is now recognized as being multi-dimensional (Firat and Venkatesh 1995; Gergen 1991; Lifton 1993). Multiple selves often involve inconsistent views that affect consumer behavior. Hence, many consumer studies have examined multiple selves and consumption (e.g., Ahuvia 2005; Bahl and Milne 2010; Firat and Shultz 2001; Firat and Venkatesh 1995; Schenk and Holman 1980; Schouten 1991; Tian and Belk 2005). However, there has been little attention given to the theme of multiple selves and self-gifting.

In addition, although past studies on SGCB have focused on Western countries, self-gifting is widespread in non-Western countries as well (Suzuki 2011; Tynan et al. 2010; Weisfeld-Spolter and Thakkar 2012). Thus, the investigation of SGCB in non-Western cultures has been added to research agendas in self-gifting research. However, initiatives exploring SGCB in Eastern cultures have begun only very recently (e.g., Joy et al. 2006; Suzuki 2011; Tynan et al. 2010).

The concept of "face" affects multiple selves in East Asia (Wong and Ahuvia 1998; Joy 2001; Qian, Razzaque, and Keng 2007). It is particularly salient for people of Confucian culture and is claimed to be a key to explaining much of their behavior (Redding and Ng 1983). Due to the importance of face, "people in Confucian cultures are more concerned with other people's perceptions of them and with the maintenance of their own status" (Wong and Ahuvia 1998, 430).

In Japan, there are two types of face: *soto* (outside; surface appearance) versus *uchi* (inside; hidden appearance). Japanese shift between the two types, adjusting their self to fit in a given social relationship and situation (Doi 1986; Suzuki and Akutsu 2012). Thus, Japanese people select certain behaviors that are consistent with social relationships and situations (Bachnik 1992).

Multiple selves are not always consistent, and people often feel uncomfortable with inconsistencies (Bahl and Milne 2010; Ahuvia 2005; Arnould and Thompson 2005; Fournier 1998). Previous studies on multiple selves and consumption find that consumers usually seek to reconcile differences and achieve coherence in their identity (Bahl and Milne 2010; Ahuvia 2005).

In this chapter, we explore the role of romantic self-gifting for these multiple selves and argue that romantic self-gifting is a gift to the "hidden true self" for Japanese women.

Theoretical Background

Self-Gifting Consumer Behavior (SGCB) and Romantic Self-Gifting

Consuming goods or services for oneself has been recognized as a common consumer behavior in Western cultures and has been noted by multiple consumer behavior researchers (e.g., Levy 1982). Mick and DeMoss were the forerunners in self-gift research and built its theoretical foundation. They conceptualized self-gifts as "personally symbolic self-communication through special indulgences that tend to be premeditated and highly context bound" (Mick and DeMoss 1990a, 328). Self-gifts can be "products, services, or experiences, and … they are partly differentiated from other personal acquisitions by their situational and motivational contexts" (Mick and DeMoss 1990b, 681). Mick (1996) noted that self-gifts can be planned or spontaneous, cognitive and/or affective, and personally symbolic; their meanings are arbitrary and culturally constituted but are also very specific to the individual. They are distinguished from other personal acquisitions partly by their strong relationship with the self (Belk, Wallendorf, and Sherry 1989). Self-gifting can be personally symbolic self-communication, are special indulgences and are embedded in a discrete context according to cultural norms (Mick 1996).

Consumers have different motivations for self-gifting: to reward oneself, to celebrate a personal anniversary, to cheer oneself up, or to please oneself (romantic) (Mick 1996; Mortimer, Bougoure, and Fazal-E-Hasan 2015). Previous studies have mostly focused on the first three types of self-gifting, and, thus, there are limited studies on romantic self-gifting (Mick 1996).

Belk and Coon (1993) suggested that the economic and social exchange paradigms are inadequate to explain many gift-giving relationships and that a paradigm based on agapic (romantic) love is needed. Referencing Belk and Coon's (1993) agapic love gift-giving model, Mick (1996) defined romantic self-gifts—they are uninhibited, whimsical, affective, and imaginative self-indulgence. According to Mick

(1991), women have a higher propensity to purchase romantic and therapeutic self-gifts, whereas men have a higher propensity to treat self-gifts as a reward.

Romantic self-gifts are often confused with hedonic consumption (Mick and DeMoss 1990b; Mortimer et al. 2015). Hedonic consumption is defined as consumer behavior related to the multisensory, fantasy, and emotive aspects of one's experience with products (Hirschman and Holbrook 1982, 92). Romantic self-gifting may also be related to these aspects of one's experience; however, it reflects more than hedonic consumption—it is a symbolic self-dialogue concerning self-regard and self-concepts (Mick and DeMoss 1990b). Hence, romantic self-gifts may be among the most affective forms of self-communication and least utilitarian consumer behaviors in consumers' daily lives (Mick 1996).

Self and Culture

Consumer researchers have recognized for decades that people consume in a way that is consistent with their sense of self (Levy 1959; Sirgy 1982). Consumers use possessions and brands to create their self-concepts and to communicate these selves to others and to themselves (Belk 1988; Fournier 1998; McCracken 1989).

The distinctions between individualistic versus collectivistic societies and independent versus interdependent self-construals are crucial for the cross-cultural understanding of consumer behavior (Shavitt, Lee, and Torelli 2008). In individualistic cultures, people value independence from others and subordinate the goals of their in-groups to their personal goals. In collectivistic cultures, in contrast, individuals value interdependent relationships to others and subordinate their personal goals to those of their in-groups (Hofstede 1980, 2001; Triandis 1989). The key distinction involves the extent to which one defines the self in relation to others. In individualistic cultural contexts, people tend to have an independent self-construal (Markus and Kitayama 1991), whereby the self is defined as autonomous and unique. By contrast, in collectivistic cultural contexts, people tend to have an interdependent self-construal (Markus and Kitayama 1991), whereby the self is seen as inextricably and fundamentally embedded within a larger social network of roles and relationships. In interdependent cultures, the self is made meaningful primarily in reference to those social relations in which it participates (Ames, Dissanayake, and Kasulis 1994; Lebra 1976). Thus, people are motivated to adjust and fit themselves into meaningful social relationships. National cultures that celebrate the values of independence, such as in the United States, Canada, Germany, and Denmark, are typically categorized as individualistic societies in which an independent self-construal is common. In contrast, cultures that nurture the value of fulfilling one's obligations and responsibilities rather than one's personal wishes or desires, including most East Asian and Latin American countries, such as China, Korea, Japan, and Mexico, are categorized as collectivistic societies in which an interdependent self-construal is common (Hofstede 1980, 2001; Markus and Kitayama 1991; Triandis 1989).

Duality of Self-Concept in Japan

Although East Asians tend to have an interdependent view of self, their self-concept is not simple. In East Asia, face affects the multiple selves (Joy 2001; Qian et al. 2007; Suzuki and Akutsu 2012; Wong and Ahuvia 1998).

The concept of face originated in China and, through the long history of interaction between China and Japan, was then introduced to Japan. Brown and Levinson (1978) conceptualized face as the public self image that every member wants to claim for himself or herself. They proposed two types of face needs, negative and positive, as the two fundamental motivations underlying individuals' concerns about face. According to Brown and Levinson, negative face needs are the individual's desire to be free of imposition and restraints from the social environment and to have control over his or her own time, space, and resources. On the other hand, positive face needs reflect the desire to possess attributes or qualities that are valued and approved of by other people. In general, people try to maintain face when they interact.

Mentsu is a face concept indigenous to Japanese culture that refers to individuals' social image of the extent to which they fulfill their ascribed social roles[1] (Lin and Yamaguchi 2007). Japanese have two types of faces: *soto* corresponding to positive face needs and *uchi* corresponding to negative face needs. They shift between the two faces, adjusting their self to fit in a given social relationship and situation (Doi 1986; Suzuki and Akutsu 2012). Thus, Japanese people select certain behaviors that are consistent with social relationships and situations (Bachnik 1992).

However, these multiple selves are not always consistent, and people often feel uncomfortable with inconsistencies (e.g., Ahuvia 2005; Bahl and Milne 2010; Firat and Shultz 2001; Firat and Venkatesh 1995). Past research has shown that consumers manage inconsistent consumption preferences across multiple selves. For example, Bahl and Milne (2010) state that the dialogical self navigates through inconsistent consumption preferences. Further, Belk's (1988) extended self concept illustrates that possessions can be part of the self and that these possessions resolve conflicts between competing identities. Thompson and Haytko (1997) and Murray (2002) find that young adults experience tension in their sense of identity as they strive to be both unique individuals and part of a group and that they use fashion to resolve this tension.

Similarly, consumers may use self-gifts to manage multiple selves. In this chapter, we focus and analyze romantic SGCB because romantic self-gifting may be the most affective self-communication and self-oriented form of self-gifting. Examining romantic self-gifting, we illustrate that Japanese women self-gift to care for their "hidden true self."

Methodology

To explore romantic self-gifting experiences, this study employed phenomenological interviewing (Schouten 1991; Thompson, Locander, and Pollio 1989; Suzuki and Akutsu 2012; Suzuki et al. 2016). This research method allows us to delve into the thoughts, feelings, and behaviors of informants and to capture the social and situational contexts of those phenomena (Schouten 1991). The study was conducted in Japan because Japan is recognized as a country with an interdependent culture, and self-gifting behavior is widespread there.

To recruit appropriate informants, we asked about their self-gifting experience within the past year and what they had bought. In-depth interviews with twenty-four Japanese women were conducted, and we selected eleven informants who had engaged in romantic self-gifting based on Mick's (1996) definition. Our criteria were women who self-gifted to please themselves *without* an achievement-oriented, celebratory, or therapeutic purpose (see Table 12.1 for the summary of informant profiles). The informants varied in age from 26 to 57 years old (the mean was 40, and the median was 35). Six informants were married, and six informants

Table 12.1 Summary Profile of Informants

Pseudonym	Age	Self-gift	Occupation	Marital Status, Children
Eri	26	Accessories	Housewife	Single (common-law marriage)
Hiroko	55	Bracelet	Housewife	Married, 2 children
Kumi	30	Accessories	Part-time job at a restaurant	Married, 1 child
Mai	32	Shoes	Stylist	Single
Meg	51	Perfume	Office Manager	Married
Nana	49	Pearl necklace and earrings	Housewife	Married, 1 child
Noe	35	Paintings	Secretary	Single (divorced), 1 child
Sachi	57	Opera	Unemployed (Caring for mother at home)	Single
Saki	28	Bag	Retail worker (on maternity leave)	Married, 1 child
Yumi	46	Bag	Office worker	Single (divorced), 1 child
Yuka	31	Paintings	Housewife	Married

had at least one child. We asked the informants to describe their most memorable self-gifting experiences, when, and why they bought self-gifts, how they felt when they bought self-gifts, and the meanings of self-gifts to the self. All interviews were conducted in the local language (Japanese). The interviews lasted approximately 60–90 minutes and were audiotaped. The informants were paid 8,000 yen (approximately $80) for their participation. The data collection process took place from April to June 2017. The data was collected as a part of a larger project.

To obtain a first-person description of consumers' experience, the interview aimed to yield a conversation with the informants. During the interview, an effort was made to allow informants to freely describe their experiences in detail. Respondents were assured of anonymity (all names are pseudonyms). These attempts were important to capture the true feelings of informants because Japanese people have a tendency to value social harmony and to not reveal their actual inner feelings (Suzuki and Akutsu 2012).

We then analyzed the text, moving from a discussion of each part to the whole (Thompson et al. 1989). We discussed each theme extensively before reaching a consensus, seeking to be open to possibilities afforded by the text (Thompson and Tambyah 1999).

Findings

Japanese Women's Recognition of the Multiple Selves

This theme illuminates Japanese women's recognition of their multiple selves.

Eri, a 26-year-old single (common-law marriage) woman, described her multiple selves as follows:

ERI: I have different faces—for my boyfriend, for my parents, for friends, and for myself. These faces are all real selves. But I sometimes feel tired [of having different faces]. When I was working as a service clerk, I think I felt more exhausted because I needed to act to match with others' expectations, to receive others' recognition. [...] I'm very pessimistic. But I think in the depth of my heart, I admit that I work hard and want to praise myself. I feel like I'm telling "It's gonna be OK" to "another me." I cannot be my favorite self and cannot live for my "true self" all the time. But I want to take good care of my "true self."

Eri has multiple selves: social selves and a "true self." Her social selves include faces for parents, her boyfriend, and friends; these are recognized as a *soto* face (face for outside). In addition, the "true self" is recognized as an *uchi* face (face for inside). She admits that these selves are all real selves; however, her "true" self is a special presence for her.

Saki, a 28-year-old housewife with a one-year-old baby, also perceives multiple selves: a social self (as a mother; *soto* face) and a "true self" (not as a "mother"; *uchi* face). She emphasized that she bought a small shoulder bag for herself and not for the mother-self.

SAKI: When I was hanging around in the department store, I found a small turquoise-colored shoulder bag. I thought it was nice and reflected carefully if I should buy it or not. And I decided to buy it. It's not a huge mother's bag or everyday use bag.
INTERVIEWER: Why did you buy a small bag and not [a] mother's bag?
SAKI: I wanted to buy something just for myself because I thought that I always bought something for oneself as a mother. [...] I was caring for my baby every day and thought I should be only doing child-raising. On that day, my husband gave me free time to spend for myself. I was very happy that I was able to spend time and to buy something just for myself.

Japanese people often have an interdependent view of self. Thus, the Japanese tend to have a strong identification with their family roles, in particular, the role as a mother (Leung 2011). However, for young mothers such as Saki, having a "true self" is gradually becoming more accepted. Hence, Japanese mothers feel inconsistencies between their multiple selves.

Romantic Self-Gift to the "Hidden True Self"

This theme highlights Japanese women's recognition of a hidden true self and their notion of romantic self-gifts to the hidden true self. Many Japanese women in our interviews described themselves as hiding their true self. For example, Meg, 51-year-old working, married women, described how only she knows her true self:

INTERVIEWER: What is this perfume for you?
MEG: It's not like my best friend ... yeah, it's like "another me."
INTERVIEWER: Is it like an ideal self or a present self?
MEG: Present self. I used another perfume called "Chance" before. It was like my ideal self. But this "Happy" is like my true self, who is natural and relaxed. [...] After all, nobody knows my true self but me. Only I know what I really like, why I am depressed.

Eri also mentioned that she is the only one who recognizes her true self:

ERI: I buy self-gifts to take good care and to love my true self. I want to love myself, including my "imperfect self." After all, only I know my true self.

INTERVIEWER. Do you show your true self to your parents or boyfriend?
ERI. Never. I think I cannot show my true self to anyone.

The true self is connected with the concepts of *honne* and *tatemae* in Japan. These words capture other notions of the face concept in Japanese. "*Honne* means one's natural, real, or inner wishes and proclivities, whereas *tatemae* refers to the standard, principle, or rule by which one is bound, at least outwardly" (Sugiyama-Lebra 1976, 136). *Honne* is contrary to what is expected by society or what is required according to one's position and circumstances. It is often kept hidden from others. In contrast, *tatemae* is what is expected by society and required according to one's position and circumstances, and it may or may not match one's *honne*. Japanese people believe that an adult should understand both sides and express the relevant side according to the situation (Orihashi 1980). They also think that *honne* should be hidden to avoid conflict with others (Doi 1986). Hence, hiding the true self is regarded as proof of maturity.

Romantic Self-Gifts for Caring for the "Hidden True Self"

This theme sheds light on the role of romantic self-gifts to care the "hidden true self." Sachi, a 57-year-old single woman taking care of her mother at home, described how she self-gifts to achieve balance between ambivalent multiple selves:

SACHI: Caring for my elderly mother is such a hard job, mentally. So, I give a small gift to myself.
INTERVIEWER: What is it [small gift]?
SACHI: For example, vanishing on Saturday evening.
INTERVIEWER: Where do you go?
SACHI: Place to escape—café, museum, opera ... Opera has very special meanings for me.
INTERVIEWER: What does opera mean to you?
SACHI: ... Well, opera is like another me.
INTERVIEWER: Why do you think so?
SACHI: I sometimes buy high-end luxury brand products, but opera is different. It is like a source of my life. It supports my sense of values.

For Sachi, viewing opera takes on the role of caring for her "hidden true self." It allows her to escape from her social self and be her true self.

Other informants also mentioned a similar role of self-gifting to care for the "hidden true self."

ERI: I feel like being bound by my ideal self—who I want to be or who I should be. I feel bad when I throw my true self away and pursue my ideal self. I buy self-gifts to reset myself; to recover my true self.

YUKA: For me, one of the meanings of self-gifts is to feel self-esteem. I can feel like telling to my true self, "you are doing well" and "you can buy nice things." [...] I can't feel self-esteem because no one praises me in daily life. So, I buy self-gifts to tell myself that I am worthy to be gifted.

Romantic self-gifts are used to care the "hidden true self" for Japanese women. They help Japanese women to accept suffering, failure, and inadequacy and to gain self-esteem. Japanese people are generally reserved and not trained to express their feelings (Benedict 1946; Matsumoto et al. 1988; Minowa and Gould 1999). Thus, self-gifting has a role in allowing them to express their feelings toward their hidden true self.

Such self-communication is particularly important for Japanese women because there is little recognition and complimentary behavior in Japan (Barnlund and Araki 1985; Matsuura 2004). Life entails many hardships, and our informants hoped to be acknowledged. A number of them reported that they buy self-gifts because no one praises them or no one gives them romantic gifts.

Discussion

In this chapter, we illuminated that romantic self-gifts help Japanese women to manage their ambivalent multiple selves: *soto* versus *uchi*. Our findings suggest that a romantic self-gift is a gift to the hidden true self for Japanese women.

According to Goldstein-Gidoni (2012), the idea of living for oneself, searching for the true self and understanding the things one likes or likes to do became a public discussion among Japanese people throughout the 1990s and 2000s. Particularly in women's magazines, the words "living for myself," "finding my true self," and "looking for my own style" proliferated. It appears that Japanese women were becoming more independent as they pursued careers following the enactment of the Equal Employment Opportunity Law in 1986. Today, it is incontrovertible that one has a true self, and Japanese women are now motivated to seek and realize their true self.

Nonetheless, Japanese women's true self is often hidden from others. They keep secrets between themselves and the self they refer to as "another me." Perhaps, Japanese women may be feeling romantic about "another me" by sharing a secret. Doi (1986) notes that romantic love seems to be precious because of the secrets implicit in it. "When love begins, secrecy must envelope both lovers. If it does not, human beings disintegrate" (140); therefore, "love is secret, and that it must be secret" (139). Secrets are an indispensable flavor for romance. Hence, for Japanese women, romantic self-gifting is a secret altruistic gift-giving behavior to solely please the hidden true self.

Our findings suggest that self-gifting can be self-oriented gift-giving for Japanese women. Tynan et al. (2010) conclude that Chinese people often do not choose purely self-oriented gifts because of the face concept. The Chinese therefore value luxury brands to visibly demonstrate their status or honor. However, for Japanese women, conspicuousness does not seem to matter. Our informants noted that it does not matter whether they choose a luxury brand or not when choosing romantic self-gifts. Rather, what truly matters is how they feel about the self-gifted object. Our findings highlight the differences of SGCB in East Asia.

This study only assessed Japanese women, which is its major limitation. We need to further explore romantic self-gifting of women in other East Asian countries, such as China and Korea. Nonetheless, this paper extends past research on self-gifting by providing a new dimension for romantic self-gifting in consumers' lives.

Acknowledgments

We thank the anonymous reviewers for their very helpful comments on this chapter. This work was supported by JSPS KAKENHI Grant Number JP 18K01889.

Note

1. The term "social role" is used broadly to include the gender role.

References

Ahuvia, Aaron C. (2005), "Beyond the Extended Self: Loved Objects and Consumers' Identity Narratives," *Journal of Consumer Research*, 32 (1), 171–84.

Ames, Roger T., Wimal Dissanayake, and Thomas P. Kasulis (1994), *Self as Person in Asian Theory and Practice*, Albany: State University of New York Press.

Arnould, Eric J. and Craig J. Thompson (2005), "Consumer Culture Theory (CCT): Twenty Years of Research," *Journal of Consumer Research*, 31 (4), 868–82.

Bachnik, Jane (1992), "Kejime: Defining a Shifting Self in Multiple Organizational Modes," in *Japanese Sense of Self*, ed. Nancy R. Rosenberger, Cambridge: Cambridge University Press, 152–72.

Bahl, Shalini and George R. Milne (2010), "Talking to Ourselves: A Dialogical Exploration of Consumption Experiences," *Journal of Consumer Research*, 37 (1), 176–95.

Barnlund, Dean C. and Shoko Araki (1985), "Intercultural Encounters: The Management of Compliments by Japanese and Americans," *Journal of Cross-Cultural Psychology*, 16 (1), 9–26.

Belk, Russell W. (1988), "Possessions and the Extended Self," *Journal of Consumer Research*, 15 (2), 139–68.

Belk, Russell W. and Gregory S. Coon (1993), "Gift Giving as Agapic Love: An Alternative to the Exchange Paradigm Based on Dating Experiences," *Journal of Consumer Research*, 20 (3), 393–417.

Belk, Russell W., Melanie Wallendorf, and John F. Sherry, Jr. (1989), "The Sacred and the Profane in Consumer Behavior: Theodicy on the Odyssey," *Journal of Consumer Research*, 16 (1), 1–38.

Benedict, Ruth (1946), *The Chrysanthemum and the Sword: Patterns of Japanese Culture*, Boston, MA: Houghton Mifflin.

Brown, Penelope and Stephen C. Levinson (1978), *Politeness: Some Universals in Language Usage*, Cambridge: Cambridge University Press.

Doi, Takeo (1986), *The Anatomy of Self: The Individual versus Society*, Tokyo: Kodansha International.

Firat, Fuat A. and Clifford J. Shultz (2001), "Preliminary Metric Investigations into the Postmodern Consumer," *Marketing Letters*, 12 (2), 189–203.

Firat, Fuat A. and Alladi Venkatesh (1995), "Liberatory Postmodernism and the Reenchantment of Consumption," *Journal of Consumer Research*, 22 (3), 239–67.

Fournier, Susan (1998), "Consumers and Their Brands: Developing Relationship Theory in Consumer Research," Journal of Consumer Research, 24 (4), 343–53.

Gergen, Kenneth J. (1991), *The Saturated Self: Dilemmas of Identity in Contemporary Life*, New edition, New York: Basic Books.

Goldstein-Gidoni, Ofra (2012), *Housewives in Japan: An Ethnography of Real Lives and Consumerized Domesticity*, New York: Palgrave Macmillan.

Hirschman, Elizabeth C. and Morris B. Holbrook (1982), "Hedonic Consumption: Emerging Concepts, Methods and Propositions," *Journal of Marketing*, 46 (3), 92–101.

Hofstede, Geert (1980), *Culture's Consequences: International Differences in Work-Related Values*, Beverly Hills, CA: Sage Publications.

——— (2001), *Culture's Consequences: Comparing Values, Behaviors, Institutions and Organizations across Nations*, Thousand Oaks, CA: Sage Publications.

Joy, Annamma (2001), "Gift-Giving in Hong Kong and the Continuum of Social Ties," *Journal of Consumer Research*, 28 (2), 239–56.

Joy, Annamma, Michael Hui, Tsong-Sung Chan, and Geng Cui (2006), "Metaphors of Self and Self-Gifts in Interdependent Cultures: Narratives from Hong Kong," in *Research in Consumer Behavior*, Vol. 10, ed. Russell W. Belk, Oxford, UK: Elsevier, 99–126.

Lebra, Takie Sugiyama (1976), *Japanese Pattern of Behavior*, Honolulu: University of Hawaii Press.

Leung, Angean (2011), "Motherhood and Entrepreneurship: Gender Role Identity as a Resource," *International Journal of Gender and Entrepreneurship*, 3 (3), 254–64.

Levy, Sidney J. (1959), "Symbols for Sale," *Harvard Business Review*, 37 (July–August), 117–24.

——— (1982), "Symbols, Selves, and Others," in *NA: Advances in Consumer Research*, Vol. 9, ed. Andrew Mitchell, Ann Arbor, MI: Association for Consumer Research, 542–3.

Lifton, Robert, J. (1993), *The Protean Self: Human Resilience in an Age of Frag-mentation*, New York: Basic Books.

Lin, Chun-Chi and Susumu Yamaguchi (2007), "Japanese Folk Concept of Mentsu: An Indigenous Approach from Psychological Perspectives," in *Perspectives and Progress in Contemporary Cross-Cultural Psychology*, ed. G. Zgeng, K. Leung, and J. Adair, Beijing: The International association of Cross-Cultural Psychology Press, 343–57.

Markus, Hazel Rose and Shinobu Kitayama (1991), "Culture and the Self: Implications for Cognition, Emotion, and Motivation," *Psychological Review*, 98 (2), 224–53.

Matsumoto, David, Tsutomu Kudoh, Klaus Sherer, and Harald Wallbott (1988), "Antecedents of and Reactions to Emotions in the United States and Japan," *Journal of Cross-Cultural Psychology*, 19 (3), 267–86.

Matsuura, Hiroko (2004), "Compliment-Giving Behavior in American English and Japanese," *Jalt Journal*, 26 (2), 147–70.

McCracken, Grant (1989), "Who Is the Celebrity Endorser? Cultural Foundations of the Endorsement Process," *Journal of Consumer Research*, 16 (3), 310–21.

Mick, David Glen (1991), "Giving Gift to Ourselves: A Greimassian Analysis Leading to Testable Propositions," in *Marketing and Semiotics: Selected Papers from the Copenhagen Symposium*, ed. Hanne Hartvig Larsen et al., Copenhagen: Handelshoskolens Forlag, 142–59.

——— (1996), "Self-Gifts," in *Gift Giving: A Research Anthology*, ed. Cele Otnes and Rechard Beltramini F., Bowling Green, OH: Bowling Green State University Popular Press, 99–120.

Mick, David Glen and Michelle Demoss (1990a), "Self-Gifts: Phenomenological Insights from Four Contexts," *Journal of Consumer Research*, 17 (3), 322–32.

——— (1990b), "To Me from Me: A Descriptive Phenomenology of Self-Gifts," in *NA: Advances in Consumer Research*, Vol. 17, ed. Marvin E. Goldberg, Gerald Gom, and Richard W. Pollay, Provo, UT: Association for Consumer Research, 677–82.

Minowa, Yuko and Stephen J. Gould (1999), "Love My Gift, Love Me or Is It Love Me, Love My Gift: A Study of the Cultural Construction of Romantic Gift Giving among Japanese Couples," in *NA: Advances in Consumer Research*, Vol. 26, ed. Eric J. Arnould and Linda M. Scott, Provo, UT: Association for Consumer Research, 119–24.

Mortimer, Gary, Ursula Sigrid Bougoure, and Syed Fazal-E-Hasan (2015), "Development and Validation of the Self-Gifting Consumer Behaviour Scale," *Journal of Consumer Behaviour*, 14 (3), 165–79.

Murray, Jeff B. (2002), "The Politics of Consumption: A Re-Inquiry on Thomson and Haytko's (1997) 'Speaking of Fashion'," *Journal of Consumer Research*, 29 (3), 427–40.

Orihashi, T. (1980), "Tatemae to Honne (Tatemae and Honne)," in *Nihonjin no Ningen Kankei Jiten* [The Dictionary of the Interpersonal Relations of Japanese], ed. H. Minami, Tokyo: Kodansha International.

Qian, Wang, Mohammed Abdur Razzaque, and Kau Ah Keng (2007), "Chinese Cultural Values and Gift-Giving Behavior," *Journal of Consumer Marketing*, 24 (4), 214–28.

Redding, Gordon S. and Michael Ng (1983), "The Role of 'Face' in the Organizational Perceptions of Chinese Managers," *International Studies of Management and Organization*, 13 (3), 92–123.

Schenk, Carolyn Turner and Rebecca H. Holman (1980), "A Sociological Approach to Brand Choice: The Concept of Situational Self Image," in *NA: Advances in Consumer Research*, Vol. 7, ed. Jerry C. Olson, Ann Arbor, MI: Association for Consumer Research, 610–14.

Schouten, John W. (1991), "Selves in Transition: Symbolic Consumption in Personal Rites of Passage and Identity Reconstruction," *Journal of Consumer Research*, 17 (4), 412–25.

Shavitt, Sharon, Angela Y. Lee, and Carlos J. Torelli (2008), "Cross-Cultural Issues in Consumer Behavior," in *Social Psychology of Consumer Behavior*, ed. Michaela Wanke, NY: Psychology Press, 227–50.

Sirgy, Joseph M. (1982), "Self-Concept in Consumer Behavior: A Critical Review," *Journal of Consumer Research*, 9 (3), 287–300.

Sugiyama-Lebra, Takie (1976), *Japanese Patterns of Behavior*, Honolulu: University of Hawaii Press.

Suzuki, Satoko (2011), "Diffusion of Self-Gift Consumer Behavior in Interdependent Cultures: The Case of Self-Reward Consumption Practice in Japan," Unpublished Dissertation, International Corporate Strategy, Hitotsubashi University, Tokyo, Japan.

Suzuki, Satoko and Satoshi Akutsu (2012), "I Don't Need an Agreement on My Inconsistent Consumption Preferences: Multiple Selves and Consumption in Japan," in *NA: Advances in Consumer Research*, Vol. 40, ed. Zeynep Gürhan-Canli, Cele Otnes, and Rui (Juliet) Zhu, Duluth, MN: Association for Consumer Research, 469–74.

Suzuki, Satoko, Saori Kanno, Kosuke Mizukoshi, and Yoshinori Fujikawa (2016), "Consuming 'To Have No Self': Kawaii Consumption in Japanese Women's Identity Work," in *NA: Advances in Consumer Research*, Vol. 44, ed. Page Moreau and Stefano Puntoni, Duluth, MN: Association for Consumer Research, 348–52.

Thompson, Craig J. and Diana L. Haytko (1997), "Speaking of Fashion: Consumers' Uses of Fashion Discourses and the Appropriation of Countervailing Cultural Meanings," *Journal of Consumer Research*, 24 (1), 15–42.

Thompson, Craig J., William B. Locander, and Howard R. Pollio (1989), "Putting Consumer Experience Back into Consumer Research: The Philosophy and Method of Existential-Phenomenology," *Journal of Consumer Research*, 16 (2), 133–46.

Thompson, Craig J. and Siok Kuan Tambyah (1999), "Trying to Be Cosmopolitan," *Journal of Consumer Research*, 26 (3), 214–41.

Tian, Kelly and Russell W. Belk (2005), "Extended Self and Possessions in the Workplace," *Journal of Consumer Research*, 32 (2), 297–310.

Triandis, Harry C. (1989), "The Self and Social Behavior in Differing Cultural Context," *Psychological Review*, 96 (3), 506–20.

Tynan, Caroline, M. Teresa Pereira Heath, Christine Ennew, Fangfang Wang, and Luping Sun (2010), "Self-Gift Giving in China and the UK: Collectivist versus Individualist Orientations," *Journal of Marketing Management*, 26 (11–12), 1112–28.

Weisfeld-Spolter, Suri and Maneesh Thakkar (2012), "A Framework for Examining the Role of Culture in Individuals Likelihood to Engage in Self-Gift Behavior," *Academy of Marketing Studies Journal*, 16 (1), 39–52.

Wong, Y. Nancy and Aaron C. Ahuvia (1998), "Personal Taste and Family Face: Luxury Consumption in Confucian and Western Societies," *Psychology and Marketing*, 15 (5), 423–41.

13 For You and for Me

Creative Experiences as Gifts

Eirini Koronaki, Antigone G. Kyrousi, and Athina Y. Zotou

Which are the psychological benefits associated with attending an engaging play? Why do consumers reward themselves by enrolling in a creative writing course through Coursera? Does one simply gift a good book to their significant other or do they ultimately offer the pleasurable stimulation stemming from the act of reading? Which are the motives underlying acts of sharing customizable tours in Tate Modern or gifting someone a visit to the Museum of Jurassic Technology? Consumption practices indicate that experiences stemming from individuals' creative engagement with esthetic products are often gifted, either to one's self or esteemed others. Despite their elusive and intangible nature, creative experiences are ubiquitous in modern consumption.

Contemporary consumers seek for and value unique and strong experiences. Experiential purchases have been linked to the notions of pleasure and self-betterment (Caprariello and Reis 2013), while consumers find delight in conversing about their experiences (Van Boven, Campbell, and Gilovich 2010). Sharing delightful experiences with others leads to positive personal and interpersonal outcomes (Lambert et al. 2013), and when those experiences are given in the form of a gift, they can strengthen social connection (Aknin and Human 2015). In fact, due to the positive emotions they provoke, experiential gifts can improve the relationship, even when the gift-giver does not consume the gift together with the receiver (Chan and Mogilner 2017). Experiences can also function as a gift to one's self: when individuals consume experiences that end well, they can derive more happiness than if they would from material products (Nicolao, Irwin, and Goodman 2009. Due to their close connection to identity (Carter and Gilovich 2010), experiences help the individual in their self-betterment efforts (Arnould and Price 1993), responding to their relentless construction of selves through products and services, creation, and self-creation (Schouten 1991) and driven by the human characteristic of self-examination and insatiableness (Scott, Cayla, and Cova 2017). Simultaneously, they respond to the individual's need to fight the "commercialization of meaning" (Arnould and Price 1993, 41), which is also in line with the prevailing tendency to let go of mundane materialism (Burroughs and Rindfleisch 2002).

Experiences are also of increasing importance because they form part of hedonic consumption (Hirschman and Holbrook 1982), which has been gaining increased interest lately (e.g., Alba and Williams 2013; Arnold and Reynolds 2012; Lim and Ang 2008). A category of products for which hedonic consumption is particularly relevant, are esthetic products, which refer to the performing and plastic arts and their corollaries (Holbrook and Hirschman 1982) and can thus function as a means to create those experiences that contemporary consumers seek for.

Apart from functioning as means through which experiences can be created, esthetic products have been linked to creativity (Aljughaiman and Mowrer-Reynolds 2005). Creativity is considered as increasingly important for in contemporary societies (Moreau and Dahl 2005). Consumer creativity has been linked to concepts such as self-expression (Schau and Gilly 2003), problem-solving ability (Burroughs and Glen Mick 2004), ability to cope with the consumption environment (Hirschman 1980), esthetics (Kozinets et al. 2004), creation of new and relevant knowledge (Beghetto and Plucker 2006), and a better idea of one's self (Runco 2004).

This chapter sets out to examine the type of experiences that can be created through interactions with esthetic products, to continue with a proposed account of how such experiences can be gifted to one's self and/ or valued others and leverage on the positive outcomes of creativity for the individual. This chapter is structured as follows: first of all, the notions of other-gifts and self-gifts, along with key concepts pertaining to creativity, are presented to introduce the conceptual foundations underlying the proposed rationale, to continue with the presentation of the concept of the creative experience and how it can be given as a gift. Then, we proceed with the motivations and consequences of such a gift.

Other-Gifts and Self-Gifts

Other-Gifts

Gift-giving has been described as a process beyond the rational (Larsen and Watson 2001), giving value to both the giver and the recipient (Areni, Kiecker, and Palan 1998). In fact, gift-giving characterizes not only the receiver but also the giver in terms of social meaning related to the gift (Belk 1976, 1996). This notion of the gift as something shared appears to underlie the three key paradigms describing gift-giving; these three paradigms nonetheless differ as to the degree to which they are emotion-driven and others-oriented. The existing paradigms can be described through a continuum including the Exchange Paradigm, continuing with the Social Exchange paradigm and reaching the Agapic Love Paradigm. The first paradigm emphasizes the exchange and perceives it as a goal-oriented act (Sherry 1983), emphasizing the egoistic dimension of human nature.

Adopting the moral economy viewpoint (Belk and Coon 1993), the second paradigm perceives the gift as something celebrating and establishing the relationship itself (Gregory 1982; Singer 1984) and valued for its symbolic worth rather than its economic worth (Ekeh 1974). According to this viewpoint, a strong connection between the giver and the recipient is created, with the former receiving part of their spiritual essence (Mauss 1954) and the latter giving part of their extended self (Belk 1988). Under such a scope, nonmaterial gifts are frequently more appreciated than material ones, acknowledging the time invested in the gift (Belk and Coon 1993) and operating as reminders of common experiences (Baxter 1987), since the recipient is symbolically accepting the giver through the process (Mauss 1954). However, the reciprocity is still a desired element in this paradigm.

Moving towards the altruistic end of the continuum and the existence of strong emotions, the Agapic Love Paradigm embraces the power of romanticism through acknowledging "the ideal of passion, the fusion of identities and the idealization of the beloved" (Belk and Coon 1993, 407) and perceives the gift as something clearly expressive and driven by the desire to give (Luhmann 1986). This is also the key differentiating factor between the Agapic Love paradigm and the two Exchange paradigms, since the former is based on expressiveness, which is linked to the relationship itself, and the latter ones based on instrumentalism, which is linked to goals external to the relationship (Gill et al. 1987). Under such a scope, the importance of investing in the relationship becomes crucial in this paradigm, rendering the giver responsible for finding something considered as valuable from the recipient, without any self-oriented motives.

Self-Gifts

Self-gifts have been defined as "personally symbolic self communications through special indulgences that tend to be premeditated and highly context bound" (Mick and DeMoss 1990, 328). It is important to note that, although any object an individual purchases for themselves is a form of symbolic self-communication, in the case of symbolic gifts self-communication is a fundamental characteristic of the gift. Self-gifts have some important characteristics that distinguish them from regular purchases. As Mick and DeMoss (1990) argue, self-gifts function as a dialog between an individual's different selves through the symbolic meanings included in the acquisitions. Parallel to that, self-gifts have been perceived as self-regulators of mood for the individual (Luomala and Laaksonen 1999). In fact, this is a commonly observed behavior that individuals invest in (Mick and DeMoss 1992), both when in a good mood and when in a bad mood (Luomala and Laaksonen 1999). They have also been proven to enhance self-esteem (Sherry 1983) and to relieve stress (McKeage, Richins, and Debevec 1993).

Consequently, self-gifts have been linked with the rise of self-indulgence (McKeage et al. 1993), which might in turn occur either in therapeutic or in reward contexts (Mick and DeMoss 1992). This reparatory or rewarding power that such gifts have stems from the fact that consumers form material or nonmaterial possession-self linkages when they are able to derive self-worth from the possessions and reflect important values (Ferraro, Escalas, and Bettman 2011). Thus, since consumers seek to signal and communicate their identity to the broader social world through their choices, they choose symbolic domains to make inferences about themselves (Berger and Heath 2007). Further, they choose to communicate those identities that are of special meaning to them, in an attempt to underline their uniqueness (Ariely and Levav 2000). Recent empirical evidence on self-gift-giving has indicated that it can be used for diverse reward and therapeutic purposes (Mortimer, Bougoure, and Fazal-E-Hasan 2015).

From the above one can conclude the shift of focus towards a more expressive and altruistic dimension in the context of gift-giving and a shift towards expressing one's desired and unique identity in the context of self-giving. In both cases, individuals in the process of giving a gift whether that is for somebody else or for the self, are in sought of a desired, valued, and precious emotion. We argue that one of the desired elements, able to function as the gift in such a setting is creativity, being an element increasingly desired in contemporary society (Schwartz 2011). Before examining how creativity can be translated and transferred through a gift, we are going to present the concept of creativity through an explanation of the dimensions it includes.

Towards an Understanding of Creativity

Creativity is a concept difficult to understand, despite it being vital to human nature. This inherent complexity yet irrevocable appeal of creativity might be plausibly argued to underline its prevalence as a topic in many fields of research such as marketing and psychology, consumer behavior and advertising.

Researchers investigating creativity have long debated whether creativity is a distinct concept or a multiple-facet assessment (Besemer and Treffinger 1981; Amabile 1982; Taylor 1988; Besemer 1998; Besemer and O'Quin 1999). That debate has been the focus of many empirical studies which present originality and usefulness as conceptually and empirically different aspects of creativity (Besemer and O'Quin 1999; Moreau and Dahl 2005). These studies also present the possible significance of stylistic and esthetic appeal in some contexts as another aspect of creativity (Besemer and O'Quin 1999; Koslow, Sasser, and Riordan 2003; Burroughs, Moreau, and Mick 2008). These multiple aspects of creativity have triggered a lot of research in what outcomes and consequences it may have (Reiter-Palmon and Robinson 2009). Therefore, creativity should be considered to have multiple facets (Mumford and Gustafson 1988; Sullivan and Ford 2010).

Some of the terms which have been used within the literature to describe creativity, include several characteristics such as creative thinking and problem-solving ability, both of which are related to creativity (Guilford 1968), imagination, which is considered a prerequisite for creativity (Arieti 1976), an essential component of creativity (Politz 1975) or merely a part of creativity (Prather 1992), innovation, which involves using and adopting original products, processes or services and, therefore, it follows creativity (Prather 1992), divergence, and relevance, which involve difference, novelty, appropriateness, meaningfulness, and functionality (Sternberg and Lubart 1999; Koslow et al. 2003; Smith and Yang 2004; Moreau and Dahl 2005; West, Kover, and Caruana 2008; Burroughs et al. 2008; Runco and Jaeger 2012). At the same time, within consumer behavior literature, creativity is commonly interpreted according to four components (4 P's) referring to person, process, product, and press (environment) (Rhodes 1961; Richards 1999; Sternberg and Lubart 1999; Burroughs et al. 2008). This means that creativity can be seen as an essential skill of any individual, and also be the basis of a purposeful behavior or activity. This activity, referred to as process, takes place in a particular environment and causes the creation of a product as an outcome that must be simultaneously unique, inventive, valuable, and useful (Csikszentmihalyi 1997, 1999; Sternberg and Lubart 1999; Burroughs and Mick 2004; Moreau and Dahl 2005; Burroughs et al. 2008; Kampylis and Valtanen 2010).

Although it has been repeatedly pointed out that creativity is very complicated to define in scientific terms (Amabile 1982; Runco and Sakamoto 1999), it is still one of the most important elements to affect persuasion and consumer behavior in general (Till and Baack 2005). Many researchers make a distinction between everyday (also called little-c) and eminent creativity (also called Big-C) (Craft 2001; Merrotsy 2013; Simonton 1999). Little-c creativity usually relates to common and everyday creativity that can be found in every person and commonly functions at a personal level, while Big-C creativity mostly refers to exceptional, eminent, and clear-cut creativity, which is kept for great people and usually works at a social level (Richards 2007; Kaufman and Beghetto 2009; Kampylis and Valtanen 2010). However, this differentiation has been questioned by some researchers (Runco 2014), while some others even propose a Four (4)-C model of creativity, including mini-c and Pro-C creativity that extends the above distinction (Kaufman and Beghetto 2009).

Given this multitude of relevant definitions, for the purposes of the present chapter, the term "creativity" will be henceforth used to refer to everyday creativity.

Within consumer behavior, creativity has been seen as relating to a task performed (creative task) and/ or the novelty of the output which results from behaviors that relate to finding novel solutions (Sellier and Dahl 2011). Similarly, Burroughs et al. (2008) distinguish between the *creative process* (the mental process that the individual engages in in order to constructively address a problem) and the *creative product* (the outcome of that process). Consumers frequently engage in activities that involve *creative products*, with such activities ranging from scrap-booking or putting together model airplanes to the production of art (Dahl and Moreau 2007). Consumers also practice *creative consumption* when they find novel yet functional approaches departing from usual consumption practices (Burroughs and Mick 2004), coming up with new ways to address the demands of their daily lives through everyday practices (Hewer and Brownlie 2010; Holt 2002). Such unconventional consumption practices might include finding a new use for an existing product, altering an existing product or combining products (Burroughs and Mick 2004). Indeed, creative consumption might be seen as one type of *creative behavior*; creative behaviors are those that result in the production of a novel and useful idea (Harrison and Wagner 2016).

An alternative way of examining notions pertaining to creativity emerges if one considers consumer behavior literature regarding esthetic products and hedonic consumption. Hirschman and Holbrook (1982) draw a distinction between traditional consumer research, which studies packaged goods and durables bought for utilitarian purposes, and hedonic consumer research, which studies emotion-laden subjectively experienced products. The authors refer to the latter as esthetic products; these include "the performing arts (opera, ballet, modern dance, legitimate theater), the plastic arts (painting, photography, sculpture, crafts) and the corollaries of these high culture products within popular culture (movies, rock concerts, fashion apparel)" (Hirschman and Holbrook 1982, 95). To experience such products, individuals process visual and other sensory cues (Krishna, Elder, and Caldara 2010) and evaluate them depending on their personal taste (Hoyer and Stokburger-Sauer 2012). It is noteworthy that esthetics and creativity are interrelated (Tinio 2013) and that esthetic products have been linked to creativity (Aljughaiman and Mowrer-Reynolds 2005). This link between creativity and esthetic products is also consistent with the notion that for hedonically consumed products, symbolic aspects are more important than functional ones (Venkatesh and Meamber 2006). For individuals, esthetic products are mostly appreciated not for their utilitarian advantages, but for their hedonic benefits (Hirschman and Holbrook 1982).

Gifts of Creative Experiences

The key premise of the present chapter is that creative experiences, namely the positive affective outcomes or hedonic benefits that stem from activities involving esthetic products, can be gifted. Esthetic products are hence seen as the *means* or *raw materials* through which gifts of creative experiences are produced (see Figure 13.1). The creative experience, in line with Burroughs et al. (2008, 1030), is a construct distinct from the creative product and the creative process and more relevant to the psychological and emotional benefits experienced by the individual. Creative experiences are internal responses and occur as a result of a wide array of activities connected to esthetic products. A creative experience might stem from the purchase/ possession of a painting or access to the latter through visiting an art gallery (Chen 2008), from passively viewing a performance or actively participating in it (Kozinets 2002, 26), from artistically creating a documentary to esthetically receiving a movie (Tinio 2013). Though conceptually distinct from other types of experiences, such as experiences stemming from brands (Brakus, Schmitt, and Zarantonello 2009), or even consumption experiences (Havlena and Holbrook 1986), creative experiences are characterized by the properties fundamental to an experience: they are subjective, and they include a substantial hedonic component (Holbrook and Hirschman 1982). The rationale underlying the latter proposition is twofold: firstly, creativity has been suggested to elicit positive psychological outcomes and secondly, esthetic products result in experiences which stem from emotional, sensorial, imaginal, and analytical responses.

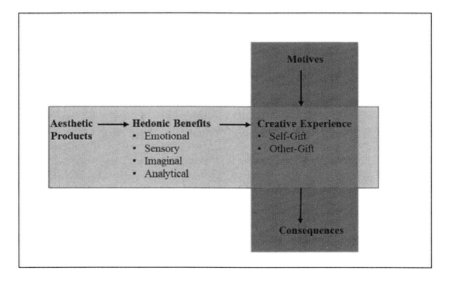

Figure 13.1 Gifts of Creative Experiences

Regarding affective responses to creativity, it would almost seem a truism to assert that creativity results in positive outcomes for individuals. Yet, little is known regarding the creative experience within the consumer psychology literature. Burroughs et al. (2008, 1030) have long acknowledged that, despite the fact that creativity is widely assumed to be related to positive outcomes for consumers, empirical evidence regarding the actual results of creativity is scarce. Apart from evidence regarding elevated positive affect resulting from engaging in creative actions (Burroughs and Mick 2004) and enjoyment felt when consumers engage in a creative task, such as recreational knitting (Sellier and Dahl 2011), the actual outcomes of creative behaviors remain largely undocumented. Interestingly, this scarcity of evidence has been remarked upon by experts in other fields. Regarding creativity in organizational settings, Kim, Hon, and Crant (2009) point out that, apart from its inherent value, creativity is assumed to, but not shown to, result in benefits; Harrison and Wagner (2016, 841) similarly assert that, when it comes to the benefits of, "researchers have primarily focused their attention on the antecedents of creative behavior often at the exclusion of the downstream effects creative behaviors might have beyond the production of the creative idea itself." Within the psychology literature, Silvia et al. (2014) have stressed the need for further understanding of the effects of everyday creativity, reporting that creative actions common in daily life performed by ordinary people can be a cause and effect of positive psychological processes. More insights into these internal processes can be gained through examining another stream of literature, that pertaining to responses to esthetic products.

As discussed above, esthetic products are thought to be prime exemplars of hedonic, experiential consumption (Lacher 1989; Lacher and Mizerski 1994). An esthetic product, such as music, can elicit emotional, sensorial, imaginal, and analytical responses (Lacher and Mizerski 1994). It is thus proposed that such responses might also be applicable to other types of esthetic products. It can be inferred that sensorial responses regard how the human senses are affected by esthetic products; indicatively, Hagtvedt and Patrick (2008) emphasize the sensory appeal of the visual arts. Emotional responses might refer to the feelings experienced when engaging with esthetic products; the notion that audiences experience feelings during arts performances (Hume, Mort, and Winzar 2007), or that visitors in museums and art galleries consider emotions and feelings of enjoyment as an integral part of their experience (Chen 2008) is almost intuitive. Lacher and Mizerski (1994) also use the term "imaginal responses" to describe mental imagery triggered by music; considering that "art has [...] the ability to arouse the imagination" (Hagtvedt and Patrick 2008, 379), other esthetic products might plausibly trigger similar responses which would correspond to the fantasy aspect of consumption (Holbrook and Hirschman 1982). Analytical responses might also be those hedonic responses that occur in the context of cognition seeking behavior, as is the case with the "objective, logical examination" of music by the listener (Lacher and Mizerski 1994, 368), given that artistic works have been thought to result in cognitive stimulation (Harrison 2009).

Having established that creative experiences refer to the hedonic benefits of esthetic products, it is further argued that such experiences can be gifted. Although gift-giving has been traditionally examined with regard to tangible products, we echo Clarke's (2006, 2008) view that experiences, intangible though they may be, can be gifted. Since gift-giving relies on the donation of something of value to the recipient (Areni et al. 1998), it is suggested that creativity is valued as a self-gift because it "is incredibly important to self-construction and positive affect" (Burroughs et al. 2008, 1030). At the same time, the cultivation of creativity can be a valuable other-gift, considering that the enhancement of creativity is considered an experiential process for the recipient; it has been recently demonstrated that experiential gifts can be even more valuable than material gifts for a relationship (Chan and Mogilner 2017). Hence, creative experiences can be seen as gifts either to one's self or to others; the motives underlying such gift-giving practices, as well as their consequences, are presented in the last section of this chapter.

Motives and Consequences of Giving the Gift of Creative Experience

Diverse motives can lead individuals to engage in gift-giving (Heath, Tynan, and Ennew 2015; Saad and Gill 2003). The underlying motives for giving the gift of creativity to another can be traced back to the very reason of existence of the agapic love gift. Characterized as something expressive (Luhmann 1986), the gift in such a context is not oriented towards achieving a specific goal—it rather serves as a celebration of the relationship and an indication of love. Such a gift carries the message of the receiver's uniqueness, showing the giver's desire to share well-being with the beloved one (Belk and Coon 1993). Additional motives can be plausibly inferred drawing on a psychological view of motivations underlying creative behaviors (Forgeard and Mecklenburg 2013): the giver might be intrinsically motivated if they focus on the benefits of the creative process for the receiver, or extrinsically motivated if they focus on the benefits of the creative outcome. For instance, a spouse gifting to their partner the creative experience resulting from reading Homer's *Odyssey* might be intrinsically motivated if they focus on the feelings experienced when reading this esthetic product; alternatively, they might be extrinsically motivated if they focus on the fact that the spouse will have read this particular book.

On the other hand, when giving the gift of creative experiences as a self-gift, the individual is primarily motivated by their creative self-efficacy beliefs, namely their ability to produce creative ideas (Tierney and Farmer 2002). Another significant motivation might relate to the individual's desire for self-actualization (Krems, Kenrick, and Neel 2017). Self-actualization is defined as "the desire to become more and more what one is, to become everything that one is capable of becoming" (Maslow 1943, 382) and is a desired end-state in contemporary globalized, hyper-real and meaning-deprived societies (Arnould and Price 2000; Beverland and Farrelly 2009). The desire for self-actualization functions as a motive for engaging in creative activities, since a self-actualizing individual is characterized by openness to experience (McCrae and Costa 1987; Mittelman 1991) and eagerness to learn new ideas and skills and try new things (Heylighen 1992). Furthermore, the extent to which the individual is predominantly intrinsically or extrinsically motivated will affect whether they will be motivated by personal growth and relevant positive feelings or obtaining rewards and gaining recognition respectively (Forgeard and Mecklenburg 2013). Illustratively, a person who rewards themselves by creatively experiencing an event in the Metropolitan Opera of New York might be motivated by the cognitive stimulation elicited; alternatively, they might be extrinsically motivated by the "collectable experience" *per se* (Keinan and Kivetz 2010, 935).Regarding the consequences of gifting creative experiences to others, it can be suggested that giving this gift can provide two types of values, not just to the giver but also to the recipient, per Larsen and Watson (2001). Out of the four types of value proposed, it can be suggested that in this context, both social value and expressive value can emerge from such an exchange. Social value can be a possible outcome created since such a gift can function as a form of celebrating the relationship, symbolizing, and conveying meaning through the creation of a bond (Belk and Coon 1993). Expressive value can also be created for both parties, considering that such a gift would be representative of the self, indicating an element of self-identity (Areni et al. 1998).

The self-gift of creative experiences can also have significant consequences for the individual. Considering the hedonic nature of such a gift, it can be perceived as an indulgence, since it would represent gratification of oneself (Kivetz and Simonson 2002). Kivetz and Simonson (2002) argue that individuals considering themselves lacking sufficient indulgence, seek to correct this imbalance in an attempt to improve and enrich their quality of life. Furthermore, the individual's need to differentiate from others and to gain some degree of emancipation can be satisfied, due to the increased levels of self-expression through those creative behaviors (Kozinets 2002).

The present chapter proposed that creative experiences, the positive affective outcomes or hedonic benefits that stem from activities involving esthetic products, can be gifted. To the best of the authors' knowledge, this is the first attempt to examine creative experiences in a gift-giving context, to identify the underlying motives for such gifts and to shed light on the emerging consequences. As such, this chapter has put forward a re-conceptualization of consumption phenomena that relate to esthetic products and creative experiences, also drawing on anecdotal experience. In an era when creativity and experiences seem more than intuitively appealing, future empirical research is called for to enhance our understanding of creative experiences as gifts.

References

Aknin, Lara B. and Lauren J. Human (2015), "Give a Piece of You: Gifts That Reflect Givers Promote Closeness," *Journal of Experimental Social Psychology*, 60, 8–16.

Alba, Joseph W. and Elanor F. Williams (2013), "Pleasure Principles: A Review of Research on Hedonic Consumption," *Journal of Consumer Psychology*, 23 (1), 2–18.

Aljughaiman, Abdullah and Elizabeth Mowrer-Reynolds (2005), "Teachers' Conceptions of Creativity and Creative Students," *The Journal of Creative Behavior*, 39 (1), 17–34.

Amabile, Teresa M. (1982), "Children's Artistic Creativity: Detrimental Effects of Competition in a Field Setting," *Personality and Social Psychology Bulletin*, 8 (3), 573–8.

Areni, Charles S., Pamela Kiecker, and Kay M. Palan (1998), "Is It Better to Give Than to Receive? Exploring Gender Differences in the Meaning of Memorable Gifts," *Psychology & Marketing*, 15 (1), 81–109.

Ariely, Dan and Jonathan Levav (2000), "Sequential Choice in Group Settings: Taking the Road Less Traveled and Less Enjoyed," *Journal of Consumer Research*, 27 (3), 279–90.

Arieti, Silvano (1976), *Creativity: The Magic Synthesis*, New York: Basic Books.

Arnold, Mark J. and Kristy E. Reynolds (2012), "Approach and Avoidance Motivation: Investigating Hedonic Consumption in a Retail Setting," *Journal of Retailing*, 88 (3), 399–411.

Arnould, Eric J. and Linda L. Price (1993), "River Magic: Extraordinary Experience and the Extended Service Encounter," *Journal of Consumer Research*, 20 (1), 24–45.

Arnould, Eric J. and Linda L. Price (2000), "Authenticating Acts and Authoritative Performances: Questing for Self and Community," in *The Why of Consumption: Contemporary Perspectives on Consumer Motives, Goals, and Desires*, ed. S. Ratneshwar, David Glen Mick, and Cynthia Huffman, London: Routledge, 140–63.

Baxter, Leslie A. (1987), "Symbols of Relationship Identity in Relationship Cultures," *Journal of Social and Personal Relationships*, 4 (3), 261–80.

Beghetto, Ronald. A. and Jonathan A. Plucker (2006), "The Relationship Among Schooling, Learning, and Creativity: "All Roads Lead to Creativity" or "You Can't Get There from Here?" in *Creativity and Reason in Cognitive*

Development, ed. James C. Kaufman and John Baer, New York, NY, US: Cambridge University Press, 316–32. http://dx.doi.org/10.1017/CBO97805 11606915.019

Belk, Russell W. (1976), "It's the Thought That Counts: A Signed Digraph Analysis of Gift-Giving," *Journal of Consumer Research*, 3 (3), 155–62.

——— (1988), "Possessions and the Extended Self," *Journal of Consumer Research*, 15 (2), 139–68.

——— (1996), "The Perfect Gift," in *Gift Giving: A Research Anthology*, ed. Cele Otnes and Richard F. Beltramini, Bowling Green, OH: Bowling Green State University Popular Press, 59–84.

Belk, Russell W. and Gregory S. Coon (1993), "Gift Giving as Agapic Love: An Alternative to the Exchange Paradigm Based on Dating Experiences," *Journal of Consumer Research*, 20 (3), 393–417.

Berger, Jonah and Chip Heath (2007), "Where Consumers Diverge from Others: Identity Signaling and Product Domains," *Journal of Consumer Research*, 34 (2), 121–34.

Besemer, Susan P. (1998), "Creative Product Analysis Matrix: Testing the Model Structure and a Comparison among Products: Three Novel Chairs," *Creativity Research Journal*, 11 (4), 333–46.

Besemer, Susan P. and Karen O'Quin (1999), "Confirming the Three-Factor Creative Product Analysis Matrix Model in an American Sample," *Creativity Research Journal*, 12 (4), 287–96.

Besemer, Susan P. and Donald J. Treffinger (1981), "Analysis of Creative Products: Review and Synthesis," *The Journal of Creative Behavior*, 15 (3), 158–78.

Beverland, Michael B. and Francis J. Farrelly (2009), "The Quest for Authenticity in Consumption: Consumers' Purposive Choice of Authentic Cues to Shape Experienced Outcomes," *Journal of Consumer Research*, 36 (5), 838–56.

Brakus, J. Joško, Bernd H. Schmitt, and Lia Zarantonello (2009), "Brand Experience: What Is It? How Is It Measured? Does It Affect Loyalty?," *Journal of Marketing*, 73 (3), 52–68.

Burroughs, James E. and David Glen Mick (2004), "Exploring Antecedents and Consequences of Consumer Creativity in a Problem-Solving Context," *Journal of Consumer Research*, 31 (2), 402–11.

Burroughs, James E., C. Page Moreau, and David Glen Mick (2008), "Toward a Psychology of Consumer Creativity," in *Handbook of Consumer Psychology*, ed. Curtis P. Haughtvedt, Paul M. Herr, and Frank R. Kardes, Mahwah, NJ: Erlbaum, 1011–38.

Burroughs, James E. and Aric Rindfleisch (2002), "Materialism and Well-Being: A Conflicting Values Perspective," *Journal of Consumer Research*, 29 (3), 348–70.

Caprariello, Peter A. and Harry T. Reis (2013), "To Do, to Have, or to Share? Valuing Experiences over Material Possessions Depends on the Involvement of Others," *Journal of Personality and Social Psychology*, 104 (2), 199–215.

Carter, Travis J. and Thomas Gilovich (2010), "The Relative Relativity of Material and Experiential Purchases," *Journal of Personality and Social Psychology*, 98 (1), 146–59.

Chan, Cindy and Cassie Mogilner (2017), "Experiential Gifts Foster Stronger Social Relationships Than Material Gifts," *Journal of Consumer Research*, 43 (6), 913–31.

Chen, Yu (2008), "Possession and Access: Consumer Desires and Value Perceptions Regarding Contemporary Art Collection and Exhibit Visits," *Journal of Consumer Research*, 35 (6), 925–40.

Clarke, Jackie R. (2006), "Different to 'Dust Collectors'? The Giving and Receiving of Experience Gifts," *Journal of Consumer Behaviour*, 5 (6), 533–49.

—— (2008), "Experiences as Gifts: From Process to Model," *European Journal of Marketing*, 42 (3/4), 365–89.

Craft, Anna (2001), "Little c Creativity," in *Creativity in Education*, ed. Anna Craft, Robert Jeffrey, and Mike Leibling, London and New York: Continuum, 45–61.

Csikszentmihalyi, Mihaly (1997), *Flow and the Psychology of Discovery and Invention*, New York: Harper Perennial, 39.

—— (1999), "16 Implications of a Systems Perspective for the Study of Creativity," in *Handbook of Creativity*, ed. Robert J. Sternberg, Cambridge: Cambridge University Press, 313–36.

Dahl, Darren W. and C. Page Moreau (2007), "Thinking Inside the Box: Why Consumers Enjoy Constrained Creative Experiences," *Journal of Marketing Research*, 44 (3), 357–69.

Ekeh, Peter Palmer (1974), *Social Exchange Theory: The Two Traditions*, Cambridge, MA: Harvard University Press.

Ferraro, Rosellina, Jennifer Edson Escalas, and James R. Bettman (2011), "Our Possessions, Our Selves: Domains of Self-Worth and the Possession: Self Link," *Journal of Consumer Psychology*, 21 (2), 169–77.

Forgeard, Marie J. C. and Anne C. Mecklenburg (2013), "The Two Dimensions of Motivation and a Reciprocal Model of the Creative Process," *Review of General Psychology*, 17 (3), 255–66.

Gill, Sandra, Jean Stockard, Miriam Johnson, and Suzanne Williams (1987), "Measuring Gender Differences: The Expressive Dimension and Critique of Androgyny Scales," *Sex Roles*, 17 (7–8), 375–400.

Gregory, Chris A. (1982), *Gifts and Commodities*, New York: Academic Press.

Guilford, Joy Paul (1968), *Intelligence, Creativity, and Their Educational Implications*, San Diego, CA: Robert R. Knapp Publisher.

Hagtvedt, Henrik and Vanessa M. Patrick (2008), "Art Infusion: The Influence of Visual Art on the Perception and Evaluation of Consumer Products," *Journal of Marketing Research*, 45 (3), 379–89.

Harrison, Paul (2009), "Evaluating Artistic Work: Balancing Competing Perspectives," *Consumption, Markets and Culture*, 12 (3), 265–74.

Harrison, Spencer H. and David T. Wagner (2016), "Spilling Outside the Box: The Effects of Individuals' Creative Behaviors at Work on Time Spent with Their Spouses at Home," *Academy of Management Journal*, 59 (3), 841–59.

Havlena, William J. and Morris B. Holbrook (1986), "The Varieties of Consumption Experience: Comparing Two Typologies of Emotion in Consumer Behavior," *Journal of Consumer Research*, 13 (3), 394–404.

Heath, Teresa Pereira, Caroline Tynan, and Christine Ennew (2015), "Accounts of Self-Gift Giving: Nature, Context and Emotions," *European Journal of Marketing*, 49 (7/8), 1067–86.

Hewer, Paul and Douglas Brownlie (2010), "On Market Forces and Adjustments: Acknowledging Consumer Creativity through the Aesthetics of 'debadging'," *Journal of Marketing Management*, 26 (5–6), 428–40.

Heylighen, Francis (1992), "A Cognitive-Systemic Reconstruction of Maslow's Theory of Self-Actualization," *Systems Research and Behavioral Science*, 37 (1), 39–58.

Hirschman, Elizabeth C. (1980), "Innovativeness, Novelty Seeking, and Consumer Creativity," *Journal of Consumer Research*, 7 (3), 283–95.

Hirschman, Elizabeth C. and Morris B. Holbrook (1982), "Hedonic Consumption: Emerging Concepts, Methods and Propositions," *The Journal of Marketing*, 46 (3), 92–101.

Holbrook, Morris B. and Elizabeth C. Hirschman (1982), "The Experiential Aspects of Consumption: Consumer Fantasies, Feelings, and Fun," *Journal of Consumer Research*, 9 (2), 132–40.

Holt, Douglas B. (2002), "Why Do Brands Cause Trouble? A Dialectical Theory of Consumer Culture and Branding," *Journal of Consumer Research*, 29 (1), 70–90.

Hoyer, Wayne D. and Nicola E. Stokburger-Sauer (2012), "The Role of Aesthetic Taste in Consumer Behavior," *Journal of the Academy of Marketing Science*, 40 (1), 167–80.

Hume, Margee, Gillian Sullivan Mort, and Hume Winzar (2007), "Exploring Repurchase Intention in a Performing Arts Context: Who Comes? And Why Do They Come Back?," *International Journal of Nonprofit and Voluntary Sector Marketing*, 12 (2), 135–48.

Kampylis, Panagiotis G. and Juri Valtanen (2010), "Redefining Creativity: Analyzing Definitions, Collocations, and Consequences," *The Journal of Creative Behavior*, 44 (3), 191–214.

Kaufman, James C. and Ronald A. Beghetto (2009), "Beyond Big and Little: The Four C Model of Creativity," *Review of General Psychology*, 13 (1), 1–12.

Keinan, Anat and Ran Kivetz (2010), "Productivity Orientation and the Consumption of Collectable Experiences," *Journal of Consumer Research*, 37 (6), 935–50.

Kim, Tae-Yeol, Alice H. Y. Hon, and J. Michael Crant (2009), "Proactive Personality, Employee Creativity, and Newcomer Outcomes: A Longitudinal Study," *Journal of Business and Psychology*, 24 (1), 93–103.

Kivetz, Ran and Itamar Simonson (2002), "Self-Control for the Righteous: Toward a Theory of Precommitment to Indulgence," *Journal of Consumer Research*, 29 (2), 199–217.

Koslow, Scott, Sheila L. Sasser, and Edward A. Riordan (2003), "What Is Creative to Whom and Why? Perceptions in Advertising Agencies," *Journal of Advertising Research*, 43 (1), 96–110.

Kozinets, Robert V. (2002), "Can Consumers Escape the Market? Emancipatory Illuminations from Burning Man," *Journal of Consumer Research*, 29 (1), 20–38.

Kozinets, Robert V., John F. Sherry, Jr, Diana Storm, Adam Duhachek, Krittinee Nuttavuthisit, and Benet DeBerry-Spence (2004), "Ludic Agency and Retail Spectacle," *Journal of Consumer Research*, 31 (3), 658–72.

Krems, Jaimie Arona, Douglas T. Kenrick, and Rebecca Neel (2017), "Individual Perceptions of Self-Actualization: What Functional Motives Are Linked to Fulfilling One's Full Potential?," *Personality and Social Psychology Bulletin*, 43 (9), 1337–52.

Krishna, Aradhna, Ryan S. Elder, and Cindy Caldara (2010), "Feminine to Smell But Masculine to Touch? Multisensory Congruence and Its Effect on the Aesthetic Experience," *Journal of Consumer Psychology*, 20 (4), 410–18.

Lacher, Kathleen T. (1989), "Hedonic Consumption: Music as a Product," *NA: Advances in Consumer Research*, 16, 367–73.

Lacher, Kathleen T. and Richard Mizerski (1994), "An Exploratory Study of the Responses and Relationships Involved in the Evaluation of, and in the Intention to Purchase New Rock Music," *Journal of Consumer Research*, 21 (2), 366–80.

Lambert, Nathaniel M., A. Marlea Gwinn, Roy F. Baumeister, Amy Strachman, Isaac J. Washburn, Shelly L. Gable, and Frank D. Fincham (2013), "A Boost of Positive Affect: The Perks of Sharing Positive Experiences," *Journal of Social and Personal Relationships*, 30 (1), 24–43.

Larsen, Derek and John J. Watson (2001), "A Guide Map to the Terrain of Gift Value," *Psychology & Marketing*, 18 (8), 889–906.

Lim, Elison Ai Ching and Swee Hoon Ang (2008), "Hedonic vs. Utilitarian Consumption: A Cross-Cultural Perspective Based on Cultural Conditioning," *Journal of Business Research*, 61 (3), 225–32.

Luhmann, Niklas (1986), *Love as Passion: The Codification of Intimacy*, Cambridge, MA: Harvard University Press, ISBN 0-679-53923-0.

Luomala, Harri T. and Martti Laaksonen (1999), "A Qualitative Exploration of Mood-Regulatory Self-Gift Behaviors," *Journal of Economic Psychology*, 20 (2), 147–82.

Maslow, Abraham H. (1943), "A Theory of Human Motivation," *Psychological Review*, 50 (4), 370–96.

Mauss, Marcel (1954), *The Gift: The Form and Functions of Exchange in Archaic Societies*, Glencoe, IL: Free Press.

McCrae, Robert R. and Paul T. Costa (1987), "Validation of the Five-Factor Model of Personality across Instruments and Observers," *Journal of Personality and Social Psychology*, 52 (1), 81.

McKeage, Kim K. R., Marsha L. Richins, and Kathleen Debevec (1993), "Self-Gifts and the Manifestation of Material Values," *ACR North American Advances in NA – Advances in Consumer Research Volume 20*, ed. Leigh McAlister and Michael L. Rothschild, Provo, UT: Association for Consumer Research, 359–64.

Merrotsy, Peter (2013), "A Note on Big-C Creativity and Little-c Creativity," *Creativity Research Journal*, 25 (4), 474–6.

Mick, David Glen and Michelle DeMoss (1990), "Self-Gifts: Phenomenological Insights from Four Contexts," *Journal of Consumer Research*, 17 (3), 322–32.

——— (1992), "Further Findings on Self-Gifts: Products, Qualities, and Socioeconomic Correlates," *NA – Advances in Consumer Research*, 19, 140–46.

Mittelman, Willard (1991), "Maslow's Study of Self-Actualization: A Reinterpretation," *Journal of Humanistic Psychology*, 31 (1), 114–35.

Moreau, C. Page and Darren W. Dahl (2005), "Designing the Solution: The Impact of Constraints on Consumers' Creativity," *Journal of Consumer Research*, 32 (1), 13–22.

Mortimer, Gary, Ursula S. Bougoure, and Syed Fazal-E-Hasan (2015), "Development and Validation of the Self-Gifting Consumer Behaviour Scale," *Journal of Consumer Behaviour*, 14 (3), 165–79.

Mumford, Michael D. and Sigrid B. Gustafson (1988), "Creativity Syndrome: Integration, Application, and Innovation," *Psychological Bulletin*, 103 (1), 27.

Nicolao, Leonardo, Julie R. Irwin, and Joseph K. Goodman (2009), "Happiness for Sale: Do Experiential Purchases Make Consumers Happier Than Material Purchases?," *Journal of Consumer Research*, 36 (2), 188–98.

Politz, Alfred (1975), "Creativeness and Imagination," *Journal of Advertising*, 4 (3), 11–14.

Prather, Ronald E. (1992), "Computer Science in an Undergraduate Liberal Arts and Sciences Setting," *ACM SIGCSE Bulletin*, 24 (2), 59–64.

Reiter-Palmon, Roni and Erika J. Robinson (2009), "Problem Identification and Construction: What Do We Know, What Is the Future?," *Psychology of Aesthetics, Creativity, and the Arts*, 3 (1), 43.

Rhodes, Mel (1961), "An Analysis of Creativity," *The Phi Delta Kappan*, 42 (7), 305–10.

Richards, Ruth (1999), "Affective Disorders," *Encyclopedia of Creativity*, 1, 31–43.

―――― (2007), *Everyday Creativity and New Views of Human Nature: Psychological, Social, and Spiritual Perspectives*, Washington, DC: American Psychological Association, 25–53.

Runco, Mark A. (2004), "Creativity as an Extracognitive Phenomenon," in *Beyond Knowledge: Extracognitive Aspects of Developing High Ability*, ed. Larisa V. Shavinina and Michel Ferrari, Mahwah, NJ: Lawrence Erlbaum Associates, Inc., 17–25.

―――― (2014), "'Big C, Little C' Creativity as a False Dichotomy: Reality Is Not Categorical," *Creativity Research Journal*, 26 (1), 131–2.

Runco, Mark A. and Garrett J. Jaeger (2012), "The Standard Definition of Creativity," *Creativity Research Journal*, 24 (1), 92–6.

Runco, Mark A. and Shawn O. Sakamoto (1999), "Experimental Studies of Creativity," in *Handbook of Creativity*, ed. Robert J. Sternberg, New York, Cambridge University Press, 62–92.

Saad, Gad and Tripat Gill (2003), "An Evolutionary Psychology Perspective on Gift Giving among Young Adults," *Psychology & Marketing*, 20 (9), 765–84.

Schau, Hope Jensen and Mary C. Gilly (2003), "We Are What We Post? Self-Presentation in Personal Web Space," *Journal of Consumer Research*, 30 (3), 385–404.

Schouten, John W. (1991), "Selves in Transition: Symbolic Consumption in Personal Rites of Passage and Identity Reconstruction," *Journal of Consumer Research*, 17 (4), 412–25.

Schwartz, Shalom H. (2011), "Studying Values: Personal Adventure, Future Directions," *Journal of Cross-Cultural Psychology*, 42 (2), 307–19.

Scott, Rebecca, Julien Cayla, and Bernard Cova (2017), "Selling Pain to the Saturated Self," *Journal of Consumer Research*, 44 (1), 22–43.

Sellier, Anne-Laure and Darren W. Dahl (2011), "Focus! Creative Success Is Enjoyed through Restricted Choice," *Journal of Marketing Research*, 48 (6), 996–1007.

Sherry, Jr., John F. (1983), "Gift Giving in Anthropological Perspective," *Journal of Consumer Research*, 10 (2), 157–68.

Silvia, Paul J., Roger E. Beaty, Emily C. Nusbaum, Kari M. Eddington, Holly Levin-Aspenson, and Thomas R. Kwapil (2014), "Everyday Creativity in Daily Life: An Experience-Sampling Study of 'Little C' Creativity," *Psychology of Aesthetics, Creativity, and the Arts*, 8 (2), 183–8.

Simonton, Dean Keith (1999), "Creativity from a Historiometric Perspective," in *Handbook of Creativity*, ed. Robert J. Sternberg, Cambridge: Cambridge University Press, 116–33.

Singer, Irving (1984), *The Nature of Love: Courtly and Romantic*, Vol. 2, Chicago: The University of Chicago Press.

Smith, Robert E. and Xiaojing Yang (2004), "Toward a General Theory of Creativity in Advertising: Examining the Role of Divergence," *Marketing Theory*, 4 (1–2), 31–58.

Sternberg, Robert J. and Todd I. Lubart (1999), "The Concept of Creativity: Prospects and Paradigms," in *Handbook of Creativity*, ed. Robert J. Sternberg, Cambridge: Cambridge University Press, 3–14.

Sullivan, Diane M. and Cameron M. Ford (2010), "The Alignment of Measures and Constructs in Organizational Research: The Case of Testing Measurement Models of Creativity," *Journal of Business and Psychology*, 25 (3), 505–21.

Taylor, Calvin W. (1988), "Various Approaches to and Definitions of Creativity" in *The Nature of Creativity: Contemporary Psychological Perspectives*, ed. Robert J. Sternberg, New York, NY: Cambridge University Press, 99–121.

Tierney, Pamela and Steven M. Farmer (2002), "Creative Self-Efficacy: Its Potential Antecedents and Relationship to Creative Performance," *Academy of Management Journal*, 45 (6), 1137–48.

Till, Brian D. and Daniel W. Baack (2005), "Recall and Persuasion: Does Creative Advertising Matter?," *Journal of Advertising*, 34 (3), 47–57.

Tinio, Pablo P. L. (2013), "From Artistic Creation to Aesthetic Reception: The Mirror Model of Art," *Psychology of Aesthetics, Creativity, and the Arts*, 7 (3), 265–75.

Van Boven, Leaf, Margaret C. Campbell, and Thomas Gilovich (2010), "Stigmatizing Materialism: On Stereotypes and Impressions of Materialistic and Experiential Pursuits," *Personality and Social Psychology Bulletin*, 36 (4), 551–63.

Venkatesh, Alladi and Laurie A. Meamber (2006), "Arts and Aesthetics: Marketing and Cultural Production," *Marketing Theory*, 6 (1), 11–39.

West, Douglas C., Arthur J. Kover, and Albert Caruana (2008), "Practitioner and Customer Views of Advertising Creativity: Same Concept, Different Meaning?," *Journal of Advertising*, 37 (4), 35–46.

Conclusion

14 Reflections on Romantic Gift Exchange

An Intersectional Conversation

Cele C. Otnes and
Robert Alfonso Arias

How might some of the issues about gift exchange raised in this book resonate, depending upon key characteristics of givers or recipients—e.g., age, life stage, gender, family composition, and gift-giving experience? From February to April 2018, we engaged in six conversations motivated by two goals: 1) to explore how our intersectionality (Gopaldas 2013) shapes our perspectives on these chapters; and 2) to generate ideas for future gift-giving research. Demographically, we are at opposite ends of the spectrum. Completing her 28th year as an academic, Cele is 58, white, married, and has one adult daughter. She grew up with married parents and an older brother in a middle-class household. Rob is 28, Hispanic, never married and with no children, and will pursue his first academic job in 2018. His parents are divorced, he has two older sisters, and his economic status has ranged from middle to lower-middle class.

Our transcripts span 45 pages—which means in this chapter, we can only represent a few topics. We focus on those we believe offer the most potential for future research. We present an abridged version of our conversations around seven topics below. We end our chapter by presenting research questions that we hope will motivate future research.

Surprise Gifts

C: Tell me how you feel about surprises.

R: I had a surprise birthday party once. It was amazing and I loved it, but at the same time it was like, "Oh man, how come I didn't see it coming? Why did I get duped?" I think a lot of it involved a combination of masculinity and growing up in an unpredictable background, where Chicago has a lot of violence. It was always comforting to have certainty or stability. I value stability a lot, and I think it's related to power. You want to feel some control, and being surprised reminds you that you don't have control.

C: I agree.

R: I still like being surprised, but at the same time, it's interesting those feelings emerged, and that's what I attribute it to.

C: And it felt negative that you didn't recognize the signs?

R: Yeah. I take pride in being able to deduce things, and maybe it's related to a need for cognition. The intensity of the emotion was very small; it was just, "They got me!" It would have been nice to see it coming. This is taking it to the negative extreme, but if you can't see something positive coming, it might be a reminder you can't perceive something negative coming.

C: So for people whose lives are more uncertain, surprise indicates they might not have as much control as they wish.

R: Maybe.

R: In Bradford's chapter, and in Gupta and Gentry, it seems they're getting at what's at stake for the giver—the investment emotionally, temporally, and economically. In both, to give a surprise, we assume it takes a lot of investment because you have to invest time to know that person.

C: That's the irony—what I would call the paradox of surprise. The fewer surprises in planning the surprise, the better; you don't want surprises as you're planning. Let's say I'm going to have a surprise party for my husband, and his favorite dessert is chocolate cake. So I get chocolate cake; it's something I know he'll love. If he hates that there are 30 people in the room and he doesn't want a big to-do, there's the chocolate cake. But what if the bakery is out of chocolate cake? I have to scramble, and suddenly the personalization of that surprise dips.

R: Jumping off what you're saying, I think there are concrete and abstract aspects of surprises. Let's say the concrete activity is that your partner likes bungee jumping. The abstract activity could be adventure seeking. So instead of getting him/her a new bungee cord, your gift is to have him/her drive a Formula One race car, or do something else that's thrill-seeking. The abstract value is like an umbrella for concrete activities.

C: What could make going from bungee jumping to Formula One racing a great surprise?

R: I think the similarities of the adrenaline rush.

C: So you're banking on giving the recipient the same emotional high.

R: I'd hope. And then, for it to be a bad surprise, it depends on the recipient's commitment to bungee jumping. If they're a die-hard bungee jumper, they're not going to get anything out of the other thing. But if they tried bungee jumping a few times and loved it, and they're just a casual person who does it, he or she will be more appreciative—scratching the surface of different thrill-seeking activities.

C: I think we need to think about whether the surprise is giver- or recipient-focused. Many times when people create something surprising, there's a tremendous rush from the planning and hiding it. That's a big deal, but it could be very contentious for the recipient: "What other secrets are you keeping from me? How did you do this without me knowing?" I think surprises can be problematic if they say more about the giver than the recipient, and I think you'd have to understand if the recipient is comfortable with ambiguity.

R: I could also imagine a person saying they don't like surprises and maybe feeling some discomfort, but a part of them does like it. It gets me thinking about multiple identities and multiple selves. A portion of myself appreciates the sentiment, and another portion doesn't like to be on display.

C: Gupta and Gentry say the American market needs to rediscover the joy of surprise since it's one of the biggest markets for gift cards—a thinly disguised version of cash. This implies money can't be a surprise, but I think it can. Webley (1983) talks about money as an unacceptable gift. I think there's been a big cultural change in this norm. In the 1980s, maybe money was considered impersonal, and it seemed givers didn't put thought into the gift. Then the recession hit in 2008, and costs for things like college have gotten out of control. I think it's time someone reinvigorates the study of money as a gift, because we still cite Webley from 35 years ago.

R: So there are certain dimensions of surprise: characteristics of the giver, characteristics of the recipient, the context, the gift itself, and the investment in the gift—which can be even further dimensionalized as economic, emotional, and things like that.

C: And you talked about the transparency of it. What I love is when a giver says, "I'm taking you on a trip, but it's a surprise." What's that about?

R: Our last pro sem speaker was talking about this ... It's showing them hints; showing the carrot.

C: I think it's a risk-reduction strategy. If you say, "I'm taking you on a trip, and it's a surprise," you give recipients time to prepare, and you might give them enough hints where it's reassuring, and you also get positive feedback earlier. You're getting them excited; you're allowing for emotional management to happen earlier in the process if you say, "I'm taking you on a trip, but it's a surprise—but pack your shorts and your tennis racket."

R: Yeah, I could definitely see it. In the instrumental sense, it's a risk-reduction strategy. In the emotional sense, maybe the giver doesn't want to delay gratification. If I have a surprise for you, I want to get you excited. I want to let you know, because I'm so excited about it. I put so much time and effort into this. I'm going to tell you we're going on that trip to get a little bit of a reaction, so I can feel good about what I've been working hard on. There are many interesting things coming out here: the benefits for givers when they disclose they have a surprise, and how from the giver's perspective, "You ruined the surprise."

C: How are surprises ruined? As the recipient, I might guess the surprise is better than what the giver got me, which then disappoints me. Sometimes my husband gets me a surprise because he buys something for himself, and he uses the surprise to deflect my disapproval. He's like, "Hey, I got you a surprise," and I'm like, "I noticed you bought $50 of vinyl albums," and he got a 45 for me of a Bobby Sherman song [1970s teen idol] I don't care about. People use surprises for all sorts of reasons so that's another question—what's the motivation behind the surprise?

R: Dimensionalizing surprise!

C: In line with this book: what can surprise do to the relational trajectory if it's successful or unsuccessful? Our article on how gifts influence relationships (Ruth, Otnes, and Brunel 1999) would imply if the relationship is rock solid, an unsuccessful surprise won't affect it. But if the relationship is vulnerable, what happens? What about a brand new dating relationship? What would a great surprise do?

R: I think it would signal the giver is quick to learn and understand the person. I have this phrase: everybody wants to be understood, but nobody wants to be figured out.

C: What do you mean?

R: People want others to understand them, but if you have somebody figured out, there's the connotation of "you think you know me; you think you know what I'm going to do." So it's an interesting paradox. But I think if it's early in the relationship, and it's a great surprise, I think it would be a signal the giver understands the recipient.

C: You mentioned earlier this masculinity aspect. When you're surprised if you're a girl, the stereotypical reaction is screaming and losing control, maybe being joyful. Are men going to scream with delight—like a "girl?" What's the difference between feminine and masculine reactions to surprise?

R: I think it goes back to the kind of masculinity, but the stoic man; you can imagine that kind of masculinity. He might signal appreciation, but he's not going to be like, "Oh, wow!"—really expressive with his gestures or voice. But other types of masculinity are probably more accepting of those kinds of expressions.

C: Is it the fear of losing control? Women can cry tears of joy and that's acceptable, but crying in guys—there always seems to be that line.

R: I do think it relates to control actually. Which is why I relate masculinity to control and psychological states of power. If you're letting everybody know you have low self-control or that things impact you so strongly, you have vulnerability or sensitivity.

Masculinity and White Day

R: Honestly, I find Minowa, Belk, and Matsui's chapter somewhat terrifying. It's interesting how they describe White Day as a tortuous experience for men. This issue of reciprocity (women buying for men on Valentine's Day; men reciprocating one month later on White Day), I found very sexist, talking about the control and how to make women seem like children, but at the same time sexually objectifying them in some way. That was odd.

C: [Quoting from an ad the authors analyze] "Oji-san seems to get [sexually] excited" about a candy necklace? That ad was bizarre.

R: A lot of it seems to be a mid-life crisis thing, and maybe more traditional beliefs being challenged with younger generations, or women becoming more empowered.

C: So it seems there might be resistance from both men and women. As an American, what does it make you think about Japanese culture or masculinity?

R: I don't think this is just a Japanese thing, but I think masculinity in general is sometimes fragile, so masculinity being dependent on one's ability to give gifts reflects this fragility.

C: If I were a man, I'd be confused [by White Day] because there's this norm of "respect men, despise women," and having to know rules about the zōtō, the gift repayment. It's interesting how many words there are for gifts, and emotions associated with gifts, in Japanese. They say, "I feel a debt of gratitude when I receive a gift." I think gratitude is definitely a double-edged emotion.

R: Even the concrete practices are complicated. So, women in your office buy men Valentine's Day gifts, and not only do men have to buy them individual gifts, but they have to buy unique gifts compared to those from other men in the office. So, you're trying to do this, and there's a romantic/sexual connotation with these gifts, but these are just women you work with. They're not even your romantic partners.

C: And the chapter says men may want to be the "oji-san," the older man who gets drunk and talks about sex! That's not anybody I want to work with! I understand why there's confusion and perhaps resentment about it. And it brought home that because work is so focal to Japanese culture, the Japanese sense of masculinity has permeated the workplace.

R: They talk about how the idealized masculine figure is the economic hero, being able to provide.

C: If I were a government official, I would be concerned from a public policy perspective. I feel like it has gotten out of hand. This brings up a question: how do you decide as a culture when enough is enough, and you start resisting these gifting occasions? Who controls the discourse of what the occasion can mean?

R: I don't know what that measurement would look like, of when enough is enough. It would be interesting to do a field experiment—so, measure workplace satisfaction or attitudes not around White Day or Valentine's Day, then when that season starts coming around, measure it again. I wonder about collaboration practices in the workplace between men and women, like in July or September, as opposed to March.

C: I was totally blown away about this idea of giving white underwear. If somebody gave me white underwear who wasn't my husband, I'd be shocked. [Reading from Minowa, et al]: "The gender power negotiation with the gift of underwear is a battle that involved exercise over the body." I guess this speaks to our cultural understanding about appropriateness and inappropriateness. Implicit in that discussion is that when you reciprocate to a woman who gave you a Valentine's Day gift, your White Day gift should demonstrate your power as a man, more than her gift demonstrates power to you. Or her gift has power over you until you reciprocate.

R: They talked about how feelings of indebtedness are more pronounced in men than women. I do think a lot of it is the mid-life crisis. They said something about, "His fantasy for enticing multiple women with material gifts suggests his fear of commitment."

C: I didn't think it was necessarily fear of commitment. I just think there is a social contract that if you get presents from women, you have to reciprocate every one of them. Then if you don't remember to reciprocate like this ad says, "I'm not going to let you go unpunished if you forget."

R: That was another thing I was interested by. How exactly are the women going to retaliate if men don't buy them a gift, or if the gift isn't that lavish?

C: Or if it doesn't meet their expectations? If you buy a woman a powerful gift after she bought you a token gift, then you have the upper hand. I think this is really a ripe context to look at gift practices in the workplace.

R: And to compare to a romantic committed context. I think it's interesting how the culture gives men a whole month to conspire [between Valentine's Day and White Day]. Like the more information you have, the more power you have. It's like if you have a debate team: it's better to go last, so you can address your opponent's points. The women go first, you sit back and see what they give you, and you have a month to plan and do them better.

C: It would be interesting to see what kinds of gifts are acceptable for Valentine's Day for women to give men, versus what's acceptable for men to give women. The discourse analysis is very interesting, but it also would be good to gain emic perspectives from participants.

R: I'm thinking of different responses to the Valentine's Day gift. One is, you just go with the flow; you buy them something nice. The other is, you want to take a jab at them, and buy them white underwear! Then there's this other option you're referring to: don't buy them anything.

C: Very dangerous. You know who's telling you it's dangerous—the retailers. Look how hard they work to keep people motivated—or scared is the better word.

R: I was really interested in this fear. So you're talking about what keeps people motivated to do this. I'm thinking about, at least from the male perspective, this fear that women can retaliate. "The ad propagandizes the disposition of women as evil beings who are immature yet demanding consumers." This fear is so real, of women retaliating against them in the workplace.

Creativity and Gift-Giving

R: If I buy the argument that creativity is a gift, does that mean any attribute or quality is a gift? Let's say I want to give someone the gift of logic, so I take them to a Marbles store and we do puzzles ...

C: Is it a gift any time you try to educate somebody?

R: Yeah, on any quality?

C: So here's the main argument of the chapter: creativity can be considered an altruistic gift. So if you give someone the opportunity to go to an artistic performance, someone else performs the creativity aspect, but you're the liaison between the gift and the giver. That disrupts the old model that the gift goes directly from giver to recipient. That could open up a line of inquiry—who are the other mediators or agents involved in gift-giving?

R: You can think about that with a lot of experiential gifts.

C: If I pay for it, I am the gift-giver, but not the gift deliverer. The actual delivery of the gift rests with a provider. So if I decide to give a gift and place it in the hands of a service provider, what opportunities exist for boundaries and roadblocks?

R: That's a good way to conceptualize it, because you can think of cases where you're purchasing the gift, but it goes badly.

C: And you don't want to be blamed. What happens in that situation?

R: Yeah, so people can still appreciate the sentiment of the gift, and it's not your fault the performer was drunk. I think that's a good way to further dimensionalize how this unfolds.

C: I like examining the role of service providers or performers or creative agents, in the delivery of the gift. If I'm performing a concert, and I think about how people receive tickets as a gift, does it make me consider the efforts I need to put into that in a different way?

R: Or even a local performer at a restaurant on Valentine's Day. You know a lot of people are taking their significant others out, as opposed to other days where's there's less pressure.

C: And how do you handle it if you're the giver? Do you have to make amends for a bad gift delivery?

R: On the receiving side, how do you receive it? Do you try to reassure the giver you appreciate it, even if it went badly? It probably depends on the state of the relationship.

C: I think it depends how much you care about the relationship. It might be your perfect exit strategy: "You took me to this performance, and the guy was drunk. We're done!" Or, "We'll laugh about this in five years!"

C: If we give the gift of enabling others' creativity, at what point does this no longer become a gift, and more of an actualization by the recipient? If I give my daughter a sewing class and she becomes a fashion designer, is her whole career a gift? Where does the gift start and end, with gifts of creativity?

R: I'm thinking about my own experience with martial arts. My brother in-law took me to my first class, and now I just do it on my own. Do I still consider that a gift? I always attribute him for my interest in it.

C: So is there some kind of erosion effect—at some point, the thing stops being a gift and starts being an everyday experience? What has to happen to remind us it was a gift to begin with?

R: Yeah, the salience of the gift fades away, and I wonder if that happens more with utilitarian gifts.

Self-Gifting

C: So, in Kanno and Suzuki's chapter on self-gifts, one informant talks about buying for herself and says, "I feel like I'm telling me, 'It's going to be okay,' to another me. I cannot be my favorite self ... all the time." I love this concept of the favorite self—Which self is getting gifts? I've got my businessperson self, my wife self, my mom self, and so on. What's my favorite self?

R: I loved that too actually; I thought about identity and identity salience. It's exactly what you were talking about: when you buy yourself something, is that the business self buying for the creative self? If a working mother buys something that helps her be a better mother, is that the professional self buying for the motherly self? You're almost conceptualizing them as different entities, which is how previous research has done it, like different selves.

C: Different but intertwined. Let's say a colleague buys me a gift. I might have thought, "Gosh, I thought we were more like friends," if he got me like, paper clips or even a nice stapler. Obviously, it's thoughtful and something I'll use, but after all the time we've spent on lunches, he's giving to my business self, not the friend self. This is something worth exploring: which identity do you make salient? How much strategic negotiation or manifestation of self do you do? Some people are calculating; they're like, "I've got to put on my work face now." Some of us have more fluid boundaries And when you're dating, how do you know which self to react to? What happens over time?

R: Has there been any work done—I'm trying to think about the definitional characteristics of what constitutes a self-gift.

C: It has been a long time—since Mick and DeMoss (1990). That topic would be ripe for the picking. I also think it's partially cultural, but maybe not, but increasingly I think a lot of self-gifts are luxury aesthetic goods. I think that's tied to a feminine perspective. What would a viable self-gift be for a young male millennial? Does it have to be luxury goods?

R: I think for the millennials and even younger, I see esthetics playing more of a role like in fashion, cosmetics even. Definitely things related to hobbies.

C: Or passions.

Chocolate as a Gift

R: This chapter by Mäkelä, Bettany, and Stevens relates chocolate to the body, and how that varies across cultures. That was my key takeaway about the materiality of chocolate and the ...

C: Carnal singularity.

R: Yeah, so you have the flesh.

C: [Quoting Mäkelä, et al] The carnal-singularity is the "processes by which the body of the woman (gifter or recipient) imbues the chocolate." So how does the woman's body absorb or use and register the chocolate, but also how does the woman's brain do it too? How is it decoded?

R: So they say chocolate is a feminine thing, but maybe you could conceptualize chocolate as a masculine food, in that it's the man trying to tempt or seduce the woman.

C: The control of the chocolate is given by the man, which is interesting given how we have all sorts of different couples now. What does chocolate mean in a gay relationship? Clearly, the authors emphasize the feminine side. But I'll bet if you look at the history of chocolate, it was probably a more masculine food because it comes from South America; it was bold and exotic. It's a darker product, and if you think about masculine colors ...

R: I thought the same about the color, actually.

C: Would a guy ever give a box of chocolates to another guy in a non-romantic fashion? Is romance inextricably tied to the meaning of certain kinds of chocolate, like these gift boxes? Except around Christmas; my family always did Whitman samplers with Christmas decorations on them. Of course, at Valentine's Day, they're loaded with symbols of love and romance. What about countries where people produce chocolate and they make five cents a day for working in the fields. What does it mean to them?

R: Maybe they don't romanticize chocolate in the same way.

C: If we want to get on the macro-level and talk about the capitalist ramifications of the chocolate industry, that could kill the romance quickly. Which begs the question, what happens when an item loses its romantic connotation and disappears from the "evoked set" for romance? Some people talk about flowers being wasteful.

R: Yeah, I was thinking about that one.

C: As a potential giver of chocolate to women, did it make you think differently about giving chocolate like, "I wonder when the right time is, what does it mean?"

R: I don't know, because I only really give chocolate for Valentine's Day.

C: So if I'm a marketer, that's a problem. I want you to give chocolate more often, as part of your masculine code of romance. So how could I make that happen? What do you think keeps it so embedded in Valentine's Day?

R: Where you associate two things so strongly together, it's hard to envision instances where you'd expand beyond chocolate's partnership with Valentine's Day.

C: The only other romance ritual I associate chocolate with is the first date: you show up with a box of chocolates. Nobody really does that anymore.

R: That's funny, because that's where my mind went when you said expanding my gift-giving practices. It seems marketers could try to bring that back.

R: I thought it was interesting that applying that feminist lens to it, they say the female is wooed by her appetite, unlike the male with his cool rationality and self-control. "Cultures perceive women as the weaker sex, perpetually assailed by moral frailties and animal urges." It's very sexist, but it's a very ancient thing, going back to Adam and Eve being tempted by the apple.

C: So the idea is you give a woman a piece of chocolate and she "melts," double entendre, into a pool of submissiveness. Then you have your way with her, so it's more of a charm. You give someone chocolate and it takes away agency; that's their argument that this is how chocolate has been perceived. So if this object is so potent, how much does it matter to dress it up? Say you're at a restaurant and the dessert tray comes by, and you present a woman with a truffle that is a work of art. Is that going to have the same desired effect as if you wrap a box of chocolates? Where does the potency come from?

R: I definitely think some of it has to do with the aesthetics.

C: Let's say you've been dating a woman for three or four months, and she gives *you* a box of chocolates. How are you going to interpret this? It's the most beautiful box of chocolates you've ever seen. And she says, "I want you to have this." How do you react to this?

R: For no occasion?

C: Yeah.

R: Of course, I would enjoy it. It would raise the question of where we stand in the relationship.

C: What's she doing this for?

R: Yeah, and I'd have to assess—do I like her as much as she likes me?

C: Gifts are dangerous, aren't they? The chocolate comes out of left field. You're dating, you're clearly getting along; everything is good. Where you are physically is not going to play a piece in that. She says, "I saw this and I thought of you."

R: Wow. I think it would definitely make me think harder about the relationship; it could be a defining moment. If I feel she likes me way more than I like her, then I will maybe try to dissolve the relationship, or slow it down. On the other hand, if she gives it to me and I like her a lot, I might reciprocate.

C: We could throw in all sorts of fun conditions here, like if she talks about chocolate 24/7, so you know it's about her, or you talk about chocolate 24/7, so it's about you. Or the most devious is— she knows you're allergic to chocolate, and she's trying to kill you! [Laughs]

R: I feel like chocolate could have a sexual connotation for men as well. I wouldn't say it's specific to women.

C: Or you might make it about her. You might say, "Is this your favorite brand?" You might be looking for excuses not to break up with her. I love how your first reaction was, "I'm going to have to rethink this relationship."

R: I could see if a woman really likes chocolate and she buys me chocolate for us to share, or if she buys me chocolate and I know there's an expectation for me to share with her. I could see how there's less expectation.

C: It dilutes the power once again.

R: Sometimes it depends on the woman and the relationship. You might have to think hard about how you feel about them, and sometimes you just know, and it's easy.

C: Also, some chocolate now supposedly has medicinal benefits. If chocolate becomes medicine, how does it impact its reception as a romantic gift?

R: It becomes this pragmatic, utilitarian product. I could see that as a potential threat to diluting the symbolic, romantic, hedonistic power of chocolate. Maybe you could try to mitigate that effect by making strong distinctions between the chocolate that's pragmatic and the type that's not.

Mother/Daughter (Parent/Child) Giving

C: So Liu, Zhao, and Hogg discuss mother/daughter giving. I was wondering if any of this is relevant to you as a man?

R: I automatically went to my sister and my mother. In the chapter, the authors discuss how daughters act as socializers to convince their mothers to engage in more experiences. But the daughters also imply that they don't want to be embarrassed by their mothers.

C: Do you see your sisters as trying to socialize your mom through gifts— trying to do things that would be beneficial to her that she mom wouldn't do herself?

R: No, I don't see it that way. I think it's more the way I give gifts to my dad, which is you buy things you think they'll like.

C: So they're doing a pleasing thing?

R: Yeah, identity reinforcement, which the authors talk about. I do that very much with my nieces and nephews; I would buy Lincoln Logs or things to make them think. I'm very cognizant of that. I do that especially with my sister struggling with depression. I buy her things I think would help transform her, or make her life easier. Do you feel your mom tried to socialize you through gifts?

C: Oh yeah. We'll get into it, but you tell me about how your mom gives gifts to you.

R: I think she tries to give me gifts I'll use, so the laptop was a big one. This year she gave me some money because I had recently bought a car, and she knew I spent a lot of money for that. And when she doesn't have as much money, she buys more symbolic gifts. So she bought me a Temptations CD for like six bucks; she knows I like The Temptations. So maybe when she has the funds the gift is more utilitarian, but when she's depleted, she'll resort to something more symbolic.

R: So taking gift-giving away from special occasions, like you're out with friends, "First round's on me." Are those considered gifts? If they are, they happen all the time, and are we accounting for them?

C: So—everyday gift-giving. Imagine if we kept a diary of all the ways we were gifted like, "Hey, I'll buy you a cup of coffee." There are figures about how much we spend on gift-giving, but I don't think they account for everyday gifts. Moms and girls go shopping a lot. Usually when Emily was in high school, shopping together meant shopping for her. So if she came home with a couple hundred dollars of clothes, I'd see that as a gift. But does it become so routinized that people don't understand it as a gift?

Let's discuss this idea of power in the gift-giving relationship. Is it ever healthy for a relationship where we use gift-giving as a mechanism of power? The sneaky thing about gift-giving is you can do things with it you can't do as normal activities, because recipients aren't supposed to refuse gifts; that's a social norm.

R: I think there are times it could be healthy. Like in the parent-child relationship, the parent says, "I'm going to put you in sports." The kid says, "No, I want to play with my friends all summer." Then it turns out the child ends up loving the sport. Obviously, there's a power and balance between the parent and child.

C: "For your own good."

R: Yeah, that's right.

C: What about adult parents and adult siblings? You're into serious manipulation territory.

R: Contention with agency.

C: Exactly. I'll tell you why this rubs me the wrong way. I was probably 38, 39. I'm a parent, I have a job, and I'm independent. My mom asks, "What do you want for Christmas?" I say, "You could get me some sets of my flatware because I'm running out of spoons ... I've taken them to work a couple of times and forgotten them." So what does she give me in my Christmas stocking, but a huge bag of plastic forks and spoons? I thought, "Are you kidding me?" First, I could fill my home with plastic spoons if I wanted to. I felt it was extremely manipulative. We had had that conversation, and I knew she was irritated—by the way, I got two sets of flatware as well—but on top, I get the plastic forks and spoons, so I don't make that mistake again. How does that strike you?

R: Two different ways: one, maybe she's poking fun at you. The other is, "I'm trying to change your routine. You're used to taking actual silverware to work, and I'm trying to make you take plasticware."

C: She could have gone to the grocery store the next day and said, "Hey, I bought you these," but to get it as a Christmas present, I couldn't

Table 14.1 Questions for Future Research on Gift-Giving

How do people's sense of security shape their enjoyment of surprises?

What motivates people to create surprise gifts?

What dimensions of the surprise-gift experience (e.g., of the giver, recipient, gift choice) shape the experience and effectiveness of surprise gifts?

How do givers' surprises unfold, and what motivates these choices?

How do people perceive gifts of money?

How are surprises ruined?

What are the relational consequences of failed surprises?

How are surprises experienced differently, vis a vis cultural constructions of gender?

How does participating in gift giving tie into one's identity, with respect to masculinity or femininity?

How do retailers contribute to people's participation in gifting rituals?

How do gift-giving and rituals in the marketplace shape workplace dynamics?

What public-policy consequences are associated with culturally-pervasive rituals?

How do people react when cultural norms of gift giving are violated?

What are the roles and responsibilities of other mediators when givers offer gifts of creativity? How do these roles and responsibilities differ for the giver, recipient, and provider?

What boundaries and roadblocks emerge with gifts of creativity?

What happens when providers don't deliver acceptable gifts of creativity?

When does a gift stop being a gift and start becoming habituated?

What giver and recipient identities are made salient during giving?

How do social identities influence the giving and receiving of gifts?

What do self-gifts mean in the 21st century? How do they differ across cultures?

How do the cultural meanings of romantic gifts differ for couples that are not heteronormative?

How do romantic gifts acquire feminine or masculine connotations? How can these connotations shape romantic relationships?

How can violating norms of romantic giving affect the relationship?

How do cultural discourses shape the meaning and desirability of romantic gifts?

How do items disappear from the normative cultural set of romantic gifts? How do their meanings change?

How can occasion-specific goods or services expand to become appropriate gifts for other occasions?

What gives seductive gifts their efficacy and potency?

How and when can gifts derail relationships?

How does gift giving differ, depending on the giver's resources?

What are everyday gifts (e.g., no occasion)? How do they contribute to relationships?

How are gifts acts of power? When are such gifts beneficial/detrimental to the giver/recipient relationship?

Is time a gift? How do consumers conceptualize it as a gift?

How can marketers promote time as a gift?

---

refuse it, and plastic forks and spoons are not exactly Christmas morning stocking stuff.

R: Also, I think the ritual audience comes into play. If it was just you and her maybe, "What are you doing, Mom? Why'd you get me plastic spoons?" but with everybody there, you're pressured to embrace the gift.

C: And to be polite, although I wasn't particularly! I knew exactly what she was doing.

Time as a Gift

C: I think time is a really interesting gift. I wonder if marketers think about how they can get on the gift-of-time bandwagon. It could be facilitated by interesting experiences and cool things to do.

R: Do you think marketers perceive Betty Crocker cake mix as a gift of time, or a dishwasher or microwave?

C: Oh, time *savings*. That's interesting. No, I think they thought of it as a benefit, not as a gift. But you could take it one step further and say, "Bake a cake with your family," and that's a gift. You know what I mean, spending time? This is how the discourse is going now about food preparation, the slow food movement and shows about loving food, and chefs, and all these businesses.

References

Gopaldas, Ahir. (2013), "Intersectionality 101," *Journal of Public Policy & Marketing*, 32 (special issue), 90–4.

Mick, David Glen and Michelle DeMoss (1990), "Self-Gifts: Phenomenological Insights from Four Contexts," *Journal of Consumer Research*, 17 (3), 322–32.

Ruth, Julie A., Otnes, Cele C., and Brunel, Frédéric F. (1999), "Gift Receipt and the Reformulation of Interpersonal Relationships," *Journal of Consumer Research*, 25 (4), 385–402.

Webley, Paul, Lea, Steven E., and Portalska, Renata. (1983), "The Unacceptability of Money as a Gift," *Journal of Economic Psychology*, 4 (3), 223–38.

Epilogue

15 Four Gift Poems

John F. Sherry, Jr.

Gift in Kind

pinching in a dented
peppermint tin
of loose tobacco,
coarse papers dampening
in persistent mist,
filters tiny and white,
elusive as pills,
sprinkling bits and shreds
along the dimpled trough, then
roll&lick&seal&twist,
a blur of fingertip
and tongue and wrist,
to bless the sacrifice,
tossing up the offering
atop the table
with a slow smile
and familiar joke
to prolong the round of stout,
warming, the radiance
of friendship beyond debit and credit,
beyond balance,
beyond ante, see, and call,
that keeps us all in play.

Marginalia

embroidering in the margin,
the scribbler tries to
edge the text like a lawn,
with filaments of
argument and assent,

and threads of
wandering *non sequitur*
hedging the published lines,
the call and response
a stichomythic tension
joining writer and inscriber
in a disembodied dance

the reader,
hanging on this cross
examination speckling each page,
pencil poised, above the fray,
wrestling with the
commentary's call to arms,
the urge to answer galling
as a gauntlet thrown for unknown cause,
commits to this pitched battle,
crimps correspondents in
cramped corners, and
fills them full of lead

the badinage of bookfolk,
a fractious throwback
in this age of Charon
ferrying across synaptic gaps
of cyberspace our
instant impulse to be
seen to mean, these
books that circulate as gifts
bear greater value for inscription,
like the sharing of kula shells,
the record of their journeys
etched in margins

Mele Hula for My Anam Cara

Scuttling around blow holes
After hours on the scarp,
Sounding the boil far below
As we sidestep jagged
Basalt clefts and bevels
Sharp as obsidian,
Scoria grabbing sandals,
Edging closer to feel the jet
Or taste the salty spume,

Knocked on my ass by
Apprehension on occasion
And by awe,
Creeping to the cliff in
Stiff breeze, leaning past ledge
To flirt with vault or flight,
The vista stills our patter
As I realize the sea,
A calm cold cobalt
Carapace far out,
Kinetic closer in,
Battering the craggy
Rockface base below,
Waves retreat apace, regroup,
Race on once more to rifts
And shelves, to shoulder pumice,
A backdraft churn of
Creamy froth, translucent
Milky turquoise left
In wake of constant carving,
Fading back, not drained,
Not madly pumped,
We linger one last moment,
A limpid tidal pool
Reflects your face, refracts
My fingers as I trace
Your image, the corona
Wavering on the ripple.

Spirit of the Gift

prometheus delivered
and relivered
and delivered again,
and so on
ad infinitum,
as god laughs

Index

Note: Page numbers in bold indicate a table on the corresponding page.

acknowledger role 145
adult daughter-mother dyads, gifting behavior within: background 141–142; research studies on gift-giving 142–144; social roles 145–149
agapic love paradigm 4, 6, 8, 37, 44, **45**, 105, 143, 150, 185, 220
aging population 39–40
altruistic giving 9–11
avoider role 145–146

capital 4, 179–182
carnal-singularity 156–159, 166–168, 245–248
chocolate: carnal-singularity by 156–159, 166–168, 245–248; as emotionally charged gift and self-gift 162–164; as gift 153–156, 245–248; giver-recipient relationships 164–166; Valentine's Day 161–162
compensator role 145
consumer behavior 39–40
Convention on the Rights of Persons with Disabilities 127, 128–129
creativity: gift-giving and 219, 243–244; gifts of creative experiences 224–226; motives and consequences of giving t gift of creative experience 226–228; towards an understanding of 221–223
credit 174, 179–182
cultural difference: common characteristics of bad romantic gift across Western and Eastern cultures 91; common characteristics of good romantic gift across Western and

Eastern cultures 88–90; common characteristics of perfect romantic gift across Western and Eastern cultures 85–86; differences between bad romantic gifts in Western and Eastern cultures 91–93; differences between good romantic gifts in Western and Eastern cultures 90–91; differences between perfect romantic gifts in Western and Eastern cultures 87–88; experiential versus material gifts 87–88; in gift-giving 82–84; literature review 81–84; online discourse on chocolate 163–167; relationship representation 86; romantic gift-giving model 81; rule of gift-giving in Asian cultures 38; rule of gift-giving in Western cultures 38; sacrifice 86; study of crosscultural romantic gift-giving behavior 84–95; surprise 87; thoughtfulness 89

delight 67–68, 72, 238–241

economic exchange 8
emotions 66–67, 162–164, 225
erotic capital 4
aesthetic products 224–226

face 204–205, 209–210, 213
flowers 133
food 41, 153–168
functionality 89–90

gender difference: carnal-singularity and 158–159; gift-giving rituals in

Japan 101–120; in giving and receiving experiences between Japanese women and men 41–58; masculinities and consumption in ritualized contexts 104–106; role in gift-giving rituals 38; surprise gifts and 71–72, 75

gift-giving: agapic love paradigm 4, 6, 8, 37, 44, **45**, 105, 143, 150, 185; chocolate 153–168; creativity and 219, 243–244; cultural difference in 38, 82–84; establishment of social bonds through 185–187; exchange paradigm 44, 45; gender difference 38, 41–58; market mediators as partners in 30–34; mother/daughter (parent/child) giving 248–251; motives for 25, 27, 205–208; occasions 3, 41, 80–83, 85, 92–93, 101–120, 161–162, 241–243; paradigms **45**, 219–220; previous consumer research on 142–144; questions for future research on **250**; rituals 41, 101–120; role of gender 38; as social exchange 25; social roles of givers 145–149; spiral 197–200; stages of 26; storgic love paradigm 44, **45**; traditional 4, 30–31; *see also* romantic gift-giving

gifts: alternative economies 4; bad 81–82, 91–93; caring about each other 196–197; chocolate 245–248; chocolate as 153–156; of creative experiences 224–228; dating 8; exchange models 8; experiential 87–88; expressive 28, 41; failure 71–73; functionality 89–90; good 81–82, 88–91; instrumental 28–29; learning from another 195; market-mediated 20–21, 26–34; material 87–88, 192–193; microloans 178–179; nonmaterial 193–197; organs 20–25; perfect 20, 22, 26–28, 44, 47, 55–57, 65, 68, 71, 81–82, 85–88; pure 8; self-gifts 162–164, 205–208, 220–221; shared experiences 195–196; sharing of interests 193–194; as social bond 143, 150; social ontology of 4; telling and listening 194–195; time as 251; types of 28; types of romantic 132–133

giver-recipient relationships: adult daughter-mother dyads 141–150; chocolate 164–166; mature consumers 37–58
gold 132–133
guardian role 147–148

hedonic consumption 205
"Housing for Help" initiative: background 184–185; engaging in material and nonmaterial practices of gift-giving 192–197; establishing quasi-family relations and friendships 191–192; gift-giving spiral 197–200; quid pro quid exchange between strangers 189–191; transforming strangers into quasi-family and friends 188–197

Japan: duality of self-concept 207–208; gift-giving occasions/rituals 101–120; role of romantic self-gifts for caring of "hidden true self" 211–212; romantic gift-giving of mature consumers 37–58; romantic self-gifting of women 204–213; romantic self-gifts to the hidden true self 210–211; self-gifting as self-oriented gift-giving 213; transformations of masculinity in 102–104; use of food as items of gift exchanges 41; White Day 101, 106–120; women's recognition of their multiple selves 209–210, 212–213

keeper role 149
kinship distance and reciprocity model 184–185, 197–199

love: existential 57–58; kinds of 5; in later life 39; nature of 4–5; styles 5; triangular theory of 5

masculinities: consumption in ritualized contexts and 104–106; gift buying and 129–132; transformations in Japan 102–104, 115–120, 241–243
mature consumers, romantic gift-giving of: aging and consumer behavior 39–40; context of research study 40–41; as expression of appreciation to beloved 44–46; as expression of

concern for well-being 51–55; as expression of empathy for the beloved's physical diminution 52; as expression of enriching everyday life 47; as expression of redefining relational closeness 49–50; as expression of reflecting meaning in life 48–49; as expression of simplifying 47–48; literature review 38–40; love in later life 39; as means of managing susceptibility to aging 52–53; as means of preparing for aging 54–55; as means of rejuvenating beloved 53–54; as means of reminiscing 50–51; method of research study 41–44; perfect gift experiences 44, 47, 55–57
mender role 148–149
microlending: background 173–175; contextualizing 175–177; credit romanticized as capital 179–181; darker side of 178–179; social relations formed by 177–178
mother/daughter (parent/child) giving 248–251

organ donation: living 23–25; organs as gifts 20–23; as perfect gift 20, 22, 26–28, 32–33; transparency in 29
other-gifts 219–220

people with disabilities, romantic gift-giving of: background 126–127; challenges facing 127–128; as compensatory behavior 135–136; masculinity and gift buying 129–132; public perception of 136–137; role of social media 133–135; sustainability 135; types of romantic gifts 132–133
perfect gift 20, 22, 26–28, 44, 47, 55–57, 65, 68, 71, 76, 81–82, 85–88
pleaser role 145
provider role 145

reciprocity 184–185, 192–199
romantic gift-giving: aging influences on **42–43**; cultural difference 38, 80–81, 84–95; mature consumers 44–46; model 81; people with disabilities 126–137; relationship

representation and 86; rituals 4, 31–32, 33; role of language 32; sacrifice and 86; social psychological perspectives 7–8; surprise and 68–71, 87; thoughtfulness and 89
romantic gifts 132–133

sacrifice 86
secrecy 28–29
self-gifting consumer behavior (SGCB): background 204–205; Japanese women's recognition of their multiple selves 209–210; romantic self-gifting and 205–208; self and culture 206–207; self-gifting as self-oriented gift-giving 213, 244–245
self-gifts: for caring for the hidden true self 211–212; chocolate 162–164; of creative experiences 226–228; definition of 220–221; motivations for 205–208; romantic self-gifts to hidden true self 210–211
self-identity 150
selfishness 9–10
self-love 9–10
singularity 157
social bonds 143, 150, 185–187
social exchange 8
socializer role 145, 147
social media: impacts on romantic relationships 133–135; romantic gift-giving and 3, 7
storgic love paradigm 37, 57
surprise: bad 71–73; conceptual framework for surprise romantic gifts 73–75; cultural difference 87; delight and 67–68, 72, 238–241; directions for future research 75; emotions and 66–67; gender difference 71–72, 75; perfect gift and 65, 68, 71, 76; romantic gift-giving and 68–71

thoughtfulness 89
time 251
triangular theory of love 5

unselfishness 9–11

Valentine's Day 3, 41, 81–82, 85, 101, 106, 107, 109, 112–113, 117–118, 161–162, 241, 246

White Day: background 101–102; as confession for the emasculated self 117–120; as event for gender performance 102, 108–111; negotiation of power and 113–116, 241–243; as rite of institution 111–113

Zimbabwe, romantic gift-giving of men with disabilities 126–127